EGYPT'S SUNKEN TREASURES

The exhibition Egypt's Sunken Treasures was opened by

Horst Köhler
The President of the Federal Republic of Germany

and
Mohamed Hosni Mubarak
The President of the Arab Republic of Egypt

This volume has been published in conjunction with the exhibition
Egypt's Sunken Treasures, held in Berlin (13 May – 4 Sept. 2006).

EGYPT'S SUNKEN TREASURES

Edited by Franck Goddio
and Manfred Clauss

Photography of the artefacts by Christoph Gerigk

Martin-Gropius-Bau, Berlin

Prestel
Munich · Berlin · London · New York

This exhibition has been organised by the Institut Européen d'Archéologie Sous-Marine (IEASM) and Hilti Arts & Culture gGmbH, in cooperation with the Martin-Gropius-Bau and Berliner Festspiele, in collaboration with the Supreme Council for Antiquities of Egypt.

Partner:

Franck Goddio and the IEASM team would like to express their gratitude to Prof. Jean Yoyotte, who, as scientific advisor at IEASM, has guided and enlightened their work thanks to his erudition, research and analytical skills. Through his judicious advice and unwavering support he contributed greatly to the success of every mission in Egypt.

LENDERS

The organisers would sincerely like to thank all lenders whose generous support has made this exhibition possible.

Egypt
The Alexandria National Museum
The Graeco-Roman Museum, Alexandria
The Archaeology Museum in the Alexandrine Library
The Maritime Museum

France
Musée du Louvre, Département des Antiquités égyptiennes, Paris
M. François René Herbin

COMMITMENT BY THE HILTI FOUNDATION

HILTI FOUNDATION

The fascination of history – researching the past, making new discoveries and presenting findings: these are the goals shared by Franck Goddio and the Hilti Foundation.

Founded and financed over many years by the Martin Hilti Family Trust, the Hilti Foundation is now supported jointly by the Hilti Corporation and the Trust. The Hilti Foundation promotes selected, sustainable projects and initiatives, especially in cultural, social and educational fields. The Martin Hilti Family Trust is the sole shareholder of the globally operational Hilti Group. Hilti is a manufacturer and supplier of state-of-the-art technological products, systems and services for the construction industry. Over 16,000 Hilti employees (including 1,600 in Liechtenstein) in more than 120 countries passionately strive to create enthusiastic customers and contribute towards a better future. The Hilti Group Headquarters and the head office of the Foundation are located in Schaan in the Principality of Liechtenstein.

The logo of the Hilti Foundation is to be found in connection with innovative projects that promise new findings – projects of international significance and impact. The provision of extensive support for Franck Goddio's work is one of the key points in the Hilti Foundation's present cultural commitment. Scientific guidance and the evaluation of projects is ensured through the cooperation of renowned experts, scientists and the Centre for Maritime Archaeology at Oxford University.

Franck Goddio and his team have worked for more than ten years on recovering and researching 'Egypt's Sunken Treasures'. The objects found and the results of the research carried out are being presented to the public for the first time in this exhibition.

www.hilti-foundation.org

Table of Contents

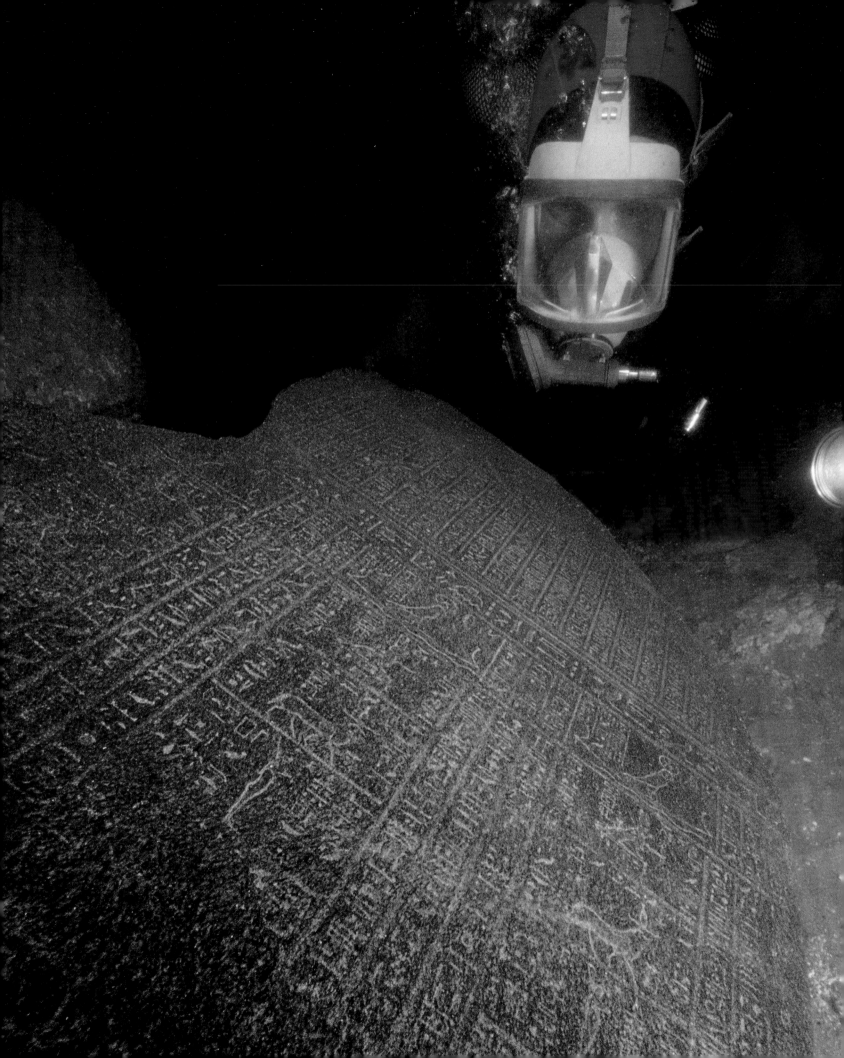

Welcoming Address

What could offer greater pleasure than reaping the fruits of the efforts? And indeed, great effort was needed to find, locate and lift the 500 artefacts of the exhibition "Egypt's Sunken Treasures". Regardless if the weight is only a few grams or a few tons, each one was lifted carefully, packed with great attention and transported to Berlin.

Now, these precious objects are gathered at the Martin-Gropius-Bau, bearing witness to 1.500 years of splendid Egyptian history. I consider these to be the pearls of the Egyptian Mediterranean coast, telling of the glory of former civilisations dramatically submerged by the sea, of a beauty and skillfulness still causing our amazement even today, at the beginning of the twenty-first century.

The exhibition has a clear message to deliver: Only if cultures are open to influence by other cultures, if they are ready to take the best of and exchange with each other on the base of joint ideals can a real dialogue, a mutual understanding between peoples, arise.

Egypt with its rich and ancient history is considered not only the cradle of civilization but also the melting pot of the great cultures of antiquity. This heritage has been preserved to the present day and is admired by thousands of guests every year, among them one million Germans in 2005 alone.

Those interested in culture and arts now have the opportunity to get an impression of the beauty of this history, in the middle of the heart of Europe from May throughout September 2006. I would like to express my deep thanks and highest appreciation to all those who have sincerely contributed with their enormous efforts to bring these "pearls" from the bottom of the sea to Berlin, especially the Egyptian Ministry for Culture, the Supreme Council for Antiquities, Mr. Franck Goddio and the Hilti Foundation, as well as the director of Martin-Gropius-Bau Mr. Gereon Sievernich.

Mohamed Al-Orabi   Ambassador of the Arab Republic of Egypt

Introduction

With the support of Liechtenstein's Hilti Foundation and in collaboration with Egypt's Supreme Council of Antiquities, French underwater archaeologist Franck Goddio has been exploring the sea at Alexandria and nearby Aboukir for over ten years. One might call underwater archaeologists the last great adventurers of the century. At any rate, the rediscovery of the cities of Canopus and Herakleion – well-known places in antiquity that gained a good press in contemporary authors such as Strabo and Herodotus – is for this century an event of the same order as the hunt for the sources of the Nile or the excavations in Pompeii were for the nineteenth century.

Parts of classical Alexandria and also the older cities of Canopus and Herakleion sank into the sea probably before 1300, no doubt as a result of earthquakes and tsunamis. 'Frozen in time' is how Goddio referred to the area – no-one had touched it for many centuries. Over the centuries Egyptian, Greek, Roman and Byzantine culture coincided here, close to one of the mouths of the Nile. Religious syncretism and scientific thinking evolved that still influence our European culture today. At the world premiere in the Martin Gropius Building, over 500 finds spanning 1500 years (from 700 BC to 800 AD, the Egyptian period to the Byzantine period) will be on show.

The ten years of support for the explorations in Egypt and the decision to exhibit the results in Berlin are major cultural feats. Such a degree of cultural commitment is certainly rare. We owe this sensational exhibition to the Hilti Foundation, and our warmest thanks are due to it. Without the considerable efforts on the part of foundation board members Michael Hilti, Georg Rosenbauer and Hans Saxer, this exhibition would not have taken place. We are indebted to them for their splendid cooperation and patient interest in bringing together the results of the long years of exploration for this exhibition. It was of course Franck Goddio who, with patience, forensic flair and a team of scientists and divers, discovered and classified the finds under the sea. Architect Philippe Delis in Paris did the design for the exhibition, which was implemented by Günther Krüger in Berlin. We should like to thank them all for the adventurous (in the best sense), very productive and always cordial cooperation.

Joachim Sartorius   Director General, Berliner Festspiele
Gereon Sievernich   Director, Martin-Gropius-Bau

Passion and Innovation

You don't need to have been on a dive with Franck Goddio to be fascinated by his work. The sight of the monumental statue of the Egyptian goddess Isis overgrown with algae is as captivating as the impressive picture of the diver lifting the massive head of ancient healing god Sarapis from the waters. He looks furious, after spending many centuries on the seabed.

The art treasures recovered from the sea – statues, ceramics, jewels and gold coins – are splendidly eloquent testimony of a glorious past. They help to clarify unanswered questions and test existing theories. For example, Franck Goddio was the first person to chart the harbour of Alexandria accurately – thereby convincingly confirming the historical records.

The care and high degree of innovation that characterise Goddio's explorations are sometimes even more impressive than the often adventurous-looking operations on the seabed. The French underwater archaeologist carries out his scientific projects with the latest equipment, which is often specially adapted to his requirements. The salvage work is performed by a specialist interdisciplinary team that includes not only archaeologists, art historians and Egyptologists but also geophysicists and electrical engineers. And his work is far from being over once the artefacts have been brought to the surface – the Institut Européen d'Archéologie Sous-Marine (IEASM) then sets to work with the Oxford Centre of Maritime Archaeology (OCMA) on the scientific assessment of the discoveries.

The Hilti Foundation has been supporting the work of Franck Goddio and his team for more than ten years. To build a better future, we need the foundation of the past. The underwater archaeologist brings us not only the splendour and magnificence of sunken dynasties – with the work he carries out with both passion and precision, he opens to us ever new gateways to understanding our history.

Michael Hilti   President of the Board of the Hilti Foundation

A Cultural Inheritance made Accessible

There was a time when French scholars such as J. F. Champollion, the inventor of Egyptology, or Antoine-Jean Letronne, who realised its contribution to our knowledge, revealed the riches of the Egyptian world. At a time when conflict between nations is more usual than mutual understanding, the treasures of Egypt will now be going round the world and contributing to bringing countries together. The discoveries of Frank Goddio and his team will not disappear in inaccessible depositories but will be within reach of scholars and ordinary people eager to extend their cultural understanding and satisfy their curiosity about two towns at the gates of Egypt – Canopus and Thonis-Herakleion – and the city of Alexandria, which have rightly excited great passion and much interest. These once submerged treasures, which have so far been seen only in pictures, have been raised and will at last be accessible for all to look at. They will travel the world and furnish the beginnings of an answer to the enigma of a city whose lighthouse and library fascinated the classical and modern world alike. The day of national, egotistical conservatism is past – this is an opportunity to make available to everyone a heritage that belongs to humanity.

An example was set in the sixteenth century. In August 1520, the city of Brussels celebrated the election of Charles I of Spain as head of the Holy Roman Empire. For the occasion, the now Emperor Charles V transported from Spain some outstanding masterpieces brought back from Mexico by conquistador Hernán Cortés. Dürer was also much taken with the splendours of Mexico exhibited in Brussels: 'I've seen many wondrous things in the custom of men . . . . All the days of my life I have never seen anything that filled my heart with such joy as these things . . . .' Some months earlier, in Valladolid, Bartolomé de las Casas and Pierre Martyr d'Anghiera had been able to study these strange gold objects at leisure – a solar disc, but also jaguar skins adorned with parrot feathers, 'a gift made up of things so rich and wrought with such art that they seemed a dream image and not the work of human hand.' This exhibition was probably the first touring exhibition in Europe, if we except the more modest one put on by Christopher Columbus after he returned from his first voyage in 1493. The admiral Cortés, who had been considered a mad visionary a few years earlier, travelled the length of Spain from Seville to Barcelona to display the Indians of the Antilles, the parrots, the gold jewellery and the strange plants. In France, it was still America that was paraded to the court and the people of Normandy on the occasion of Henri II's ceremonial entry into Rouen on 1 October 1550. Fifty Brazilian Indians and 250 sailors, all naked and painted with genipap powder, made a colourful sight.

In the sixteenth century Egypt likewise provided objects for display, not only mummies or exotic animals such as budgerigars, macaques and baboons but also a whole paraphernalia of talismans and miraculous products such as eagle stones (*aetites*), stellar stones, serpent stones, Lemnian earth, bezoars, petrified wood, *theriac*, and so forth … souvenirs recalling the East and its colours and evoking countries beyond the Suez isthmus, the Far East or the African interior. But among them were also objects charged with power and effect whose mere presence on board could engender irreversible catastrophes. In the twentieth century, the development of museography and improved transport have made it easier for artistic or wondrous objects to be lent out, the most emblematic certainly being the *Mona Lisa*, which has been round the world, arousing extraordinary excitement particularly in the USA and Japan. Incidentally, in many countries it has long been understood that the public shouldn't be expected to go to exhibitions – exhibitions should come to the public. In the domain of painting, and indeed sculpture and architecture as well, works appear before their admirers and awake new passions in neophytes. We are witnesses to an opening up of knowledge that can only be beneficial to both artists and lovers of art.

An object is always more evocative than an image, however perfect the latter might be. Though the men of the Renaissance had some remarkable painters, they fully understood that, to believe in the existence of a New World, you need to show a real sample of it. The drowned treasures of the port of Alexandria, like the marvels of the Aztecs, are pieces that have never been seen Thus their presentation in the travelling exhibition throughout Europe should be seen more as a journey of discovery than as mere cultural tourism. These stones rescued from the sea, over and beyond their intrinsic aesthetic and archaeological value, also bear witness to a site, a city now under the waves, an ensemble of monuments that allows us to reconstruct part of what was the most famous city in antiquity, one which has never ceased to fascinate us.

Thanks to the exhibition in which these buried treasures are shown, a new world is revealed to us, and viewers become as it were carriers, caretakers and messengers of the new. Active efforts are now demanded of those who are not content simply to admire but want to explore in their turn and arouse enthusiasm for what cannot remain shrouded in veils of purple where dead gods sleep. New muses – curiosity, the imagination, understanding – welcome the spectator and open up the portals of universal culture.

The Old World, unfortunately disparaged unjustly, never ceases to move us and show us what civilisation is essentially all about.

André Bernand   Professor emeritus

LEGENDARY PLACES

AN INTERVIEW WITH
FRANCK GODDIO
BY MANFRED CLAUSS

Franck Goddio's team and their
colossal discovery of
the stele of Ptolemy VIII and
the statue of a Ptolemaic
Pharaoh

previous double page:
An encounter with myths
on the sea bed – the head
of a Pharaoh from the Saitic
Dynasty. (cat. 3)

MANFRED CLAUSS: Franck, after your underwater expeditions in the South China Sea, where from 1985 you and your team located Chinese junks, Spanish galleons and British East Indiamen and recovered their cargoes, you turned to a different cultural area – Egypt. What fascinated you about the country? How did your expeditions there get going?

FRANCK GODDIO: I first thought about doing underwater archaeological excavations in Egypt in 1984. That was when I first heard that there might be sunken buildings in the waters off the Nile Delta. I went with archaeologists from the Supreme Council of Antiquities [in Egypt] to visit Jacques Dumas, President of the World Underwater Diving Federation, who was carrying out excavations in Aboukir Bay. His interest was in Napoleon's fleet, especially the flagship. Meantime, the Egyptian archaeologists told me that Prince Omar Tousson, a great authority on the Delta, had discovered the remains of ancient buildings more than a mile offshore in 1933. Legendary names such as Canopus, Herakleion and Thonis cropped up in the conversation.

MC: What did you do about it?

FG: It stirred my curiosity. I collected all the information available about archaeological discoveries in the area, which once bordered on the now vanished westernmost arm of the Nile.

MC: But the name Canopus was already known and the city had been excavated, hadn't it?

New discoveries are added
to maps in meticulous detail

FG: Some researchers reported that ruins of the famous city of Canopus had been found along the coast of Aboukir Bay, around twenty-four miles north-east of Alexandria, though archaeologists had not found any trace of the important shrine of Sarapis. So where could this temple of Sarapis have stood, that once attracted pilgrims from the whole world of antiquity and had served the Emperor Hadrian as a model for his villa in Tivoli? It was known that the early Christians had destroyed it and built a major monastery nearby, and a building to house the relics of Saints John and Cyril.

MC: And what was known about the city of Herakleion?

FG: That city was built at a place near the Canopus mouth of the Nile, where according to legend Herakles, the demi-god and son of Zeus, had set foot on Egyptian soil in order to perform his famous labours. It was also said that Helen of Troy stopped there with Paris, and the slaves in her retinue had found refuge in a large temple dedicated to Herakles. Of course, the existence of the city was only known about from inscriptions on steles and a few rare references in the writings of ancient authors. All real trace of it had vanished.

MC: You mentioned Thonis earlier – what is this mysterious name really about?

FG: Whereas in the writings of Diodorus the historian (90–30 BC) Thonis is still mentioned as the great gateway harbour of Egypt, the memory of the place had largely faded by the time Greek geographer and historian Strabo arrived in Egypt around the end of the first century BC. So Strabo's written references to the situation of the port near Herakleion are not really clear. One had to wonder whether the city really ever existed, or whether it was mythical fabrication.

MC: How did you come on the idea of looking for the cities on the seabed?

FG: Well, all these places had vanished from human sight – but how? Had they been inundated, perhaps? That was a possible explanation, because countless archaeological finds along the coastline of Alexandria provided clear proof that a considerable part of the famous grand harbour that underpinned the power and wealth of the Ptolemaic capital lies at the bottom of the bay. The discoveries near the coast of Aboukir Bay in 1934 refer to particular buildings that were inundated by the sea.

MC: What motivated you when you were looking for these ancient buildings that had sunk under the sea so long ago?

FG: It was my greatest dream to do excavations at legendary places such as Herakleion and the ancient harbour of Alexandria. I wanted to reconstruct the ancient topography of the region, discover cities and historic structures beneath the sea, measure the Portus Magnus, the large port, of the sunken part of Alexandria and research the history of these places.

MC: Didn't that ambition seem rather unrealistic?

FG: Before I could get into any venture like that in the early 1990s, I had to wait for work I was doing with the French nuclear energy authority (CEA) to be concluded. It involved developing highly sensitive location equipment and adapting its application protocols to the techniques of underwater exploration. The current ongoing research work should be regarded less as underwater exploration than archaeological excavations that happen to take place underwater. They must satisfy the requirements of an historical approach. Also, they not only require exploration and excavation techniques to be adjusted to the marine environment but also demand extensive technical skills and downright athletic stamina among all concerned. A long-term scheme like this can only be successful if you work as a team made up of experts from a wide range of disciplines. And when you know you have a first-class sponsor behind you.

MC: How is a team like this put together?

FG: Our work demands interdisciplinary collaboration among Egyptologists, archaeologists, historians, geophysicists, restorers and curators. In addition we need divers, photographers and cameramen specialising in archaeological work, plus staff to handle the logistics on land and at sea.

MC: How did you set about the actual job?

FG: Based on very complex electronic sweeps, we were able to draw up maps charting the ancient topography of the submerged region. During these search operations we discovered ancient ruins, which were then identified more precisely during archaeological excavations.

MC: Let's talk about these excavations, Franck.

FG: Every excavation changes the condition of the excavation site. That means you have to photograph and record all relevant data during the work. Extracting samples, drawing plans of the buildings and recording the dimensions and locations of the objects in space and relative to each other require absolutely meticulous accuracy. Every day we get new insights that extend the areas of our knowledge about the region, its various ways of life and its trade a bit more. In the course of a dig, the expedition ship is transformed into a floating museum.

MC: What happens with the objects when they come to light?

FG: The first steps towards conservation are taken immediately the objects reach the surface. That's when the prolonged work of conservation, restoration, registration and systematic study begins.

MC: You must have experienced impressive moments during the discovery of such treasures.

FG: Yes, diving to these submerged places is full of unforgettable moments. As the objects are uncovered bit by bit, they steadily grow out of the semi-darkness of the murky water. For many centuries they lay hidden beneath silt and sand. Because of encrustation, some of the objects acquire strange shapes. It's an indescribable feeling to slowly approach them through water clouded by sediments.

MC: Do you enjoy not only being able to see these discovered treasures but also to be able to touch them?

FG: Many of the objects we bring to light are pure masterpieces. It's a privilege to be able to admire them at leisure. Other objects are ordinary utilitarian things, fragile messengers from the past that nonetheless often convey valuable information. But the true importance of all these objects is only revealed though scientific study carried out by respected researchers.

MC: You mention respected researchers with whom you cooperated on several occasions. Did you have difficulties in gaining acceptance among the specialists since you don't have an academic qualification as an archaeologist?

FG: Getting specialists to accept me was indeed rather difficult at first, for the reason you mention, but I was prepared for that. In my own previous specialist area – as an advisor in business and financial matters – an underwater archaeologist who suddenly wanted to carry out development projects in Arabia or elsewhere would have encountered the same scepticism. With the development of the location methods I mentioned earlier, I managed to win over even prominent scientists.

MC: What on balance was the result of your underwater expeditions in Egypt?

FG: The rediscovered city of Herakleion-Thonis provides us with knowledge that had been lost for two millennia and solves one of the mysteries of historical geography. The excavations of buildings, ports and canals enable us to gradually resurrect the beauty of these sunken cities. The Portus Magnus of

Alexandria is now mapped. On our charts and plans, its infrastructure appears larger and more substantial than earlier researchers had probably imagined.

MC: The archaeological work here and in Canopus, which was already partly investigated in 1934, has brought further astonishing finds to light.

FG: The uncovering of numerous sculptures, extensive epigraphic materials and a wide range of objects from all excavation sites in the region contribute new knowledge about this part of Egypt. We now know more about a region that experienced many changes in the period between the last native dynasties and the end of the Byzantine period, when the places finally vanished under the waters.

MC: The 'Egypt's Sunken Treasures' exhibition in Berlin shows the results of your work in recent years in Egypt, doesn't it?

FG: Diving in the sea and dipping into the past have brought a good deal of the history of this region to light. The objects we discovered and brought to the surface are now being presented to the public for the first time. The exhibition at the Martin Gropius Building is the best reward the team could have after spending fourteen years on the job in order to bring the past of sunken cities and ports back to life. These places are now like the statue of a queenly beauty found in Canopus, who seems to have been born like Aphrodite from the foaming billows, emerging from the waters of the Mediterranean.

Manfred Clauss is professor for Ancient History. His publications on Egypt, Alexandria and Cleopatra have been translated into several languages.

Franck Goddio is founder and director of IEASM (Institut Européan d'Archéologie Sous-Marine) in Paris.

following double page:
View of present-day Alexandria from the expedition ship

Recovery of the Pharaoh's torso

I. THE REGION AND ITS HISTORY

MANFRED CLAUSS

Alexandria and the Nile

THE NILE

It is one of the longest rivers on earth. It is one of the oldest waterways on earth. It is one of the most fertile rivers on earth. It is the river Nile.

The Nile rises in the volcanic mountains of equatorial Africa – a vast and lonely wilderness that for a long time was deemed impassable and hence left unexplored. The search for the river's source began thousands of years ago so that even for the Romans, 'searching for the source of the Nile' was a byword for any futile quest or endeavour. Not until the late nineteenth century did explorers advance as far as the source itself and begin the arduous task of charting its headwaters.

With a length of 6,500 kilometres, the Nile is the longest river in Africa and one of the longest rivers on earth. What it loses to evaporation in the blazing heat of northeast Africa is constantly replenished by its numerous tributaries. Most important of all are those that flow into it from the Ethiopian highlands for it is these that supply the fertile silt that makes the river so important. The Nile is Egypt, or rather, 'Egypt is a gift of the Nile' – as the historiographer Herodotus put it after travelling there in the fifth century BC. And this is what makes it is so essential to our understanding of Egyptian history.

Until the building of the Aswan Dam in 1971, the sky was invariably blue, yet the waters of the Nile continued to swell even without a single drop of rain. Every year, the people of Egypt's 1,100-kilometre-long Nile Valley would wait anxiously for the return of the annual floods. After all, the waters of the Nile are the main source of food for the flora and fauna, and hence the people, who live along it. Without these waters, the valley would be doomed. That a reverence for the river eventually turned into a religion is therefore not surprising. The Nile was worshipped as the deity that brought the Egyptians the dark earth after which their country was named – the name Kemet meaning 'black land', as opposed to the 'red land' of the desert, which also explains how the Red Sea got its name.

Ancient Egypt comprised more or less the same territory as it does today. Circumscribed by the Mediterranean to the north and Red Sea to the east, the first cataract marks Egypt's southernmost border, while the vast stretches of uninhabitable desert in the west provide no natural dividing line between it and Libya. Here, too, topography was to have a formative influence on Egyptian thought: The idea of a Realm of the Dead to the west can doubtless be attributed not just to the analogy the ancient Egyptians drew between death and the setting sun, but also to their dread of the unknown and seemingly boundless desert lands of western Egypt.

Father Nile and his sixteen children

sow. Egypt is a like a green emerald in the months of January, February and March, when the grasses and plants shooting up out of the soil lend it the splendour of this precious gem. And Egypt is like a bar of red gold in the months of April, May and June, when the seeds ripen and the grass takes on a reddish hue so that the land not only looks like gold, but is as bountiful as gold too.'

Although the annual floods were always very plentiful, they were not without fluctuations. If the Nile rose no more than one metre above its normal level, the consequence was drought and famine. If it rose higher than usual, however, dams burst and fields were ruined. People therefore prayed for just the right amount of water, which meant sixteen cubits of water (one cubit equals 44.43 centimetres). This, incidentally, is the significance of the sixteen infants on the allegorical marble of the River Nile now in the Vatican Museum.

The Nile certainly had to rise by more than eleven cubits, for as the typically laconic Pliny the Elder put it, twelve cubits meant hunger, thirteen sufficiency, fourteen joy, fifteen security and sixteen superfluity.

Egypt covers an area of almost one million square kilometres extending over more than seven and a half latitudes. Of this area, however, only some 35,000 square kilometres is habitable, cultivated land – a figure that translates into a mere 3.5 per cent of the total. Since time immemorial, Egypt has been divided into Lower Egypt, an area of some 24,000 square kilometres extending from today's Cairo to the coast and comprising the large and fertile marshlands of the Nile Delta, and Upper Egypt, which comprises the remainder of the Nile Valley from Cairo as far as Aswan.

It is to the tenth-century Arab writer, Al-Masū-dī, that we owe the following very vivid description of Egypt's exceptional fecundity:

'A wise man once described Egypt as follows: For three months it is a white pearl, for three months black musk, for three months a green emerald and for three months a bar of red gold.

Egypt is a white pearl in the months of July, August and September, when it is immersed in water and the villages built on hilltops and elevated land look like stars surrounded by a shimmering white sea and one can travel from village to village only by boat. Egypt is black musk in the months of October, November and December, when the waters recede to the riverbed, leaving behind black soil as fragrant as musk that the peasants then till and

The area around Alexandria (drawing by G. Seidensticker)

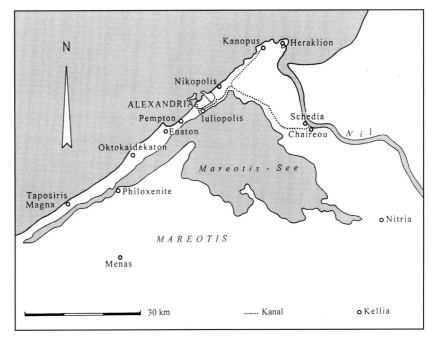

EGYPT'S MAIN ARTERY

Whereas Herodotus' famous description of Egypt as a 'gift of the Nile' is rightly understood to be a reference to the exceptionally fertile soil of the Nile Delta, it also holds true of the river's second function as a waterway and the country's most important artery. Vessels travelling northwards down the Nile have always been carried along by the river itself, while traffic in the other direction has profited from the prevalence of northerly winds. For the trading port of Alexandria and the surrounding region, it was essential to have at least one direct link to the Nile. As the port developed, therefore, so too did a dense network of canals on which the bulk of the cargo could be shipped.

If Alexandria and its satellite ports of Juliopolis, Nikopolis, Canopus, Menouthis and Herakleion was considered the 'greatest trading centre' of the ancient world, this was true not just because of its favourably situated Mediterranean port, but also because of the numerous canals linking it to the Nile. The map shows only the largest of these vital arteries, but it should be remembered that there were a lot of canals linking Lake Mareotis to the Nile as well. Various ancient river ports such as Schedia/Chaireou can also be said to belong to Alexandria, for it was here that grain shipped down the Nile on large grain vessels was transferred onto canal barges to be taken to the granaries of Alexandria. Indeed, it was above all the export of grain that made Alexandria and the surrounding region so rich and its ship owners the most powerful group in this most affluent city.

The Grecian settlements of Canopus and Menouthis had been in existence for several centuries before Alexandria itself was founded and Herakleion, from which Herodotus began his tour of Egypt in 450 BC was probably even more important than even these two ports. The poet Poseidippos who in the third century BC sang the praises of the famous Pharos lighthouse of Alexandria, also eulogised the port of Herakleion. Situated on Cape Zephyrium, a limestone spur extending from the Libyan desert as far as the sea, it provided a natural harbour which 'made the sea as smooth as oil even when storms were raging.'

Herakleion may have served well enough as a port, but Cape Zephyrium was nowhere near such an effective bulwark against the north-easterlies to which it owed its name as Poseidippos claimed, for it left the Bay of Aboukir, completely exposed. The main problem with Herakleion, however, was that being at the mouth of the Nile, it was constantly silting up and hence required endless dredging; after all, the Canopic branch of the Nile was the largest in the entire delta, which is why Ptolemy of Alexandria (second century BC) referred to it simply as the 'great river'. As Canopus was not in fact situated on the river of that name at all, the distributary that would later form Alexandria's eastern boundary was sometimes named after Herakleion instead.

Alexander the Great can indeed take credit for having in 331 BC chosen such a perfect spot on which to found his city. Plutarch reports how the idea came to Alexander in a dream – a story the people of Alexandria have always been happy to tell: 'After conquering Egypt, he wanted to found a large and populous Greek city to which he could give his name and acting on the advice of his architects had a site larger than any that had preceded it staked out and enclosed for that purpose. Then one night, he had a wonderful vision in his sleep. A man with hoary locks and with a countenance most venerable appeared to stand by his side and recite these verses from Homer:

> "There is an island in the surging sea,
> off the shore of Egypt and Pharos is its
> name . . .
> It conceals a harbour with good anchorage."

Alexander thereupon rose and crossed over to Pharos that in those days really was an island just above the Canopic estuary, though now it is joined to the mainland by a causeway. And when he saw the outstanding natural advantages of the site – for it is a strip of land that forms a natural bridge between a large lake (Mareotis) and the sea, ending in an expansive harbour – he said he saw that Homer was not only an admirable poet, but also a very wise architect.'

That Homer, as the greatest Greek poet who ever lived, had deemed the site favourable would have been grounds enough for Alexander, although it is likely that Greek merchants and seafarers who knew the area well confirmed him in his decision.

Numerous ancient writers saw in Alexander's choice of location a stroke of genius – which is not surprising, given how successful his enterprise was. For the two-kilometre-wide strip of land between the Mediterranean Sea and Lake Mareotis did indeed prove an ideal site for a port. While the Mediterranean served as a gateway to the world, Lake Mareotis, which in those days was much larger than it is now, fed numerous canals that in turn led to the Nile and the Egyptian interior. Furthermore, the lake had an abundant supply of fish and seemingly endless papyrus marshes to provide the raw materials for what would soon be one of the city's most important industries. The lake eventually became so important to the city that in his *Historia Ecclesiastica* of 450 AD, the Christian author Sozomenos described Alexandria simply as 'a city on Lake Mareotis'.

Not only were huge quantities of goods transported down the Nile to Alexandria and from there dispatched throughout the Mediterranean region, but the city itself attracted large numbers of visit-

ors, most of whom travelled along the same routes. Canopus, Menouthis, Herakleion and Alexandria all had cultic sites and their temples of Isis, Osiris and Sarapis in particular had long proved a magnet for pilgrims from all over the world. To these pagan sites were later added rival or substitute Christian ones so that Alexandria became a popular base for Christian writers wanting to visit convents both in the city itself and in its satellites. Travellers also used Alexandria as a starting point for trips across Lake Mareotis to the convents of Menas, Kellia and Nitria.

Water, whether from the Nile, the Mediterranean, Lake Mareotis or the countless canals, dictated the life of the entire region. For some parts of the region, however, the Nile and Mediterranean would determine their fate in quite a different way. In the final days of the first millennium, the great port of Alexandria and parts of Canopus, Menouthis and Herakleion were engulfed by the sea. Thanks to state-of-the-art technology and painstaking under-sea exploration, however, important parts of this lost world have at last resurfaced. The purpose of this exhibition is to give visitors an impression of what life in the region was once like, even if the most lasting impression is likely to be of how much was lost and may forever remain so.

Wall of a Byzantine building

AS DARK AS THE RIVERBED
FATHER NILE

The bust was found at the temple site at Canopus and is remarkably well preserved and of the highest quality. It represents a long-bearded divinity with vigorous ideal features, carrying a cornucopia on its left shoulder. This attribute and the divine 'portrait' best suit a river god, while the material and context best suit a representation of the god Nile. The semi-circular lower edge, the flat back with a wide-gauge dowel hole, and the forward lean of the head all show that the bust was mounted inside a frame in the form of a shield. A deep oval dowel hole in the back centre is still partly filled with lead and was used for attaching the bust to this frame. A hole for attaching a metal attribute – probably a lotus flower – was drilled into the headband above the centre of the forehead.

The character of the river god as an old but vigorous man is represented by the thick long beard, by the muscled brow, and by light aging lines beneath the eyes. Such virtuoso sculptures of Greek divinities in dark Egyptian stones were products of specialist workshops located probably in Alexandria that catered to a sophisticated clientele in Delta communities as well as in Rome and central Italy. These workshops made purely pharaonic-looking statuary and figures in 'mixed' Greek-Egyptian style, as well as figures – such as this new bust – in purely classical style but of dark stone.   R.R.R.S.

29   Bust of the Nile god
Greywacke
Roman period (2nd cent. AD)
H. 67 cm | w. 56 cm | d. 30 cm

MANFRED CLAUSS

The History of Alexandria and the Surrounding Area

Myths and sagas stand at the beginning of the histories of many peoples and nations; we have been handed down tales about some of the most famous figures of ancient times from the area between Alexandria and the mouth of the Nile. Herakles was definitely the most famous traveller of antiquity. In order to perform his universally known labours, he had to travel across all of the known (Mediterranean) world of the time. Of course, he also visited Egypt. There, the Nile had just overflowed its banks and was threatening to destroy everything. Herakles brought the river under control, repaired the embankments and, in this way, saved the country. As a sign of gratitude, a Herakles temple was erected – the Herakleion – to which the most easterly of the three cities dealt with in this exhibition, owes its name.

The most famous love story of antiquity also leads us into this region. A beautiful woman succumbed to the charm of a dashing hero and, at his side, deserted her husband and homeland; the result was a war of previously unknown dimensions. Everybody knows the story and the names: we are talking about Helen and her lover, Paris, as well as her husband, Menelaos. The lovers also passed through the harbour of Herakleion when they were on their way from Sparta to Troy. When Thonis, the guardian of the Nile mouth, discovered just who the couple was, he refused to give them refuge. After Menelaos had been successful in bring-ing his wife back from Troy, the married couple, their helmsman Canobos and his wife, Menouthis, got caught in a storm and ended up in Egypt. While he was repairing the damaged ship, Canobos was bitten by a snake and transformed into a god. The married couple, Canobos and Menouthis, have been immortalised in two cities near the mouth of the Nile, to the east of the later Alexandria. In the meantime, underwater archaeologists have rediscovered the city of Canapus. However, Menouthis still lies hidden on the sea floor.

In spite of their charm and morality, such stories are, etymologically and historically, without significance. The important thing is that they form a connection between the area around Alexandria and the Trojan War, which the ancient storytellers thought to be historical. This tradition created a link between the region and Greek history – making the Nile delta a part of Greece, as it were – and this already at a very early stage. At that time Greek seafarers created the mythological figure that was to become an expression for the Egyptians inhospitality and unfriendliness towards all foreigners. The name of this figure stems from a place in the Nile delta: Busiris. Busiris, one of Poseidon's sons, was to kill many people until Herakles went to Egypt and brought an end to his deeds (p. 122).

Soon, northern Egypt was so familiar to Greek seafarers that more and more mercenaries and merchants, as well as scientists, showed an interest in this area which promised all of them a gigantic profit. Even at that early stage of dealing with Egyptian culture, the 'European' side developed the opinion that the land on the Nile was the source of all wisdom.

THE AGE OF THE PHARAOHS

The Egypt of the late period, which one calls the last millennium BC, was no longer able to play the role in the field of power politics it did in the times of Thutmosis III (1479–1425 BC) and Ramesses II (1279–1213 BC), when the pharaohs managed to extend their sphere of influence far into the Levant. But Egypt's riches were still legendary whenever the central government was able to organise the labour force of the peasants in such a way that the canals, through which the Nile silt was led to the fields, were regularly taken care of and cleaned. A strong royal power was often lacking in those last thousand years. From 945 to 722 BC, Libyan tribal chieftains, who had become indispensable to the Egyptians as leaders of the mercenaries and felt themselves, both culturally and from a religious aspect, to be Egyptian, ousted their lords and assumed control of the country. After this period, the centre of power was located entirely in the delta region. Under these kings, Egypt increasingly became a link between the countries of the Mediterranean from Libya to Palestine.

The Libyan dynasty was toppled by the Ethiopian (712–664 BC). During this epoch, there were two events which created much attention far beyond the borders of Egypt. In 685 BC, the country experienced the largest known Nile flooding of ancient times. Even though it obviously caused severe damage, the contemporaries exalted in the glory of the gods who they saw symbolised in the unbridled masses of water. The second event was the conquest and destruction of Thebes, the centre of the country for thousands of years, by the Assyrians in 664 BC. This was a forewarning that Egypt's destiny would be in the hands of foreign powers for the following centuries.

These phases of foreign rule, as well as the permanent threats from the major powers of the Middle East – whether Assyrian or Persian – were interrupted by the pharaohs of the Saite dynasty

3   **Portrait of a Pharaoh**
Diorite
Saitic dynasty (664–525 BC)
H. 35 cm | w. 30 cm | d. 29 cm

This is a portrait of pharaoh with a nemes headdress. The *uraeus*-snake rises above in an indistinct section. The body of a cobra forms two symmetrical long flat curves ending at the back of the head. The smooth and supple, but precise, modelling of the face is characteristic of the so-called 'Saite Renaissance'.   Z. K.

(664–525 BC) (cat. no. 3). Towards the end of this period, Pharaoh Amasis (570–526 BC) intensified the Greek elements in Egypt. The fact that he gave the Greeks the city of Naukratis, which had been founded by Milet, in the western delta as a trading base, proved to be especially significant for the future. Naukratis became the first Greek polis on Egyptian soil and was to make a decisive contribution to the amalgamation of Egyptian and Greek culture. Herakleion, Egypt's gateway to the Mediterranean world, played an increasingly important role, alongside Naukratis (cat. no. 424).

Following the Saite, the Persians took control of Egypt for 120 years before a local dynasty, with the help of Greek mercenaries, once again prevailed in 404 BC, further increasing the integration of the country with the other nations of the eastern Mediterranean. Quarrels within the royal family led to its downfall. Nektanabo II (360–343 BC) was the last pharaoh in a series of thirty dynasties (cat. no. 102).

After the country once again fell to the Persians in 343 BC, Nektanabo II flew to Nubia, never to return – at least not in his human form. Later legends transformed him into one of Alexander's 'fathers'. Through magical powers, Nektanabo took on the guise of Zeus and, in this form, coupled with Alexander's mother Olympias. In this way, the legend reconciled the Egyptians with the conqueror Alexander whom posterity would dub 'the Great'.

102 **Sphinx**
Black granite
4ᵗʰ cent. BC
H. 98 cm | w. 147 cm | d. 58 cm

The sphinx is composed of numerous pieces. The presence of a *uraeus*-snake on the *nemes* headdress proves that we are in the presence of a royal person. The lion with a human head is in its traditional pose: the front section with the front paws on the top of the stone base, the rear paws folded, the tail rolled on the right leg.   Z. K.

424 **Fragment of a red-figure vessel**
Ceramic
4ᵗʰ cent. BC
H. 12 cm | w. 7 cm

The fragment of a *krater* is decorated with the bust of a man dressed in a cloak.   C. G.

FROM ASTRONOMY TO ASTROLOGY
THE NAOS OF THE DECADES

The shrines known as *naos* were niches meant for statues of deities and were set up at the rear of temples, the holiest part. Their façades were provided with doors that the officiating priests opened in order to carry out daily rites specifically dedicated to the deity. Originally of wood, these chapels were later carved from stone, in the Egyptian late period from monolithic blocks. Franck Goddio's marine-archaeological mission in the Bay of Aboukir revealed numerous side sections of a remarkable *naos* known as the *Naos of the Decades*, parts of which were already in the possession of museums in Alexandria and the Louvre in Paris.

The uppermost section, in the form of a pyramidal roof, was found on land in the Canapus region and entered the Louvre as early as 1817. A sizeable piece consisting of the plinth and the back wall was discovered in 1940 in the Bay of Aboukir and donated by its finder, Prince Omar Toussoun, to the Graeco-Roman Museum in Alexandria. The fragments discovered most recently contribute a substantial piece of the left lateral façade, as well as part of the right, although considerable bits of the latter are still missing (fig. p. 50, *top*).

The *Naos of the Decades* is a monolith of very dark granite, magnificently decorated both inside and out. It was erected by Pharaoh Nektanabo I (380–362 BC) for Schu-Soped, who represents a special form of the god Schu worshipped in a town in the east of the Nile Delta and who delivers the eastern enemies to the pharaoh. Schu is a personification of the gaseous atmosphere that the Egyptians

The roof of the *Naos of the Decades* is now in the Musée du Louvre, Paris

imagined existed between sky and earth; he is often portrayed as a man standing with his feet on the ground (embodied by his son Geb) and with his arms stretched upwards in order to support the sky, personified by his daughter Nut (fig. p. 50, *bottom left*).

An associated text mentions the dimensions of the actual figure ('height four hand widths', that is, around thirty centimetres) and the material from which it was made: silver covered with fine gold.

31–34
Naos ot the Decades
Black granite
380–362 BC
H. 178 cm | w. 88 cm | d. 80 cm

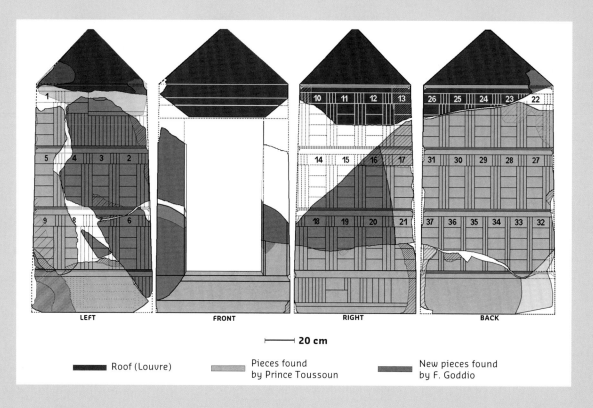

LEFT   FRONT   RIGHT   BACK

⊢————⊣ **20 cm**

▬▬▬ Roof (Louvre)   ▬▬▬ Pieces found
by Prince Toussoun   ▬▬▬ New pieces found
by F. Goddio

The four external surfaces of the *Naos of the Decades* with the parts found, their origin and the arrangement of the thirty-seven decades (reproduction to scale by L. von Bomhard)

New theory to explain the figures of the decades
• The arrangement of the *decan* stars as they appear in each decade according to the *Book of Nut*.
• The relevant figures on the *naos* show the various aspects of Schu corresponding to the sections of the night sky as can be seen throughout the year in each decade.

(Egyptians orientated themselves to the south, so east lies on the left.)
(After A. S. von Bomhard, *The Naos of the Decades*)

The direction for reading the texts on the outer sides

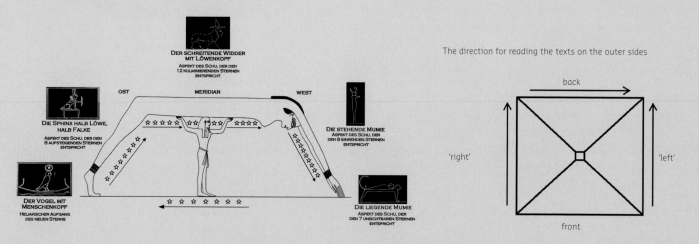

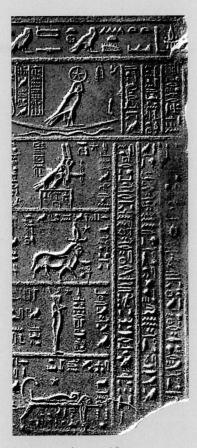

Arrangement of texts and figures of each decade on the *naos*, example of second decade, left side, second (middle) register.

Undoubtedly, when the doors were opened, this impressively realistic golden lion must have caused people to catch their breath, both because of the fearsome appearance of the predator and its shininess, which must have stood out particularly well against the dark stone background. This colour contrast was intentional, since Schu in this lion form embodied the power of the radiant sun, while the dark walls of the shrine symbolised night.

In the outer sides of the *naos* is chiselled a calendar that divides the Egyptian year into ten-day periods or decades. The start of each of these is introduced by special stars, rising one after the other, known as *decan* stars. The framed decade fields are distributed on the left, right and rear façades of the chapel and arranged in three registers on each side. The registers are in turn separated on each side by bands of hieroglyphic texts. These nine lines provide a continuous text, which deals with the *decan* stars. Just like the fields of the decades, this text is read in order on the left, then the right and finally the rear façade (fig. p. 50, *bottom right*).

The thirty-six large, vertical fields are devoted to the thirty-six decades of the year, thus a total of 360 days. A thirty-seventh field is inserted for the five leap days that the Egyptians added to the 360 days in order to complete the 365-day year.

The same five figures appear in each of these thirty-seven fields from top to bottom (*left*): a human-headed bird, a falcon-headed sphinx swinging a bow, a ram in motion, an upright mummy and a mummy laid on a bier.

These figures refer to the various sections of the annual cycle of *decan* stars from their appearance (human-headed bird) to their disappearance (mummy laid on bier).

A new theory about the interpretation of these figures is based on a very ancient Egyptian book, produced at least eight centuries before the time of Nektanabo I, the *Book of Nut* or *Book of the Sky*. In this one reads that the number of *decan* stars that can be seen in the night sky always remains constant, since every ten days one of these stars rises in the east and another one disappears in the west at the end of its course. The book furthermore states that every night eight stars rise in the eastern sky, a further twelve culminate 'in the middle of the sky', nine sink in the west and seven are invisible. According to the new theory, the five deities are references to the various sections of the night sky as they can be observed throughout all the decades (fig. p. 50, *bottom left*): The bird refers to the new star that opens the decade, the sphinx to the eight stars rising in the eastern sky, the ram to the twelve stars that wander across the zenith during the night, the upright mummy to the nine stars that sink towards the west and the recumbent mummy to the seven stars that are invisible during the relevant decade.

Thus each of the deities would represent an aspect of the god Schu relating to one section of the night sky so that, over the course of each decade, the entire night sky would be represented.

In front of the bird there are three small text columns. These define the ten days of the year that fill the decades and mention sacrificial offerings made by the king in order to protect the country from evil.

Three further columns along the four remaining figures contain historical data: wars, massacres, epidemics reach foreign peoples, rebels or animals and plants. Illnesses are usually accompanied by fever, since these were infectious diseases caused by germs spreading through the air. These calamities are caused by a 'great god'. This great god is Schu himself who acts via all the stars in the decade (including the invisible ones). In order to convey an idea of the content of these texts, here is a literal rendition of the commentary relating to the fourth decade:

'The Great God, the First Time; he it is who brings death to the peoples of Asia, he makes all plants die. The appearance of one exposed to his diseased breath is like a human with stomach ache; his fever lasts for five days. Sacrifices of dogs are being made.'

The expression 'the First Time' gives us to understand that the year described follows directly on the creation of the world, the splendid telling of which can be found in the uppermost section of the fragment of the left side recently discovered by Goddio. This creation text – of which we have no further version – stands at the beginning and as introduction to the fields of decades. It recounts the creation of the sky and the stars by the god Schu, who separates sky and earth and, standing between them, embodies the atmosphere. After the sky had been created, Schu set the *decan* stars in motion and became their ruler. Accordingly, he must be the 'great god' of the astrological commentaries that accompany each decade and, together with the *decan* stars that he controls, is responsible for disease and death, primarily affecting Egypt's enemies.

From the time of the Old Kingdom it was incumbent on Schu-Soped to protect Egypt against conquerors from the east. The renewed danger from the Persians, of whom the country had only just rid itself, could be one of the reasons why Pharaoh Nektanabo I had this holy place built for the god.

Since it divides astronomical facts into ten-day periods or decades, the monument might appear to be the ancestor of modern astrology, which divides the twelve signs of the zodiac into ten-day sections, *decans*. However the zodiac is not of Egyptian origin: it is found in Egypt only in the Ptolemaic period (318 – 30 BC). When it does appear in the land of the Nile, three of the ancient *decans* are incorporated into each of the twelve zodiac signs.

On the other hand, the oldest source for the concept of *decans* does undoubtedly lie in Egypt; as early as the Ninth Dynasty (around 2100 BC) one finds lists on sarcophagus lids recording the observed rising of *decan* stars and connecting them with a period of ten days. But this division of time into decades on the basis of astronomical observations about the rising of *decan* stars apparently dates back very much earlier and probably underpins the entire division of time in the Egyptian calendar.

The *Naos of the Decades* is an incalculable witness to the evolution of ideas because it sheds light on how astrology and mythology developed out of scientific observation of astronomical processes and not vice versa.   A. S. v. B.

PTOLEMAIC PERIOD

Alexander was welcomed in Egypt as the country's liberator from the Persians. The foundation of Alexandria was an enormous success for him. The authors of antiquity are unanimous in their praise of Alexander's fortuitous decision. The, approximately two-kilometre-long, sandstone spur between the Mediterranean and Lake Mareotis proved to be an ideal location. The speed at which this metropolis grew was breathtaking. Already at the beginning of the third century BC, the city probably had more than 100,000 inhabitants. Around 200 BC, at the very latest, Alexandria was the largest city in the known world and, at the same time, the largest trading metropolis. In comparison, Herakleion rapidly sank into the background. That Herakleion maintained its position as a harbour until late in the ancient era was principally due to the fact that ships were located there with which one could cross the mouth of the Nile or travel up river.

In Egypt, three hundred years of rule by the Macedonian kings began under Alexander's general Ptolemy. The empire was expanded and rebuilt by three kings who, in total, ruled for more than 100 years. After Alexander's death, Ptolemy I Soter, 'the Saviour', founded the dynasty (323–283 BC) and secured control over Kyrene (cat. no. 428). Ptolemy II Philadelphos, his sister's lover, extended the empire (283–246 BC) (cat. no. *450*) and it reached its greatest extent under Ptolemy III Euergetes, 'the Benefactor' (246–221 BC).

Just as the first Ptolemy successfully established his position of power, the second was the creator of a religious stylisation of this sovereignty. He incorporated the ritual reverence of the dynasty so strongly in everyday life that, in spite of the later decadence of individual kings, this was never questioned by the populace. We are indebted to the first Ptolemies for the numerous buildings and facilities which laid the foundations for the fame which the new capital city Alexandria and its surroundings still enjoy today. Here, the harbour must take pride of place. The great lighthouse, the symbol of Alexandria as the gateway to the Mediterranean, later became one of the seven wonders of the world. The university was world famous and remained one of the major educational institutions of the world until the late ancient era.

Philetas of Kos and Zenodotos of Ephesos, the first great philologists, edited the *Iliad* and *Odyssey* here and created the foundations of their science. Eratosthenes of Cyrene, called the 'global surveyor' in ancient times, used measurements made here to calculate the circumference of the earth. Euclid, the mathematician of all peoples and generations up to the present day, taught in Alexandria as did Apollonius the 'great geometer' whom we must thank for the mathematical theorem for the conic section. Ctesibios was the most prominent representative of applied mechanics. In the area of medicine it was Herophilos who created the foundations for the teaching of anatomy. This later disappeared – as did so much other knowledge from ancient times – and had to be reacquired, at great pains, in modern times.

The 'great library', as the institution was appropriately named in antiquity, was no less famous than the city's symbol – the lighthouse. It is estimated that the library was in possession of as many as half a million scrolls. And, one must not forget the temples – the most famous being those of Isis and Sarapis.

428 **Stater from Cyrene**
Gold
c. 310 – 306 BC
Diam. 1.74 cm | wt. 7.14 g

left: Head of Ptolemy I decorated with a diadem; he is wearing an aegis around his neck.
Reverse : ΠΤΟΛΕΜΑΙΟΥ ΒΑΣΙΛΕΩΣ – (coin) of King Ptolemy – in two lines above Alexander the Great, bearing a lightning bolt in his right hand, on a chariot drawn by four elephants marching towards the left; inscribed with three monograms.   B. L.

97 **Coin**
Bronze
Cleopatra VII (51–30 BC)
Diam. 2.5 cm

The coin is a bronze 80-drachma (?) piece of Cleopatra VII from the mint of Alexandria.
Obverse: Head of Cleopatra facing to the right wearing diadem.
Reverse. Eagle standing left on thunderbolt; behind, Π(?) (=80). ΚΛΕΟΠΑΤΡΑΣ ΒΑΣΙΛΙΣΣΗΣ – (coin) of Queen Cleopatra.   A. M.

Greek intervention had long turned these Egyptian gods into universal ones and their most important shrines were the Sarapis temples in Alexandria and Canapus (cat. no. 19). In addition, this was also the location of one of the most famous Isis shrines of the age.

The Ptolemies had long managed to keep themselves removed from the disputes between the Romans and the Greeks but, after the middle of the second century BC, this was no longer possible. Egypt had been a Roman clientele state since the reign of Ptolemy VI Philometor (180–145 BC), 'his mother's lover', and every successor to the throne made great efforts to be regarded as a friend and confederate of the Roman people. The wealth of the country was reason enough for the Romans to intervene in the internal affairs of Egypt and it was precisely this wealth which saved it from a direct takeover by the Romans for so long. Nobody in Rome thought that anyone else was entitled to these rich pickings. Therefore, it was hardly a coincidence that, towards the end of Roman Republic, the final battle between the contenders for the imperial crown was fought before the gates of Alexandria.

Ptolemy XII (80–51 BC) (cat. no. 462), called 'the flautist' because of his obsession for accompanying choirs on the flute, had divide the country between his oldest daughter and oldest son while he was still alive. He had solemnly promised the Roman people to regulate his succession. The children who ascended the throne in this manner – the famous Cleopatra VII and the comparatively insignificant Ptolemy XIII – soon began a civil war which the Romans were dragged into. The final decision was reached when Caesar entered Alexandria. His love affair with Cleopatra assured her of the throne, which she soon shared with Ptolemy Caesar (cat. no. 463) her son from Caesar.

After Caesar's assassination and the ensuing battles, Cleopatra (cat. nos. 97, 96) went over to the side of Mark Antony who had selected the east when dividing the Roman empire between himself and Octavian, the later Emperor Augustus.

Antony needed Egypt in order to assert himself and Cleopatra needed him to be able to rule. She contributed the wealth of the country and he the experience of a Roman officer. However, both led to nothing. When Octavian entered Alexandria on the first day of a month in 30 BC, the three-thousand year epoch of Egyptian independence came to a close. Due to the exceptional importance of Egypt for Rome, the month in which Octavian/Augustus set foot in Alexandria was named August.

463   **Colossal head** (illus. p. 55)
Grey granite
Caesarion (?), 1st cent. BC
H. 80 cm | w. 60 cm | d. 50 cm

This fragment of a colossal statue is an example of a specific group of Ptolemaic royal representations with both Greek and Egyptian features. Statues that were Egyptian in their style but which adopted key Greek features began to be produced during the reign of Ptolemy V (204–180 BC) and continued to be made until the time of the last Ptolemaic ruler, Ptolemy XV. Some Roman emperors continued this tradition but only sporadically and often in Italy, where the audience needed a portrait in order to recognise the statue.
The statue is broken at the shoulders, only the head and part of the headdress are preserved. The face is that of a youthful subject and is naturalistic in appearance, thus suggesting a Greek rather than Egyptian model. The inclusion of hair is not Egyptian, but is a feature that appears on many of the Ptolemaic statues with Greek features. On the fringe is a worn *uraeus*-snake.
The head-cloth, a *nemes*, was worn by male rulers and some youthful gods, such as Horus, and is usual of Egyptian representations of the king. There are two sets of holes in the nemes which would have once supported a dowel. The first is at the top of the head and would have held a crown or the combined crowns of Upper and Lower Egypt. The second is in the form of a pair of dowel holes positioned in the folds of the head-cloth, above the ears. Perhaps the holes had once supported ram's horns, thus associating the subject with the Greco-Egyptian god Amon and by association the Greek Zeus.
The portrait features (not a true likeness of the subject but following a naturalistic Greek model that had been developed as the acceptable image of a ruler) are distinctively youthful. There are a number of statues of male rulers with similar youthful features, often interpreted as images of first-century princes, wearing either the traditional *nemes* head-cloth or diadem; some have a *uraeus*-snake, others are without it. The similarity of this particular statue with others that are recognised as late Ptolemaic suggests that the subject is a late king of this period. The youthful appearance provides further clues to the identity of the subject. Since the subject of the Alexandrian statue is shown as king of Egypt, it seems likely that it represents Cleopatra's eldest son, Ptolemy XV, whom she had with Caesar and who was named Caesarion (little Caesar) by the Alexandrians, and it is likely that there was once an accompanying representation of the queen herself.   S.-A. A.

462   **Sphinx**
Grey granite
1st cent. BC
H. 70 cm | w. 150 cm

It is almost completely preserved but its surface has suffered extensive erosion through its long sojourn on the seabed. The sphinx is shown in its traditional pose: the front paws stretched forwards, the hind paws under the belly. The head is adorned with a *nemes* with the two extended side-panels falling in front of the two sides of the chest. The royal *uraeus*-snake can be seen in front of the royal *nemes*. The sphinx could be a royal effigy of the father of Cleopatra VII, Ptolemy XII.   Z. K.

EMPIRE PERIOD

Following the death of Cleopatra and the capture of her capital, the period of Roman sovereignty began for Alexandria and its surroundings. Alexandria was no longer the metropolis of a kingdom but merely the capital of a province. However, it soon became clear that Egypt was vital for Rome. The tax revenues from the country alone amounted to more than eight times those from all of Gaul. In order to guarantee the smooth administration of the province, Augustus founded Nikopolis, the victory city, on the site of his conquest of the Egyptians and stationed 20,000 soldiers there. The battles under Caesar had devastated the formerly populated island of Pharos and also affected individual areas in northern Alexandria. This had the result that, under Augustus, a 'new city,' which was connected to the 'great harbour,' was constructed on the foundations of the former royal palace. Large-scale granaries, also incorporating the cemetery area of Alexander the Great, were built here. The tomb of the city's founder was not infringed on but, due to its encompassing walls, the entire area was predestined to be a storage place for goods which needed safekeeping – here, first and foremost, grain. In the vernacular, this new city district was called 'Brucheion' – wheat warehouse.

For example, one third of all the grain distributed in the city of Rome was delivered from Alexandria and its 'great harbour'. The amount of grain which left Alexandria every year must have been approximately 250,000 tons. This was the equivalent of 2,700,000 sacks which had to be loaded and reloaded several times within the city and transported from south to north. Augustus had a new port built on Lake Mareotis in the south of Alexandria which was named Iuliopolis after the emperor's family name.

Even though the golden time of the university was during the Ptolemaic period, it still maintained its high reputation in some faculties during the imperial period. This was particularly true of the medical department; the most famous doctor of the second century, Galen, studied in Alexandria. In addition, Alexandrian astrologers were in great demand and, among other things, they are to be thanked for our calendar. The Romans made comparatively few changes to the economy of Egypt and Alexandra but did, however, place more emphasis on private initiatives.

The peace which now prevailed around the Mediterranean provided Alexandria with even greater possibilities. Even though, as a provincial capital, its political importance had diminished compared with its time as a regal residence, this was compensated for by the fact that Alexandria had now become the undisputed largest trade metropolis of the Mediterranean world. This applied to the export of grain and other Egyptian and Alexandrian products as well as for intermediate trade with goods from the east. In order to improve transportation from and to the Nile as well as circulation within Alexandria, Augustus had the Emperor's Canal constructed in the south of the city. Three canals branched off from this within the city limits in a north-south direction; one of them led to Canapus.

Small and large manufacturers provided the city and province, as well as distant lands, with papyrus, textiles, glass and numerous other products. Red porphyry, from the Egyptian mountain of the same name, was the most expensive stone of antiquity and also left the country by way of Alexandria. In order to increase trade with the Far East, Emperor Trajan (98–117) had a canal constructed which, starting in today's Old Cairo, connected the Nile with the Red Sea near Suez. Trade with India was given new impetus through the results of research carried out at the University of Alexandria. Around the beginning of the common era, Alexandrian scientists described the monsoon winds and their influence on shipping to India and, after this, it became possible to benefit from these findings. Eventually, merchants from Alexandria reached China by way of India. It was possibly his origin in Alexandrian Menouthis which caused a voyager to India to name an island in the Indian Ocean Menuthias.

Along with their wares, merchants came into the region – an unparalleled mixture of ethnic groups. In addition, the region between Alexandria, Canapus and Herakleion was famous for its temples and the luxurious entertainment offered in the city was enormously attractive. The Caesareum, located in Alexandria, was a temple to the emperor as God. It enclosed a gigantic area with covered walks, libraries, rooms, sacred groves, portals, spacious squares and open courtyards. The large Sarapeum in the south-west of the city was even more immense in size, the Sarapis temple in Canapus was only slightly smaller. Along with the Sarapis temple, others were dedicated to Osiris, erected by Ptolemy III, and Isis and Anubis. The main religious festivals were not only popular with the Alexandrians; until far into the late ancient period, all of these temples, with their oracles and healing cults, attracted thousands of pilgrims from all over the world.

Life in this Egyptian provincial city was, therefore, characterised by the numerous visitors who came to the region in droves on any number of occasions. This was everyday life, but the occasional visits by the Roman emperor represented outstanding events. When we speak about the Roman emperor, the ruler of the world, travelling we can assume that the military and civil entourage of the regent consisted of approximately 5,000 persons. Following the death of Emperor Nero in 68, several aspirants

Phoenix, Byzantine mosaic from Daphnis

to the throne appeared in the Roman Empire; eventually, Vespasian (69–79) prevailed. One of the first and most important stations in the consolidation of his still fragile reign was Alexandria. Numerous troops were stationed there and Egypt was the granary of the Mediterranean world. His miracle cures, where the emperor, as the living manifestation of Sarapis, made it possible for a lame person to walk again and a blind man was given back his eyesight, were spectacular and celebrated throughout the empire.

The visit by the 'travelling emperor' Hadrian (117–138), who stayed in Egypt for approximately eight months, left the strongest impression. In Alexandria, he deliberated with scholars from the university and undertook an expedition into the Libyan desert to hunt lions. One of the main attractions of Alexandria, which hardly a single tourist omitted, was a visit to 'disreputable' Canapus, located twenty-four kilometres to the east of the city. This was not only the location of the holy district of Sarapis, but also the largest entertainment area in the world. Whoever wanted to amuse himself and live life to the full came to Canapus. There were gourmet restaurants and brothels for all tastes and within everybody's means. Here, one could find dance and theatre performances ranging from high-class drama to vulgar burlesque. A person who had not experienced Canapus could be accused of not having experienced life. Hadrian was also there and a 'facility' in his large villa in Tivoli near Rome was called Canapus as a reminiscence of his visit.

A special reason for visiting the Alexandria region was given in 139 when Egypt celebrated an event which occurred only once every 1,461 years. In order to appreciate it fully, one must go far back into Egypt's past. In the period of the Old Kingdom, probably during the reign of King Djoser (2624–2605 BC), Egypt had a calendar year of 365 days. Shortly thereafter, the Egyptians connected the beginning of the new year with an astronomic date: with the ascent of the brightest of all the fixed stars – the dog star – when this can once again be seen, shortly before sunrise, at dawn. Seeing that the civil calendar year was approximately a quarter day shorter than the astronomic stellar year, the beginnings of both years only fell on the same day once every 1,461 years and this long interim period makes it understandable that so much importance was placed on this concurrence. At that time, coins depicting the phoenix were minted in Alexandria. The bird which, according to the legend, miraculously rises from its ashes can really be seen as the symbol of the city which, following the disastrous blows of fate it experienced repeatedly after the beginning of the third century, always managed to recover.

At the beginning of the empire period, the region, if one ignores a few exceptional moments, experienced a comparatively peaceful period. However, confrontations between the Greek and Jewish inhabitants of Alexandria, in addition to the large Egyptian population, were a permanent factor of trouble. Time and time again, bloody conflict flamed up and, at the beginning of the second century, a regular war broke out at the end of which the Jewish population of the city was annihilated. The population living in the swamp area surrounding Lake Mareotis was also another danger. They lived from the lake and raiding which made them such a threat to the cities of Alexandria, Canapus, Menouthis and Herakleion that, occasionally, the military had to be sent into action. In 172, they were finally conquered in a veritable land battle.

At the beginning of 200, a Roman emperor – this time, Septimius Severus (193–211) along with his family – once again visited the city. Science, religious matters and antiquities were among the emperor's passions, and where could he better indulge these hobbies than in Alexandria and Egypt? Caracalla, approximately fifteen years old at the time (cat. no. 495), was a member of the family and was later to succeed his father (211–217).

A gloomy chapter in the history of Alexandria became linked with his name when he made a return visit to the Nile in 215. Whereas Caracalla was greeted in the suburb of Canapus by the officials of the city with a festive procession, and returned the favour with a magnificent banquet, rioting broke out in the centre of the city during which the statues of the emperor were toppled. Caracalla crushed the revolt and principally punished the officials whom he deemed responsible for the events which had occurred in their city; in addition there were victims among the rest of the population. It seems that life soon returned to its normal trot. Inscriptions of honour from the time after his visit can be seen on the harbour island Antirhodos: 'For the ruler of the world, Emperor Caracalla, the devotee of Sarapis'. No city could afford to fall out with the emperor for too long and no ruler could do without Alexandria.

After the middle of the third century, the situation became much more difficult as the weaknesses of the Roman central administration emboldened usurpers throughout the empire. In the east, Zenobia the ruler of Palmyra, was one of them. In 270, she attempted to conquer Alexandria and was finally successful. A Roman counterattack was soon started which brought Alexandria, once again, under the control of the emperor. Each of these occurrences resulted in serious destruction to the civic infrastructure: the Brucheion district became deserted in this period.

The next similar revolt was experienced by Alexandria and the region in 297. The emperor Diocletian (284–305) appeared personally in Alexandria and smothered the usurpation in a bloodbath. Once again, the city had to be conquered by military force which led to destruction throughout the entire region. In 298, Diocletian celebrated this success with a victory monument which he had constructed on the Sarapeum hill. This memorial, quite literally, towered above everything. An almost twenty-nine-metre-high column soared above a square pedestal; it is one of the largest preserved monoliths and one of the most impressive memorial columns which, today, still dominates the appearance of the city.

The reform measures undertaken by this emperor in so many areas mark the beginning of the late ancient era which can also be seen as the beginning of a new chapter in the history of the region around Alexandria.

495 Aureus
Gold
Caracalla (206 AD)
Diam. 2 cm

This is a gold coin of Caracalla (198–217 AD) from the mint of Rome.
Obverse: Head of the emperor laureate facing right.
ANTONINVS PIVS AVG(VSTVS) Antoninus Pius (the pious) Emperor
Reverse: Mars standing facing to the right, wearing helmet and holding spear.
PONTIF(EX) TR(IBVNICIA) P(OTESTATE) VIII CO(N)S(VL) II – Priest, eight-time bearer of the tribunal power, two-time consul.   A. M.

Diocletian column in Alexandria

A VISIT BY A GOD
CARACALLA IN ALEXANDRIA

473 **Column with Greek inscription**
Red granite
Caracalla (211–217 AD)
H. 160 cm | diam. 105 cm

Translation: "(For the) Master over the earth and the sea
and all places inhabited on the earth, the Ruler of the
Cosmos, the worshiper of Sarapis, who is blessed with
eternal life, the emperor Marcus Aurelius Severus
Antoninus (called Caracalla) . . . on Phamenoth 25."   E. B.

474 **Column with Greek inscription**
Red granite
Caracalla (211–217 AD)
H. 85 cm | diam. 105 cm

Translation: "(For the) Master over the earth and the sea,
the Ruler of the Cosmos, the worshiper of Sarapis, who is
blessed with eternal life, the emperor Marcus Aurelius
Severus Antoninus (called Caracalla), the God."   E. B.

476 **Column with Greek inscription**
Red granite
Caracalla (211–217 AD)
H. 150 cm | diam. 105 cm

In the fourth line some twenty letters have been lost. After the year in line 6, the last digit of which is missing, the beginning of the emperor's title is indicated and continued in line 7. Only M(arcus) Aur[elius . . .] however has survived.

Translation: "(For the) Master over the earth and the sea, the worshiper of Sarapis, who is blessed with eternal life, the emperor Marcus Aurelius Severus Antoninus, the Pious (called Caracalla), the people of Rome and Alexandria (have dedicated the statue) to the citizens [of . . .] in the year . . . [of the Emperor]."   E. B.

475 **Column with Greek inscription**
Red granite
Caracalla (211–217 AD)
H. 155 cm | diam. 105 cm

Translation: "(For the) Master over the earth and the sea, the woshiper of Sarapis, who is blessed with eternal life, the emperor Marcus Aurelius Severus Antoninus, the Pious (called Caracalla), the Antoninans . . . the people of Rome and Alexandria (have) dedicated (the statue) as a sign of their devotion."
In the fifth line some fifteen letters have been lost. The inscription names the dedication being made by the Antoninans, who are described as people of Rome and Alexandria. These could have belonged to a guild whose aim was to uphold reverence to the emperor, its members coming from two different ethnic groups or, what is probably more likely, from Roman citizens of Alexandria. The term 'people of Rome and Alexandria' can be found in texts from the third century and was used to define a privileged group of people living in the city.   E. B.

476

LATE ANTIQUITY

Among the changes made in the Diocletian time were the downsizing of many administrative districts into smaller entities, which also had an effect on the former province of Egypt. The most obvious change in the appearance of the city of Alexandria and its suburbs came from the Christian churches, the earliest of which were founded in the third century. The most impressive of these buildings was the bishop's church of Alexandria which, due to its dimensions, was called the 'Great Church'. Its second name, 'Emperor's Church,' originated from its location as it was built within the confines of the former Caesareum. While still out at sea, voyagers arriving in Alexandria could see a prominent Christian building located on the harbour alongside the lighthouse.

Several Christian sects had spread throughout the city and surroundings and were fighting amongst themselves about the one true path to salvation. One thing they had in common was their battle against the pagans and the Jewish community which was once again in the process of establishing itself in the city. Quite often, these quarrels ended in bloody fighting in the streets.

The date 21 July 365 marked a profound turning point in the city. Alexandria had been stuck by earthquakes on more than one occasion but that which battered the metropolis and the neighbouring cities on this day reached dimensions which had never before been experienced. A gigantic tsunami hit the coast and washed ships ashore onto the roofs of the houses. Centuries later, this day was remembered in Alexandria as the 'day of fear'.

Many of the major controversies of Christian theology and the entire history of the empire had their genesis in Alexandria seeing that the city was, in many respects, the religious centre of the eastern Mediterranean area. It was still the home of one of the most important educational institutes of the day and so it comes as no surprise that the theological discussions of the Christians were significantly influenced by the bishops of Alexandria. These arguments, which often split Christianity into two opposing camps, dealt with questions of faith concerning the salvation of the individual as well as of mankind. However, they were also about Episcopal sees, benefices, religious following, and politics in the widest possible sense especially because, since the time of Emperor Constantine (306–337) the expansion of Christianity had become an increasingly governmental matter.

Over the centuries, Alexandria, Canapus, Menouthis and Herakleion had developed into centres of pagan cults which attracted believers from all over the Mediterranean world. In the late ancient period, the same applied to the Christian churches and, above all, to the monasteries which had been constructed on the area of the destroyed and deserted Brucheion district. Here, particular attention must be drawn to the institutions in the suburbs of Canapus and Menouthis.

The Christian pilgrims drawn to Alexandria came, on the one hand, to visit the metropolis itself but mostly because of the monasteries in the surrounding area. At times, there were up to 2,000 monks in the immediate vicinity of the city and as many as 5,000 in Nitria at the far end of Lake Mareotis. Somewhat further south lay the great hermitage centre of Kellia where there were 1,600 buildings in the sixth century. Each of these consisted of two separate rooms for the monks, a reception room, kitchen and prayer room, all around a walled courtyard with fountains, a garden and, occasionally, a small chapel. An impressive crowd assembled whenever the bishop of Alexandria called upon the monks of the neighbourhood to help him against the Jews, pagans or even the authorities.

All of these small and large monastic sites were dwarfed in importance by the famous shrine of Saint Menas to which was attributed tremendous magical powers – healing powers, above all. The monastery where, according to legend, Menas was transported through the skies, lay one-and-a-half days journey from Alexandria on the other side of Lake Mareotis at its western end and, up to the sixth century, had developed into a city and the largest early-Christian place of pilgrimage of antiquity (p. 35).

The growth of the Christian communities in the city led to an increase in the readiness of the faithful and their patriarchs to be aggressive towards the pagans and Jews. Since the beginning of the fourth century, Alexandria had had a series of bishops who were absolutely unparalleled in their will to power and self-assertiveness. A major, spectacular incident occurred in 391. The pagans protested when the patriarch had their idols paraded through the streets in order to subject them to mockery. This was followed by a counter from the Christians and they soon came to blows which, once again, had bloody consequences. During the commotion, a large group of Christians encircled a number of pagans on the area of the Sarapeum. After vicious fighting, the Christians forced their way into the temple, overpowered the pagans and began their work of destruction by hacking off the hands and feet of the great statue of Sarapis. The individual limbs were taken to different districts of the city and burned there.

After the destruction of the Sarapeum – which Christian historians liked to deal with, in great detail, seeing that it filled them with pride – the counterpart in Canapus suffered the same fate. Once again, the Sarapis cult changed its location, moving this time to Menouthis where its holy shrine experienced a considerable boom, principally as a place of in the history of Alexandria. In order to weld his own followers together against competitive Christian groups, Patriarch Kyrill used a tried and tested method: a battle against a common enemy such as the Jews. The pogrom of 415 began in the theatre of Alexandria with a fight between Christians and Jews. When the Jews were threatened by the patriarch, they carried out a massacre among the Christians on the following night. On the next day the patriarch retaliated. The pogrom meant the end of the history of a group of people who had lived in Alexandria since the very beginnings of the city 700 years previously. When the prefect of Egypt asked the female pagan philosopher Hypatia, who was well-known far beyond the borders of the city, to attempt to calm down the population in a public speech, the bishop's rage increased immeasurably. Nursing staff of the Alexandrian church, who had long since turned into a gang of thugs, attacked the philosopher, killed her brutally and finally burned her body as was customarily done with idols.

Even after the terrible fate of Hypatia, the university remained an educational institution for prominent pagans. Horapollon taught grammar and philosophy until the eighties of the fifth century. He finished his teaching following persecution by the Christians, was forced to flee and, towards the end of his life, appears to have converted to Christianity in order to avoid further oppression. His treatise on hieroglyphics became famous. When his work was discovered and published, in the fifteenth century, it triggered a passion for hieroglyphics which soon swept over the whole of Europe. After the sixth century, Christians played an increasingly important role in the university. One of their most outstanding representatives and, at the same time, the most important theologian of his time was John Philoponos (495–575). His epithet Philoponos, work lover, came from his immense diligence and his enormous literary productivity. His commentary on Aristotle's physics, which cemented his fame for all time, originated in 517. In the sixteenth century, Latin translations of his works were published in Venice. Galileo Galilei was aware of them and his studies of the works of John Philoponos played no small part in stimulating his development of the laws of the free fall of objects.

Pressure on the pagans in the region did increase somewhat in the fifth century without leading to the complete elimination of the old religion. However, these pagan cults increasingly moved to the surroundings of Alexandria. For example, there was a lively practice of pagan cults in the sanctuaries at Menouthis until the end of the fifth century. Canapus had also long since developed into a focal point in the confrontation between pagans and Christians. In spite of all their attacks and the foundation of monasteries, some of the sanctuaries had remained preserved and offered refuge to pagan intellectuals. This also drew pagan priests from all regions of Egypt to Canapus where they brought their otherwise threatened cultic objects to safety. The *Naos of the Decades* is a fascinating witness to these rescue attempts (p. 49 ff.).

From the fourth to the sixth centuries, Christianity was characterised by a confrontation with implications reaching far into the political sphere. Theologians managed to find agreement on the subject that two natures (Greek, *physeis*; singular, *physis*), the human (Jesus) and the divine (Christ) were united in the Son

Hypatia, as imagined by Charles William Mitchell, 1885

healing. In 414, the destiny of this temple was also sealed. In order to take advantage of the attractiveness of the location and cult, the patriarch transferred the remains of Saint Cyrus there. According to the legend, Cyrus was a famous doctor who had a high reputation among the poor because he treated them free of charge. It appears that he was eventually executed as a martyr. The entire story greatly resembles a fairytale but this did nothing to affect its popularity. The name Cyrus lives on in the contemporary designation Aboukir (= Father Cyrus).

The controversies within the individual Christian groups played an increasingly important role of God, in Jesus Christ. However, there was a difference of opinion as to whether both natures had remained independent in their characteristics – two natures (*dyophysites*) – or had become completely amalgamated into a single entity (*miaphysites*). In principle, this dissent ruled out any discussion. Mediation between the *miaphysites* and *dyophysites* was impossible seeing that there could be no solution such as 'one-and-a-half' natures. Anybody who attempted to find a compromise had both sides against him.

The opposition between the two major Christian groups led to some bishops of Alexandria only to appear in public accompanied by their bodyguards; the insurmountable differences even found their way into miracle tales. A rich young man, a *miaphysite*, who expected assistance from Saint Cyrus, a supporter of *dyophysist* Christianity, had to first take communion in one of the *dyophysist* churches in Alexandria before being helped by the saint contributing, from his point of view, to the victory of the 'true' religion. This sanctimonious legend teaches us that the conflict between the Christian cults also affected Alexandra and its environs. The capital itself was, more or less, *miaphysic*, Canapus and its monasteries, however, *dyophysic*.

Whenever a theological controversy arose in the Greek east, the bishop of Alexandria, sooner than later, became involved. His most important rival had his seat in the capital of the eastern empire, in Constantinople. Dogmatic disputes were often connected with special national interests. *Miaphysitism* was also partially an expression of local dissatisfaction, particularly in Syria and Egypt. Here, there was resentment towards Constantinople, the political and religious parvenu. Its belief, *dyophytism*, was seen as being an instrument of a foreign power.

The disputes described, on both the national and regional level, weakened the resistance of the Byzantine Empire which it especially needed in the early seventh century. In 619, the Persian king, who had been Rome's opponent in the Near East for centuries, conquered Alexandria following a lengthy siege. The rural land and the numerous monasteries also suffered a great deal from the plundering Persian soldiers. It was not until ten years later that Emperor Heraclius (610–641) (cat. no. 91) was able to reconquer the city and to extend the phase of Roman control over Alexandria for an additional decade.

ISLAMIC PERIOD

The Arab conquest followed rapidly after the Persian. After he had laid siege to Alexandria for fourteen months and finally hoisted Mohammed's banner above its walls, Amr ibn al-As, the caliph of Oman, wrote: 'I have conquered the greatest city of the Occident.' In 646, Omar was forced to put down a rebellion which groups sympathising with Constantinople had instigated against Arab rule. During the battle, part of the old city wall was destroyed. Seeing that there was a danger of a re-conquest by east Rome, the Arabs transferred a force of 12,000 men to Alexandria.

Life in the city and region continued – even Christian life. Pilgrimage tourism was hardly affected, Alexandria remained an important station on the way to the Holy Land. The Arabs also continued trading activities following well-trodden paths; still using the Trajan canal, for instance. This meant that golden Christian crosses (cat. no. 55) and Islamic coins (cat. nos. 438, 94, 95) could be found alongside each other on the ocean floor in Aboukir Bay.

The changes in the landscape were much more grave than those in politics. Arabic texts record extreme Nile flooding in the years 741 and 742 which was definitely responsible for some damage in the suburbs of Alexandria. As early as the seventh century, some buildings in Canapus were so close to the coastline that they were in danger of sinking into the sea. Herakleion, Menouthis, parts of Canapus and the harbour of Alexandria disappeared as a result of different natural catastrophes. They rested on the floor of the ocean until modern technology made their rediscovery possible.

During underwater excavations at Canapus, two Umayyad gold coins and an Abbasid gold coin (Arabic *dinar*) were found together with Byzantine coins. These three coins date from the second phase of Islamic coin-minting following Caliph Abd al-Malik's monetary reform in year 77 of the Hegira (696 AD), suggesting a possible first attempt to unite his empire by means of currency.

The coins display no names at all, and the legends adorning the obverse and reverse are (except for the date) of a purely religious nature. Under the Umayyad and first Abbasid caliphs, coins were initially minted anonymously. It was only later that the governors added their names, at first on some copper coins and then on their silver dirhams. The title caliph was added only under the Abbasids.

The dates featuring in the marginal areas occasionally enable us to attribute these coins to the rule of a particular caliph. The Umayyad dinar, half-dinar and third-dinar may be the equivalent of the Byzantine solidus and its fractions (*semissis* and *tremissis*). Unlike on the silver coins, the mint is generally not mentioned. They were probably made in Damascus, the caliphate capital. Supporting this notion is that authority for minting gold derived from the sovereign jurisdiction of *sikka*, the Arabic term for minting coins. The obverse of these three coins is identical, and bears the inscription *kalima*, the confirmation of the uniqueness of God. In the margin is the 'prophetic mission' or second symbol, an extract from *sure* 9,33 of the Koran. This proclaims the supreme position of Mohammed in Islam, his role in the revelation and the pre-eminence of Islam vis-à-vis other religions.

91

438

94

95

55

The script on the coins is Kufic. It is square and angular, and was likewise reformed during the rule of 'Abd al-Malik, and has no diacritic symbols.

Umayyad and Abbasid dinars were always minted with great care and are generally well-preserved. 'Abd al-Malik's reform introduce a statutory weight of one *mithqāl* (*c.* 4.25 g) for the dinar, and this remained the standard weight for the coins of succeeding dynasties.

It is certain that gold and silver were in circulation in Egypt both before and after the Arab conquest of Egypt, as minted gold was the only recognised payment method for the settlement of taxes. Nonetheless, all the monetary finds from Umayyad and Abbasid Egypt have hitherto been exclusively copper coins. As far as we are aware, no find from the pre-Tulunid period (pre-868 AD) has been published for Egypt.

Although the Egyptian collections have a wealth of Umayyad and Abbasid dinars, their origin remains unknown. They are undoubtedly coins found in Egypt, but where they were found and in what circumstances is not known. On the other hand, these dinars have been found in great quantity in Syria, where Umayyad dinars were minted, also in Iraq and south-east Turkey.   C. B.

previous page:

91   **Tremissis**
Gold
Heraclius (613–641 AD)
Diam. 1.69 cm | wt. 1.31 g

Obverse: Bust with a diadem, [D(OMINVS)] N(OSTER) [H]EPACLIVS T P(ER)P(ETVVS) AVG(VSTVS) – Our Lord Heraclius, perpetual emperor; the T cannot be explained
Reverse: Cross potent, VICTORIA AVGVS(TORVM) – Victory to the emperor.   C. M.

438   **Abbassid dinar**
Gold
785 AD
Diam. 1.9 cm | wt. 4.2 g

Abbassid gold dinar from the reign of Al-Mahdī or Al-Hadī (year 169 = 785).
Obverse and Reverse: 'There is no God but God. He is unique, There is no associate. Muhammad is the Prophet of Allah.'
Legend on the side of the obverse : 'In the name of God, this dinar was struck in the year 169.' Legend on the edge of the reverse: 'Muhammad is the Prophet of Allah, he sent him the good direction and the true religion to make it triumph over all others.'   C. B.

94   **Umayyad dinar**
Gold
729–730 AD
Diam. 2 cm | wt. 4.25 g

Gold Dinar from the reign of Hish_m, (year 11 = 729–730).
Obverse: "There is no God but God. He is unique, There is no associate." Reverse : "God is unique, God is eternal, He has not engendered, nor was he engendered" Legend on the side of the obverse : "Muhammad is the Prophet of Allah, he sent him the good direction and the true religion to make it triumph over all others." Legend on the edge of the reverse: "This Dinar was struck in the year 111."   C. B.

95   **Umayyad third-dinar**
Gold
718–719 AD
Diam. 1.37 cm | wt. 1.43 g

Golden third-dinar from the reign of Umar II (year 100 = 718–719). Obverse: "There is no God but God." Reverse : "In the name of God, the merciful, the clement." Legend on the side of the obverse: "Muhammad is the Prophet of Allah, he sent him the good direction and the true religion." Legend on the edge of the reverse : "This third-dinar was struck in the year 100."   C. B.

55   **Cross pendant**
Gold
6th – early 8th cent. AD
H. 1.51 cm | w. 0.94 cm | d. 0.1 cm

The arms of the cross are engraved with circular forms and tear and sickle shapes.   Y. S.

FRANCK GODDIO

The Rediscovery of the Sunken Cities

The glorious past of the city of Alexandria makes it a fascinating subject. During the Hellenistic era, its influence radiated across the entire ancient world. But the historical interest of this region of Egypt situated directly west of the mouth of the Nile's westernmost branch goes altogether beyond the domain and issues of Alexandrian studies to embrace Egyptology as a whole. Even before Alexander the Great founded the glorious city and its ports, the region around Canopos had already been the favoured point of contact between the Aegean world and the kingdom of the pharaohs in the eastern Mediterranean for more than four centuries. It was in fact almost exclusively by ascending the western arm of the Nile that the Greeks and their products penetrated Egyptian territory to reach Memphis, the seat of royal power and river junction linking the Nilotic branches to Upper Egypt.

During the second millennium BC, this waterway does not seem to have acted as a general channel of communication. The Egyptians contented themselves with keeping pirates out of it. The principal axis of trade at the time was the Pelusian (easternmost) branch, used by Egyptian convoys going to Asia and Canaanite merchant ships entering the kingdom. That way came the luxury products of the Aegean world, shipped via Cyprus and the Levantine coast or Asian entrepot ports. Then, during the eighth century BC, conquering empires established themselves in Asia. Assyrians, Babylonians and sub-

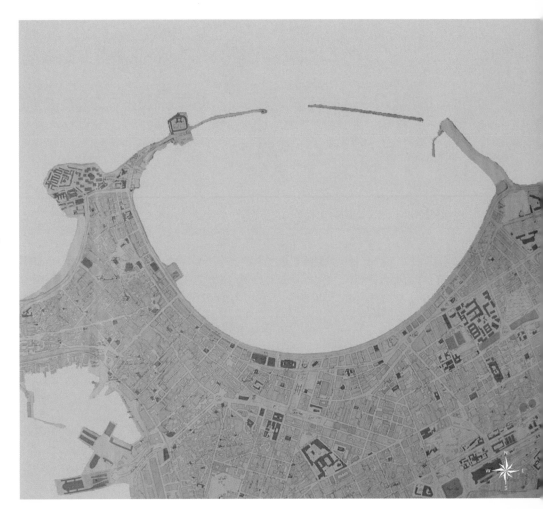

The excavation site off Alexandria's eastern port

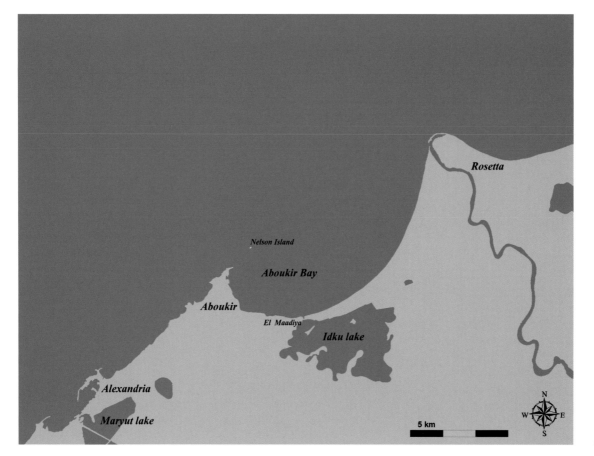

Alexandria and Aboukir Bay

sequently Persians reached the Mediterranean and threatened Egypt on its Asiatic frontier by land and sea so that the Greeks of the Balkan peninsula and Asia Minor headed directly for Egypt, steering clear of coasts controlled by the Phoenicians. At this juncture, the region around Canopus acquired a new historical dimension.

It has long been accepted that the ruins of Canopus should be sought on the present-day peninsula of Aboukir. This assumption was largely based on the distance that separated Alexandria from Canopus, according to the antique geographer Strabo, and the apparent survival of the name of St Cyril in the Arabic place name (Abū Qīr), his relics having been (according to Christian tradition) preserved in Canopus. However, placing and demarcating on the map the neighbouring city east of Alexandria which we call Canopus is not as straightforward as one might think. It is therefore more appropriate to speak of the 'Canopus region', since the distance between the eastern gate of the capital (the Canopus gate) and the western branch of the Nile was only around twenty-two miles (thirty-five kilometres). Moreover, identifying the whereabouts and configuration of the oldest Canopus, the city the Greek texts begin to speak of at least two centuries before the founding of Alexandria, turns out to be very difficult given the present state of our investigations.

Numerous surveys and discoveries of remains and sites were carried out in the eighteenth, nineteenth and twentieth centuries on the Alexandrian and Aboukir coasts. Attempts at locating the sites were made from the nineteenth century on. Several hypotheses were put forward regarding the whereabouts of different cities mentioned in ancient texts. Scholars such as Mahmoud bey El-Falaki and the Rev. J. Faivre situated them on terra firma, along the shore of Aboukir Bay (p. 76).

However, the discovery of ruins there prompted some people to consider the possibility that natural phenomena could have caused the waters of the Mediterranean to swallow up lands that stood proud of the sea in antiquity. The clues in the texts therefore needed reconsideration. In 1929, G. Daressy put forward the theory that the distances indicated in the ancient texts should be transferred to the extension of the coastline from Alexandria to Aboukir rather than following the present-day shore of the bay. He thus situated the lost city of Herakleion in a theoretical location in the bay.

A vital discovery in support of such reasoning was made in 1933. Alerted by Group Captain Cull, commander of the RAF base at Aboukir who thought he had seen an area of ruins in Aboukir Bay when taking off from the military aerodrome, Prince Omar Toussoun, a scholar and expert on the Delta, came to look for himself. Not finding anything on the spot, he asked local fishermen if they knew anything about submerged ruins. Following their information, the prince identified an important archaeological deposit just over a mile from the shore made up of 'columns of marble and probably red granite'. A diver brought to the surface the white marble head of a statue of Alexander the Great. It was thus proved that the remains of important monuments were lying at the bottom of Aboukir Bay. These discoveries were vital as far as future exploration of the Canopus region was concerned because they proved that a part of this inhabited zone had been well and truly submerged by the waves.

The exploration project launched by the European Institute of Underwater Archaeology in 1992 set an initial objective of accurately fixing the topography of the submerged zones of Alexandria's eastern port and the Canopus region. It seemed logical to extend the studies of the great port to the estuarial region of Canopus lost beneath the waves, since these places are linked by geography and history. The results obtained also served to show that the entire historical geography of the Alexandria region was affected by the discoveries made in Aboukir Bay.

The fundamental aim of the work was to reconsider methodically the problems of physical geography raised by the submersion of the shoreline in the Alexandria region and the chronology of the phenomena that caused the submersion. Exploration of the places in the Canopus region lost beneath the sea and the submerged part of the great port was thus of necessity coupled with a study of the circumstances that caused their drowning.

The plan that was adopted aimed to carry out geophysical and geological exploration, the results of which would then be enriched by archaeological findings from scientific excavations. The study of

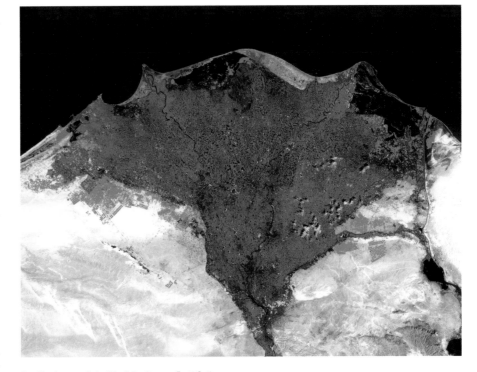

Satellite image of the Nile Delta (Image: EarthSat)

these finds would be done in the light of the documentary evidence from papyruses and epigraphs, following a critical philological analysis of these sources. The study could thus then lead on to an analysis of the sites discovered and possibly even identify them.

But the project had first to deal with specific problems, because an archaeological study of submerged sites had never been carried out on such a scale.

As far as Alexandria is concerned, there are numerous detailed descriptions supported by eyewitness accounts such as those of Julius Caesar, Hirtius, Strabo, Josephus and Philo. As a known ancient spot that could be used as a reference, we had the well-established location beside the entrance to the Caesarium, marked in the past by the two obelisks called 'Cleopatra's Needles', one of which arrived in London in 1877 and the other in New York in 1879. We also knew that modern Cape Silsileh had to be a remnant of the ancient Cape Lochias. This provided us with an eastern limit to the ancient great port. Bearing in mind the ruins found on land and the descriptions of the great port given in the texts, there could be no doubt that parts of the ancient port infrastructure and former terra firma lay under the waters of the port of Alexandria and that these were where famous monuments had been located in antiquity. The area that we explored in order to locate the sunken part of the great harbour covered 400 hectares of the present harbour basin. (p. 371).

With regard to the Canopic mouth of the Nile, writers in antiquity referred to two places on the coast; one bore the Greek name Herakles, the other a name

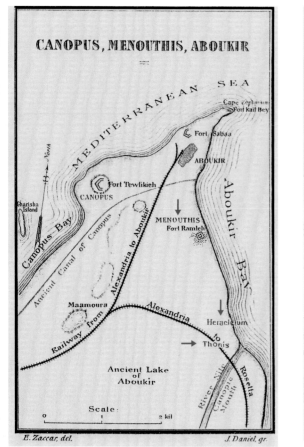

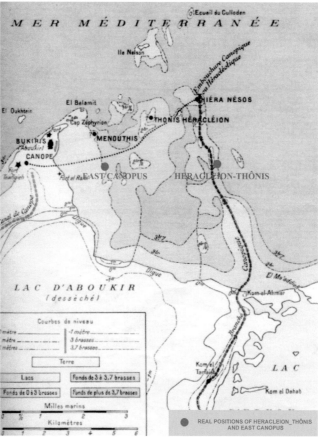

left: Chart produced by E. Zaccar in J. Père Faivre's 1917 publication *Canopus, Menouthis, Aboukir* showing the presumed locations of the towns of Thonis, Menouthis and Herakleion on the coast of Aboukir Bay.

far left: Chart produced by G. Daressy in 1929. Menouthis and Thonis-Herakleion are located offshore.

in the local language, transcribed as Tonis. From their context, it can be assumed that both lay to the east of Canopus near the mouth of the western arm of the Nile known as the Canopic or Herakleion mouth or estuary. Reports by contemporary writers about the former port of Canopus are so numerous that, these alone, give an idea as to how important this town must have been in the Hellenistic and imperial periods. A considerable number of texts and an abundance of information of various degrees has been available ever since Hecataios of Milet recorded his thoughts at the end of the sixth century BC, and since the port was mentioned by tragedians such as Aeschylus or included in reports by Herodotus in the fifth century BC, in the poems of Callimachus, Poseidippus and Nicander or in descriptions made by Strabon (66 BC–24 AD), Aelius Aristides (129–172 AD), or Pausanias (c. 110–180 AD), right up to mentions by the church fathers of late antiquity such as Epiphanius of Salamis, Rufinus of Aquileia, Eunap, Hieronymus, Zacharias Rhetor or Sophronios of Jerusalem (seventh century AD). Collectively, these reports hinted at the discoveries to be made.

A MISSION UNDER DIFFICULT CIRCUMSTANCES

Works carried out on land had led to discoveries identifiying certain ruins of the city of Canopus. The finds made by Prince Omar Toussoun indicated clearly that a portion of this region had been drowned (p.119). Bearing in mind the underwater discoveries and relative positions of the different cities mentioned in the texts, the bay seemed to be where the ancient Egyptian shore zone needed to be and where towns and monuments lay whose existence was known to us but which had never been found. However, instead of having (as in Alexandria) precise landmarks nearby that we could easily relate to the submerged sites, all we had as reference points for the drowned area were vast zones of remains on land and beneath the sea that were vague in outline and a long way apart.

Another formidable handicap was soon revealed. The quality of the water at Aboukir is as awful as in Alexandria, making underwater work extremely difficult. Visibility is often extremely poor because of the alluvial deposits carried down by the Nile and sand from coastal currents, and this is aggravated by various kinds of pollution. The fact that the bays are not very deep and are poorly sheltered likewise means the water constantly churns up sediment and carries it along. Thus underwater visibility ranges most of the time between two and three feet (50−100 centimetres). Sometimes it is almost zero; in exceptionally favourable circumstances it may reach a few yards (metres). But there is also an advantage to these factors. The poor visibility and the thick deposits of sediment have kept the remains hidden from human sight and thus preserved them.

Our project concerned only the western part of Aboukir Bay because the ancient texts indicated that the sites of Canopus, Thonis and Herakleion were situated to the west of the Canopus branch of the Nile. The mouth of Edku Lake, at the level of the recently blocked present-day port of El Maadiya seemed on the evidence to be a relic of the ancient, now vanished branch of the Nile. Bearing in mind all the information available to us, a search zone was established for investigation in the water that covered an immense area of almost seven by six miles, that is, forty-two square miles.

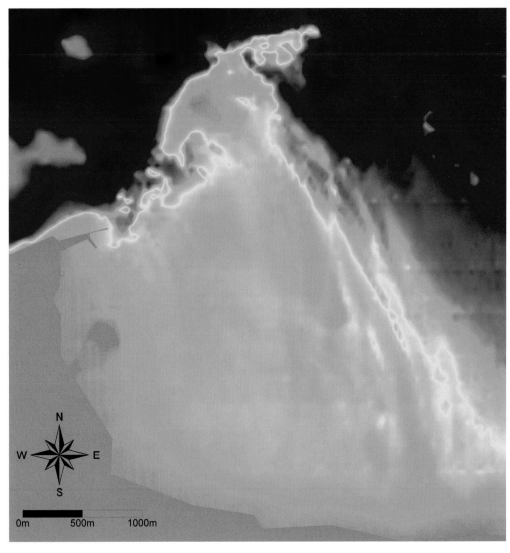

Bathymetric chart of the excavation site

THE RESOURCES USED
FOR THE EXPLORATION

The scientific approach relative to the exploration we had defined beforehand had to take into account the specific topography of the zones studied. The ancient surface of the land now under the sea has been completely changed over the centuries by factors of a seismic (earthquakes and tidal waves), hydrographic (floods and changes in sea levels) and geological (subsidence) nature. The process of change went on even after the sea took over. Once underwater, the former terra firma was still subject to seismic events, to which were added the action of sediments, currents, swell and waves. The simple observation of the current state of the seabed by any one of the instruments available today for geo-

physical and geological exploration (bathymetric sounder, lateral sonar, sediment sounder, magnometer, geological core drilling) would not in isolation be enough to discover the entire reality of the antique topography. It was necessary to cross-reference data collected by different methods available in order to obtain an image as close as possible to what the land looked like in ancient times.

Moreover, the top layer of the bottom of Aboukir Bay consists mainly of sand and Nile alluvium brought by currents from the east. The seabed at Alexandria likewise suffers from substantial sedimentation, sand having been accumulating for centuries on the west side of the port. It is incidentally this silting which has filled the zone of the Heptastadion built by Alexander the Great, on which a whole city district has now been built. We had to assume that many archaeological remnants in these areas would have been covered with sediment.

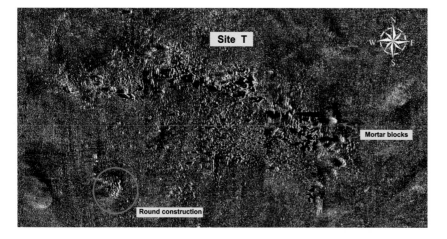

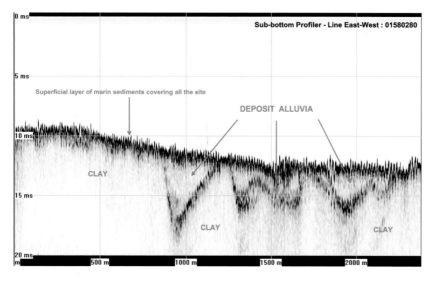

top: Side-scan sonar image of excavation site T showing important architectural features projecting through the sediment

above: Sub-bottom profiler of the sediment including extended areas covered by the Canopic branch of the Nile near Herakleion

We first pursued the indication in the texts that the city of Thonis was situated at the mouth of the Canopus branch of the Nile. This piece of information about the ancient emporium allowed us to approach the problem geologically because the existence of this water channel and its outlet into the sea had probably left geological traces we could spot.

An effective way to find archaeological remnants underwater that are covered with sediment was to draw up a detailed magnometric map with very high resolution. On a map of this kind geological phenomena would also be visible: faults, trenches, channels, the beds of water courses filled with sundry materials differentiating them from the surrounding terrain. All these features would provide evidence about ancient topography and could suggest possible reasons why the sea took over.

Coverage with a side-sweeping sonar, providing an electronic image of the bottom and showing up features sticking out of the sediment layer, was a useful additional tool for finding archaeological sectors not yet completely discovered.

Exploration done with the help of a sediment sounder would meantime provide precise information about the different geological layers making up the ground in the zone. It could supply information about phenomena of a seismic nature that took place in that area (local existence of inclined sedimentary layers, horst, diapirics). Possibly it would also detect areas containing fossils if we looked for specific sediments that would pinpoint the respective courses of the channels and main arm of the Canopus branch in ancient times.

The different technologies thus had to be deployed in a complementary manner in order to achieve the topographical, geological and archaeological objectives we had set ourselves. Both in Alexandria and Aboukir Bay, the combined use of different instruments and methods of exploration proved particularly fruitful in the event, each technique adding a specific contribution to the investigation of the seafloor.

The results show that the sites were struck at different periods by cataclysmic geological events and natural disasters. It has been shown that a slow subsidence movement in the ground affected this

In this case, uncovering them would involve difficulties. Though it is possible to localise artefacts on poor surfaces by accurate mechanical soundings carried out in a systematic fashion, this approach was unrealistic there bearing in mind the immensity of the zones considered. Only exploration with electronic detection instruments using hi-tech devices such as nuclear magnetic resonance magnetometers could enable us to attain our objective.

When any archaeological remains are found, they form part of the topographical definition: ruins indicate terrain that was once dry land, while wrecks or ancient anchors generally mark watery zones. Conversely, the discovery of certain topographical features could help locate archaeological deposits.

part of the south-east basin of the Mediterranean; also the rise in sea level – confirmed since antiquity – contributed significantly to this. Geological observations we carried out with the help of the Smithsonian Institute in Washington and Stanford University helped us to trace these phenomena by locating seismic effects in the substratum of the seabed. Geological analysis of the sites also revealed scars indicating liquefaction of the ground in certain spots, especially in Aboukir Bay. Local events of this kind can be triggered off by substantial pressure bearing down on clayey soils. The weight exercised by the ancient monuments, combined with excess weight resulting from, for example, exceptional water levels or a tsunami, is capable of sufficient compression to expel water contained in the structure of clays. The latter therefore suddenly lose some of their volume, which creates sudden subsidence. An earthquake can also bring about such an event. Such factors arising independently or together could cause major destruction, explaining the disappearance of the great harbour of Alexandria and a large portion of the Canopus region beneath the sea.

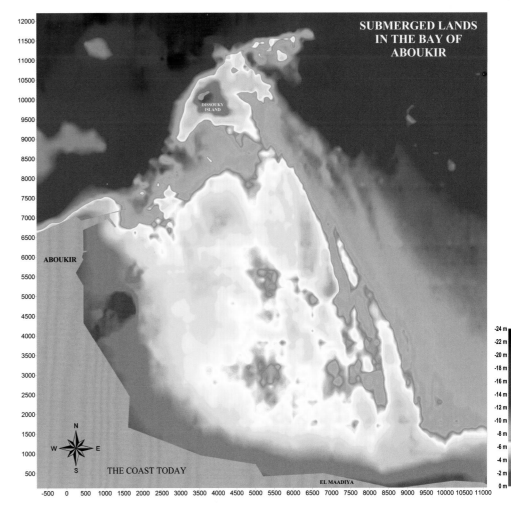

Chart of the submerged Canopic Region as revealed by IEASM surveys and excavations. The present-day coastline is shown in dark grey.

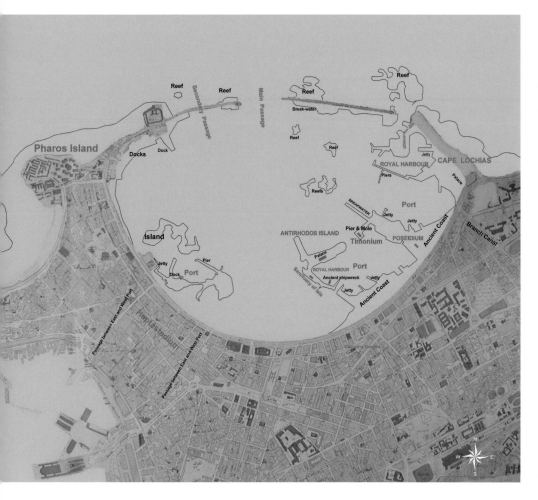

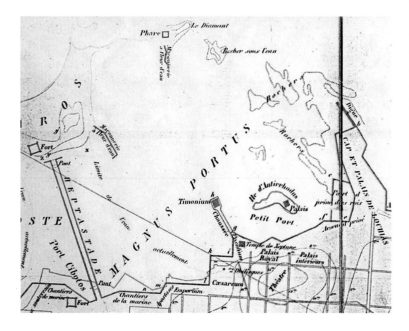

ALEXANDRIA

In Alexandria, topographical campaigns, soundings and archaeological excavations enabled us to provide the first complete panorama of the famous great harbour based on observations made in the area (p. 370). The topography obtained was very different from the versions that scholars had previously imagined based on the texts.

We observed that the submerged land and infrastructure of the port was at a maximum depth of twenty-one feet. If we bear in mind that this infrastructure was originally probably at a minimum height of six or seven feet above sea level in antiquity, we can conclude that successive subsidences combined with rises in the sea level have caused an effective shift of over twenty-six feet since ancient times. The area of the great harbour is now mapped in its entirety. For the first time, we have an accurate vision of how it was in the Roman period, before the great destruction that changed the topography of the area.

The royal districts began at Cape Lochias, which enclosed the great port in the east. Hemmed in by the cape was the galley port, reserved for the use of the royal fleet. The port infrastructure appears on our maps with its moles and long protecting seawall which, according to Strabo, hid it from public view. The island of Antirhodos, the private property of the kings, was equally part of the royal districts. This island, entirely paved over, has been rediscovered in a completely different location from the one historians imagined. Its central arm was 330 yards long and had a vast central esplanade facing the site of the Caesarium. The entrance to the latter on the ancient coast is known from the spots where the famous 'Cleopatra's Needles' once stood. On the esplanade, the remains of the foundations of

previous double page: A diver investigates fissures caused by the liquefaction of clay. Photographs taken following the removal of a 2.5-metre-thick layer of sediment

top left: Chart of the submerged areas, buildings and monuments around Alexandria's *Portus Magnus* produced on the basis of IEASM surveys and excavations

bottom left: Map of Alexandria's *Portus Magnus*, produced in 1866 after ancient texts by Mahmoud Bey El Falaki at the request of Emperor Napoleon III for a history of Julius Caesar

View of the coast at Alexandria in 1860. One of *Cleopatra's Needles* still stood on the shore at the end of the nineteenth century.

a palace have been uncovered whose existence at the end of the Lagid era is confirmed by Strabo. They have been dated to the third century BC. The central arm is dotted with numerous remains such as shafts of columns in pink granite. On a secondary branch of the island a fine statue of a priest of Isis was found, carrying an Osiris vase (p. 215), and two sphinxes, one of which represents the effigy of King Ptolemy XII, father of the great Cleopatra (p. 157). This suggests that there must have been a small sanctuary dedicated to Isis on this royal island.

A small port, magnificently sheltered, was included between the two arms of the island and a jetty. It is lined with quays and the large esplanade on which the palace stood. Investigations have shown that this island was probably settled before the foundation of Alexandria and that major works were subsequently carried out there around the mid-third century BC. That this island was occupied already during imperial times is borne out by the archaeological discoveries of emperors Commodus (180–192 AD) and Caracalla (211–217 AD) (p. 63).

The Poseidium peninsula looked a bit like an elbow of land sticking out towards the port. At its northern extremity, a large breakwater protected the royal galley port. The remnants of a Roman-period temple have been uncovered at the point where this neck of land joined the ancient shore-line. At the extremity of a seawall on the peninsula and developing towards the centre of a dock, excavations have uncovered base levels dating from the end of the first century BC and reorganisation in the Antonine period. What the ruins represent is not certain, but thanks to Strabo again it is known the Mark Antony had his Timonium (a little sanctuary-palace) constructed at the end of a seawall of the Poseidium. After being defeated by his rival Octavian, he retired there. Could the late-Lagid period ruins be those of the retreat described by Strabo? Excavations now underway may possibly provide more information about this in the future.

Several large docks were fitted out between Cape Lochias, the Poseidium peninsula, the island Antirhodos, the breakwater and the seawalls. Ships, even those with deep draughts, could comfortably be berthed along the numerous quays.

The ancient coastline was found to have abutted the whole length of the royal districts. This shows that the seaward encroachment of embankments during development works carried out in the nineteenth and twentieth centuries did not entirely cover over the areas submerged following the subsidence events and collapse of the land. The ancient coastline, visible throughout the entire eastern part of the great port, is occasionally well paved and features numerous remains and fine relics of statues.

In the western part of the great port opposite the Heptastadion was a complex that protected the long causeway built to the Pharos island, its seawalls being constructed of large blocks of limestone that formed a bulwark against the assaults of the sea. It contained docks perfectly suited to accommodating ships at anchor in transit from the great eastern port to the western port giving access to traffic heading for the Egyptian interior, because, according to the texts, two passages controlled by forts gave access through this seawall and linked the two ports. At this spot, large naval yards were also located,

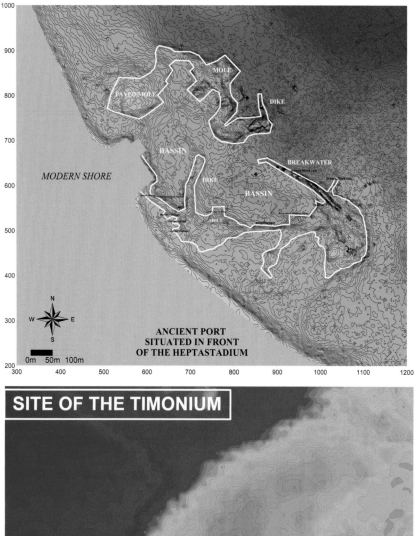

ANCIENT PORT
SITUATED IN FRONT
OF THE HEPTASTADIUM

0m 50m 100m

MODERN SHORE

SITE OF THE TIMONIUM

● WOODEN POST
□ LIMESTONE BLOCK
■ MORTAR BLOCK
● CERAMIC
● BRONZE COIN
● GOLD COIN
◆ RED GRANITE COLUMN
▼ LIMESTONE ANCHOR

0m 10m 20m

on account of which this part of the great port was called the Navalia.

The two channels giving access to the great port have been mapped. The main channel towards the middle between Pharos and Cape Lochias was confined on the western side by a large submerged rock. The secondary channel was narrower, and allowed ships to navigate between this rock and the island of Pharos. The famous lighthouse must have stood very close to this. At present, bearing in mind the topographical and geological results obtained by our mission and comparing them with the ancient sources, and since there are no certain archaeological discoveries suggesting a different position, we may put forward the hypothesis that the lighthouse must have stood on this rock located between the two channels.

Today, there is nothing visible left of this prestigious monument which so captured the admiration of contemporaries. Its remnants are probably covered by the enormous mass of the modern breakwater to the west, which links the fort Qait Bey to the great central rock, now submerged and likewise largely covered by blocks of modern work.

The layout of the complex is thus now known in all its splendour. Its organisation was evidently more functional than historians have allowed us to believe. As discoveries were made, it became clear that Lagid and later Roman engineers had exploited the natural features of the site with remarkable intelligence, turning the site into a powerful high-capacity port facility capable of handling dense shipping traffic. With the astonishing complexity of the interior docks and the numerous sumptuous monuments alongside, this great port and emporium of Egypt must have been an extraordinary sight in the Lagid and Roman periods.

above left: Structure of the ancient port opposite the former location of the Heptastadium

left: Location of the Timonium on a dike protruding from the Poseidium peninsula.

opposite: A statue of King Ptolemy in the form of Hermes was found and cleaned in the port of the royal island (cat. no. 108)

following double page: Hypothetical reconstruction of the Portus Magnus based on results from surveys and excavations

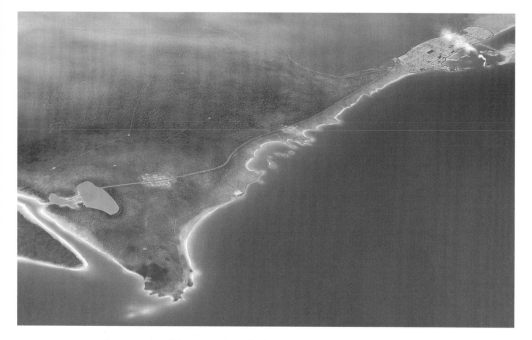

Reconstruction of the stretch of coastline from Alexandria to the Canopic arm of the Nile based on work by IEASM

THE SUBMERGED REGION OF CANOPUS: EAST CANOPUS

'Canopus is a city lying 125 *stadia* (around twenty-four kilometres) from Alexandria by the land route, and is named after the pilot Menelaos Canopus, who died in this place. It has a temple of Sarapis, which has a great following and produces cures such that even men of the greatest merit lend credence to them and come to sleep there to be healed or else send others to sleep there in their place. Some people record in writing their cures, others the proofs of the efficacy of the oracle of Sarapis.' (Strabo, Geography, 17.1.17)

The work done in Aboukir Bay from 1996 onwards enabled us to determine the contours of the submerged part of the Canopus region, the position of the main archaeological deposits and the course of the ancient western branch of the Nile. It appears that a huge triangle of land with sides of six miles (ten kilometres) each was swallowed up by the sea as a result of geological faulting and slow subsidence. It was in this drowned area that the cities mentioned by the ancient texts once flourished.

The analysis of these discoveries and their incorporation into our knowledge of the geography and history of antiquity plus the studies of the archaeological finds have added essential information to our knowledge of the Canopus region also known as Heracleiotic branch in allusion to the large temple of Hercules close to its shores.

Just over a mile to the east of the modern port of Aboukir, a zone with numerous remains was identified, some of which obviously corresponded with those examined by Prince Omar in 1933. The site explored between 1933 and 1940 shows up as an alignment of ruins 164 yards long (150 metres). Broken shafts of smooth pink granite columns of varying diameter were found together with construction blocks of limestone and other architecture. The excavations on this site, which only gave rise to a few recoveries at the time, led to some interesting new discoveries. Numerous bits of jewellery, including rings, crosses and earrings of the Byzantine period (mainly the sixth and seventh centuries) were brought to light (p. 278). These objects were associated with seals and amulets of lead from the same period. Byzantine and Islamic coins were likewise discovered at various locations. While the sediment was being cleared, fragments of pharaonic, Ptolemaic and Roman statues also came to light. The presence of these heterogeneous objects at one location seems to indicate that numerous items dating from earlier periods were probably extracted from a nearby site for reuse. Pieces of granite with hieroglyphics on them turned out to belong to a famous and unique monolithic chapel called the *Naos of the Decades* (p. 48).

In the west, this site is linked by a number of secondary structures to a rectangular edifice 100 feet (thirty metres) long. The latter still preserves walls buried in the sand up to a surviving height of nearly ten feet (three metres). Bearing in mind their masonry, these structures can be dated to the Byzantine period, in conformity with the archaeological chattels, jewellery, crosses, coins and seals recovered not far away. The likelihood is that the structures are the remains of a large Christian establishment.

North of this ensemble under six or seven feet (two metres) of sand, the well-preserved foundations of the magnificent walls of a temple enclosure were found, 112 yards (103 metres) long and constructed of large blocks of limestone. This monument was by far the most imposing in the area. The presence of these remains reveals that on this drowned site stood the largest Egyptian sanctuary so far found in the area of the town of Aboukir, either on terra firma or underwater.

Between this magnificent monument and the Christian architectural complex was a waste dump where statues were thrown, probably to be cut up and re-used as raw material. The statues from the era of the last indigenous dynasties as well as the Ptolemaic and Roman periods are remarkable for their quality. The statues of gods, pharaohs, queens, individuals and numerous sphinxes rival one another in beauty. Among them is a remarkable marble head of the god Sarapis dating from the Ptolemaic period, which used to belong to a statue over thirteen feet (four metres) tall (p. 233). This statue must have been the cult statue of a temple.

Comparison of the ancient texts and archaeological findings suggests a theory. The finds indicate that an important structure, a Christian establishment, was constructed near a large pharaonic sanctuary. Couldn't these remnants correspond to the base of the church of Sts John and Cyril, which, according to Tyrannius Rufinus of Aquileia, was constructed near the Sarapeum? 'In the sepulchre of Sarapis, when the profane buildings had been levelled, a martyrium was built on one side, a church on the other.' (Rufinus, *Church History*, 2, 26–27).

The hypothesis that the large pharaonic sanctuary is the Sarapeum of Canopus is supported by several observations. Its distance from the temple of Herakleion matches that which separated the sites according to the texts. The substantial size of its temple district shows that this monument was indeed a major site. The most imposing item among the statues found in the vicinity was the large head of a colossal statue of the Sarapis cult just mentioned, very probably the most important statue in the temple (p. 233).

The artefacts brought to light in the precinct show that it was still occupied in the Roman period. Excavations indicated that the temple was destroyed and razed by human hand before the Christian structures collapsed. Almost all the building blocks from it have disappeared with the exception of the foundation levels, the monument apparently having served as a quarry. The construction of the Christian establishment thus appears to have served it as a source of building materials in the immediate neighbourhood. The Christian establishment obviously enjoyed a period of prosperity in the seventh century and seems to have continued to exist into the Islamic period, surviving until the mid-eighth century.

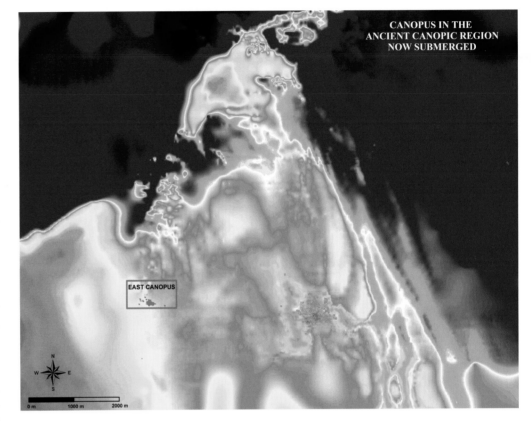

CANOPUS IN THE
ANCIENT CANOPIC REGION
NOW SUBMERGED

EAST CANOPUS

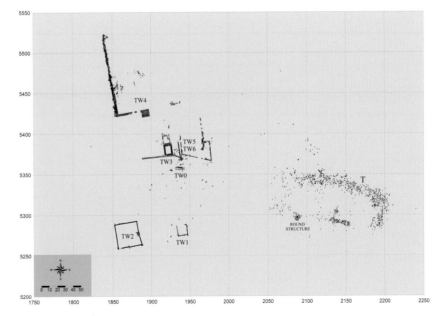

top: Chart of the Canopic Region based on surveys and excavations by IEASM. The present-day coastline is marked in brown; traces of East Canopus submerged in the sea

above: Layout plan of the preserved remains of buildings at East Canopus

The excavation teams have so far not brought to light any epigraphic documents that could identify the site in a formal way, but the topographical and archaeological evidence and comparisons with the texts suggest the designation East Canopus for the site, which very probably housed the large sanctuary of Sarapis, then the Christian complex of the monastery of Metonoia.

above and opposite page: Plan of a section of the enclosure wall around the great temple at East Canopus.

The foundations of the large temple's enclosure wall are well preserved.

Hypothetical rendering of the centre port of Herakleion with its main temple to Amun-Gereb

THONIS-HERAKLEION

A vast concentration of ruins was discovered four miles (over six and a half kilometres) from the coast, directly east of the East Canopus zone. In these surroundings, explorations revealed the ancient bed of the Nile that was once the Canopus branch. Excavations were carried out on the archaeological deposits. Substantial traces of walls constructed of large limestone blocks were uncovered. They belonged to the enclosure of a substantial monument over 160 yards (150 metres) long. Clearly this was a temple site. One of the first objects discovered in the temple area was a pink granite *naos* (monolith chapel that contained the image of the principal god in a sanctuary). Its inscriptions confirmed the dedication of the temple to Amon-gereb, in conformity with the text of the Decree of Canopus Stele, and that the city in which it stood was Herakleion (p. 127).

A rare find served to confirm the identity of the site, if confirmation had been needed – a gold plaque inscribed in Greek indicating that King Ptolemy III had founded (or renovated) a sanctuary dedicated to Herakles at this site (p. 188). Another extraordinary discovery was an intact stele made of black granite, the counterpart of the stele of Naukratis, which was discovered beneath a wall very close to the *naos* in the same sanctuary. It dates from the reign of Pharaoh Nektanabo I and gives us the Egyptian name for the site: 'Pharaoh

ordered this to be recorded on the present stele erected at the mouth of the Greek Sea, in the city called Thonis of Sais' (p. 316).

The simultaneous – and improbable – discovery of these two epigraphic documents confirms the identities of the places found and immediately resolves a puzzle of historical geography. It clarifies the texts of ancient writers – the Herakleion of the Greeks was the Thonis of the Egyptians.

The archaeological excavations carried out at the city and the large temple give a precise idea of the topography of the city and its surroundings and reveal their major features. The city was a peninsula situated between several basins, functioning as interconnecting ports in the east and a lake in the west. The port areas were separated from the Canopus branch of the Nile by a string of dunes. A narrow channel provided a passage joining the port to the river. A more substantial channel, called by the team the grand canal, linked the port areas to the lake in the west, passing through Thonis-Herakleion on the way. Rich votive offerings were discovered there that establish the religious nature of this great channel that served the sanctuary. They are a reminder of the intensive cultic activity that went on at these places and are a relic of the celebrations of the ceremonies for Osiris-Dionysus in the month of the Nile flood (p. 195).

The temple was built on a huge central esplanade, fringed on the north side by this canal. Excavations in the area of the temple district uncovered a great variety of objects. Dishes and gold, silver and bronze ritual objects, fine pottery, plaster vessels, numerous amulets and coins confirm the past opulence of the area. The excavations also showed that the temple was a centre of manufacturing (p. 256). The monumental complex extended over several acres and with its substantial mass dominated the port to the east. It was this port that boats put into in order to pay customs duties. Seafarers made their

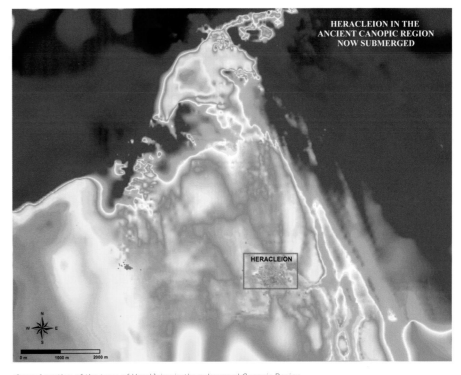

above: Location of the town of Herakleion in the submerged Canopic Region

below: Herakleion lay near the mouth of the Nile on a peninsula between the port to the east and a lake to the west.

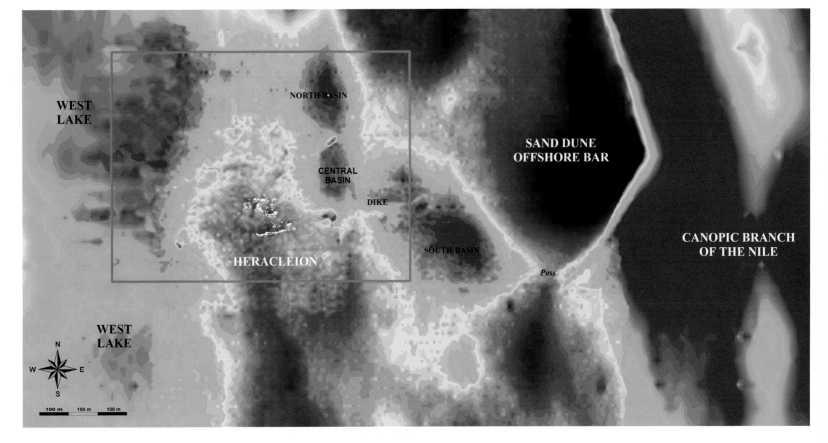

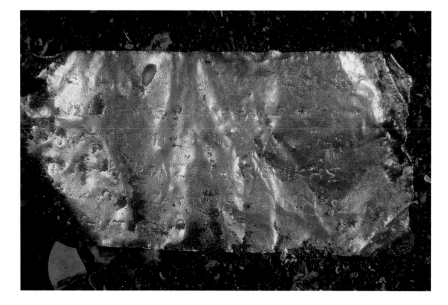

above: Discovering a gold foundation plaque from a shrine to Herakles (cat. no. 161)

right: The site of a hoard of coins, an amphora, a bronze platter and a ladle,
as well as a votive deposit with offerings

votive offerings to the gods there after a dangerous voyage. Very numerous relics of their gifts were scattered over the bed of the harbour and the channels. Small votive anchors made of bronze, lead or stone rubbed shoulders with cups, miniature vessels and amulets, fragile and moving proofs of wishes granted.

In terms of materials uncovered, the excavations show that this port was made up of several large basins, an indication of intensive commercial activity that contributed towards the prosperity of the city. More than seven hundred ancient anchors of various shapes and sixteen wrecks dating from the sixth to the second centuries BC lying on the seabed are eloquent witness to it (p. 100).

Substantial monuments were still to be found in the precinct of the temple. Near the *naos*, for example, a large bowl made of pink granite was uncovered, which was probably used during the celebrations of the mysteries of Osiris (p. 194). Three colossal statues over sixteen feet (five metres) high and made of pink granite depict a king, a queen (p. 165) and Hapi, the god of fertility, plenty and the Nile flood (p. 311). They are imposing witnesses to the majesty of the temple. High-quality statues of gods and royal persons, numerous bronze statuettes of deities and ritual instruments illustrate the practices and rites of the sanctuary. The archaeological material excavated at the site of Thonis-Herakleion confirms that this city was very busy in the fifth and fourth centuries BC. An immense bilingual stele made of pink granite dating from the reign of

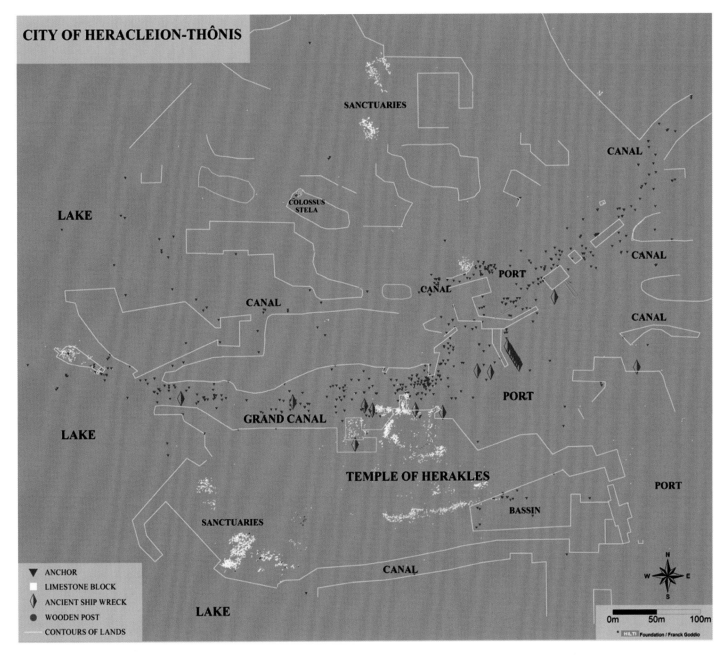

CITY OF HERACLEION-THÔNIS

SANCTUARIES

CANAL

COLOSSUS
STELA

LAKE

CANAL

PORT

CANAL

CANAL

CANAL

PORT

LAKE

GRAND CANAL

TEMPLE OF HERAKLES

PORT

BASSIN

SANCTUARIES

CANAL

LAKE

▼ ANCHOR
☐ LIMESTONE BLOCK
◇ ANCIENT SHIP WRECK
● WOODEN POST
— CONTOURS OF LANDS

N
W · E
S

0m   50m   100m

HILTI Foundation / Franck Goddio

Map of Herakleion based on surveys and excavations by IEASM

next double page, left: Following its recovery, the great *naos*
of the temple of Amun-Gereb is re-erected where it was found
(cat. no. 117).

right: Monumental pink granite statues graced the main temple
of Thonis-Herakleion. An impressive statue of Hapi, god of fertility,
the inundation of the Nile and abundance. The statue
of this god is the largest yet found in Egypt (see p. 311).

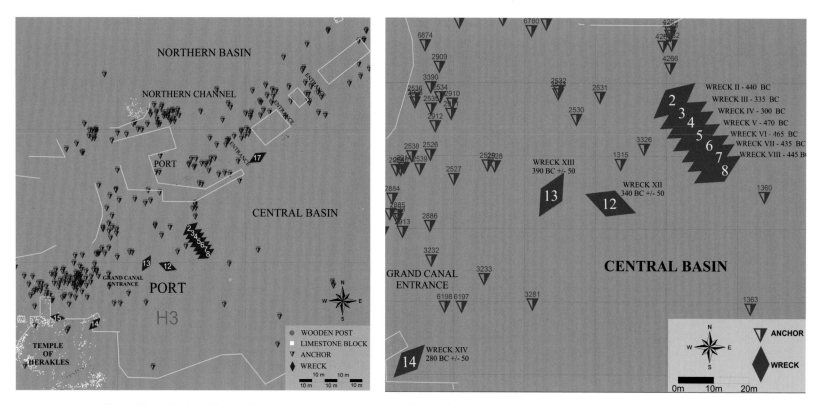

NORTHERN BASIN

NORTHERN CHANNEL

ENTRANCE

ENTRANCE

ENTRANCE

PORT

17

CENTRAL BASIN

2 3 4 5 6 7 8

13 12

GRAND CANAL
ENTRANCE

PORT

H3

15

14

TEMPLE
OF
HERAKLES

● WOODEN POST
■ LIMESTONE BLOCK
▽ ANCHOR
◆ WRECK

10 m   10 m
10 m   10 m   10 m

6874   6780   426
426 2
4266

2909

3390
2536 2534
2535 2910
2912
2532
2531
2530
3326
1315

WRECK II - 440 BC
WRECK III - 335 BC
WRECK IV - 300 BC
WRECK V - 470 BC
WRECK VI - 465 BC
WRECK VII - 435 BC
WRECK VIII - 445 BC

2 3 4 5 6 7 8

2538 2526
2521 2539
2527
252 2928

WRECK XIII
390 BC +/- 50

WRECK XII
340 BC +/- 50

1360

2884
2885
2913
2886

13   12

3232
3233
1363

GRAND CANAL
ENTRANCE

6198 6197   3281

CENTRAL BASIN

WRECK XIV
280 BC +/- 50

14

▽ ANCHOR
◆ WRECK

0m   10m   20m

Charts of the port basins to the east of the great temple showing anchors and shipwrecks from antiquity

Ptolemy VIII demonstrates that the sanctuary at Herakleion continued under the Ptolemies. They had become pharaohs, which was of religious importance for the Egyptians just as much as for the Greeks (p. 183). The small number of objects from the Roman period indicate that its importance did not continue into this time period, but the great sanctuary of Amon-gereb (identified with Zeus) and his son Chons (identified with Hercules) was a privileged celebratory site of dynastic continuity for the conquered Egyptian kings. The site continued to be occupied until the end of the eighth century, and the Byzantine presence, known from texts, is illustrated by the discovery of modest architectural items, a few bits of jewellery and coins (p. 258).

With the continuing work, the plan of the great emporium of Egypt is gradually being completed, recording a site that was active several centuries prior to the foundation of Alexandria. The city extended all round the majestic temple, criss-crossed by a network of canals that must have given it a lakeside appearance. The numerous docks connected to the Nile provided anchorage for ships of all tonnages. Goods were carried in transit via the cross canals towards the lake in the west, which itself was linked to the city of Canopus by a long canal. This water channel was certainly the outlet of the canal which linked Alexandria and Canopus during the Lagid era. On these islands and islets there were secondary sanctuaries, esplanades with pavilions allowing for a view over the watery world, as well as homes.

Thonis-Herakleion, placed near the mouth of the Canopic branch that linked it with Naukratis, was perfectly situated to control the maritime traffic of ships entering or leaving Egypt. It also acted as an interface with the interior of the Canopus region in the redistribution of goods, thanks to a network of canals which ensured easy interconnection between the docks and the hinterland.

All in all, the geophysical and geological approaches followed by systematic location and evaluating procedures and archaeological excavations have made possible a first global vision of the drowned Canopus region and the great port of Alexandria. The discoveries made, thanks to the work of a multi-disciplinary team and a novel approach in underwater archaeology, remain encouraging in more than one respect. The plans of the cities and monuments are becoming more accurate year by year. Of course, major archaeological sites, localised and identified with certainty in some cases as a result of the discovery of epigraphic evidence and

In its lower section, the Nile mosaic of Palestrina shows the landscapes of the Nile delta (end of 2nd cent. BC).

following double page: Found near the *naos*, this pink granite basin was probably used during ceremonies held during the 'Osiris mysteries'.

remarkable artefacts, demand excavations and analysis, which in turn need decades of research. The results also raise numerous questions to which future research will try to respond. However that may be, they are the first fruits of discoveries to come which will enable an entire facet of the history of the Nile Delta to be rescued from the obscurity of the past.

II. RELIGION AND BELIEFS

A JAR BRINGING HOPE FOR ETERNAL LIFE
THE OSIRIS-CANOBOS

A sort of oval jar of white marble, filled, broken at the top, with severely worn walls decorated in relief, was found in the vicinity of two sphinxes. Luckily, the missing top of this jar was found not far away, in the form of a male head wearing the *nemes*. This is an example of the iconographic type known as 'Osiris-Canobos' from its geographical origin, or 'Osiris *Hydreios*' from its attributions.

The head with regular, relatively worn features is surrounded by the tripartite wig with bands delimited by incisions. On top of the head a round hole served for the attachment of a supplementary component; the slight lump under the chin is probably the remains of an artificial beard, judging from known examples.

This Osiris-Canobos is characterised by the religious scene which decorates the belly of the vessel. In the middle, a scarab beetle holds up the sun-disc flanked by two antithetical *uraei*. It is set on a reed boat the prow of which, consisting of three bundles of sticks, can be discerned on the right. Further to the right, on the same level, a cynocephalus, its head topped by the solar disc, squats on a plinth. Above, the upright heads of the snakes support a rectangular *naos*. Two falcons are set facing each other in the upper corners of the *naos*.

On two sides of the *naos* we can distinguish two pairs of naked figures of childlike proportions. A child is shown advancing towards the *naos*, right foot on the prow of the boat that supports the scarab. His right arm hangs down beside his body, his left arm is bent at the elbow and raised. The child is touching his mouth with his left index finger. The second person on the left, also naked, is represented following the same convention, but the left arm is held forward. If the identification of the first figure – Harpokrates – poses no problem, the second, perhaps slightly more slender, figure presents no characteristic features at all. On the right of the *naos*, the heavily blurred scene seems to develop in symmetry with the preceding one.

The general compositional scheme agrees perfectly with that of known images of Osiris-Canobos.

Z. K.

In Egypt the depiction of deities in the form of human-shaped water jars probably began in the first century AD. The form of the vessel draws on its connotations as a container of thirst-quenching water to emphasise the rejuvenating role of the deity depicted, in this case most likely Osiris, wearing a modified *atef* crown (cat. no. 68). Squat objects like this were also an ideal shape for weights.　T. H.

28　**Osiris-Canobos**
Marble
1st-2nd cent. BC
Vase: h. 24 cm | diam. 21.2 cm |
Head: h. 13.3 cm | w. 12.6 cm | d. 11.1 cm

68　**Amulet in the shape of Osiris-Canobos**
Lead
Roman period
H. 6 cm | w. 2.2 cm | d. 1.9 cm

HELENA-ISIS AND HORUS-HARPOKRATES

Images of Isis brought to light in the Bay of Aboukir, from modest figurine to beautiful statuette, show the goddess in the pose of *mater lactans*. Isis appears in her role as divine mother suckling the infant Horus. Clad in a long robe, she offers her left breast with her right hand to the baby sitting on her lap. This pose, in which some people have wished to see a prototype of Virgin and Child depictions, is a reminder that, according to a tradition handed down by Plutarch, Isis the widow sat watching over her son in the marshes of the Delta until he was able to accede to the throne. Isis was thus an important link in the transmission of royal power.

The poet Nicandros of Colophon in the early second century BC relates how, having stretched out 'on the sands of Thonis', Menelaos' steersman was bitten by a viper of the kind called 'that which makes the blood run'. Helen could do nothing but crush the ghastly reptile under her foot. Nicandros was not the first to tell this dramatic story. The great Apollonius of Rhodes (295–215 BC) had himself written a poem entitled *Kanopus*, only three fragments of which have survived, one evoking precisely the gaping wounds caused by the specific reptile. It is not known at what period of his eventful life his erudite curiosity led Apollonius to compose such a poem, but one can assume that the composition met the particular interest felt by Lagid rulers in the steersman turned god. It is revealing that among the new establishments created under Ptolemy II in the western part of the Fayum was a village called Kanopias whose name is formed in the same way as Dionysias, a place under the protection of Dionysos, and whose demotic name, Pegouti, indisputably denotes that this was an offshoot of our maritime Canopos. And it is known what role Ptolemy III held in the development of Canopos; evidence of this is provided by the foundation plaque in his name (cat. no. 161, p. 190) and the Dionysio-Osiriac rituals practised in the region.

We cannot recall the death of Canopos and Helen's avenging intervention without bringing the fate of Horus to mind. Isis had given birth to the young god in the Borollos marshes and kept him hidden until, emerging from adolescence, he came out of the marshes to fight Seth, the killer of his father Osiris. His refuge may have been hard to find, but it also held all sorts of dangers: vipers in the sand, cobras between the papyrus stalks, scorpions on the islets of silt and crocodiles in the river branches of the Delta. Magic formulas intended to cure people who had been bitten by a scorpion consisted of identifying them to little Horus who, as a baby, had been fatally stung by one of these creatures but whom Isis, the clever magician, had just managed to save.

It is attested that near the mouths of the Nile there were cults to the goddess Isis, often represented in the monstrous form of Thoueris (Tawaret) but sometimes in human form, mastering handfuls of snakes and treading on two crocodiles.

She was also a loving wife and protective mother (cat. nos. 182, p. 105; 183–184). No doubt it was the same at Canopos. In any case, in the Roman period, when the Canopic goddess received the completely human appearance that she inherited from the Lagid queens, Isis is shown grasping a snake with her right hand while her left foot rests on a reduced-scale model of a crocodile.   J. Y. | D. F.

183 **Statuette of Isis _lactans_**
Bronze
Late period – Ptolemaic period
H. 11.8 cm | w. 2.8 cm
(cf. cat. no. 182, p. 105)

184 **Statuette of Isis _lactans_**
Bronze
Late period – Ptolemaic period
H. 10 cm | w. 3.5 cm
(cf. cat. no. 182, p. 105)

BACK TOGETHER AFTER CENTURIES
ISIS AND HARPOKRATES

The fragment of white marble recently discovered in Canopos represents a Harpokrates. A large hand is resting on the back of his head; only the thumb with its pronounced nail, the first phalanxes of the index and middle finger and the base of the wrist remain. It follows therefore that the sculpture is definitely not of a single figure, but part of a life-sized group. The position of the wrist and the thumb identify this as a figure who was holding the slightly backwards inclined head of a child in its left hand, the child was as high as the chest of the adult figure.

The statue represents a woman sitting on a simple smooth, rectangular seat. A roll suggests that there may have been a cushion. The left side of the sculpture has disappeared, as has the right side, but a long horizontal crack under the right breast seems to show the line of the forearm pointing towards the missing left breast, under which three slender fingers of the right hand remain, supported beneath by the remaining three slender fingers of the right hand. This is the precise image that is seen in representations of the goddess offering her breast for Horus to nurse from: Isis *lactans*. In fact, the broken lower part of the child's body rests on the left thigh of the goddess and the smooth side of the left buttock can be made out. The right leg of the divine infant also remains, stuck to his mother's stomach.

Z. K.

HISTORY OF A REDISCOVERY In April 1988, I was asked by the authorities to inspect a statue at the region of Aboukir. The area, more than a hundred years ago, had been subject to archaeological activities whether on land or under the waters of Aboukir bay. The only prominent person who left his mark on the area was the Prince Omar Tousson, whose underwater activities gave us various antiquities and a lot of information about ancient Canopos in particular. As a result of his activities many antiquities were scattered inside his palace and around it. It is well known that his property included the beach of Aboukir.

On arriving at Aboukir, to the south of the so-called 'Cleopatra's Bath', I realised that I had to walk in the sand for a few hundred meters in order to arrive at the site of the statue. I was quite impressed when I saw from afar a shining white marble statue of a seated woman hidden behind a building, at a distance of about twenty metres from the waters. When I came face to face with the statue, I realised at once that it was the statue of Isis suckling her son Harpokrates. For bureaucratic reasons I could not manage to receive and remove any of the items there except the statue of Isis.

The statue was not found in situ, but in the precincts of the property of Prince Omar Tousson in the region. He was the one who salvaged the statue from the water, during the course of his underwater activities of salvaging underwater monuments from the bottom of the bay, after the year 1933. The statue was discovered in the area corresponding to ancient

26 Isis
Marble
Roman period
H. 130 cm | w. 63 cm

Statue of Isis in Prince Omar Toussoun's garden

Canopos. It seems that the prince had kept it in his palace and it had remained there till it was transported to its current place after the confiscation of the prince's property. Hussein Bey Toussoun, the grandson of the prince gave us a rare photograph of the prince beside the statue.

After many years a strange coincidence occurred, when Franck Goddio discovered at the bottom of Aboukir bay, in the same site where the statue had been discovered, a missing part of it which consisted of the head of Harpokrates and a part of the body that was darker than the rest of the statue.   A. A. E–F. Y.

24 **Harpokrates**
Marble
Roman period
H. 15 cm | w. 34.5 cm | d. 20.5 cm

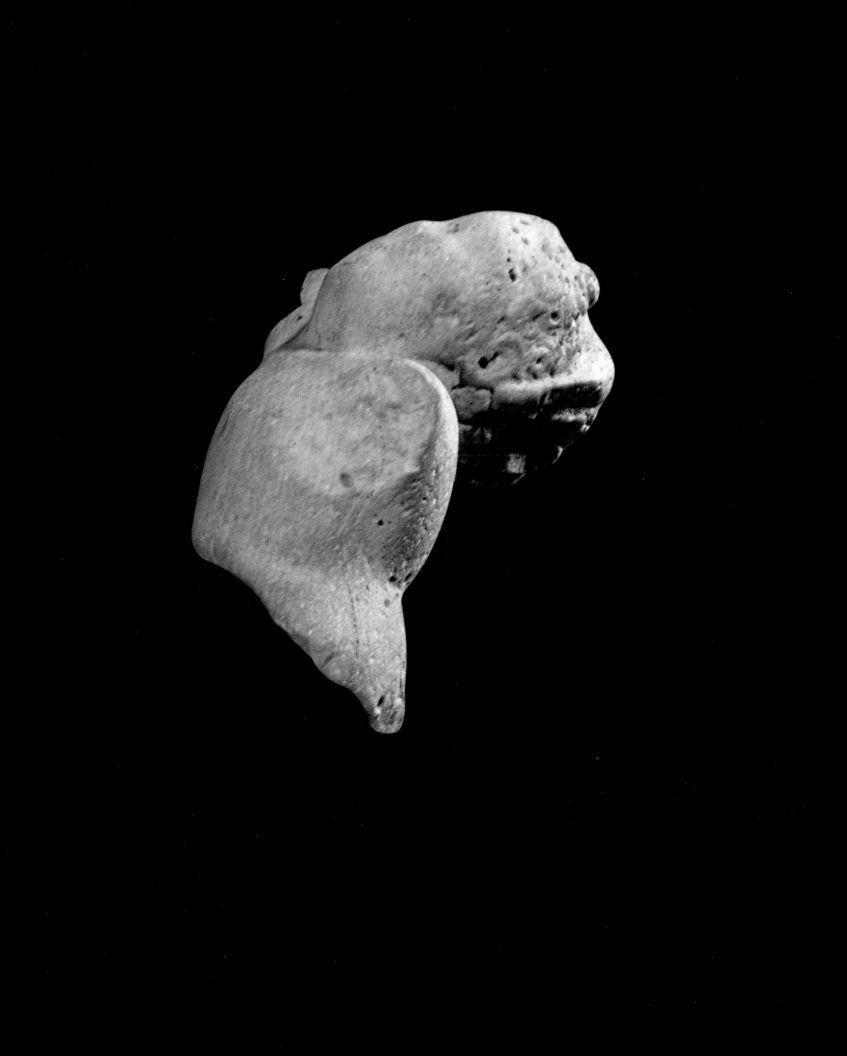

HERAKLEION, HERAKLES AND CHONS

HERAKLES: 'THE GREEK MAN AND HIS IDEAL' If any male figure from mythology is famous nowadays, it must be Herakles, whom the Romans followed the Etruscans in calling Hercules, the initiator of the Olympic Games whose twelve labours remain proverbial. This demigod enjoyed enormous popularity in antiquity. A prestigious, but pathetic incarnation: the invincible athlete, capable of visiting hell and coming back again, would end up, all man that he was, as the husband of his wife Deianeira and would then put an end to the intolerable sufferings caused by the poisoned cloak of Nessos by sacrificing himself on a funeral pyre. This would bring him apotheosis.

Greek and Latin authors give a large number of variants for his twelve labours and multiple side exploits regarding places, partners or the various circumstances. Herakles, son of Zeus himself, would father countless sons with many different women, to the extent that Greek rulers just as barbarian dynasts found enough points of contact to claim to be his descendants and emulators. The demigod certainly employed violence to commit more or less justified murders, but more often than not this was in order to let justice and security prevail for the benefit of the weak and the oppressed, accomplishing the duties supremely incumbent on a man. He slew monsters that terrorised cities and countries and he killed despots who were murdering the population. His beneficent activities were not confined to the Hellenic realm. They extended to Europe, Anatolia, the shores of the Black Sea and the coast of the Levant. Herakles was active throughout the Mediterranean, rampaging towards the west even beyond the straits where the Pillars of Herakles would stand.

HERAKLES IN EGYPT The rediscovered Herakleion is a reminder that the hero was induced to deploy his muscles and his famous club on the continent of Africa. Having accomplished the eleventh of the labours imposed on him by bringing back the golden apples of the Hesperides after killing the dragon guarding the orchard, he set off to travel all over Libya, where he exchanged burdens with the giant Atlas, triumphed over Antaios, another giant, and captured a handful of pygmies who attempted to put him in chains... Passing through the oasis of Amon, he sacrificed to his father Zeus 'and from there passed into Egypt, following which' the first town along the Nile that he came to 'was called Herakleion'. According to some anecdotes, Osiris put him in charge of Libya and Ethiopia and he is said, moreover, to have ensured the safety of the region by building dykes to counter the effects of excessively strong Nile floods.

Nevertheless, according to a newer paradoxical tradition, Herakles did not only enjoy good relationships with the Egyptians. Busiris, who was then in power, had the custom of sacrificing on the altar of Zeus all strangers who entered his kingdom, until the day our hero slew the king along with his priests and henchmen. The story of this secondary exploit of the demigod was famous throughout the Hellenic world. In the sixth century BC, picturesque scenes showing Herakles in the course of killing the sacrificers adorned beautiful vases in the Attic style, not without a hint of pastiche of Egyptian representations of the pharaoh triumphant over his enemies. The victory over the wicked Busiris was crowed over – in epic compositions of the fifth century BC, and Johann Gottfried Schadow depicted it much later in the reliefs on the Brandenburg Gate.

Within a short time, however, the historicity of this story was already being questioned. Herodotus refused to believe that the Egyptians, a pious, hospitable people who scrupulously regulated the immolation of animals, would ever have been capable of human sacrifice. Diodorus, however, would report it as a fact that ancient kings killed or enslaved foreigners who penetrated into Egypt. The Greek rhetors, Polykrates and Isokrates, proclaimed Busiris' innocence and turned his image around to make him a founding example of the wise institutions and high culture of the blessed Egyptian state. Rational explanations were given for the origins of the legend. Busiris was said to have been one of the helpers whom Osiris had charged with defending the maritime borders. Strabo supposed that the myth actually symbolised the difficulties that sailors encountered on reaching the shores of the Delta, the concept of 'sacrifices' covering the putting to death of smugglers and pirates by the wild inhabitants of the littoral marshes. Following upon Herodotus, historians, confident in the classics, and Egyptologists, sympathising with their good Egyptians, wished to exonerate the latter from an accusation attributing to them a practice as horrendously barbaric as human sacrifice.

However, from Egyptian sources it would appear that the invention by the Greeks of the figure of Busiris reflects reality and that ritual immolations of foreigners resulted from an authentic pharaonic notion. People who rebelled against the king were considered in doctrinal terms to be auxiliaries of Apopi, the snake that threatens the equilibrium of creation, or accomplices of Seth, killer of Osiris. Until the abolition of this practice in the sixth century BC, it happened that troublemakers were condemned to be burned alive at one of the numerous sanctuaries where a reproduction of the mummified corpse of Osiris at the point of resurrection was watched over and tended while being

Harpokrates (cat. no. 329)

burned alive. The fact of redness was for men, as for animals, a mark of their genetic kinship with Seth and Apopi. As a consequence, Greek pirates – blond or red-haired – who presented this mark underwent this death sentence, which was theologically based and ritualised.

There is every reason to suppose that the legend of Busiris originated in these executions, which took place in a locality where there was a 'House of Osiris'. All across Egypt there were many places bearing this name which the Greeks recorded in the form *Bousiris*. The evil king is nothing but the personification of one of these localities. One thinks readily of the House of Osiris in Canopos, close to the place where Herakles' compatriots were captured by the border police. It is evidently out of the question that the Egyptians would have invented the person of Busiris, this symbol of vanquished royalty made man in the Greek manner. Whether the Greek and Latin authors of the imperial period be-

lieved it or not, the alleged Egyptian origin that local people were said to confer on Herakles derives from a theory put forward by Herodotus according to which all the figures in the Hellenic pantheon had come from Egypt, a theory that certain priests of mixed culture would go on to support in their turn at the time of the Ptolemies. Herakles' typical attributes, however, the club and lion skin which make him recognisable, and the circumstances of his major labours and minor exploits do not find any direct counterpart in the traditional iconography of the Egyptians nor in myths relating to the gods of the pharaonic pantheon.

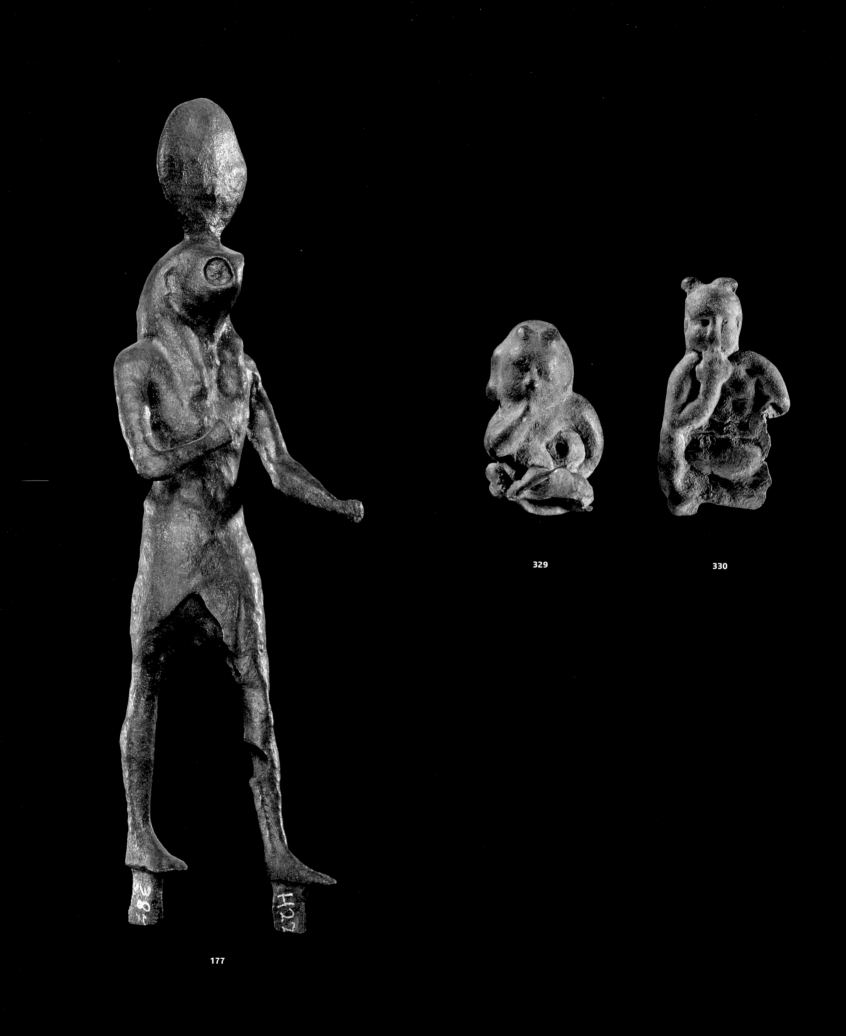

177

329

330

181   180   178   179   213

177   **Statuette of Chons with a lunar disc on his head**

Bronze
Late period
H. 21.5 cm | w. 6.5 cm

Chons is represented here in the form of a man with a falcon's head. Despite the heavily corroded surface of the metal, the main figural characteristics of the god are identifiable: He wears a short loincloth and has his left leg, now with damage to the calf, stretched forward. Two stems extend the lower limbs in order to fix the statuette to a plinth, now lost. The head is covered by the tripartite *nemes* headdress topped by a moon-disc. Chons was likened to the left eye of his father Amon, the star providing nocturnal light. The eyes, now vanished, consisted of small inlays corresponding to a technique observable in the Late period.
A. A-R. R.

329   **Statuette of Harpokrates**

Lead
Ptolemaic period
H. 4 cm | w. 2.5 cm | d. 0.5 cm

Harpokrates is portrayed as a chubby naked child, crouching, left leg bent on the ground, one finger of his right hand raised to his mouth. Under his left arm he holds a vessel.   D. F.

330   **Statuette of Harpokrates**

Lead
Ptolemaic period
H. 5 cm | w. 2.5 cm | d. 0.5 cm

This representation of Harpokrates shows a Hellenistic interpretation of his iconography. He is less formally posed than the Egyptian figures and his side-lock of youth has been re-styled as two tufts above his forehead. His finger is now raised to his mouth in consequence of the pot of food by his side.   T. H.

181   **Statuette of Harpokrates**

Bronze
Late period – Ptolemaic period
H. 10.4 cm | w. 2.8 cm | d. 1.8 cm

180   **Statuette of Harpokrates**

Bronze
Late period – Ptolemaic period
H. 8.8 cm | w. 2.7 cm | d. 1 cm

178   **Statuette of Harpokrates**

Bronze
Late period – Ptolemaic period
H. 10.6 cm | w. 4.4 cm | d. 2 cm

179   **Statuette of Harpokrates**

Bronze
Late period – Ptolemaic period
H. 9.2 cm | w. 2.7 cm | d. 1.3 cm

213   **Amulet of Harpokrates**

Bronze
Late period – Ptolemaic period
H. 3.3 cm | w. 1.3 cm | d. 1.3 cm | d. 0.6 cm

116   Naos

Pink granite
Ptolemaic period
H. 110 cm | w. 53 cm | d. 63 cm

Small monolithic chapel intended to hold an effigy of a deity.
Discovered not far from the large *naos* of Amon, it might come
from the 'holy of holies' of the temple of Chons.   D. F.

117   Naos from the Temple of Amon-gereb

Pink granite
Ptolemaic period
H. 174 cm | w. 93 cm | d. 100 cm

Among the large monuments discovered at the temple district of
Herakleion, was this monumental monolithic chapel. The two
uprights framing the door of the niche bore vertical hieroglyphic
inscriptions, orientated normally. The upper part of both texts
was so heavily eroded that nothing can now be read. What survives below contains on two sides the end of the titulature of a
god and, because the latter signs the word 'loved by …', one can
deduce that at the top of each column there appeared the name
of the pharaoh making the dedication, in conformity with the
usual formula: "King X, loved by the god Y".
In the lower section of the right upright, the last two titles of the
deity for whom this large monolithic chapel was made are
clearly legible: ' … he who presides over the mekes case, the
noble god of the House-of-Rejoicing'. From the time of the Egyptian Late period, the *mekes* symbolises a case for a document confirming the right of rulership over Egypt. On the left upright one
can read: ' … the god of Lower Egypt. He erected it as King, by
designating it … of the country', the pronoun 'he' referring,
obviously, to the ruler named higher up, in the eroded section.
These few confirmed words permit one to resolve the problem
posed by the local name of the main temple at Herakleion.
It is known that the first Greeks to become established in Egypt
likened Amon-Re, king of the Egyptian gods and tutelary deity of
the famous Thebes, to their Zeus, king of the gods on their
Mount Olympos, and that, more curiously, they identified Chons,
the young moon-god, son of Amon, with Herakles, son of Zeus.
From the tenth century onwards, Chons gains great popularity
as a saviour god, healer and oracle-giver, and it is undoubtedly
this that would explain fairly well why his cult supplanted that
of Amon in the Canopic town, to the point that foreigners saw a
sanctuary of Herakles in his temple.   J. Y.

116

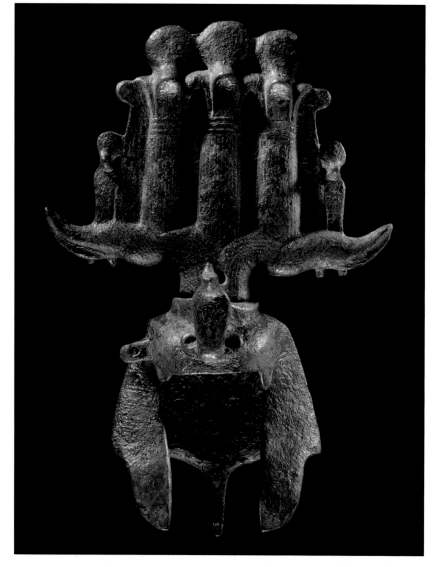

209 Hem-hem crown of Chons
Bronze
End of late period – early Ptolemaic period
H. 15 cm | w. 10 cm

This interesting component of pharaonic statuary in bronze was found at the site H1 in Herakleion (p. 312). This is a complete headdress made up of the *nemes* headdress and the *hem-hem* crown. The *nemes* is hollow in order to fit the head of the wearer. Its side panels are short and trapezoidal, ending in two tongues with a rounded outer rim, each pierced by a small hole for attachment. On the upper right-hand side of the headdress, a small rectangular tenon must likewise have served for attachment of a component that has disappeared. On the front of the *nemes* there was a large, heavily corroded *uraeus*. The *hem-hem* crown is that of the warlike form of the god Horus of Edfu. It is also sometimes seen on the heads of kings. But most importantly, the *hem-hem* crown is the attribute par excellence of a young Horus, Somtus, the tutelary deity of Heracleopolis. In the Graeco-Roman period the young Horus, Harpokrates, is often represented wearing this form of headdress.
Judging by the dimensions of the crown, the size of the complete effigy may be estimated as fifty to seventy-five centimetres. Z. K.

CHONS THE CHILD, THE EGYPTIAN HERAKLES AND AMON-GEREB One might consider the extravagant stories associating Herakles with the western mouth of the Nile to be restless creations of the Hellenic imagination, if the Egyptians themselves had not admitted that one of their gods was identical to the Herakles of the Greeks. From the fifth century BC, as Herodotus attests, Amon-Re, the main god of Karnak, recognised everywhere as the 'king of the gods' of Egypt, was identified with Zeus, ruler of Olympus. Greek documents of the Ptolemaic period confirm that Amon's companion Mut, who is simultaneously maternal and formidable, was Hera and that Chons, the son-god, was Herakles.

The identification of Chons with Herakles is logical in formal terms but, as far as everything else goes, disconcerting. Well known in Thebes from the time of the New Kingdom to the Roman period, Chons is a lunar deity who at first sight has nothing in common with the Greek Herakles. Under his formal title 'Chons in Thebes Neferhotep' he is most frequently portrayed with a mummiform human body, the same size as adult deities, although he displays the plaited side-lock on his temple as worn by children and adolescents. When represented as 'Horus, master of joy', he is also a man with the head of a falcon sporting the lunar disc (cat. no. 177, p. 124).

The god identified with Herakles must indeed have been Chons, but under a different form: that of 'Chons the Child', one of those specifically childlike aspects in which all Egyptian gods were likewise doubled by a Harpokrates, a 'child Horus', in recent periods (cat. nos. 178–181, 213, p. 125; 329, 330, p. 124).

For convenience, the custom developed of referring to the various god-children or child gods, which are among the most commonly depicted deities in bronze, generally as Harpocrates. Reproduced in seated, standing or walking positions, their youth is represented in the iconography in canonical fashion: nakedness, a youthful curl over the right temple and often the index finger of the right hand at their mouths. They sport various hairstyles and crowns that bear witness to the variety and richness of the mythology of divine childhood, and became common in most late official and popular Egyptian religion from the first third of the first

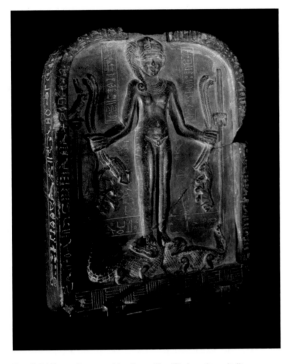

The Child Horus Supported by Crocodiles (Ptolemaic period)

millennium BC. The model was the small Horus, the son of Isis and Osiris, who was threatened and had to hide, but was ultimately promised triumph. Their bronzes are therefore classified less on the basis of their poses than by the various hairstyles or crowns that the Harpocrates statues display. Two types were discovered in Aboukir – god-children wearing *pshent* crowns and others wearing long robes. The head is missing on the example shown, with only the end of the childish pigtail being discernible. The child is naked and depicted in seated posture. Several parts of the body- the right arm, the left hand and the feet – are incomplete (cat. no. 178, p. 125).

All the Harpokrates of the countless local groups of deities were characterised primarily through their head adornment. The complex helmet called the *hem-hem*, placed over the *nemes* wig cover, distinguished the young Chons, son of Amon-Re, both at Tanis and at Canopic Herakleion. The *hem-hem* is made up of two ram's horns with three bundles of papyrus, each topped by a sun; the papyrus bundles are flanked on either side by an ostrich feather and a menacing upright *uraeus* cobra. As far as we know, the *hem-hem* symbolised the radiant power of the sun. In the great temple dis-

trict at Herakleion the IEASM found a few votive offerings for the god Chons. It seems reasonable to attribute to him the small monolithic granite chapel found not far from the large chapel which has a definite attribution to Amon, his father (cat. no. 116, p. 126).

In addition, at some distance within the area of the great temple district important remains of the idol formerly installed in this small *naos* were recovered: a *nemes* topped by a *hem-hem*, the whole thing measuring fifteen centimetres in height by ten in width (cat. no. 209). Here we are dealing with a retrieved bronze element which fitted on to the head of a statuette of the young god, itself made of wood, undoubtedly plated with gold as well as inlaid with stones or glass. The usual braided side-lock, presumably made of lapis lazuli, was suspended from the ring that one sees on the right temple. Below the horns of the crown, the linked rings must have supported long cobras – *uraei* – which fell above the shoulders. The dimensions of the object suggest that this Chons the Child, if it was in an upright pose, measured sixty centimetres in height, a suitable size for a cult statue.

We now have to ask ourselves which personality traits of Chons the Child led the Greeks to recognise Herakles in him. The birth of the local Harpokrates, the homologue of the young king Horus, was celebrated in each temple every year. This celebration renews the myth according to which Amon himself impregnated the respective goddess of the place, the homologue of Isis. In these sanctuaries, low reliefs represented a band of illustrations on the subject of the divine triad which, in the New Kingdom, related that Amon took on the appearance of the ruling pharaoh to make love to the queen so that she would give birth to a predestined heir to whom would evolve the powers of the creator and organiser of the universe. Thus, Amon-Re, who was at once sun, creator god and monarch of whom all the local gods were nothing but manifestations and of whom every pharaoh must really be the son, disguised himself as a man in order to beget the future depository of his supreme power. The text of the *naos* discovered in the area of the temple district illustrates this perfectly (cat. no. 117, p. 126). The rite celebrating the birth of the child-king ensured by magic means that there would always be a genetically divine pharaoh, predestined by the eternal father to guarantee order down on earth. And just as the king of the Egyptian gods assumed the appearance of the father of a future king, so had Zeus in Greece assumed the appearance of Amphitryon to father a child by Alcmena – Herakles.

Another feature of the iconography of representations of the child Horus has strengthened the adaptation. The 'magic steles' covered with figures and formulas permitting survival from reptile bites and scorpion stings depict the young 'saviour Horus' as a naked adolescent who, his feet placed on two crocodiles, stands holding snakes in his hands (p. 129).

Herakles in the cradle, for his part, had strangled two snakes that threatened him before going on to kill large numbers of wild animals and monstrous creatures when he was older. The symbiosis of Chons and Herakles is pictured by occasionally showing the Greek hero holding a crook in one hand and the legendary club in the other.

Herakleion, which is a 'House of Amon' for Egyptians, became for Hellenes a sanctuary of Herakles, as if the latter were in their eyes the principal deity of the place. J. Y. | D. F.

EXCURSUS: PUMIATHON, BENEFACTOR OF HERAKLEION – BETWEEN MYTH AND HISTORY

To date, only a single Greek image of the eponymous demigod has been found at Herakleion, but this evidence is particularly replete with historical significance. It appears on a gold coin (cat. no. 427), which was recovered from the north wall of the great temple district. It is a good example of the type of coin created for the use of vassal rulers of the Achaemenid Empire by artists working in the Greek manner while adapting themes from local mythology and regional iconography. These rulers sometimes marked their coins using the official language of their administration: Aramaic for a satrap (including the satrap of Egypt), the Cypriot dialect in syllabic or Phoenician script, or Greek for the kings of Cyprus.

Our remarkable gold coin was left behind at the site by the Phoenician Pumiathon; it is far from being the only piece. An exceptional quantity of his bronze coins, around fifty, have been excavated by the IEASM. On the obverse, an animal walks towards the left; on the reverse a lion, face turned towards the viewer, walks towards the left surmounted by a star with eight branches. Two examples were reported at the east and west ends of the 'central wall' to the south of the great temple district; another was found fifteen metres from the northeast corner of its enclosure. On the other hand, it seems possible to interpret a small group in H2 (p. 289) and ten or so examples along the façade and in the monumental complex to the north as coming from the foundation deposits.

Pumiathon, who ruled for half a century (362/363–312 BC), is an important figure in the history of the Cypriots and in the political landscape of the Near East at the end of the so-called 'Persian' period. In the fourth century BC, these states were in the possession of the Achaemenid Empire. In theory, they had to pay the great king of the Persians and Medes a regular tribute as well as make occasional gifts and provide him with the support of their military and naval forces. But in fact, just like the satraps of the coastal provinces of Anatolia and the kings of Phoenician cities, Cypriot dynasts, both Greek and Phoenician, conducted their own political affairs. They fought each other or entered into coalitions with their neighbours, sometimes allied with the great king, sometimes in open rebellion in concert with his adversaries of the time. The main powers on the island of Cyprus were the Greek kingdoms of Paphos and Salamis and the Phoenician kingdom of Kition.

The relatively great power of the king of Kition lay in the city's port and the fleet he kept there, facing south, at the start of the route towards Egypt. The wealth and the well-founded claims of Pumiathon are illustrated by the fact that, following his father, he multiplied his issues of gold coins. Pumiathon of Kition ruled from around 392 to 362/361 BC during a period when the pharaoh Tachos (362–360 BC) launched his armies victoriously against Asia but was dethroned in the same period by his nephew Nektanabo II (360–343 BC). Under his administration, the material wealth and defensive strength of Egypt would not merely be retained, but even increased. His well-stocked treasury permitted him to recruit legions of Greek mercenaries to oppose the mercenaries of the great king. Even more than his predecessors, Nektanabo II accompanied military armaments with spiritual armaments, paying more attention than ever to his ancestors, the deities who guaranteed the prosperity and security of the kingdom, pressing ahead with the enlargement and embellishment of the temples of Upper and Lower Egypt and gaining the loyal services of priestly associations and the great notables of the provinces. Nektanabo II himself glorified the divinity of his person by likening himself to Horus the falcon, while magical conjurations likened the war in progress to a cosmic battle aiming to drive the satanic monster Apopi and Seth the murderer, as well as foreigners, their stooges, back into Asia. The adversary whom Nektanabo II had to face was Artaxerxes III (359–338 BC), whom the Egyptians saw as a reincarnation of Seth, accusing him of having, like the latter, mistreated sacred animals. It was only after twenty years that the armies of the Persians brutally crushed in the field those of the 'last indigenous pharaoh' who, withdrawing to Meroitic Nubia in 343, disappeared from the scene but lived on in the memory of mankind as one of the fathers of Alexander the Great.

Whatever the horrors that the Greeks attributed to the ghastly Persian king, whatever the brutalities supposedly committed, the conqueror was recognised by the administrative offices and notaries as 'Artaxerxes Pharaoh', as is written in demotic script on the coins struck at Memphis. When, in 332, a new great king ousted the satrap of the last Persian pharaoh, Darius III (335–332 BC), 'Pharaoh Alexander' succeeded him automatically both in the deeds and on the monuments. Kleomenes of Naukratis, whom he appointed administrator of Egypt, was succeeded abruptly in 320 by the satrap Ptolemy, later king, who would soon eliminate the Cypriot dynasties and put our Pumiathon to death (312).

The construction of the great temple district was started between 355 and 353, the date of the gold coin, and 312 at the latest: around forty years that were packed with events in which the Cypriots must have been involved. We do not know if Pumiathon took part in the general revolt against the Persian king. It seems plausible that his ships and soldiers would have participated in his victory over Nektanabo II and that, like the other kings of Cyprus, he would have rallied to Alexander, the victor at Issos. In any case, taking the part of the diadoch Antigonos against the diadoch Ptolemy caused his loss. In short, except under the reign of Pharaoh Alexander, Pumiathon sided with the objective adversaries of Egyptian power. Nevertheless, his intervention in the affairs of Herakleion arose from a peaceful relationship.

If the situation was clear as regards military matters – Egypt was entrenched against the Persians – it was much more flexible as regards its commercial relationships with their Phoenician, Cypriot, Carian and Greek vassals. The conflicts between pharaohs and Persian kings had by no means loosened the bonds of devotion shared by the Egyptians and the Greeks, the Carians and Phoenicians settled in Memphis and the foreigners resident at Naukratis. The main indigenous cult at Naukratis was that of Amon (Zeus), Mut (Hera) and Chons, in other words Herakles, also dear to the dynasts of Cyprus. An inscription on a now vanished statue, dedicated by a certain Aristion 'to Herakles', was 'made by Sikon of Cyprus'. Now, it appears that the generosity of the king of Kition, evident at Thonis, extended as far as Naukratis.

In the end, it seems likely that Pumiathon's dealings at Thonis/Herakleion and Naukratis were not motivated by political, military or even commercial aspects but can be explained instead by cultic motives. Since the deities of others were considered to be true and real and one's own gods could be recognised in them, we should not be surprised that Pumiathon, despite being a devoted vassal of Persia, displayed his devotion to the Egyptian Herakles, even though this venerable form of his god Melkart or Baal was in enemy country. The identification of the protector deity of Canopic Herakleion with the Phoenician Baal would endure. Under the Lagids, a Syrian named Barthybas calls Herakles – and not Harpokrates – the son of Sarapis and Isis on a stele that he left at Canopos. And deep in the Roman period, an inhabitant of Palestine who had come from Ashkelon deposited in the Sarapeum there an image of the 'god of (his) homeland, Herakles-Belos, the invincible'. J. Y.

427 Hemistater from Cyprus
Gold
Pumiathon (c. 355/354 BC)
Diam. 1.4 cm | wt. 4.10g

On the obverse Herakles, clad in his lion skin, holds his bow and brandishes his club. On the reverse, a lion leaps on the back of a stag and bites it in the neck. The Phoenician inscription extending above and in front of the scene names 'the King Pumiathon', and dates the issue to the seventh or eighth year of his reign (i.e. 355/54 or 354/53 BC). J. Y. | B. L.

GODS, GODDESSES AND PHARAONIC ROYALTY

HERITAGE OF THE GODS, HERITAGE OF THE KINGS

The site of Thonis-Herakleion takes the form of a town located between a side channel of the Nile and a lake, with its buildings and harbour pools built of large blocks of limestone and a temple in the style of the pharaohs. In the sanctuary were three colossi of pink granite – a Ptolemy and his royal spouse (cat. nos. 106, 107, p.165) plus an extraordinary image of Hapi, the god personifying the Nile in flood (cat. no.103, p. 311), as well as various other statues alongside fragments of statues, large and small monuments of stone, ritual utensils and bronze figurines, gold and bronze coins and pottery; the dates of most of the artefacts range from the fourth to the first pre-Christian centuries, indicating the prosperity of the temple during the Ptolemaic period. Certain objects, like the pretty perfume burner in the shape of a sphinx (cat. no.136, p.351) or the imported pottery (cat. nos. 402, 411, 418, pp. 336, 402), take us back to the sixth century before Christ. Other more spectacular discoveries such as a stele with the decree by Nektanabo (cat. no.118, p.318), the counterpart of the stele of Naukratis (p.319), illustrate the Late Dynastic period.

In Canopos, excavations have uncovered a dump area between the main temple and a Christian architectural zone where statues were thrown, probably to be cut up as material for re-use. These statues of the late indigenous dynasties (cat. nos. 3, p. 43; 4) or even older (cat. no. 2) and also the Ptolemaic (cat. no.101, p.136) and Roman periods (cat. no. 25, p.136), are remarkable for their quality. The statues of gods, pharaohs, queens, individuals and numerous sphinxes vie with each other in aesthetic appeal, even if they are only fragments such as a wig (cat. no. 24, p.136).

Over and above their aesthetic value, the statues constitute new landmarks in the study of divine and royal iconography. And, even more happily, epigraphic material provides instant and more or less conclusive answers to problems of geography that had remained unsolved. The texts engraved on a *naos* monolith under one of the Lagid rulers serve to confirm that we are indeed at Herakleion, in the 'temple of Amon of the Gereb', as the famous Decree of Canopos calls it. As king of the gods, this Amon-gereb had a role in passing on to the new worldly rulers the inventory of the universe, or else his title as sovereign over the world. In fact, in the years that followed the Macedonian conquest, Alexander and then his young son would always be officially considered legitimate rulers, which implies that worship was carried out in their names, and that they were felt to be the foundations of the stability and prosperity of Egypt. And the same applied to their

4 **Portrait of a Pharaoh**
Black granite
30th Dynasty (380–343 BC)
H. 37 cm | w. 17 cm | d. 14 cm

The *uraeus*-snake and blue crown or *khepresh* confirms the royal origin of the figure. The style and treatment of the snake, crown and face date this statue, discovered in East Canopus to the fourth century BC.   Z. K.

2 **Portrait of a Pharaoh**
Quartzite
25th Dynasty (712–664 BC)
H. 38 cm | w. 31.5 cm | d. 34.5 cm

Despite a very worn rear, the stump of hair enables us to attribute this head to a sphinx. On the front of the *nemes* above the forehead is a *uraeus*-snake, on which we can now only distinguish two loops formed by the body of the cobra. Despite the respect for iconographical conventions in ancient Egypt, this piece has characteristics of 'Ethiopian' style statuary of the twenty-fifth dynasty.   Z. K.

214

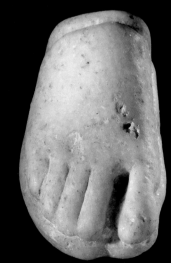

25

101

previous double page:

214 Wig
Bronze, silver, electrum
Late period – Ptolemaic period
H. 25 cm | w. 13 cm | d. 18.5 cm

This is the left half of a bronze striated tripartite wig, with *modius* and decorative collar for the statue of a queen or deity; it is hollow cast (p. 366). It was broken at its centre and has a substantial hole at the shoulder. The sockets and tenons on the underside of the shoulder show that it was intended to be a section of a larger statue. A flat recessed section at the front with a slot provided a back for a face that was either separately cast or made from another metal, wood, or stone. A rough area at the front of the wig suggests that a decorative element, probably a *uraeus*-snake, is missing. The plain *modius*, which is broken at the top, was possibly the support for an another crown element.
The use of polychromy, especially by adding elements in metal, was a common practice both in Pharaonic and Graeco-Roman art. Monumental metal sculpture, or the attachment of metal to pieces of sculpture, had been practiced in Egypt since the Early Dynastic period. The intention of such composite statuary was to create a more striking visual effect and to highlight specific attributes. E. L.

25 Fragment of base with foot
Marble
Roman period
H. 2.9 cm | w. 6.7 cm | d. 3.8 cm

This is the fragment of a foot, approximately to the springing of the ankle. The toes are well modelled, but wear on the surface prevents us from determining how the nails were indicated. The toes form an arc broken only by the hollow between the big toe and the next toe. The gaps between the other toes are simple grooves. The foot rests directly on a thick 'sole' that projects slightly, but without any trace of a sandal. The foot is bare
and the 'sole' is probably only a survival of the base it was attached to.
It was probably from a statue 75–100 cm high. The slender narrow, bare foot suggests a female figure. The skill of the sculptor suggests a date in the Roman period. Z. K.

101 Statue of Horus as a falcon
Black granite
Late period – Ptolemaic period
H. 68 cm | w. 23 cm | d. 54 cm

The iconography of the falcon standing and resting, as a manifestation of the god Horus, is perfectly recognisable. These effigies were common at the time; large and medium-scale statues of falcons were set up in courtyards of temples. Z. K.

Ptolemaic successors. The Roman conquest would have brought little change to this picture. Although the priesthood had supported the power of the Lagids, it also considered the Roman emperor to be a new Horus, the successor to Osiris, responsible for the order of the world and society. The texts of temples built in honour of the Egyptian gods in the Hellenistic and Roman periods glorified the Lagid king or Roman emperor in terms that were very close to those that had previously been used for the pharaohs.

Two statues of Sethos II (1203–1196) bear out this desire for ideological continuity (cat. nos. 99, 100, p. 138). These works are a particularly interesting case of *pharaonica*, objects from the time of the Egyptian dynasties being transferred to a Ptolemaic context. The phenomenon existed at Herakleion just as it did at the Sarapeum in Alexandria and the temple of Canopos west – pharaonic statues dating from ancient indigenous dynasties found a place in monuments of the Ptolemaic period. As in other structures in the capital, stones taken from old temples were re-used at Herakleion: a large block in the name of Ramesses II (1279–1213 BC) was re-cut on a grindstone when the monuments of idolaters were exploited as quarries after 391 AD (cat. no.143, p. 356). But these monuments, as little in Herakleion as in Canopos and Alexandria, do not prove that the sites were occupied from the fourteenth or thirteenth centuries BC and that the pharaohs of the New Empire built temples there. Around 1200, in the time of Sethos II, the ground along the coastal fringe was not yet consolidated enough to support structures.

One question remains open: in what period were the architectural elements and statues taken from the inland sites and carried to the new sites founded in the Hellenistic period or shortly beforehand, which continued to prosper under Roman domination? Two theories exist: the one that, for example, the blocks of granite submerged in front of the island of Pharos are the remains of the lighthouse and the one that would go to show that these pharaonic antiquities were brought to the temples in Alexandria only under the Romans. Undoubtedly one can imagine that transfers of this kind took place in both periods, since it is evident that the Ptolemies admired ancient Egyptian works of art in

Alexandria. The Sethos II pair of statues could thus well involve a new element for consideration. Up until the present, the site of the temple of Herakleion, a sanctuary that owes its importance to the dynastic ideology of Lagid rule, does not manifest any traces of a substantial presence during the Roman period. It would thus be plausible to suppose that this evidence of divine predestination of the rulers was brought to Herakleion under the Ptolemies.

However that may be, these works enable us to think about the fates of the temples in the Canopos region. They give us an idea of the complexity of processes and activities, and creation and destruction that took place over this lengthy period and the diversity of meanings and uses of things in the temples. We need therefore to distinguish the *pharaonica* dating from the Egyptian dynasties and obviously brought from elsewhere from works which, in material, style, attitudes, clothing and hieroglyphic inscriptions are equally 'pharaonic' but were made during the reigns of the Ptolemies or Roman emperors. We have also to distinguish works created in the name of a pharaoh to embellish the temple of a deity from those works consecrated by individuals and installed in these temples so that they might personally benefit in their lifetime and after their deaths from the rites practised there. Whoever the king may be whose names sign and date a statue or a scene of offering, his image represents him as being in the presence of the god to whom he is performing the worship. Additionally, these ancient effigies materialise the presence of earlier kings, who enjoy daily rites performed to the god, symbolising a dynastic continuity exceptionally well. The sphinx in particular, where the human head symbolised intelligence and the leonine body the physical power of the pharaoh, remained in fashion throughout the Empire and beyond (cat. no.102, p. 44, cat. nos. 1, 5–16, 104, 105, 461, pp.144–59).

As far as religious architecture and art and ritual were concerned, however, the traditions of the Egyptian and Greek cultures were different. The Egyptian temple, for example, is enclosed, the Greek temple open. The conception of the layout and sculpture of the images differs radically, and can have had little or no reciprocal influence. The Greeks did of course recognise the local gods, and in some case accepted them as their own gods in an *interpretatio Græca*. In the long term, there was much borrowing of symbolism. An image of Chons, the counterpart of the Greek Herakles, carries a club in a representation in a purely Egyptian style. A Greek-style Harpokrates will have a *pschent* hairstyle or a *hem-hem* crest. These exchanges are purely iconographical and are a long way from constituting a mixed style. Greek taste in representing the gods for the personal use of the population would continue into the Roman period. Egyptian tradition retained its individuality inside the large temples down to the end of the antique period, even if annexes tailored to Greek styles of worship found their way into the interiors of the sacred enclosures. That is the situation in the matter of art, architecture and official rites. However, we should not therefore be tempted to overlook the perceptible Hellenisation of the indigenous priestly elite, nor the devotion of the inhabitants of Greek status and Greek culture to the gods of their native places.

The religious zone of an Egyptian temple was enclosed in high outer walls, but the royal monuments of large dimensions, obelisks, colossi and sphinxes lining the access way were arranged in pairs in front of the façades. It should be noted that the remains of colossal sculptures discovered in Alexandria show that the Ptolemies and the Roman emperors did not lock away pharaonic art from the area around Alexandria as they installed it in the interior of indigenous temples (cat. no. 462, p. 57, cat. no. 463, p. 56). Retaining the hieratic iconography and gigantic manifestations of their predecessors for their own purposes, they exhibited the superhuman nature of their divinity to the eyes of all the world, whether or not they were of Greek status, mores and taste.   J. Y.

99   **Statue of Sethos II (A)**
      Black granite
      1203–1196 BC
      H. 127 cm | w. 60 cm | d. 30 cm

100   **Statue of Sethos II (B)**
      Black granite
      1203–1196 BC
      H. 112 cm | w. 50 cm | d. 30 cm

These are the remains of two sculptures that both represented a life-size man; all that is left of both statues is the major part of the body, namely the torso and pelvis, broken in two at waist height in both cases but nonetheless still fitting together. Judging from the dimensions, proportions, posture, shape of the dorsal pillar and style of dress of what survives, it would appear that the two images were practically identical, or in other words represented the same person, or at least the same iconographical type.

The figure is in the normal walking posture, the left leg forward, the arms hanging beside the body. On neither A nor B are there any vestiges of hair moulding that would enable us to deduce whether the figures were either wearing a short wig, with or without a crown on top, or were wearing a crown directly on the head. We cannot identify these figures as deities, given the absence of a divine beard.

The torso is nude; above the navel, the belly is clothed in a simple loincloth held in place by a belt. About halfway up the back, the dorsal pillars of the two statues are shaped as slender pyramids; the two figures thus stand leaning against an obelisk.

These dorsal pillars were covered from top to bottom with a complex decoration of hieroglyphics. Of the total, we are largely missing more than two thirds of the inscribed surface, and can only make out more or less damaged remnants of the latter. On A, the whole left half of the pyramid has disappeared, but what is carved on the right half has remained perfectly comprehensible. Fortunately, on both figures, at the back a central area preserves a substantial group of signs, almost all readable in A, much more damaged on B.

But these vestiges are sufficient to enable us to identify the shape and style of the hieroglyphs and the written forms of typical words of the monumental writing of the Ramessid period. There is enough evidence to confirm also that the arrangement and content of the decoration was identical on both. The conspicuous oddity of these twin inscriptions is the layout, which achieves a studied complexity; the 'model' invented by the scribes requires three parts placed vertically with differing layouts and signs taken from different scales in each, arranged in decreasing size from top to bottom. This exceptional feature allows us at least to conclude that the two monuments were created to constitute a pair.

At the top, on what is left on A, the left half of the surface is covered by large superposed signs which make up a text listing the classic promises of eternal existence that the gods allowed the pharaohs: *'an infinity of jubilees, tens of thousands of years as (Re)'*. These large hieroglyphs are ranged right (i.e. to be read right to left).

In the middle, below, clearly separated by a strip, is an inscription made up of smaller hieroglyphs distributed over three columns. Those in A are very readable, and those in B can be easily made out. Fortunately the inscribed surface is so well preserved on A that we can see that this part contained an elaborate list of the titles of the king for whom the pair of statues was made; in this case the hieroglyphs here are ranged left, i.e. read from left to right.

Towards the bottom, following this panel, three columns of text begin, made up of still smaller signs. Of the few groups of signs that have survived, virtually nothing can be learnt that would enable us to define the contents of these statements. The fact that they are ranged left like in the centre part suggest that they describe the acts or virtues of the pharaoh. In accordance with the normal known standards of arrangement of such inscriptions the convergent orientations would relate a dialogue between two people; the king who receives the gift of long life, and the donor god whose name would be in the now destroyed half of the upper area.

It remains to identify the ruler in the centre part of the decoration, where four of these five names that formally defined the identity of a pharaoh were written. These titles were arranged in the usual fashion on the two statues, in the form of two panels one above the other: A title is clear in A and can be guessed in B: *'The king of Upper and Lower Egypt, Master of the Two Lands, Master of the Performance of the Rites.'* The cartouche follows, then a subsequent qualifying term clearly visible in the two versions, *'living as Re'*.

The identification of the pharaoh involved is not obvious at first glance. Certain Ramessid rulers possessed, either at the same time or successively, two 'canonical' sets of titles, effectively formal identity cards that can be read on the majority of their monuments. However, sometimes 'occasional' stylings were invented for them in which the first three of these traditional titles depart from any canonical examples; there are cases where such extraordinary stylings coexist with the canonical set on one and the same monument. Our pair of statues carry this rather exceptional category of stylings.

On A, one can ultimately read the throne name of Sethos II: 'ouser-kheperou-Re, Re's chosen one, beloved of Amon', the Horus-name 'Horus our pehty, great in vigour', can be found on our statue A.

The two following formal titles laud the king's physical strength and military prowess and the overarching theme behind the design of the statues, Sethos II's struggle to gain power and defend the kingdom. The absence of a beard is typical of such statues and drawings featuring the king wearing the blue crown, a head covering associated with the ruler's recent accession to power. The pair of statues from Herakleion thus add a new element to the exceptionally large repertory of images of Sethos II.   J. Y.

99

100

A SEEMINGLY ENDLESS NUMBER
THE SPHINXES

Sphinxes were a major sculptural form in Egypt from the fourth dynasty (c. 2600–2450 BC) through the Graeco-Roman period as representations of the king's image. The standard sphinx composition has a recumbent lion's body with the hindquarters gathered in a crouched position and the forelegs stretched straight out from the body. The lion's body is rendered with decorative additions that vary from the realistic to the stylised. On the examples from Herakleion and Canopos, there is a full and dynamic range of renderings of bodily detail. In particular, the body's separation from the plinth, the position and height of the drawn-up haunches, the sculpting of the ribs in order to highlight a lean abdomen, the rendering of muscle groups on the flanks and forelegs, the sculpting of the claws, and the occasional sexing of the creature by depicting testicles, reveal a complicated and lively visual vocabulary for the body.

The head of the sphinx is human, a representation of the monarch, and normally wears a *nemes* headdress with a *uraeus*-snake in the middle of the brow. The *nemes* headdress is an integral signifier of royal iconography and has a solar meaning. The *nemes* is fitted tightly to the temples with a band, so that the cloth outlines the skull from which it flares out in a triangular shape behind the ears and falls in lappets at either side of the shoulder. The *nemes* headdress can either be plain or banded, although this decoration is less common in the Ptolemaic period.

The headdress is usually accompanied by a single or double *uraeus*-snake, a stylised depiction of a cobra with a rearing head attached to the brow. The *uraeus* is perhaps the most common sign of kingship in the Egyptian artistic canon, which affirms both the legitimacy of power and protection for the wearer. At the back of the headdress, an ornamental pigtail gathers the remaining hair not covered by the headdress and displays it on the back.

The sphinxes recovered from Canopos and Herakleion represent a rich and varied group from the Late Dynastic through the Roman period. Sphinxes were traditionally used to create a monumental processional way or *dromos* to the pylons of temples, such as can be seen at Sakkara and between the Karnak and Luxor temples. The sphinxes at Canopos and Herakleion highlight the Egyptian character of these sacred architectural spaces and the Ptolemies' willingness to have themselves represented in traditional ways. Evidence from Canopos shows that in the Byzantine period, statues and sphinxes were re-cut to be used in later constructions after the pieces ceased to be significant for the inhabitants. In the area at Canopos designated T1, numerous sphinxes were found with cuttings and chips that signalled either a workshop for hard stone carving and/or a dump for sculptures which were reused as construction material in the later centuries. In Herakleion, sphinxes, as well as other types of statuary, were found across the whole site.

E. L.

Ram-headed sphinxes in Karnak, 19th dynasty (1295–1188 BC)

following double page:

104   **Sphinx**
Pink granite
Ptolemaic period
H. 139 cm | w. 36 cm | d. 68 cm

The head of the sphinx carries a short wig. A bulge on the front may suggest the presence of a *uraeus*-snake. The identification of the person, also the style and dating of the sculpture, are impossible to determine.   Z. K.

105   **Sphinx**
Pink granite
Ptolemaic period
H. body 40.5 cm | h. head 31 cm | w. 124 cm | d. 42.5 cm

Many pieces of this sculpture that would define the body of the sphinx from his plinth, such as at the hindquarters or between the front paws, have not been adequately worked, giving the impression that the body mass is only roughly defined from the original block of stone. The head is blocky and without any discernible facial features except the flaring but lopsided *nemes* headdress.   E. L.

461   **Sphinx**
Diorite
1st cent. BC
H. 75 cm | w. 140 cm

1   **Sphinx**
Quartzite
Rameses II, 1279–1213 BC
H. 53 cm | w. 142 cm | d. 70 cm

All raised features such as the tail and the *nemes* pigtail have been damaged. The proper left side of the body has suffered considerable surface deterioration as a result of underwater exposure. At the front, the lappets of the *nemes* headdress are carved in raised relief and there can be seen the remains of the beard support scar. On the chest are the remains of an inscription, '*Son of Re, lord of appearances*' above a cartouche. The cartouche's contents may suggest a Ramessid ruler, although possibilities also include that the cartouche was re-cut with a later dynast's name. The piece was probably moved from another site to Canopos during the Graeco-Roman period.   E. L.

104

105

461

11

13

In the close attention to the features of the face, care has been taken to model the ears in a naturalistic manner. The eyes lack the round or surprised expression of many of the other sphinxes recovered due to a flattened lower lid. Both the pursed mouth and the chin have prominent drill holes, a technique used to accentuate these features.   E. L.

462   Sphinx
Grey granite
1st cent. BC
H. 70 cm | w. 150 cm
(cf. page 56)

11   Head of a sphinx
Pink granite
Ptolemaic period
H. 27.5 cm | w. 18.5 cm | d. 23 cm

13   Head of a sphinx
Pink granite
Ptolemaic period
H. 30 cm | w. 22 cm | d. 23 cm

The double *uraeus* juts prominently from the *nemes* headdress. With cat. nos. 11 and 15 this piece shares the rounded eyes and small pouty lips, which have been accentuated with drill holes and a prominent chin.   E. L.

14

10

14   **Head of a sphinx**
Pink granite
Ptolemaic period
H. 28 cm | w. 21 cm | d. 23 cm

10   **Head of a sphinx**
Pink granite
Ptolemaic period
H. 31 cm | w. 27 cm | d. 29 cm

The head has puffy cheeks and a jutting squarish jaw, which is reminiscent of the corpulent portraits of the later Ptolemies.   E. L.

following double page:

12   **Head of a sphinx**
Pink granite
Ptolemaic period
H. 26.5 cm | w. 31 cm | d. 24.5 cm

Due to the *nemes* headdress the ears are very far forward.   E. L.

15   **Head of a sphinx**
Pink granite
Ptolemaic period
H. 27.5 cm | w. 26 cm | d. 23 cm

This piece shares the benevolent wide-eyed expression, the small pouty lips and the prominent jutting chin of cat. nos. 11 and 13.   E. L.

15

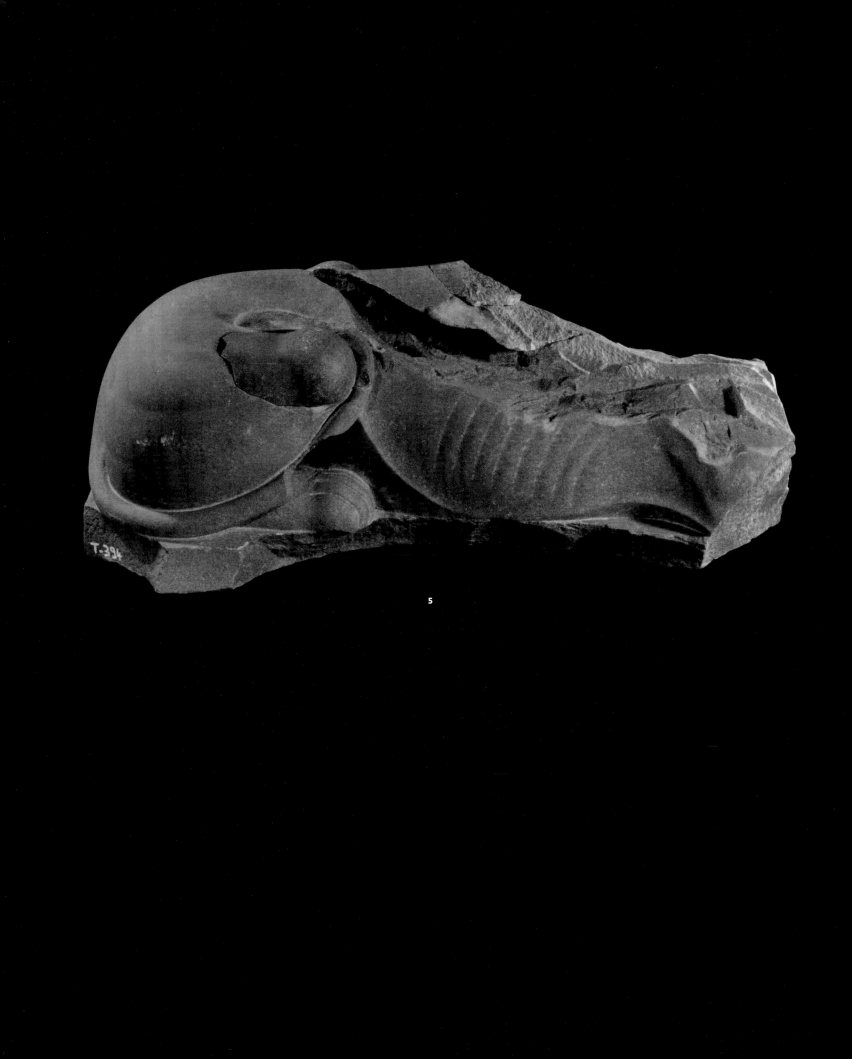

5

8

6

previous double page:

5 Sphinx
Diorite
End of late period – Ptolemaic period
W. 115 cm | d. 50 cm

This middle and back section of a sphinx body is composed of five pieces; the fragments from the hindquarters and lower torso were discovered in a three-metre radius around the main piece. Although the piece has sustained significant damage, the bottom and back section reveal that the piece was of high quality stone with particular attention to decorative and naturalistic detailing. The testicles are rendered distinctly and tucked underneath the tail, a feature that emerges in the Egyptian Late Dynastic period.   E. L.

8 Sphinx
Pink granite
Ptolemaic period
H. 46 cm | w. 114 cm | d. 36 cm

The intact sphinx body with plinth; from the missing head, however, the back edge of the *nemes* headdress is visible.   E. L.

6 Sphinx
Black granite
End of late period – beginning of Ptolemaic period
H. 65 cm | w. 145 cm | d. 50 cm

The front section of the forelegs and the back forelegs share stylistic and material similarities with cat. no. 5, although the damage makes it difficult to determine if they are from a similar workshop.
E. L.

7   Sphinx

Black granite
End of late period – beginning of Ptolemaic period
H. 28 cm | w. 75 cm | d. 23.5 cm

9 **Sphinx**

Pink granite
Ptolemaic period
H. 44 cm | w. 120 cm | d. 36.5 cm

The surface has deteriorated, as has the surface detail due to underwater exposure. The lappets of the *nemes* headdress are visible in low relief on the chest.   E. L.

FOREIGN PHARAOHS
AND EGYPTIAN ARTISTS

The stiff poses, gait, stylisation of musculature, royal dress and added crowns: all these are pure pharaonic tradition. The knot with the flap ends falling from the belt of the queen in Isis is the only sign of Hellenistic innovation. It is not unknown for royal faces to be individualised, but the only trace of a Greek feature consists of the occasional curly hair sticking out beyond the *nemes*. All the signs indicate that these sculptures came from the hands of good Egyptian sculptors. And sometimes it was a Greek work carved in hard Egyptian rock that was ordered by a Lagid ruler to decorate a sanctuary (cat. no. 17).

The desire of the Ptolemaic rulers to present themselves to their new subjects as successors to the last Egyptian kings induced them to show themselves as following their traditions. In fact, it must have been inconceivable to represent them other than as pharaohs in these places of worship. The same phenomenon is found on the reliefs of temples where Egyptian conventions were always strictly applied and where it is even more difficult than with sculpture in the round to distinguish one Ptolemy from another. There were numerous effigies of this kind. The Mendes Stele tells us about the erection of statues of Arsinoe II deified after her death in 270 BC by Ptolemy II: 'His Majesty ordered her statue to be erected in all the temples – which was acceptable to their priests – because these intentions were known to the gods and her kind deeds to all men.'

The Rosetta Stone, dated Year 9 of Ptolemy V Epiphanes (196 BC), has still more details. 'A statue of Pharaoh Ptolemy was ordered to be built, living eternally, god apparent, whose goodness is manifest, and he is called Ptolemy, protector of Egypt, which means Ptolemy defending Egypt; it is opposite a statue of the local god, who is giving him the scimitar of victory, in each temple, in a place visible to all, in the Egyptian style.'

The collection of representations in the round of Ptolemaic kings and queens ranges from colossi to statuettes carved in all sorts of materials, and juxtaposes masterpieces alongside very everyday products. Intact monuments are extremely rare. Everything is broken or reduced to the state of debris – bodies without feet and heads; heads capable of being identified thanks to Hellenistic-style portraits and coins are separated from bodies. The locations of the finds and the contexts are largely unknown or only vaguely known. There is an ample bibliography, but the opinions of specialists frequently differ. The typological criteria used by each to determine the date of the statues, selecting a detail considered important, are not very convincing, so that the monuments thus listed do not constitute a statistically useable database.

The influence that the Greeks – of the classical and then Hellenistic periods – had on Egyptian art has long been a matter of debate among archaeologists. Others have looked for traces of interaction between the two aesthetics. In fact, certain items of female clothing and the hitherto unknown way the hair is handled for both sexes indicate a reciprocal influence in the statues of Ptolemaic kings and queens produced by Egyptian sculptors.

It should be borne in mind that the artists of Egyptian origin who sculpted these hard stone statues were governed by very different conditions from Greek sculptors working in marble, trained in reputable workshops and recruited by the Ptolemies. Egyptian sculptors were very much at the service of the Graeco-Macedonian pharaoh, but in an indirect fashion. They were part of the technical staff of the temples just like the carvers of reliefs and engravers of hieroglyphs, the carpenters and metallurgists who made furnishings and ritual instruments. The temples were run by associations of priests under the direction of leading notables. These notables were the educated clergy who planned the architecture, furniture and wall decorations of buildings locally. Doctrinally the pharaoh, the heir and substitute for Re, was the only one anywhere to perform the rites, as one can see in the scenes lined up on the walls. His virtual presence had also to be made tangible by representations in the round of his person. Pharaohs of foreign origin were no exception, religious sculptors even authenticating their models by integrating into their works elements of exotic finery from the masters of the day.

Queens were the first to benefit from iconographical cross-referencing of this kind, which was in fashion down to Cleopatra VII's day. The first to be represented in the round in a pharaonic style was Arsinoe II, wife of Ptolemy II, very shortly after she died.

It is surprising to note that all these sister-wives have the same anatomy, impersonal but splendid. From the third millennium, Egyptian art had always immortalised women by installing them for good in an ideal body. Goddesses and princesses, like the mothers, sisters and daughters of the deceased as well, are endowed with perfect shapes clad in a tight dress. There is thus no cause to see the dress innovations as resulting from an 'influence' of Greek art. The Egyptian artists were content to accept reality in combining two formal traditions, perhaps to order but in any event with talent.

Does this mean at least that the oldest works owe nothing to their Greek colleagues? Undoubtedly there are grounds for detecting inspiration drawn from the works of the latter in the soft, fluid curves of folds, at least in the best works, in stark contrast to the static rigidity of Ramessid antecedents.   J. Y.

17   Portrait of Berenice II
Diorite
3rd cent. BC
H. 13.7 cm | w. 11.4 cm | d. 9 cm

If this sculpture manifests stylistic features similar to effigies of queens Cleopatra II and Cleopatra III, the wavy treatment of the hair above the forehead and the relatively soft contours of the face are more in the style of images of Berenice II, the mother of Ptolemy IV, who established a cult in her honour in 211/210 BC.   Z. K.

SUPERHUMAN DIMENSIONS
A PTOLEMAIC RULING COUPLE

Abu Simnel, the temple of Nefertari

We are here in the presence of a king and queen, both nearly five metres (over sixteen feet) high, shown erect in a walking pose, both built against a pillar. This royal couple is not the biggest, but they are much the best preserved of the large effigies of the Ptolemaic rulers in a pharaonic style that have come down to us. These are two original variants of the genre, and thanks to the excellent state of preservation and knowledge of the archaeological context they will form an important reference point in research relating to the iconography and deification of the Ptolemies. Their role is the same as that of the colossi that the kings of the New Empire erected in front of temple façades. The deified king guards the temple and manifests himself in his grandeur to accept the adoration of his subjects. The most convenient parallel is provided by the colossi of Ramesses II and his great spouse Nefertari sculpted on the façade of the small temple of Abu Simbel.

The colossus of the king was found in five pieces but is virtually complete. Its right fist grips the mysterious little cylinder that statuary always put in the hands of important men. His dress is

106 **Colossus of a Ptolemaic king**
Pink granite
Ptolemaic period
H. 500 cm | w. 150 cm | d. 75 cm | wt. 5.5 t.

107 **Colossus of a Ptolemaic queen**
Pink granite
Ptolemaic period
H. 490 cm | w. 120 cm | d. 75 cm | wt. 4 t.

utterly simple and classical: the upper body is bare, while the lower body is clothed in the traditional loin cloth. His head is coiffed *pschent*-style with a cobra *uraeus* on the forehead, its body being stylised to form two coils.

The double crown that expresses the union of the two lands of Egypt and at the same time symbolises the necessary unity of the *oecumene* under the control of the pharaoh, now features on the great royal figured sculptures in the round made during the New Empire, but it is usually placed on the nemes and rarely sits directly on the head. An element of updating is clearly visible in the 'personalisation' of the face. Although the nose is unfortunately broken off, the shape of the eyes and mouth will enable specialists to determine which of the Ptolemies it would be appropriate to see here in this toned down Egyptian-style portrait.

The colossus of a queen was discovered broken into three fragments, which fit together exactly. The Hathor crown worn by the queen was an added piece. It is intact, and happens to fit perfectly in the hollowed mortice in the centre of the head. The face with the frontal part of the hair and the start of the neck has come away, but the fracture was so clean that they fit together perfectly.

In accordance with tradition as a lady dressed in a pencil dress, she makes a measured step forward with the left foot. The modelling of the belly is discreet and delicate. The two breasts form very prominent hemispheres, and the protuberance of the nipples is very pronounced, as is generally the case in Egyptian statuary of the Hellenistic era.

The queen wears a classic tripartite wig, with the plaits shown in minute detail. An unusual *uraeus*-snake, represented only by the front part of the body of an erect cobra, stands upright in the centre of the forehead. The female body is sheathed in the normal tight-fitting robe that falls to just above the ankles, the robe being decorated with fine pleats. Around the shoulders is a shawl, the end of it passing diagonally between the breasts and attaching to the girdle below the right breast in a rather discreet knot. From the belt, two very long tails fall each side of the navel almost to the bottom of the robe.

The high hairstyle combines the orb of the sun between the horns of Hathor the cow and the two long raptor remiges. From the New Empire on, this was a sign of divinity among both royal women and goddesses 'of the great spells' that provided the force to go with their rulership. The crests of the ruler of Herakleion and Nefertari are practically identical.

Like the king's, the queen's face has individual features which will enable her identity to be discovered.

Of a general type and dress, these two colossi are imitations of Ramessid models lacking any symbol borrowed from Hellenic iconography. Only certain details and a number of refinements in the modelling reveal their Ptolemaic origin. The rendering here is softer and more natural. The transparency of the

Abu Simbel, portrait of Nefertari

clothing is rendered differently. The folds engraved on the fall of the skirt curve so as to show the natural movement of the fabric better.   J. Y.

GOD KINGS AND GODDESS QUEENS

'The last drops of water trickled down the black granite body. After more than a millennium spent at the bottom of the Mediterranean, just a few cables' lengths from Alexandria, a statue of the Egyptian goddess Isis was being recovered by the underwater exploration team directed by Franck Goddio. Immodest in her stone guise, she offers herself to the sun after years of darkness . . . Isis saved from the waters and other riches from Menouthis could well open the way to other discoveries.' (Claude Guibal, *Libération*, Tuesday, 6 June 2000, p. 27)

The photo that illustrates these words was taken at the moment when the team was bringing the sculpture trussed up in transport belts into the light of day. Taken from below, it was an outrageously provocative take on the creature's belly and *mons veneris*. The Egyptian and European presses alike refrained from publishing the image, which was taken to shock the public, and when later a frontal view of the magnificent creation appeared, the impression of majesty that the work conveys from the front banished the memory of her accidental shamelessness. With a very erect body, her arms glued to her sides and her left foot forward, her pose presents the same quiet dignity displayed by all the figures that pharaonic sculptors left behind (cat. no. 18, p. 173).

The statue was found on the western edge of site T (pp. 78, 89), explored in 2000, where the IEASM had removed a group of sculptures lying on or below a Byzantine and Islamic-period floor and which was covered by sixty to eighty centimetres of marine sand. The discovery area extended over an area measuring forty by ten metres. On the periphery and in the middle, there were no less than nine remnants of decapitated and mutilated sphinxes (p. 142); the splinters all around showed that we were on the site of workshops making tools of hard stone from dethroned gods. All the mutilations were visibly the result of vigorous dry blows applied with blunt instruments. This was the normal treatment meted out by Christians to deprive the demons that the pagan gods embodied of all capacity for perception, apprehension and movement. But since that time neither the anatomy nor the surface of the statue have suffered any violence, nor do they appear to have suffered seriously from marine erosion. The contrast between the all too obvious deterioration of the sphinxes and the condition of this statue, which the stonecutters did not attack, is perplexing. One wonders whether these remains of images of gods were not in fact hidden under the workshop floor, buried by the last pagans to safeguard them until the hoped-for day of the return of the ancestral gods.

The masterpiece is undoubtedly the representation of a queen of the Ptolemaic dynasty that a master sculptor fashioned from rock cut from an Egyptian quarry. It was no doubt decided too quickly that all representations of Isis as a queen date from the Roman period and that the type is a direct consequence of the assimilation to the goddess proclaimed by Cleopatra VII. In fact, the assimilation of the queen-mothers who ultimately ruled the kingdom independently for Isis, considered as regents of the kingdom during the absence of the king Osiris and the minority of Horus, was already evident in the second century before Christ. Moreover, the images in Dendera representing the sacred statues

conserved in the temple of Hathor and Isis and two of the wooden statues from there show that the principal cult image of Isis had the appearance of a queen.

More generally, these divine assimilations were part of a religious programme underpinning Lagid power. The Greek concept of the conquering god and his taking of power found an echo in the oriental concept of the sovereign ruler. Miraculously strong and victorious, the kings were obliged to defend the people. The king was a saviour, benefactor and restorer of peace. Conquest was conceived of in terms of liberation and restoration. It included the restitution of institutions that had been changed. The king's duty was to bring back a past considered excellent. Alexander launched himself against the Persian Empire and entered Egypt, which had never really come to terms with the second period of rule by the Achaemenid kings. The Macedonian became Horus the liberator and pharaoh. In Siwa in 331 BC, the conqueror was greeted by the priests as the 'son of Zeus'. Alexander came to the temple of Amon to get confirmation of his divine origin, but also the god's recognition of his aspirations for universal domination. As the 'son of Zeus', he had conquered sovereignty like his father had done after the victory over the Titans and also against Typhon/Seth; as the new Dionysos (Osiris) and heir of Horus, he was the conqueror of Seth (p. 106). Alexander and the new Lagid pharaohs that succeeded him discovered a useful propaganda tool in the myths.

Particularly Ptolemy II mobilised an enormous propaganda apparatus in support of his dynasty when he married his sister Arsinoe II and after her death conferred divine status on her. The king proclaimed that the incestuous relationship was confirmation of the divine nature of the royal couple. This marriage enabled the dynastic cult, which both Egyptians and Greeks would feel comfortable with, to be placed on an original footing. A highly mythical dynasty evolved from the relationship constituting the archetypal divine couple, pairing Osiris and Isis for the Egyptians and Zeus and

Hera for the Greeks. Royal theologians identified the rulers with the gods. Cleopatra III was 'Isis, the great mother of the gods' and Ptolemy XII (80–51 BC) designated himself a new 'second Dionysos'. And when Cleopatra VII (51–30 BC) paired up with Mark Antony, likewise a second Dionysos, who had summoned her to him, she featured as Isis-Aphrodite.

The Ptolemaic sovereigns were the heirs to the pharaohs and as Hellenistic kings successors to Alexander. This double aspect of Lagid power recurs in figured representations, and the taste for allegory shows through in the royal figures. During the Ptolemaic period, the kings fashioned on the Graeco-Egyptian model felt they were bearers of divine roles, and attributed to their enemies the role of Titans, the mythical enemies of the gods, who had to be eliminated. Thus the Lagid kings and queens integrated themselves into the ritual system worked out by the priests. This 'double' religion expresses the contact between the two concepts of the world, two types of cult and two types of thought. The myths were adapted and underwent changes, and prove that creation in the realm of legend is intimately bound up with the vicissitudes of history.   J. Y. | D. F.

The black granit body of the queen emerges
from the water after many hundreds of years.

AS BEAUTIFUL AS APHRODITE
A PTOLEMAIC QUEEN

Cut in hard, dark stone, this feminine body has a startlingly sculptural quality. Complete, it must have been slightly larger than life-size. The statue does not represent the goddess Isis. The detail that confirms this identification is the knot that joins the ends of the shawl the woman wears.

The knot is located, as elsewhere on numerous statues of Lagid rulers, above the left breast or even between the breasts. Since these sister-wives, mothers of the heir to power, tended to be compared with Isis, sister-wife of king Osiris and mother of Horus, scholars frequently talked of an 'Isis knot'. This expression certainly gives rise to a degree of confusion with another, different kind of object described as an 'Isis knot' – the amulet known as a *tyet*, made up of different ribbons and known since archaic times. Undoubtedly the latter originally represented the belt buckle on the abdomen of women. Thus the statue is certainly one of the queens of the Ptolemaic dynasty.

THE MANIFESTATION OF APHRODITE The handling of fabric recalls the marble work of Hellenistic artists showing Aphrodite in 'wet drapery'. Frontally, the folds undress the figure more than they clothe it. From the rear, a mass of fabric falls heavily, like a sheet saturated with water. The edge clings obliquely across the left leg.

Great goddess of fertility though she may have been, she was born from the foaming seas off Palaipaphos (old Paphos), on the south coast of Cyprus. One is immediately reminded of the queen who was especially considered as a notable earthly manifestation of Aphrodite – Arsinoe II, wife of Ptolemy II, who loved her brother, a woman whose fortunes, during her life and after her death, were an extravagant adventure.

A NAVAL APOTHEOSIS Ptolemy II (283–246 BC) not only did a lot for letters, the arts and sciences. By force of arms he was able to retain the conquests his father had achieved beyond Egypt, such as Cyprus and the Syrian coast, and even to intervene in Greece. He instigated the initial fitting out of the military port of Alexandria and the construction of the lighthouse. Arsinoe, who because of her past was always ready for a fight and had travelled widely, took an active interest in the navy and maritime routes, with the result that, if we take her devotees' word for it, she was much admired by admirals and adored by most sailors and indigenous oarsmen.

To stick to the domain of underwater archaeology, we shall limit ourselves to the religious sites created by Ptolemy II for Arsinoe on the seashores that she was especially interested in. In Alexandria itself, in the large port, an immense obelisk dedicated to her was raised in the proximity of the dockyards. In its Arsinoeion, an engineer had planned to put in place an iron statue which was supposed to have floated in the air by virtue of a magnet, and a statue carved from a block of chrysolith would have been installed. The choice of this material, brought from an island in the Red Sea, was of great symbolic

18 **Statue of a queen**
Black granite
3rd cent. BC
H. 150 cm | w. 55 cm | d. 28 cm

The Isis knot
(detail of cat. no. 18)

Roman copy from the Augustan period after a Greek original
by Praxiteles

power. Having repaired the canal joining the Nile to the Gulf of Suez, Ptolemy founded at its outlet a town which he called Arsinoe. The ships that set out from here and returned thither were those that, *inter alia*, conveyed the hunters who set off to capture war elephants in the eastern plains of Sudan.

And most extraordinary of all: as mistress of the seas, Queen Arsinoe II benefited from a specific form of apotheosis – she was Aphrodite in person. It turned out, in fact, that the great Cypriot goddess, source of the fertility of the fields, gardens and humans, had also acquired the role of protectress of navigators and mistress of the seas. Her sanctuary is perched on a promontory. As Strabo made clear, it was a little building established on a peak, thus clearly visible from the open sea. It was arranged to be 'sheltered from the waves', and was named the Zephyrion, the 'place of Zephyr', Arsinoe herself being termed 'Zephyritis', belonging to the zephyr. She was 'the one who loves Zephyr'. Zephyr signifies the wind when it is calm and regular, favourable to fortunate navigation.

At the same time, to judge by its quality the statue was intended for a very important temple and sculpted, one may imagine, in accordance with the express wish of Ptolemy II Philadelphos, who loved his sister, and who must have invited an Egyptian master to create an expressive image of sister Aphrodite-Arsinoe showing her as she was born, in order to serve as a model for the planned religious statues. The king no doubt put the artist in touch with Alexandrian workshops or at least showed him the types of statues of the goddess the Greeks made in marble. The *Aphrodite of Knidos* by Praxiteles, entirely nude; the *Venus Genitrix*, attributed to Callimachus of Athens, whose left breast was totally bare, and the Aphrodite in 'wet drapery', a type that went back to the end of the fifth century BC.

The artist fixed his Aphrodite ritually in the pharaonic attitude of all time – she steps out with dignity, left foot forward. At the front, he borrows from the Greeks the damp drapery that shows the body in all its beauty but allows the nipples of the two breasts to be made out. From the rear, in a radical break with tradition, it dispenses with the back pillar and replaces it with a naturalistic rendering of the water-saturated lines that fall obliquely because of the forward position of the left foot. Possibly this statue is the prototype of the costume, more or less well rendered, that all the Lagid queens would wear, then the images of Isis, even if the drapery later ends up not being transparent any more and looks as if it had been starched.

In any event, this statue does not represent a simple synthesis of clothing styles, but rather a real, pure invention – not a combination of formal insignia but the intimate fusion of two aesthetic concepts placed at the service of a cultic project.   J. Y.

GODS, TEMPLES AND ROYALTY

The so-called Satrap Stele of 311 BC, erected while the later king Ptolemy I still ruled the land as Satrap, or governor, for the official king Alexander IV, illustrates the religious politics of the new master of Egypt. The monument commemorates the return of an agricultural area to the temple at Buto in the Delta. The area had originally been given to it by an indigenous pharaoh but was subsequently confiscated by the Persians. Ptolemy thus restored an indigenous foundation and at the same time established his role as successor to the pharaohs of old.

As a general principle, the Ptolemies needed to secure the support of the clergy since they played such a leading part in the political, economic, social and cultural life of Egypt. Lagid rulers were fully aware that the sacerdotal class were the sole mediators documenting relations between the royal power and the religious authorities and in getting an authority accepted that was alien in language, customs and culture. The long-term domination of the country was effected by the clergy recognising the new pharaoh as a man-god predestined for the throne by the Creator, and thereby in turn securing the recognition of the gods and at the same time the allegiance of the entire Egyptian people.

The loyalty of the priesthood was ensured by granting them the revenues they needed to perform the rites and maintain the temples and their personnel. That was a matter of preserving the old order of things – each temple had a rather large college of priests. The upkeep and feeding of this cult personnel and the food offerings intended for the gods were assured by the temple being granted lands and benefiting from pious foundations established by the pharaoh himself. However, the Lagids chose to exercise stricter control over the lands devolved to the temples. Their estates remained the property of the king, who could dispose of them as he wished, encumbering them with the same taxes as other estates or partially exempting them when he wished to favour a particular deity and his priests. In fact, there was a progressive move towards these estates being administered directly by royal officials, attracting in compensation a payment of allowances by the state to temples thus dispossessed.

The structures at Edfu, Dendera, Kom Ombo and Philae, work on which was started during the period of the first Ptolemaics, illustrate the prosperity of the Egyptian temples under the Ptolemies, and also the deliberate policy of favouring certain priesthoods to the detriment of others. From Ptolemy II's time onwards, the devoted loyalty of the sacerdotal authorities was achieved by stressing the dynastic cult. To the same end, the Lagid sovereigns instituted annual synods, bringing together delegates from all the temples in Egypt, initially in Alexandria or nearby townships such as Canopos, and later in Memphis. These meetings were commemorated by spectacular steles, the most famous of which is the Rosetta stone.

The best preserved of these trilingual decrees is nonetheless the one at Canopos issued on 7 March 238 in honour of Ptolemy III. Among the beneficial acts for which the pharaoh is praised is the decision to introduce bissextile years. And as an exemplary instance of these occasional councils, it also illustrates the national celebrations, including one concerning the ritual ceremonies for the deification of the infant Berenice:

'...and seeing that a daughter was born to King Ptolemy and Queen Berenice, benefactor gods, and immediately proclaimed queen, and that it happened that the latter, still a virgin, suddenly departed for the eternal world while the priests accustomed to coming to the king were still with him, who immediately led the great mourning following this event and who, after having submitted a request, persuaded the king and queen to bring the goddess with Osiris in the sanctuary at Canopos, which is not only among the sanctuaries of the first rank but is among those which are most honoured by the king and all the inhabitants of the country; and that the ascent of the sacred barque of Osiris to this sanctuary is made every year from the sanctuary of Herakleion on the twenty-ninth (the fourth flood month), all the priests of the sanctuaries of the first rank celebrating sacrifices on the altars that they have set up on behalf of each of the sanctuaries of the first rank on each side of the road; and after that, the ritual ceremonies for the deification of Berenice and the closing of the mourning were accomplished by them with magnificence and care, as it is customary for it to be done for Apis (the holy steer of Memphis) and Mnevis (the holy steer of Heliopolis), and it was considered good to render unto Queen Berenice born of the benefactor gods (her parents) eternal honours in all the sanctuaries of the country.'

The decrees voted by the priests were thus posted in all the temples, written in three scripts – hieroglyphs, current Egyptian (demotic) and Greek. In gratitude for the benefits, real or imaginary, dispensed by the sovereigns of the country and to its gods, the priesthood thus multiplied the divine honours due to their foreign master in the form of ordinations, statues and crowns as so many proofs of loyalty towards the dynasty. The right of asylum featured among the various privileges accorded to temples and their priests; in many places one received the king's permission to publish this right granted to their sanctuaries on steles placed all round the sacred enclosure. Notices of this kind, which reassured the priests and enhanced the prestige of their temples, equally served royal propaganda in displaying to the public gaze the image of the ruler who was aware of the misfortunes of the weak, respectful of the prerogatives of local gods, but who did not hesitate to crack down on the abuses of his subordinates. The stele of Ptolemy VIII Euergetes II (cat. no.119, p.183), rescued from the seabed by Aboukir of antique Herakleion, is an exceptional echo of these public notices that instituted ritual honours in favour of the Lagid monarch and enumerated the benefits that the pharaoh, as Euergetes, benefactor, had conferred on Egypt, its gods and its inhabitants.   D. F.

Four colossal objects being transported on a barge

UNDERLINING THE GOOD DEEDS OF A RULER
THE STELE OF PTOLEMY VIII

This monumental stele, which stood in the vicinity of the temple district of Herakleion, has unfortunately suffered from the depredations of time. Broken into numerous fragments, its inscribed face of hieroglyphic and Greek texts has not stood up well to erosion by seawater. Approximately a quarter of the document has survived. The beginning of every line of hieroglyphics has been lost, while of the Greek text only a few letters remain. But between the numerous gaps that stud the document, the content of some individual passages can be gleaned.

The stele was erected under the joint reign of Ptolemy VIII Euergetes II and his two wives Cleopatra II and III, sometime between either 141/140 and 131 or 124 and 116 BC. The three beneficent gods are shown in the left part of the image that is still preserved, officiating in front of Amon, Mut and a line of deified predecessors beginning with the sibling gods Ptolemy II and Arsinoe II. Fortunately, the presence of Neos Philopator Memphites, son of Euergetes II and Cleopatra II, in the list of deified Lagids enables us to pin down the dating more closely. After his assassination in 130, the deification of the young Memphites in the year 118 was intended to seal the great reconciliation within the ruling family. Our stele was thus made prior to the issue of the amnesty decrees of April 118 BC.

The text is laid out in traditional fashion: royal protocol (l. 1) and royal eulogy underlining the good deeds of the ruler with regard to the temples and his warrior qualities in the fixed topoi of royal phrase-ology (ll. 2–11). Line 12 appears to mark the end of the royal eulogy and the start of the narrative.

Line 13 tells us that the Lagid brought the 'statue of Amon-Re, king of the gods, to the Thebes of the North', a place name which probably indicates Diospolis Kato (present-day Tell el-Balamoun). Nothing has been preserved of the reasons for this celebratory procession. Euergetes II's interest in Egyptian temples continues with the mention of the annual granting of corn to the gods in general and in particular to the 'god, master of the waters,' that is, Amon (ll. 13–14).

Line 15 is an account of an achievement possibly attributed to ancestors of the king, an achievement which is localised with the help of a succession of topographical indications, on the edges of the shores of the Delta – the place is situated within the confines of the region of the gods to the west and 'within the borders of the country, on the [edge] of the sea,' a localisation that matches Herakleion.

In line 16, Chons is put in touch with the islands of the sea, in a passage whose reconstruction takes us back to the alliterative wordplay setting out the attributions of the god – he is the one who has 'travelled the islands of the sea in his name of Chons'.

In line 17, the text continues with the evocation of royal good deeds in honour of a goddess, who is now installed in her dwelling place again. This probably refers to the re-establishment of worship or the operation of a sanctuary sacred to this

119 **Stele
of Ptolemy VIII
Euergetes II**

Pink granite
2nd cent. BC
H.. 610 cm | w. 310 cm |
d. 40 cm | wt. 15.7 t.

goddess. The king has paid a visit to Herakleion, located not far from the capital Alexandria.

Line 18 begins by mentioning a gift of land and continues by recalling a visit paid by 'the king of Upper and Lower Egypt Ptolemy, the god Philopator', that is, Ptolemy IV (221–205 BC), to 'the extreme (?) territory of the borders of the country, called the Temple of Acacia, in order to discharge the tax.'

Line 19 seems to refer to a conflict prior to the reign of Euergetes II, when rebels are said to have 'transgressed an order/decree' promulgated by his father, Ptolemy Epiphanes (204–180 BC), an probable allusion to troubles that broke out somewhere in Egypt.

Line 20 finally tells of an assembly of leading figures in the country convened by the king. However, this was a meeting of a synod not of priests but of administrative personnel and officials. We learn that this delegation went to

Alexandria but what they discussed with Euergetes II is not recorded.

Line 21 instances an appeal to ancient writings, probably to explain the ownership of land up to year 44 of Pharaoh Amasis (570–526 BC), on the eve of the first Persian takeover of Egypt.

In a very unclear passage in line 22, the king places people 'in the presence of the master of Gereb' and has his scribe called, probably to make known publicly all the decisions he has taken in the form of a decree.

Line 23 contains mention of a gift of money. The rest, lines 24 to 33, only consists of remnants

and cannot be interpreted. In sum, the mighty stele contains facts relative to the local affairs of the priests of Herakleion, in this case, the recovery of a benefice and asylum.   C. T

CULTS AND RITES

A GOLD FOUNDATION PLAQUE AND AN ENIGMATIC DEPOSIT

A gold plaque bearing the stippled dedication in Greek to King Ptolemy III was discovered at Herakleion (cat. no.161, p.188). It provides clear proof that the city's sanctuary was consecrated or reconsecrated by this Lagid pharaoh. Given its sacral character, the temple could not, in effect, have been built without abiding by very precise rules governing foundation and consecration rites to the gods. The king, assisted in his proceedings by the goddess of the art of writing, Seschat, would have set the position of the building's corners, and hollowed out the foundation trenches, into which pure sand was poured, with foundation deposits used to mark the corners. This plaque from Herakleion fits perfectly into the pharaonic tradition of construction and consecration to the gods. Such objects, plaques in gold, silver, glass and earthenware, inscribed with dedications, were placed in niches in the substructure's corners. In Herakleion there was also an enigmatic example, discovered under the corner of a limestone block to the south of the canal and to the west of the east basin that corresponded in all respects to the Chons sanctuary. This batch of very high quality amulets and figurines, including a wooden *naos* (cat. no. 454) and a statuette of a child-god (cat. no. 374), may derive from a consecration rite to the divinity of the son of Amon (who is comparable to Herakles), along the lines of those numerous, and modest, foundation deposits in the temples of the Nile Valley (cat. nos. 338, 376, 378, 380, 396).   J. Y. | D. F.

338 ***Uraeus* amulet**
Ceramic
Late period
H. 1.6 cm | w. 3.7 cm | d. 1 cm

396 **Double ewer**
Ceramic
Late period
H. 7.3 cm | w. 3.2 cm | d. 1.6 cm

380 **Plaque**
Faience
Late period
H. 8.4 cm | w. 3.6 cm | d. 1 cm

453 ***Naos* figurine**
Wood
Late period
H. 13 cm | w. 6 cm | d. 7 cm

Naos of wood with a principal parallelepiped part, in which a
rectangular niche has been cut into the front, and which is surmounted by a pyramidal part (with four equal sides). D. F.

374 **God-child**
Faience
Late period
H. 7.9 cm | w. 2.2 cm | d. 1.8 cm

The divine child, naked, is standing upright, its left leg forward,
holding a finger from its right hand to its mouth; in its other
hand is a cylindrical object, in all probability the 'testament of
the gods', making the god-child into the model of the predestined heir. The context seems to indicate that this is a Chons,
likened to Harpokrates (p. 128).

378 ***Oudjat*-eye amulet**
Ceramic
Late period
H. 5 cm | w. 4 cm | d. 0.9 cm

379 **Papyrus-shaped amulet**
Ceramic
Late period
H. 13 cm | d. 3,6 cm

376 ***Uraeus* amulet**
Faience
Late period
H. 4.2 cm | w. 2.2 cm | d. 1.1 cm

The amulet is fitted with a suspension ring.　D. F.

GOLD FOR THE HOUSE OF THE GODS
PTOLEMY III FOUNDATION PLAQUE

This gold object was found during the preliminary exploration of the northern sector of Herakleion, during the 2003 campaign. It is engraved with a Greek text of five and a half lines, produced through stippling. It is an example of those plaques that act as a signature for foundation deposits, buried under the corners of the enclosure and sanctuary walls, and in the name of the king responsible for building. It is clear that the plaque is at some remove from its original location and in the course of its travels, has suffered very rough treatment. Its four corners have been bent over. There are three undulations, suggesting the effect of lateral blows, and water pressure has resulted in a partial protrusion of little pointed dots. As a result of these alterations, some letters, in places, have completely disappeared, are wearing away or, worse, are distorted to the point of being unrecognisable.

Despite the gap in the middle of line one, the first two lines are easily understandable: 'King Ptolemy son of Ptolemy and Arsinoe, the sibling gods, the …'. Likewise, lines four–five: 'of himself and of Queen Berenice, his sister and wife, and of (their) children.'

The author of the foundation is therefore Ptolemy III, probably before he received the surname Euergetes in 238 BC; he announces himself as the offspring of the sibling gods Ptolemy II and Arsinoe II.

He connects his sister and wife, Berenice II, with his action and the blessings he expects as a result. In fact, she was his first cousin whom he had married in around 246. He also includes their children, without naming them. It is known that the couple had six children, including the future Ptolemy IV (221–204 BC), born around 244, his future sister-wife, the intrepid Arsinoe III, who even took part in military campaigns, and finally the ephemeral little Berenice deified by the decree of Canopus (p.178).

We can observe that the properly legible lines contain neither the name of the monument nor the name of the god to whom it is dedicated. This information must be sought in line 3, which has greatly deteriorated, to the point that establishing the text is problematic. What can be made out relatively clearly in the second half of this line, at least, is the Greek letters [.]ΡΑΚΛ[…], which can be expanded to '[H]eracl[…].'   J. Y.

following double page:

161 Ptolemy III foundation plaque (246–222 BC)
Gold
H. 11 cm | w. 5 cm | d. 0.1 cm

439 Coin
Silver
Alexander the Great (336–323 BC)
Diam. 2.4 cm | wt. 11.85 g

Silver tetradrachm of uncertain mint
Obverse: Head of Herakles in lion skin facing right.
Reverse: Zeus seated facing left on a throne, holding sceptre and eagle.
ΑΛΕΞΑΝΔΡΟΥ ([Coin] of Alexander)   B. L.

440 Tetradrachm
Silver
Ptolemy I Soter (310–306 BC)
Diam. 2.7 cm

Obverse: Head of Alexander the Great, with a headdress of elephant's hide, a ram's horn and an aegis. Beaded circular border.
Reverse: ΑΛΕΞΑΝΔΡΟ[Υ]. ([Coin] of Alexander) Athena Alkidemos advancing right, carries a lance in her right hand and a shield in her left; in front of her is an eagle; in the area to the left is a monogram, to the right, ΔI. Beaded circular border.

445 Coin
Bronze
Pumiathon (361–312 BC)
Diam. 1.8 cm

Obverse: Lion walking left; ram's head above.
Reverse: Horse walking left; above, star and Ankh-character.
B. L.

COINS AS FOUNDATION DEPOSIT A huge number of coins dating from the fourth to the first centuries BC have been collected at Herakleion, both throughout the exploratory dives, and during exploratory excavating in the canal: there are bronze coins in abundance, relatively rare silver coins, and several gold coins. The precise location of each has been noted, but mapping them does not have any real significance, given that these objects were found on ground that has been dramatically disturbed by tectonic movements, swells, flora, fauna and modern trawling. The bronze coins and some of the silver coins were, with some exceptions, in a barely legible state. This leaves the gold coins and a number of silver coins whose provenance in terms of period, and sometimes the actual date, can be determined. It should be remembered that those dates of issue that are known, with greater or lesser precision, for some of them,

only provide us with a *terminus post quem*, the coins having been sent to Herakleion long after they were struck. Aside from the coins of Alexander the Great (cat. no. 439), of the first two Lagids (cat. nos. 440, *450*) and of the Cypriot king Pumiathon (cat. no. 427, p. 131, cat. no. 445), there are also coins carrying on the obverse a profile of Athena wearing a helmet and on the reverse a little owl bearing right (p. 295).

The coins in question were collected from the interior or close surroundings of the temple area (H 1), where they were more or less scattered (p. 289). They offer important chronological information concerning the history of the cult of Amon-gereb and Chons-Herakles maintained by the sovereigns. It would scarcely have been a surprise to discover a hidden treasure trove in a wall or buried in the ground.

On the other hand, the discovery of this dispersal of valuable coins is quite disconcerting. The question remains as to what these gold and silver coins, some barely grouped together, others isolated and scattered far and wide, were doing there. There has been no shortage of hypotheses: coins lost by inhabitants wanting to save their belongings and themselves at the same time, during the panic of the final catastrophe; disparate objects from votive offerings that had originally been buried; and finally, foundation deposits, in other words objects from amongst those carrying the founder's name, and those ritually placed under the corners of surrounding walls and sanctuaries.

This last hypothesis would imply the possibility that coins in a foreign style, even if not produced outside Egypt, might have played the same role in these deposits as those rectangular plaques engraved with the pharaoh's royal title in hieroglyphics. The idea is not totally new. It was put forward already upon the discovery in Memphis of a haul of thirteen tetradrachms similar to our two examples (cat. no. 440), believed to have been issued by an Egyptian coin-maker. This batch, originally contained together in a bag, had been emptied out at the foot of the platform, where the Apis embalming workshops were located. The hypothesis that coins found in the great temple area of Herakleion might be elements dispersed from foundation deposits, is actually worth considering.

This hypothesis appears to be validated by the discovery of four coins grouped together underneath a segment of the so-called central wall (cat. no. 450). All four are from Ptolemy II Philadelphos and are as yet the only examples from this king that originate there. It is quite possible that the rubble forming the west portion of the so-called central wall as being the remains of a chapel built by Philadelphos.

Leaving aside the isolated coins collected a good distance from the great temple area, let us consider the constellations of coins that were scattered in the north part of H2 and within the perimeter of the *naos* (p. 289). One can assume that the coins that were discovered in contact with the massive limestone blocks came from beneath the walls, which had been demolished by later quarriers and which were damaged by telluric phenomena.

By far the most numerous coins are those sent to the Egyptian sanctuary of Herakles by the Phoenician king of Kition on Cyprus, Pumiathon (362–312 BC, p. 130): four of these bronze examples were found together with the two Athenian coins in the excavated part of the H2 stretch to the north of the great jetty. Several limestone blocks suggest that a building once existed in this location, separated from the northern face of the temple area by a dozen metres or so, but now destroyed. The discovery continues along the western extremity of this side, then the length of the south side. In addition there are seven bronze coins (cat. no. 445) and a single gold hemistater that was found squeezed between two blocks in the western side (cat. no. 427, p. 131). Two further examples were discovered in the west part of the interior wall, in front of the *naos*. The following temporal connections would be possible: to the west, a coin of Pumiathon, a tetradrachm of Alexander the Great, who became ruler of Egypt in 332 BC; to the east a tetradrachm dating from the period when Ptolemy, son of Lagos, carried out the functions of governor in the name of the Macedonian dynasty (323–306 BC). Three tribol coins of the same, who became king, were found in the *naos* zone. The hemistater, issued in the seventh year of Pumiathon's reign, fixes a *terminus post quem*: the earliest possible date of Pumiathon's activity in the construction of the southern temple of Amon and Chons would have been 355 BC.

It becomes clear from all of this not only that Pumiathon enriched Egyptian Herakles, but that he was the patron who contributed to the construction of the façade of the great temple area, followed by Ptolemy first as governor and later as king. Beyond the construction of an outlying chapel, Ptolemy II does not appear to have occupied himself with the great temple area. According to research, although Ptolemy III Euergetes I was an active promoter of the region of Canopus, he seems not to have been interested in this imposing sanctuary, instead he had an edifice built for Herakles some 140 metres further north, as the gold foundation plaque verifies (cat. no. 161, p. 190).   J. Y.

146 Vat
Pink granite
Ptolemaic period
H. 63 cm | w. 205 cm | d. 90 cm

RITES AND FORMS OF OSIRIS WORSHIP IN HERAKLEION AND CANOPUS

In March 238 BC, delegates from all the temples in Egypt, who had assembled at Canopus to celebrate the anniversaries of both the birth and accession of Ptolemy III Euergetes, issued a decree enumerating the benefits that the king had bestowed on the country and defining the honours that were to be accorded this 'god benefactor' and his sister-wife Berenice. The decree was published in Egyptian hieroglyphics, demotic and Greek (undoubtedly the original language of the text), and it was decided to have it posted in the three languages in all the temples. Two virtually intact copies have been discovered, and numerous fragments have been recovered in various sites north and south.

The synod was still sitting when the daughter of the rulers, called Berenice like her mother, happened to die. The priests were the chief mourners and performed the traditional funeral rites for the princess, who by her death immediately became a goddess. They decided to venerate her as consort to the god in the temple of Osiris in Canopus. The young girl would have thus been called to accompany the god who died and was resurrected every year during his 'ascent', that is, his trip aboard the sacred barque, departing from the 'temple of Amon-gereb, the forth month of the flood, on the twenty-ninth day,' or as expressed in Greek, 'setting out every year from the sanctuary of Herakleion on the twenty-ninth of the month of Khoiak' to finish up in the temple of Osiris in Canopus (about the text p. 178).

A portable statuette featuring the deceased Princess Berenice, adorned with a crown symbolising the growth of bread-making cereals, would be a burnt offering, while sacred virgins, representing the deities of the country, would address hymns to her, since the whole pantheon was supposed to participate in the vigil for the dormant body of Osiris after offering incense to him. It is stated that this ceremony would have taken place before the navigation of Osiris in the 'sacred boat'.

The barque of the deceased god bore the name of the mythical boat in which the sun travelled through the night. It was in fact a model boat, in all likelihood made of wood coated with gold, hauled on a sled from an altar of repose in Herakleion to the canal, then on to the holy of holies at the Osiris temple in Canopus. This ceremony, in which the delegates from the other great temples took part, was part of the mysteries of the vigil and reawakening of Osiris. This festival is familiar from an ensemble of figures and texts in chapels constructed in the first century on the roof of the temple of Hathor at Dendera. In the first phase of these mysteries a 'vegetating' Osiris – a mummy-shaped silhouette made of barley (which they watered) – was placed in a stone vat on the twelfth of the month. Once the grain germinated, the figure was dried out and buried in the necropolis. Though the stone vat described in the Dendera text is of modest dimensions, the same does not apply to the one on which a ritual of the mysteries of Khoiak was engraved during the Shoshenq period (early first millennium BC), following the draft drawn up in the reign of Thutmosis III (1479–1425 BC). It contains a picturesque allusion to the navigation of a barque and the beer that made the goddess and her followers drunk.

As it happens, in the holy of holies of the great temple at Herakleion, behind the two Ptolemaic *naos* of Amon-gereb and Chons-Herakles (cat. no. 116, p. 126), a vat of pink granite was found (cat. no. 146). Its walls are pierced by two holes, one resulting from subsequent reworking, the other relating to its use as an Osiris vat. It was in here that Osiris germinated before he was exposed to sunlight and dried out, then transported on the gilt barque which would perform the ascent to his temple, which was suitably situated somewhere in the necropolis of Canopus. At that point the now redundant corpse was got rid of, either by being buried with its predecessors in a collective hypogeum or by being thrown in the water (p. 105).

Apart from the simulacra of Osiris mummies, a series of *ex voto* statuettes scattered around the site confirmed the popular fervour of the cult of Osiris, the king-god – from whom help could be expected after one's own death – who died and was resurrected. Undoubtedly thousands of copies of the sheathed silhouette of the Osiris mummy were produced, the murdered king-god with the *atef* headpiece – the crown of Upper Egypt flanked by two ostrich feathers, sometimes embellished with two curly rams' horns – who clutched the insignia of his immortal power: the shepherd's crook with a hook at the end, and the flagellum whisk used to dispel emanations. These bronzes – ranging from statuettes of fine proportions down to minuscule amulets – have also been found in their thousands and have gone off to fill museums and private collections. The intact copies found in the bay of Aboukir invariably show the mummy-shaped god standing.

The notoriety of the mysteries of Osiris at Canopus explains the numerous finds of *ex votos* to him, confirming the lively belief in him among the general populace. (cat. nos. *185–192*, 199 and 215).

The route followed by the god's boat in the direction of its temple was in all probability the great canal explored by the IEASM from 2003. It is extended

125

122

124

126

to the west, first by the further canal that crossed the urban site of Canopus located in 2004, then via the canal that took pilgrims and revellers from Alexandria to Canopus. The canal between Canopus and Herakleion yielded a considerable number of oblatory dishes (cat. nos. 122, 124–126; *123, 127*), votive barques and lamp dishes, as well as some small ceramic pots (cat. nos. 404, p. 199, *408*) and a bronze pail (cat. no. 255, p. 199). Among all these objects, apparently evidence of religious processions, there was also a small gold pendant (cat. no. *164*).

The texts mentioned above refer to small barques – one cubit and two palms (sixty-eight centimetres or twenty-six inches) – made of papyrus. A good many boats were reproduced in lead or bronze in the late period, but the apparent simplicity results mainly from the loss of figurines formerly present on the bridge. The examples discovered between Canopus and Herakleion might suggest (in the shape of *ex votos*) the divine procession in the month of Choiak (cat. nos. 334–337, p. 199).

The nautical procession they took part in was made up of a flotilla of thirty-four units of various types, to judge from the different names they have, which were divided into two groups. On board was the Chenti Amenti, the basin of the divine flame, plus thirty-four deities who kept watch over the precious sacred images. They also carried 365 lamps. A nice example is the circular lead oil lamp pinched at one point of the lip to shape a handle for it. The shape is perfectly attested in the typology of pottery oil lamps (cat. no. 346, p. 199).

The procession route was lined with a whole series of what appear to be places of individual worship: deposits grouping bronze cups, food offerings (animal remains), strainers (cat. nos. 278–280, pp. 201–02) and especially ladles (cat. nos. 260, 270, p. 202; 257, 258, p. 398; *259, 261–269, 271–273*): these were objects called *kyathos* by the Greeks (from the verb *kuo*, 'draw') used to decant wine into drinking cups.

The simple type of these ladles consisted of a little vase with a handle. However, by analogy with the ladles the Romans used for libations at banquets, the duck or Nile goose-head handles are designated *simpulum*. A great number of them have been found in Egypt, but others have turned up at various Mediterranean sites (Cyprus, Etruria). The motif of the head of a duck suggests immediately that this type of ladle is of Egyptian origin.

In any event, the oldest datable example, made of silver, features among the wealth of Psusennes I's objects (1040–990 BC). Such items were

The head is adorned with the
atef crown.   D. F.

The beard undoubtedly belonged to a
statue of Osiris. The upper part has a
fastening tenon.   D. F.

334

337

335

336

404 Big-bellied *lekythos*
Clay
End of 5th–mid-4th cent. BC
H. 8.3 cm | diam. 5.4 cm

The decoration of this vase, which contained perfumed oils, depicts a stylised panther, an animal associated with Dionysian processions.   C. G.

255 *Situla*
Bronze
Ptolemaic period
H. 25 cm | diam. 28.5 cm | d. 0.4 cm

The bucket, or bell *situla*, so termed because the shape resembles a bell, has a slightly flared rim and a sloping shoulder. The handle is surmounted by a projecting floral design. Around the top of the vessel run a series of unevenly spaced incised lines. The Greek letters BAKOI (= Bacchos = Dionysus = Bacchus?) have been clumsily etched on one side. The vessel rests on a cylindrical foot; it was clearly designed for holding and/or transporting liquid and was perhaps connected with feasting or symposia and used for mixing wine and water, taking over from the Classical *krater*. The *situla* is perhaps one of the most widespread and numerous metal vases of Hellenistic times. In the Egyptian religion, *situlai* were used for cult libations and were often donated by individuals. A second *situla* included in this catalogue has a hieroglyphic inscription linking it to the cult of Isis (cat. no. 253, p. 224).   Z. C.

346 Oil lamp
Lead
5th – 4th cent. BC

334 Votiv barque
Lead
Ptolemaic period
W. 12.1 cm | d. 1.6 cm

River-based imagery was central to the Egyptian religion. The gods travelled trough the sky seated in papyrus skiffs above the heavens, and on earth the shrines housing their cult images were carried in elaborate barques.   D. F.

337 Votive barque
Lead
Ptolemaic period
W. 44.5 cm | d. 3.7 cm

335 Votive barque
Lead
Ptolemaic period
W. 21.5 cm | d. 3 cm

336 Votive barque
Lead
Ptolemaic period
H. 6.2 cm | w. 37.3 cm | d. 3.3 cm,

There are grooves in the metal suggesting the twisting of the papyrus used to prepare the boat. In the middle, it has a throne engraved with various motifs.

still being made in Egypt around 300 BC. The motif of the duck with its head turned round was a familiar motif of Egyptian artists. Familiar in images found in rural parts of the marshes where people bathed, went boating or hunting in the verdant areas, ducks are symbols of pleasure. This fowl is often associated with the agreeable consumption of an intoxicating drink. One of the older examples dates from the Amarna period: Nefertiti in person, watched by her three daughters, pours out a drink for Akhenaton. The scene takes place in a pavilion supported by columns whose capitals are shaped like three papyrus plants, whence three duck hang, their heads turned round. A later example of the association of the duck with a drink is found in a stone cup from the treasures of Persepolis and engraved on the rim with the name of 'Xerxes the great king'. The rim is decorated with twelve ducks' heads, as many of them as the months of the year, with their beaks turned towards the cavity of the cup.

The symbolism of these fowl associated with the consumption of alcoholic drink and their possible identity with some deity in the Egyptian pantheon can only be the object of speculation. However, the same type of ladle, identical in every way with the Egyptian models, appears in scenes of Dionysian rites on fifteen or so Attic vases dating from the fifth century BC. These vases are vessels intended to hold wine. On the vases can be seen a similar cup placed on a low table in front of the idol of Dionysus. The ivy-crowned priestesses dip their ladles into them to decant the liquid of inebriation into a cup intended for the bacchants.

The Greeks were still very familiar with the name of Osiris, and had, as Herodotus clearly relates, assimilated him to Dionysus. Certain similarities between the adventures of the two gods lent themselves to the identification: both had been dismembered and brought back to life, both had escaped death thanks to the masters of knowledge, Thoth and Hermes respectively. Herodotus

goes into the subject of Dionysus at length, whose name and personality were known to the Greeks through the Egyptians, since according to his theory Greece got the names of almost all of its divinities from them. The kingdom of the dead also belonged to him and Demeter, identified as Isis. Pigs, as abominable animals, were only sacrificed to the moon and Dionysus. The immolation of this abominable animal and consumption of its flesh took place on the feast of the god, which concluded in the countryside with popular processions in which Herodotus recognises the prototype of the *phallophoria*, the transport of an erect penis, of the Greek worship of Dionysus.

These celebrations, he says, 'go off in Egypt like in Greece. Instead of the phallus, they have another symbol, a kind of jointed mannequin; this was carried by the women through the villages causing the virile member to move, which is no less great than the rest of the body. A flute player leads the procession, and the women follow singing hymns to Dionysus.' Although we find in the Egyptian texts no trace of this popular celebration similar to the Hellenic *phallophoria*, there is no reason to accuse the father of history of deceiving himself when he makes a phallic entity of the king of the dead. Osiris was dead when he procreated his son Horus, and traditional imagery shows him making Isis pregnant after she has taken the shape of a kite and mounted the stiffened sex of her mummified husband.

The Ptolemies who were descended from Dionysus on the maternal side did not fail to encourage the worship of Osiris in Canopus, while their encouragement of the worship of Dionysus conquered the crowds from the Greek populace of Alexandria and cult communities of this god were set up among groups of Greek colonisers all across Egypt. The pomp of the great procession enacted by Ptolemy II Philadelphos was Dionysian in inspiration: an immense phallus seventy meters long (230 feet), painted in gaudy colours and trimmed with ribbons, was one of its attractions. The rowdy, inebriated casualness of the processions of Alexandrians along the canal leading towards Canopus, that is described time and again, could be compared with the fury of the bacchants and maenads. Mark Antony, as Ptolemy X, proclaimed himself a 'new

Alexandria and its environs (drawing by G. Seidensticker)

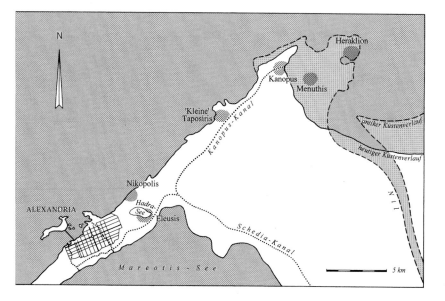

Dionysus' beside his wife Cleopatra-Isis and let himself lead a dissolute life before going off to his Timonium, named after an Athenian predecessor.

Osiris could do nothing about it, except that he had long been considered in Egypt as the god whose vitality made the vines bear fruit. According to the Greeks, Dionysus, also a tree expert, had made the world familiar with wine. The same civilising action was attributed to Osiris during the syncretism worked out under the Graeco-Macedonian dynasty. As a result, the Egyptian god borrowed from his Greek counterpart the role of 'lord of drunkenness'. The astonishing series of ladles found along the canal can thus undoubtedly be easily explained. During the procession returning Osiris to his temple, the followers of Dionysus added a libation of wine to their sacrifices and oblations. J. Y. | D. F.

279 Strainer
Bronze
6th – 2nd cent. BC
H. 2.7 cm | l. 22 cm, diam. 9.1 cm | d. 0.1 cm

The handle of this strainer terminates in the back-turned head of a goose. Two fine or rested on the edge of the recipient vessel intended to receive the filtered substance. They also evoke in profile the tail of the fowl.   D. F.

278 Strainer
Bronze
6th – 2nd cent. BC
H. 1.4 cm | l. 17.6 cm | diam. 8.6 cm

The strainer comprises a contoured ring with two curved cylindrical handles terminating in swans' heads.   D. F.

259 *Simpulum*
Bronze
Ptolemaic period
L. 26.5 cm | diam. 6.1 cm

280 Strainer

Bronze
Ptolemaic period
H. 3.1 cm | l. 28.8 cm | diam. 14.6 cm,

The strainer has a rounded corpus and its
edges curve inwards; the lower part is missing and only a small part with round holes is
extant. The handle terminates with a hook in
the shape of a bird's head. Both the handle
and corpus are of beaten metal.   D. F.

260 *Simpulum*

Bronze
6th – 2nd cent. BC
L. 52.2 cm | diam. 6.7 cm

The long handle has a square cross-section
and terminates in a crook in the shape of a
vulture's head. The figured features of the
bird are detailed.   A. A-R. R.

270 *Simpulum*

Bronze
Ptolemaic period
L. 51.8 cm | diam. 4.2 cm

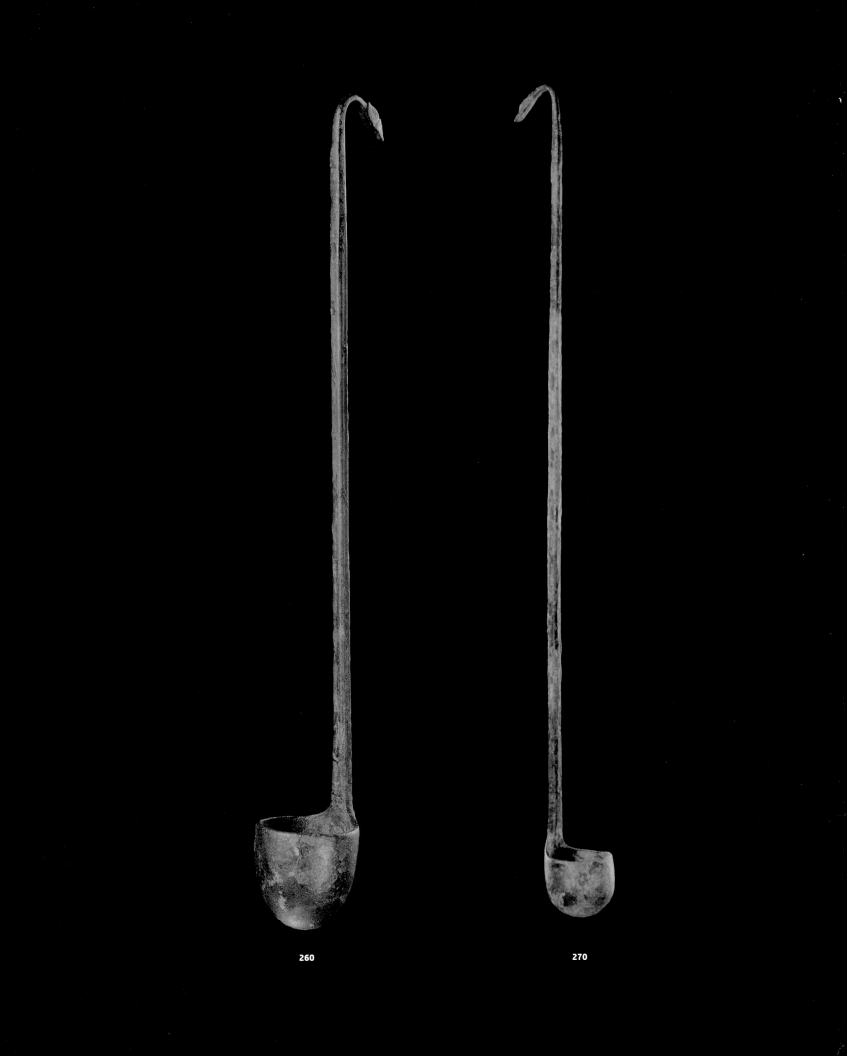

260   270

GREAT GODS

'Of all those who came before and those who are living today and leaving their mark in the dust of this region, only he has built temples perfumed with incense in praise of his beloved mother and father; in these temples he himself erected splendid statues of gold and ivory in their honour as protector of all those on the earth; over the course of the month he and his noble wife roast the legs of many fatted cattle on their bloodstained altars. She is the best among women, she who as a young spouse held him in her arms in their marital bedchamber, cherishing with all her heart this man who is her brother and her husband.'
(Theokritos, *In Praise of Ptolemy*, 17.120–130)

Alexander, supreme chief of the Hellenic coalition, had founded a Greek city. His architects designed it in the Greek style. During the reign of the Macedonian kings Alexandria quickly became the seat of the central government of Egypt. Greek was the language written and spoken at court and in offices, among private individuals, and citizens of the diverse territories. As in the entire Hellenistic Orient this would have been the language of everyday conversation and it would have been used for administrative and business purposes and in any written material. During the reign of the Lagid kings, Alexandria became a pinnacle of Hellenistic culture, attracting scholars, thinkers and men of letters from throughout ancient Greece. Town-planning, residences, Alexandrian *objets d'art*, mosaics and ceramics were Hellenistic, as were the way of life and the names of the places and the inhabitants. The royal household was constructed around the Greek model; the priests of the deified sovereigns were Greek. Temples were built in honour of Zeus, Poseidon and other Olympians and the iconography presents us with entirely Greek façades. Certainly, at a very early stage Alexandria adopted as its patron and installed on its acropolis the Memphite god Osiris-Apis, under the name of Sarapis, whom the Greeks and Carians living in Egypt at the time of the Saite pharaohs (664–525 BC) already worshipped. Several shrines were established for worship of the goddess Isis, a sorceress with the power to protect people and resurrect the dead (p. 105). However, these indigenous divinities were re-clothed in Greek fashion by the Alexandrian artists. The effigies of Sarapis resembled those of Zeus, Hades and Asklepios, and a cult specific to Isis in form and language developed, which enjoyed a theological importance that it had not achieved among the Egyptians, and which would soon spread around the entire Hellenistic Mediterranean. There is no need to give any further examples. Alexandria was, and remained in body and spirit, a Greek city on the margins of Egypt.

Underwater excavations in the eastern port have revealed remarkable remains of statuary that give much food for thought regarding religious practices in ancient Alexandria. The torso of the god Hermes is a magnificent example of the talent of the sculptors of the Hellenistic period (cat. no. 108). Preserved almost complete, the image of a priest clasping the vase containing the relics of Osiris seems to express an almost tender feeling of piety towards the saviour god who resurrected the followers of Isis (cat. no. 464, p. 215). In the area of the buildings that once stood on the harbour, a royal colossus of Caesarion (cat. no. 463, p. 56) and two classical sphinxes (cat. nos. 461, 462, pp. 57, 147) are works in pharaonic style carved in granite during the Graeco-Roman period. They announced the divine power of the sovereign on the façades before which they stood. When the cult of sovereign worship was established a number of original and diverse adaptations developed, as the Greek and Egyptian gods came together.

In the same discovery area there is the gigantic head of an enormous sphinx with the face of a bird of prey, an image that is the embodiment, it would appear, of a universal god protector specially evoked by theologians and invoked by the sorcerers of Roman Egypt (cat. no. 458, p. 206).

Further away, two statues of animals, a Hellenistic serpent in granite (cat. no. 459, p. 387) and a typically Egyptian limestone ibis (cat. 460, p. 208), were found probably not far from their original positions; they represent gods that were particularly venerated by the Alexandrians, firstly the Good Genie – Agathodaimon – on whom the fate of the city depended, and secondly, Thothh, the master of knowledge and wisdom, *alias* Hermes Trismegistos. According to Pseudo-Callisthenes the worship of Agathodaimon dates back to the foundation of the city by Alexander the Great. When a shrine was erected small snakes would appear and would then scatter throughout the city, where the Alexandrians would protect and honour them. The origin of this seems to be linked to the Egyptian serpent Schai, a very popular protector god, in whom the Greeks would have recognised the agrarian and domestic role of Zeus. Schai's partner goddess, Renenutet, having been assimilated into Isis Thermoutis – Isis in the form of *uraeus* – often appeared alongside Agathodaimon on reliefs. This association also contributed to the bringing together of the Good Genie

108 Statue of Thoth-Hermes
Marble
Ptolemaic period
H. 170 cm | w. 60 cm | d. 50 cm

The torso was discovered at the foot of a scree slope on the southern branch of the Island of Antirhodos. The figure is wearing only a cloak fastened at the right shoulder with a fibula; the torso is naked, the musculature of the chest softly modelled. The image of the god Hermes as a young man is well known; behind him there may also be the image of a king. This god was a popular choice of deity assimilated by the Ptolemies. Ptolemy III has been recognised in several lead figurines representing Hermes the fighter.   Z. K.

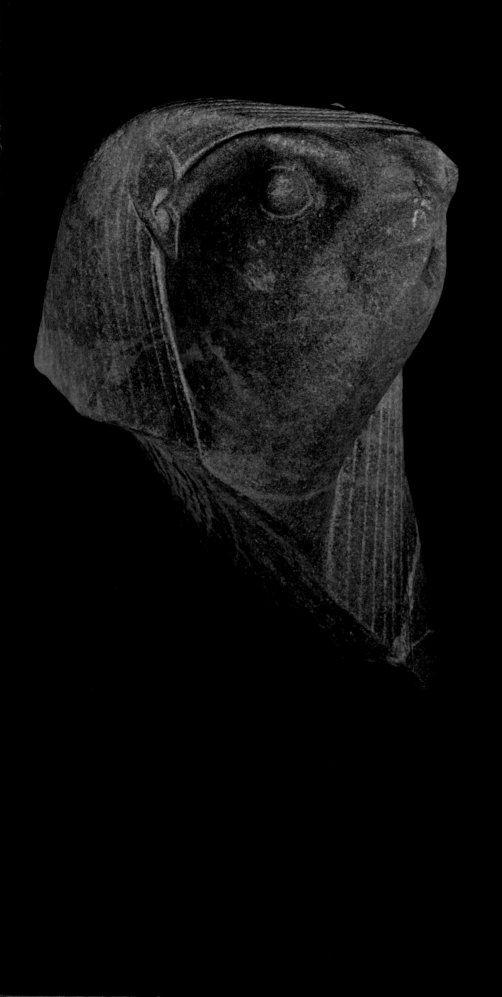

458   Falcon-headed crocodile

Black granite
7th – 6th cent. BC (?)
H. 70 cm | w. 43 cm | d. 70 cm

Despite its fragmentary state, the falcon head is in a good state of preservation. The compact head on the massive neck appears to be slightly lifted. The beak is broken and marked by a horizontal ridge. Above the very large eye is a long fold forming the arch of the eyebrow. Above it, the wig of the Egyptian deities, made up of large locks, covers the animal's head.

Human ears are fixed to the bird of prey's temples, slightly overlapping the wig, as though the completely anthropomorphic mask of the gods had been replaced by the mask of an animal. Now the ears give a precise indication of its date. As far as we know there are no free-standing representations of falcon-headed gods, whether in stone, wood or metal, with human ears. On the other hand, from the twenty-sixth dynasty (664–525 BC) onwards they are found attached to the wig on an appreciable number of bronze votive statuettes of Horus and other falcon-type gods. Moreover, this addition, which is found on statuettes of other gods with a human body and the head of an animal wearing a large wig, could be considered a typical feature of those gods that people hold sacred, such as gods 'who listen to people's prayers'. It can be deduced that the head could not have been made before the seventh century BC. Too little of the work, which shows quality workmanship and polish, remains to be able to establish whether it was made before or after the arrival of the Graeco-Macedonian kings. Under the indigenous dynasties, then under the Ptolemies, superhuman-sized effigies of kings and even certain important dignitaries were carved in stone; one giant divine statue, from whichever period it might originate, remains an uncomfortable exception.

The difficulty can be resolved on closer observation of the statue. The locks of hair in the wig, instead of falling vertically at the nape of the neck, curve horizontally away, as though resting on the back of a reclining body. This seems to be confirmed by the curve of the shoulder, as though the front limbs were positioned stretched out in front. These observations point to two possible reconstructions:

– The head belonged to a great falcon-headed sphinx. In order to represent the king as a manifestation of the warrior god Montou, or of the sun god of the Horus Nubians guarding the door of a holy place and protecting the king, the New Empire invented a variety of sphinxes by placing the head of a falcon wearing the divine wig on the body of a reclining lion. The Alexandrian monument would have been a great sphinx representing Re or Horus. It can be noted that it is almost as large as certain classical royal sphinxes dating from the thirtieth dynasty or the time of the first Ptolemies.

– The head could be the remains of a god represented in the form of a 'falcon-headed crocodile sphinx'. An alabaster figure (5.33 metres at the base, by 1.05 meters) can be seen amongst the monumental sacred statues in the Theban temple of Amenhotep III (1391–1353 BC), which has the front end of a lion and the rear end of a crocodile. Since there is no inscription, the name of this mixed entity is unknown, and as the head has disappeared it is not known whether it was that of a man, a falcon or another animal. In any event, this sculpture prefigures a type of iconography that is well attested later and of which the earliest evidence dates from the fifth century.

Various drawings show a deity with the appearance of a composite animal with the front end of a lion, the rear end of a crocodile and the head of a falcon, often placed on a high plinth in the shape of a temple. There are several variants of this imagery: the crest on the headpiece varies, but the structure of this type of composition comprising various attributes of divinity, is typical. It acts as a kind of 'umbrella' for the aspect of Horus 'that links everything together', an ancient god found in the Sohag region, known everywhere since the Ancient Empire as a redoubtable magician, who cured the sick and annihilated wicked enemies. It is found, for example, among the deities on statues and magic columns, stone objects inscribed with curative formulae that in the fourth and third centuries were placed at the disposal of the sick. Figurines and amulets were made with this idol and they can be found among the deities modelled in relief in the shallow depressions in votive paterae made of steatite. It became one of the cosmic powers on Graeco-Roman talismans. The magician Horus of Sohag was invoked in incantations recited for the protection of the cosmos as of the state and for the safe-keeping of the people during the Ptolemaic period. All available evidence points to an idol endowing the omnipresent saviour god with the power of the falcon who ruled the skies, the lion who ruled the earth and the crocodile who ruled the waters, and which was supposed to safeguard eternity, as enjoying exceptional popularity in later years in ancient Egypt. It is also not unreasonable to imagine that a giant example of this idol could have been brought in from elsewhere, or indeed newly sculpted, during the Ptolemaic or Roman era to protect the pharaoh and the well-being of the Alexandrians.   J. Y.

and Sarapis. This could perhaps be the reason for the presence of the stele representing Isis-Thermoutis in Canopus (cat. 30, p. 390).

Be that as it may, these finds clearly must have been very close to other effigies of gods that were discovered earlier in adjacent parts of antique Alexandria and which today are hidden below the coastal road – a small statue of Harpokrates and one of Isis and the lion-headed Sachmet. But this does not mean that there were as many temples in this quarter as there are gods in question. For the main patron of each major temple, whether it was in the Egyptian or the Greek tradition, accommodated images and worship of other partner deities. It is easy to imagine that the falcon sphinx, the Good Genie of the city and the Master Thoth-Hermes were situated in the open parts of large buildings or in chapel annexes. The two sphinxes and the statue of the priest representing Osiris in the form of a canopic jar, found in the same location at Antirhodos, would have been situated in a chapel similar, for example, to the small Sarapeum built in the time of Hadrian in front of the façade of the temple of Luxor. In order to gain some idea of the great number of statues of gods in this area one simply

has to refer to the description of the temples for the Roman Emperor Augustus given by the Jewish author Philo of Alexandria (*Legatio ad Gaium* § 150–151):

'Temples, propylaea, vestibules, porticoes that so many new and ancient cities contain in the way of splendid structures are surpassed by the beauty and grandeur of the buildings erected in honour of Caesar, especially in our city of Alexandria. For there is no shrine comparable with the one known as the 'Sebastion', the temple of 'Augustus of the Safe Haven', which towers to a great height opposite harbours with excellent moorings and can be clearly seen, filled like no other with consecrated gifts, decorated throughout with paintings, statues, objects in silver and gold; a great shrine with porticoes, libraries, meeting rooms, groves, monumental doors, spacious areas, esplanades and everything possible to create the most sumptuous layout giving hope of safety to those who take to the seas and those entering the port.'

New ways of representing Egyptian gods were thus created, probably in the Alexandria region. A typical example is that of the Nile. According to Egyptian tradition the floods were depicted as an apparently androgynous being with a masculine face, but with drooping breasts and an obese body, painted in green or blue; the colours of water and vegetation. This Hapi was not a god in the strictest sense, he was a power that created life and was therefore bisexual (cat. no. 103, p. 311).

Now, in Alexandrian art the Nile is represented in the style in which river gods were depicted by the Greeks and Romans, that is, as a bearded old man carrying a cornucopia, the Greek symbol of fertility (cat. no. 29, p. 41). He is usually lying on a bed of rushes surrounded by little children playing, the number of whom, sixteen, corresponds to the number of cubits considered to be the ideal level for the height of the floodwaters (p. 35). This figure occurs very widely in the statuary, and it is found on the Alexandrian coinage of the imperial period, which thus document that the Nile god is the incarnation of the country's prosperity, guaranteed as much by the return of the floods as by the wise government of the emperors.

The iconography of the Nile god is not entirely dissimilar to that of Sarapis. Therefore it is no surprise to discover his busts in the same sector, that of the shrine at Canopus, whose beneficiary had an exceptional future (cat. no. 20, p. 233, cat. no. 19, p. 55). Under Ptolemy I Soter the priest Manetho transferred the ancient worship of Osiris-Apis from Memphis to Alexandria, where the Greek name Sarapis was adopted. Thus the city was given a new god, who in the Hellenistic form united the characteristics of the Egyptian Osiris-Apis and the Greek gods Zeus, Hades and Dionysos. As god of the dead, healing god, god of fertility and protector of seafarers, Sarapis assumed the characteristics of Zeus, the king of the Olympian gods, and like him was depicted wearing a beard and sitting on a throne. In the Egyptian quarter of Rhakotis a modest temple was built in honour of Sarapis: the Sarapeum, of which no trace remains today. Its foundation during the reign of Ptolemy III Euergetes (246–222 BC) is only confirmed by bilingual plaques in Greek and hieroglyphics made of gold, silver and bronze. During the imperial period, this building became part of a prestigious shrine containing a great many works of art. The interior courtyard was decorated with columns: at the eastern side there was a great staircase at the bottom of which the Column of Diocletian, also known as Pompey's Pillar, was erected in

460 Ibis

Limestone
Ptolemaic period
H. 40 cm | w. 55 cm | d. 21 cm

The long legs are bent; the whole of the lower limbs rest on the plinth. Three long toes, bulging at the extremities, end in claws. The fourth shorter toe is extended backwards towards the side edge of the plinth. This is the statue of an ibis, the sacred bird of Thoth, which was widespread in Egypt until the Graeco-Roman period during which the god was identified as Hermes.   Z. K.

298 AD. The courtyard also contained sphinxes and many fountains. The worship that took place there was lavish, if one can believe the imperial-period poet Achilles Tatius (*Leucippe and Cleitophon* 5.1–2):

'By good fortune it happened to be the time of the monthly feast of the great god called Zeus by the Greeks and Sarapis by the Egyptians, and there was a torch-lit procession. I had never seen anything so grandiose; it was evening and the sun had set, but it was not dark – another sun had risen, but it was fragmented; that day I saw that the city rivalled the heavens in beauty…'

Sarapis similarly reigned in Canopus, endowed here, like Asklepios, with the power to heal; people hoped he would perform miracles and they came from afar to consult him (Strabo 17.1, 17): 'Canopus possesses a temple of Sarapis that is the object of such great devotion that even the most important men put their faith in him and come to sleep there or even send others to sleep in their place.' The oracle attracted crowds and incubation was practised, as in the great Asklepion shrines of Epidauros, Kos and Pergamon in the Greek world. During the night, which the pilgrims spent in an area close to the shrine, the appropriate recipe or therapy for a cure would be delivered in a dream. On waking the effects could be rapid and the miracles of Sarapis are recorded in the temple archives (cat. no. 67, cf. pp. 240, 369).

Associated with Sarapis, the goddess Isis enjoyed a flourishing cult as is shown by the temples devoted to her. For example, the temple of Isis Pharia is situated on the island of Pharos. Further within the city a shrine was built in honour of Isis Plousia and on the heights opposite Nikopolis (p. 200) a building was devoted to Isis Demeter. While still maintaining her Egyptian origins, Isis also underwent many metamorphoses. The diversity in her appearance points to her assimilation into other deities. She still always remains the devoted mother to her son, whom she breast-feeds, but the image of the goddess undergoes some notable transformations. During the Ptolemaic period a rather different image began to occur in the statuary, steles and bronze and terracotta figurines from that which continued to appear on the walls of temples and also in the 'minor' arts. It is characterised by a different, more 'realist', treatment of the body, a pursuit of a variety of more natural attitudes; hairstyles and clothing are different: the hair is in layered curls instead of the Egyptian wig, and the tunic and cloak are draped in the Greek style (cat. no. 24, p. 121).

The 'Alexandrian' Isis, who retained the appearance and powers that she had in Egyptian circles, became increasingly universal; this universality is proclaimed in one of the hymns (in Greek) in her temple in Narmouthis (first hymn of Medinet Maadi, *Narmouthis*, 14–24):

All mortals who live on the infinite earth,
Thracians, Greeks and barbarians too,
Utter your beautiful name, honoured by all,
Each in his own tongue, each in his own country.
The Syrians name you Astarte, Artemis, Nanaia,
And the people of Lykian Leto, sovereign,
The men of Thrace name you Mother of the Gods,
The Greeks Hera, enthroned on high, or even Aphrodite,
Hestia the benevolent, Rhea, or Demeter,

But the Egyptians call you Thioui, because you, and you alone,
Are all the goddesses that people know by other names.

At the end of the fourth century, and even more so during the third century BC, individuals and even cities in the Mediterranean region worshipped Isis and Sarapis. In Greek circles a form developed that could commonly be qualified as 'Isiac', which came from features and rituals of Egyptian mythology. These went so far as to transform what was initially a form of magic intended to assure the people of a divine afterlife into a global doctrine of salvation, reserved for people initiated into the mysteries.

In fact, in Alexandria itself, the numerous idols and sphinxes show that the indigenous works of art publicly expressing the superhuman nature of the king were part of the urban landscape during the Ptolemaic period. However, it should be questioned whether the presence of pharaonic art and ideology in the city that was founded by Alexander and was supposed to have remained an important seat of science, thinking and Greek aesthetics was simply restricted to such ostentation. In other words: even if Egyptian cosmology had had no influence at all on the intellectual activity in the museum and the library, and even if Alexandrian art had been purely Hellenistic, would it still not have been the case that the Ptolemies, in their capital facing the Greek sea, would have accorded important status to the deities popular with their subjects in the interior, which they themselves worshipped in Memphis, the other cosmopolitan capital that they had inherited from previous dynasties? They accepted these gods as they were, with their own names and forms, and admitted them into temples with their own deities. And their distinguished followers would eventually sit alongside Sarapis and Isis and assimilate the images and symbols of a thousand-year-old and long-prestigious religion adopted by the kings and queens. Describing in Greek the *rhyton* that Ctesibios the engineer offered to Arsinoe-Aphrodite in her temple at Canopus, the poet Hedyle of Samos presented the god Bes, 'the Egyptian dancer', who summoned the divine waters of the Nile and gave the signal for feasting and holy drinking sessions. Now, it was the same demon Bes,

67 **Amulet in the shape of a temple**
Lead
Ptolemaic period
H. 1.1 cm | w. 1.2 cm | d. 0.42 cm

bered remains of Osiris to be reunited, as far as Osiris-Canobos, those who knew the sacred texts skilfully reinterpreted the authentic indigenous traditions to pass on to the Greeks. Intercultural exchanges did not happen by osmosis between abstract cultural entities but through dialogue between people. The attributes of the Isis cult can only be understood as the result of traditions passed between Egyptian priests who knew Greek and Greeks who were interested in sacred things, which developed into a reciprocal interpretation of their respective pantheons, myths and rituals. Under Ptolemy I, according to reports by Plutarch, a committee was formed around the Egyptian priest Manetho, who retold the history and religion of his people in Greek, and around Timotheus, interpreter of the Eleusian mysteries, to identify a strange statue brought from Sinope. It is possible that other symposia of a similar kind drawing together people from the Sarapeum and other Egyptian and Greek shrines established in Alexandria dealt with Isis and Demeter, Dionysos and Osiris, Apis and the sun, Anubis (the guide of souls in the realm of the dead) and Thothh Hermes, water and wheat, rethinking the model for the sacred knowledge of Egypt to produce a Greek version.   J. Y. | D. F.

the joyful trumpeter and tambourine player, who used to lead the drunken feasts held in the towns of Egypt to celebrate Hathor, whom the Greeks recognised as Aphrodite. Therefore, were a Hellenistic *objet d'art* and the ceremonial from a Greek shrine from the Alexandrian region mixed with the Egyptian in the third century BC?

If the existence of Egyptian temples and the permanent presence of priests safeguarding pharaonic traditions in Lagid Alexandria are accepted, it can clearly be imagined how the Hellenistic forms of the Greek gods were created. The worship of these gods, with their so-called 'Isis' rites, their appropriate theology and their mysticism, spread, as we know, from the beginning and throughout the whole of the Hellenistic period in the countries bordering on the Aegean, the Black Sea and the Mediterranean.

It is commonly accepted that the 'Isis' cult exported from Egypt could just as easily have been called 'Alexandrian', that its theological ideas, its iconographic models, and its ritual practices were exported by Greek sailors from this great emporium throughout the world. The fact that there were Greek temples in Alexandria at the same time allows a lively picture to be formed of the way in which this cult was developed amongst the residents of the capital. From the 'new waters' of the floods that the priests of Karnak presented in procession to Amon in ewers and jars with lids in the form of rams', falcons' or human heads, to the vases in which the regional deities brought the dismem-

DO NOT TOUCH
PRIEST WITH OSIRIS-CANOBOS

This sculpture was found on the south-west shore of the island of Antirhodos in an area with paving and fallen rocks a short distance from two sphinxes from the Ptolemaic period (cat. nos. 461, 462, pp. 57, 147). The figure is wearing a cloak tightly wrapped around the upper body, including the arms, over a long pleated tunic. Seen from the back, the head appears to be carefully shaved. It is well known from texts and pictures that both in Egypt and in temples of Egyptian deities throughout the Greek and Roman worlds priests were required to have their heads shaven and wear no beards.

In his hands, hidden under the folds of his cloak, the young man is holding a round-bellied vase with a lid in the form of a human head at shoulder height resting against his cheek; the front of the vase is decorated with the relief of a crown. The masculine head, wearing a beard and the *nemes* headdress under the edge of which a fringe of hair can be seen, allows the object to be identified as what is generally known as Osiris-Canobos (p. 114). This is clearly a representation of a priest carrying a divine image, most likely during a procession, or in any case a cultural ceremony.

Several ancient writers refer to the liturgical use of vases, which can vary in type, in Egyptian processions, and this use is confirmed by the statue in Alexandria. But the object carried by the priest is not just a ritual object: it concerns the very image of the deity himself. The preserved images of Osiris-Canobos are representations of one of the manifestations of the god: 'Osiris-in-the-jar'. In fact, several quite large versions of this image have been discovered in Hellenic-style temples, where their role was clearly that of statues to be worshipped. On the other hand, canopic jars with the heads of Osiris and Isis in a temple, or even in a portable *naos*, or shrine, carried on a stretcher, appeared on Alexandrian coins from the time of Hadrian (117–138 AD), which clearly shows them also to be cult images.

Therefore, this statue is part of an iconographic development and a theological context specific to the early stages of the imperial era. But its exceptional aesthetic quality particularly highlights the sacred status of the divine image, which the priest is not allowed to touch with his bare hands for fear of defiling it, or because to touch it might be dangerous. What is expressed in the gesture of the veiled hands is perhaps the religious fear of forbidden contact. But the almost tender gesture of the priest in resting the image he is carrying against his cheek can also be just as well interpreted as love for the god and the desire, so often evoked in Egyptian texts, to remain in his presence.   F. D.

464 **Priest with Osiris-Canobos**
Black granite
1st cent. BC
H. 122 cm

CULT INSTRUMENTS AND TEMPLE FURNISHINGS

Everyday rites, the celebration of annual festivities, religious singing and offerings, as well as the sumptuousness of the processions, made an incalculable number of cult instruments necessary. The most important duty of an Egyptian priest was to perpetuate the completeness of the divine hypostasis through the precise performance of rites prescribed since the origin of the cult, the only manner of permanently preserving the equilibrium of the world, threatened by the powers of chaos. The texts and depictions which cover almost the entirety of the walls of the temples provide a precise description of the complex theology of the holiness of the place as well as details of the rituals performed there. The cult instruments discovered in the bay of Aboukir disclose a little about the requirements placed on the servants of the gods for fulfilling their liturgical activities as described on the famous Rosetta stone. 'The priests shall serve the statues of each temple three times a day, they will present them with all necessary things and they will also perform all that is required to do to honour the gods on their festive and processional days.'

It is still difficult to say whether the objects found were necessary instruments for the proper sequence of the events of a rite or if they represented the function of the rite itself in the form of offerings or other votive donations. In addition many rites could be celebrated indifferently for the majority of the gods in the pantheon, whereas other, more specialised rites, were intrinsically directed towards this or that god, because the object either had an exclusive connection with him or stood in a close symbolic relationship with the god.

If one considers the events in the temples, without making a comprehensive list, one can divide the majority of them into major categories. Offerings of food were extremely numerous, including conventional 'offerings' of meat, plants, bread, liquids, water, milk, beer wine and the like as are revealed to us on the offering tables and the plates of the sacrificial offerings (cat. nos. 36, 122, 124, 125, p. 196; 140, 142, p. 354; *123, 127, 141*).

Perfume products are present in the forms of oil and incense, of frankincense offered ritually to the god with the assistance of an incense burner, a brazier or a censer (cat. nos. 226, 286, 274, p. 218; 287, 289, 281, 282, p. 219).

In ancient Egypt, purifying powers were ascribed to both incense and water, and funerals and temple ceremonies often began with the burning of incense. Before a priest entered the temple, he required purification by means of the incense burner. The rite of offering incense cleansed the air of all evil and led the officiants and favoured ones into the sacred area. In the Hellenistic world, incense was an expensive commodity, and in Egypt its scent was considered to be the smell of the gods, so that it was often burnt in temples. Many vessels were shaped like charcoal dishes whose three feet were arranged like a stool's (cat. no. 290). Cloven hoofs or lion's paws were particularly popular for such items.

In antiquity, the main purpose of lamps was to illuminate houses and shops. But the results of temple excavations bear witness to a widespread secondary function. Lamps were frequently used by the Greeks during religious ceremonies. They were not only lit in temples but could also function as votive gifts for the gods (cat. nos. 283, 284, p. 220). Apuleius's view was that they were particularly connected with the cult of Isis, and describes a golden light in the shape of a goblet that was carried around in processions. St Clement of Alexandria ascribes the invention of lamps to the Egyptians. Although archaeological research has not confirmed this, the oldest known lamps having been found in Mycenaean and Minoan environments, the claim indicates the great importance that they had for Egyptian culture.

Flowers, ornaments, jewellery, fabrics and mirrors must also be included (cat. nos. 217–221, 223, pp. 222–23; *222*). Other types of rites, where the object itself is offered, appear immediately symbolic: the *oudjat* eyes (cat. nos. 170, 378, pp. 187, 242), the sistrums, situlas and especially Maat (cat. no. 194, p. 220).

The sistrum is probably one of the most important musical instruments made of bronze found in the burial sites of Canopus and Herakleion (cat. nos. *291–293*). The shaft of ornate Egyptian sistrums almost always terminates in a head of Hathor, who would have appreciated the harmonious sounds of the bars the priests moved. The Egyptian sistrum is a kind of rattle with metal bars set in a frame

36 Offering table
Black granite
Ptolemaic period – Roman period
H. 17 cm | w. 61.5 cm | d. 59 cm

Offering tables were integral to the architecture and equipment of temples to Egyptian deities, providing both a symbolic and a physical location for commodities intended for the god's consumption. From the third millennium through the Graeco-Roman period the top surface of the offering table had incised or relief representations of the sort of objects sacrificed to the deity, such as bread, beer, linen, fowl, meat, oil, papyrus and flowers. Representations of this kind can be seen on the offering table that the colossal Hapi holds (p. 311). The shape of the offering table can be compared with a hieroglyphic sign, which depicts a loaf on a reed mat. The top surface of this offering table is surrounded by a trough, which has an outlet on the front central protrusion. There is minor damage to the edges of the trough as well as to the relief decoration. The trough almost divides the stone into two halves but terminates at the front in a U-shaped symbol, which may suggest that the offering table is unfinished. Two heraldic lotus plants facing each other decorate the interior top surface of the table. The two cartouche-shaped troughs provide a place to hold physical offerings. D.F. | E. L.

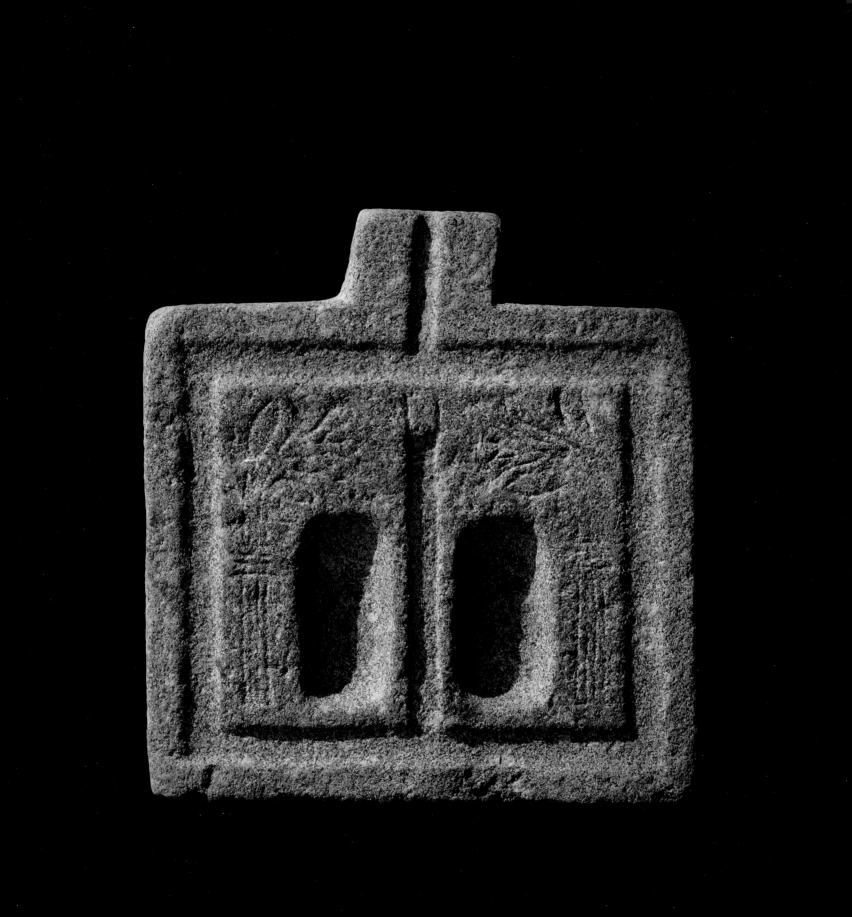

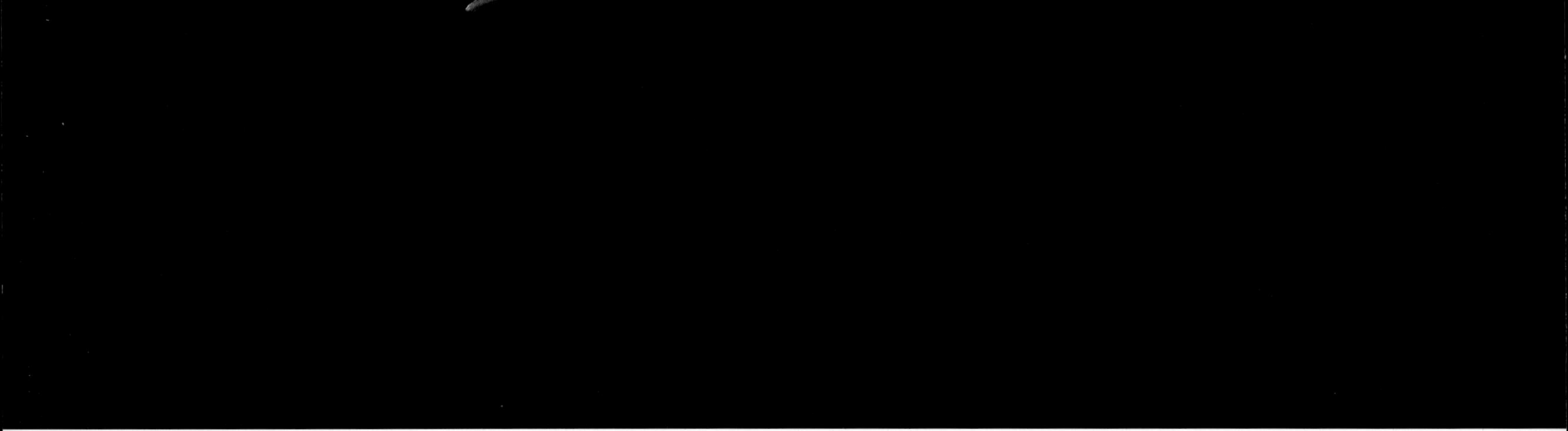

226 Vessel

Bronze
Ptolemaic period
H. 10.3 cm | diam. 5.1 cm

The vessel is decorated with a series of raised areas around the neck, shoulder and towards the bottom. The small hole in the top could have originally had a stopper. The object most probably belonged to the toilette, perhaps once containing perfumes or scented oils or eye make-up. The small opening and ridge surrounding it would have prevented spillage or waste of the precious contents.   D. F. | Z. C.

274 Spoon

Bronze
6th – 2nd cent. BC
L. 27 cm | diam. 10.2 cm

The large round, quite shallow spoon may originally have been attached to a wooden or ivory handle; the joining point of the two parts is decorated with a floral motif (lotus?).   D. F.

287 **Incense burner**

Bronze
6th – 2nd cent. BC
H. 9.6 cm | diam. 8.7–9.9 cm

289 **Incense burner (?)**

Bronze
6th – 2nd cent. BC
H. 8.3 cm | diam. 13 cm

The rim of the vessel is wide and flat. About one centimetre
below the edge a raised band, fashioned out of the same piece of
material as the main body, contains eighteen evenly spaced
'bolts', two of which are now missing. Two flat, heart-shaped
pieces of bronze have been bolted to opposite sides of the bowl to
serve as decorative handle attachments.   Z. C.

281|282 **Candelabra**

Bronze
6th – 2nd cent. BC
H. foot 18.8 cm | diam. 3.2 – 3.8 cm (281)
diam. bowl 9.5 cm (282)

The upper part of the hollow circular foot, which
possibly imitates a palm-like column, is decorated with
a cylindrical tenon which is inserted into the second
element, a circular bowl, receding at the sides to a flat
base with a perforated opening intended to take up the
tenon.   D. F.

parallel to each other and in several layers above each other. These bars are easy to use, and even when touched lightly, the bars move, striking metal discs or small cymbals that move and percuss together. The examples found in the burials are of the curved sistrum type. They consist of a cylindrical grip that always ends in a double head of Hathor and must have been crowned by a longish belt-shaped curve. To judge from the known examples, this curve was provided with two series of holes which could be fitted with metal bars. The small rings on these bars produced a sound as soon as the instrument was shaken.

194　**Base of figurine of the goddess Maat**
Bronze
6th – 2nd cent. BC
H. 8.5 cm | w. 2.5 cm | d. 1.9 cm

This is most probably a figurine of the goddess Maat; the protuberance visible at the top of her head could represent the beginning of an ostrich plume, the symbol of this deity.　D. F.

283 | 284　**Lamp and handle**
Bronze
Ptolemaic period
H. 11 cm | w. 13.2 cm | d. 7.6 cm (283) |
L. 36.4 cm | d. 1.1 cm (284)

Most lamps from the site of Herakleion-Thonis comprise little more than simple oil dishes and the majority are of lead or ceramic. The lamp highlighted here is of a more unusual type. It has an elongated oval body with a wide opening at the narrower end, supported on three hoofed feet. The narrow end has been cut off obliquely. This part of the lamp would have originally had a lid. A long suspension bar rises almost vertically and terminates in a duck's head.
Z. C.

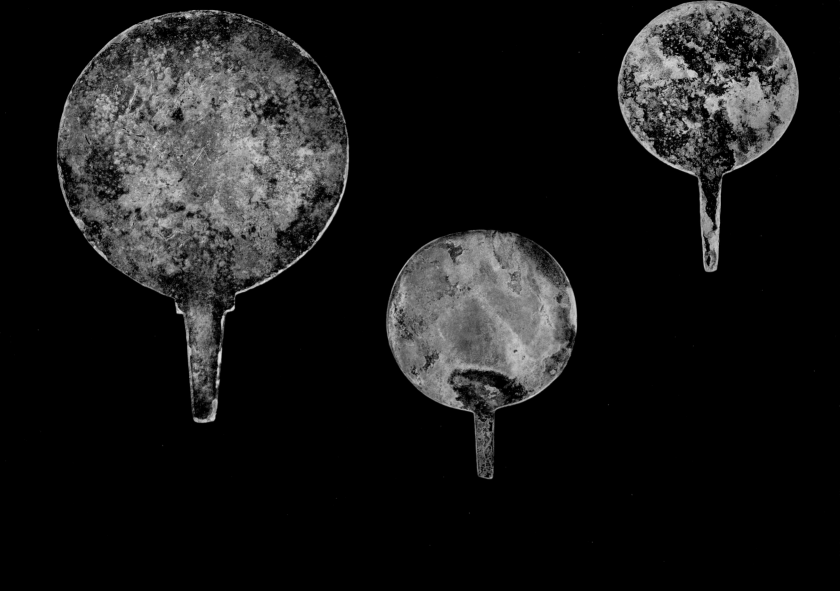

220 Mirror
Bronze
6th – 2nd cent. BC
H. 19.9 cm | diam. 18.2 cm | d. 1 cm

The shape of the mirror was widespread – what is unusual however is its weight of 1,700 g making it much too heavy to be carried around or held in the hand. It may have been mounted on a wall or held in place by some other means. It is equally possible that the mirror was acquired as a consecratory gift or made on commission. Literary sources and inventories of temples in antiquity clearly show that metal objects were valued on account of their weight. In this respect, the mirror must have been of some value to the person who used it for consecratory purposes and for the respective god and the temple.   Z. C.

218 Mirror
Bronze
6th – 2nd cent. BC
H. 15.1 cm | diam. 11.9 cm | d. 0.4 cm

217 Mirror
Bronze
6th – 2nd cent. BC
H. 16.3 cm | diam. 11.2 cm | d. 0.4 cm

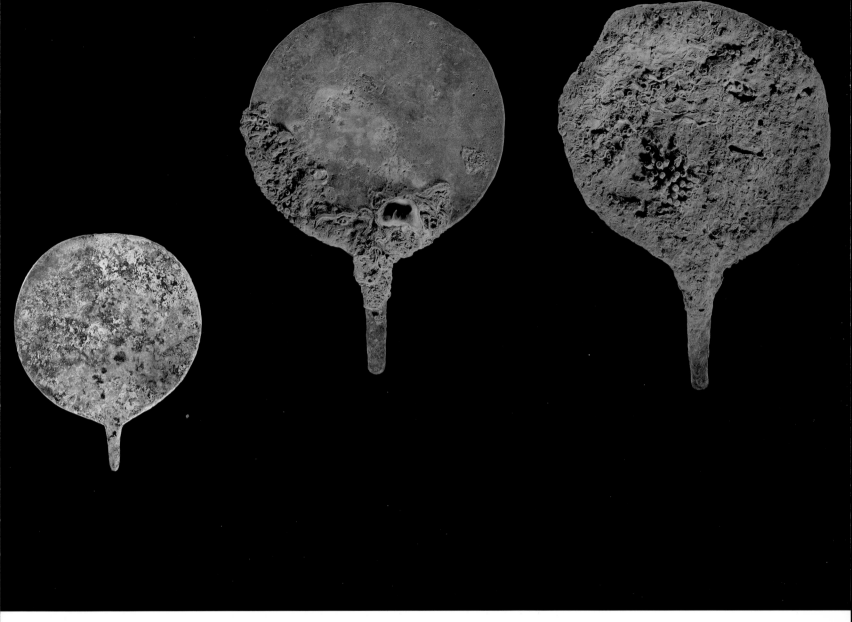

219 **Mirror**
Bronze
6th – 2nd cent. BC
H. 14.4 cm | diam. 11.8 cm | d. 0.3 cm

223 **Mirror**
Bronze
Ptolemaic period
H. 22.6 cm | diam. 16.2 cm | d. 0.5 cm

The surface of the object is damaged in parts from its long
sojourn under water.   Z. C.

222 **Mirror**
Bronze
6th – 2nd cent. BC
H. 23.6 cm | diam. 17.2 cm | d. 1 cm

The surface of the object is destroyed in parts from
its long sojourn under water.   Z. C.

As an instrument of the goddess Isis-Hathor, the sistrum spread over the Mediterranean region at the same time as Isis worship. At that time, the instrument was decorated with countless symbolic figures. Besides burial ceremonies, it played an important part in religious ceremonies such as dances for Hathor, sacrifices for the gods and processions of sacred boats. Nonetheless, it would be exaggerating to say curved sistrums were used exclusively for religious purposes. They were much more likely to be used for overtly secular celebrations as well, for example in public assemblies and to welcome VIPs.

Situlas were also part of the equipment of a temple, and were used during sacred rites and liquid offerings on the occasion of funerals (cat. nos. 253, *254*, 255, p.199). They and sistrums were essential features of the cult of Isis in the Graeco-Roman world. The Isis statue in the temple at Pompeii carries examples of both, and they are also visible in the hands of the priests of Isis on a fresco there. Initially the mystic nature of these vessels was less marked. It became pronounced only later and then in a way that had been possibly less obvious to start with. Situlas created a connection between the beneficial waters of the Nile and Osiris, who according to an inscription in the temple of Dendera 'brings forth the corn by the water contained in him, so that men may live.'

Phialae were saucer-like vessels used throughout the Hellenistic world both for drinking and to hold liquid offerings. There is a wealth of documentary evidence for this function in ancient sources and in countless scenes in Greek art, with the vessel in the hands of gods or men and women. Liquid offerings were the most popular form of sacrifice in antiquity, during which two vessels were used – the wine pitcher and the sacrificial drinking bowl or phiale. The wine was poured from the pitcher into the bowl, which was subsequently tipped up so that the liquid ran out on to the ground. We know from the sources that phialae, especially those made of gold (cat. no.152), were also used as diplomatic presents.

One must imagine the temples provided with wells where one could draw the water for ritual purification, a 'pool' for the purification of the priests, crypts to preserve idols and divine figurines, doors dedicated to the gods (cat. no.204, p.227), as well as any number of different instruments: tongs (cat. no.303, p.227), spoons (cat. nos. 274, p.218; *275–277, 302*), bells (cat. nos. 295–296, p.227), and gold (cat. no.152, p.226), silver (cat. no.153, p. 228), bronze (cat. nos. 224, 240, 242, p. 228; 227, 252, 288, p. 229; *65, 66, 225, 229–238, 243–245, 247–251, 256, 300*) and stone (cat. nos. 35, 137, p.230) vessels. All of these objects were used every day and in the rites of the Egyptian sanctuaries.   D.F. | Z.C.

Young woman with *sistra* from a Theban tomb, 1401–1391 BC

253   *Situla*

Bronze
Late period – Ptolemaic period
H. 3.4 cm | diam. 3.4 cm | d. 0.4 cm

The upper fragment of a *situla* has two suspension rings with lateral holes. The instrument contains an inscription that is difficult to decipher. The hieroglyphics precisely follow the contour of the lip. It could concern an offering to Isis: *'Powerful Isis (grant) life to Payn … legitimised by voice.'*   D.F.

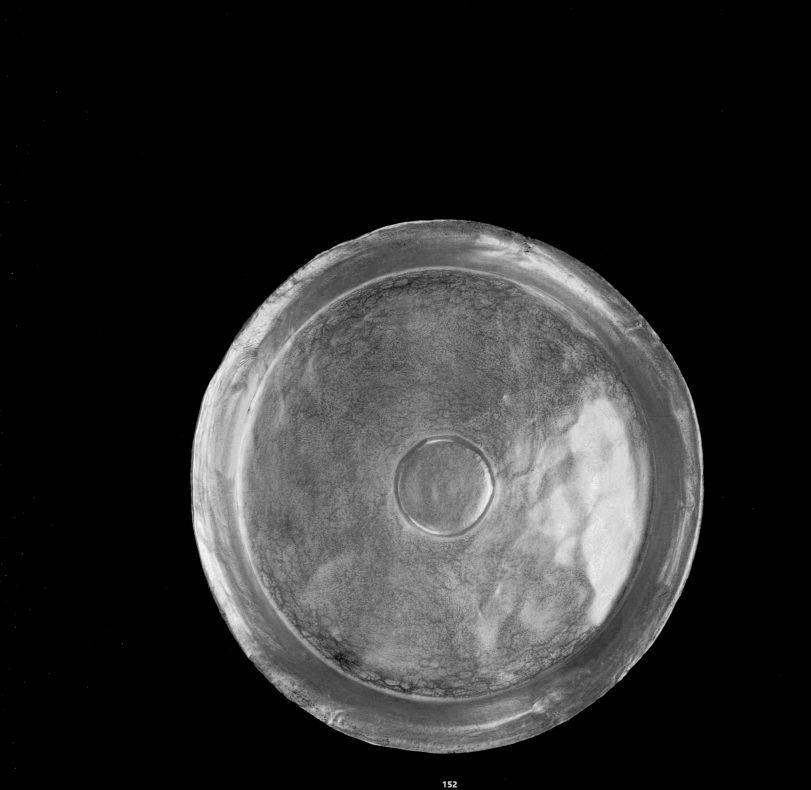

296

295

204

303

152   Phial

Gold
6th – 2nd cent. BC
H. 1.5 cm | diam. 18.9 cm | d. 0.1 cm

The phial, the only gold vessel to have been recovered from Herakleion, is complete and in a good condition, although with some
very small dents in the sides and base. The phial is made from
one sheet of gold, most probably hammered into shape and then
finished with a lathe.
In the middle of the phial an *omphalos* seems to be suggested.
Traditionally, the *omphalos* was intended to enable the dish to be
held more securely; two fingers were inserted into the boss from
below, the other fingers spread under the inside and the thumb
lay alongside the rim or stretched over the top. This hold can be
seen in reliefs, statuary and on painted potteries.
The phial was found trapped beneath construction blocks of a
structure identified as a traditional pharaonic-style temple and it
is tempting to conclude that the object was used at this site, as a
part of the rituals taking place there or a consecration.   Z. C.

303   Tongs

Bronze
6th – 2nd cent. BC
L. 45.9 cm | d. 0.4 cm

The tongs, in an excellent state of preservation, are terminated
by two taut hands. This implement may have been used for hand-
ling burning coals.   D. F. | Z. C.

295   Bell

Bronze
6th – 2nd cent. BC
H. 7.5 cm | diam. 4.3 – 5.2 cm | d. 0.2 cm

The main body is surmounted by a thick rectangle, fashioned out
of the same piece of metal. A hole has been punched through the
rectangle, slightly off centre, presumably to attach it to a rope or
chain.   D. F. | Z. C.

296   Bell

Bronze
6th – 2nd cent. BC
H. 7.6 cm | diam. 4.5 – 5.2 cm | d. 0.4 cm

204   Emblem

Bronze
6th – 2nd cent. BC
H. 13.6 cm | w. 7.9 cm | diam. 23.3 cm

The ensign comprises a hollow cylindrical handle with a projecting rim at the bottom, a horizontal platform and the beginnings
of a surmounting statue of an ibis (Thothh). The feet of the ibis
are very detailed, the scaly skin and nails carefully brought out.
It stands on a thin rectangular piece of bronze with rounded
short edges, a shape reminiscent of a cartouche. This has been
inserted into a rectangular plate, formed from the same piece of
metal as the cylindrical handle. Originally, a pole would have
been inserted into the bottom of the cylinder, possibly of wood.
Ensigns were carried aloft in processions and as attributes of the
deities.   D. F. | Z. C.

153   **Bowl**
Silver
6th – 2nd cent. BC
H. 6.4 cm | diam. 11 cm | d. 0.1 cm

This is the only silver vessel to have been recovered from the site. A simple loop pattern runs around the circumference of the vessel, approximately two and a half centimetres below the rim. Z. C.

240   **Bowl**
Bronze
5th – 2nd cent. BC
H. 6.4 cm | diam. 10.5 cm | d. 0.35 cm

A double incised line runs around the circumference of the vessel approximately half a centimetre below the rim. The rim has been flattened on top.   Z. C.

242   **Bowl**
Bronze
Ptolemaic period
H. 7 cm | diam. 12.2 cm | d. 0.2 cm

A large part of the body of the big-bellied vase is corroded. The two handles are missing but parts have been preserved in the form of two small tubes. Swinging handles would have probably been attached to these.   A. A-R. R. | Z. C.

224   **Vessel**
Bronze
5th – 2nd cent. BC
H. 13 cm | diam. 41.5 cm | d. 0.3 cm

Rectangular handles are soldered onto the edge of the circular vessel with a narrow, triangular beak-like spout.   A. A-R. R.

227   Cauldron

Bronze
Ptolemaic period
H. 18 cm | w. incl. handles 45.4 cm | diam. 27.9 cm

The cauldron has two horizontal handles of round section, attached directly to the body through two holes and hammered from the interior. It has no base or feet and was probably intended to be placed on a stand over a fire.   A. A–R. R.

252   Bowl with handle

Bronze
Ptolemaic period
H. 9.6 cm | diam. 25.2 cm

The deep bowl with handles seems to have appeared in metal ware around the second half of the fourth century BC in western and northern Greece. Such bowls were probably used during meals as containers for food or liquid. Given their size, it is unlikely that they functioned as wine *kraters*. This example is missing one of its two handles and the foot, but the position of both can be clearly seen by the presence of irregularities on the surface of the bowl. The handle comprises two parts: a swinging bronze half-ring, thinned at the corners, and a cylindrical flared tube with which it could have been attached to the body of the vessel.   Z. C.

288   Brazier

Bronze
6th – 2nd cent. BC
H. 23 cm | diam. 46 cm

The brazier comprises a truncated conical section riveted in four places to a large plate with a rim. The handles are attached to the outer edge of the plate by two strips of metal, bolted to the underside. At the inner end the metal strips have been left unfinished, the other end has been curled into a ring shape to form the handle attachments. The cylindrical handles have been threaded through these loops and then folded back on themselves, a simple, unelaborated method of securing them. They swing easily, facilitating lifting, and are contoured for an easy grip. A central circular section, with a diameter of twenty-four centimetres, roughly corresponding to the diameter of the top of the conical section directly beneath, has been pushed down by approximately one centimetre, to create a central depression. This circle contains the four evenly spaced rivets connecting the plate to its stand. The indentation in the centre of the plate, although perhaps a little shallow, could have been used for coals, the heating vessel perhaps on a small tripod or grill above. If turned upside down, it may have been possible to use the conical section as a bowl, economising on space in the kitchen. The handles, however, would be rendered useless if the object were used this way up. The vessel needing to be heated would sit atop the bowl, which held the coals. The ash collected at the bottom of the stand.   Z. C.

137   Bowl

Stone
Ptolemaic period
H. 5.3 cm | diam. 14 cm

35   Console or table-leg

Black granite
Ptolemaic period
H. 70 cm | w. 21 cm

The part of a console or table-leg has the form of the
hind leg of a large animal, perhaps a bull. From the
thigh sprouts an acanthus leaf with two curved volutes
and single lotus leaves marking the rear and upper
edges of the support. The rear surface has a large
rectangular cutting, evidently intended to house a
beam to secure the leg to a wall, or a brace linking it
to another leg of a three-legged table. The lower leg
and hoof are missing: surviving complete examples
suggest that such legs sometimes combined the features
of more than one animal.

The object was evidently intended to support either
a sculpture, of which no trace of any attachment has
survived, or more likely a table-top: for this latter role
the lack of any rectangular support at the back below
the level of the mid-thigh is unusual. The place of
discovery at Canopus suggests that it might have
furnished the sanctuary of Sarapis, for which context
a bull's leg would be appropriate.

A GUARANTOR FOR FERTILITY
SARAPIS AND CALATHOS

On the top of the head is a slightly raised, horizontal, circular surface. In the centre of this disc a square hole has been drilled as a fixing point for a feature mounted on top of the head. This detail and the imposing size of the head prove that this is the image of a god. The powerful face adorned by a thick flowing beard and mass of hair is characteristic of the effigies of Sarapis. The shape of the disc on top of the head exactly matches the base of the basket, or *calathos*, a fruit basket that the god is commonly represented wearing.

The *calathos* belonging to this sculpture was found further away on the seabed at ancient East Canopus. Its outer wall is decorated with a slight relief of two similar plants with thick stems and short side shoots ending in large lanceolate leaves. This is a stylised but unmistakable representation of olive trees, the form of decoration most commonly found on the headgear of the god Sarapis.

The scale of the sculpture also plays an essential part in its identification. In its current state, with the *calathos*, it is eighty-three centimetres tall. The only head that is any larger is that of Crocodilopolis in the Egyptian Museum in Cairo, which is ninety centimetres tall! The method of fixing at the rear of the sculpture implies that it was most likely part of a canonic-type statue of the god – that is, one in which he is sitting on a throne. Therefore it can be assumed that this was a colossal statue of between four and four-and-a-half metres tall. The size means that this is clearly not a simple votive statue. There could only have been one statue of

such a scale in a Greek temple: the statue central to the cult. Of course it was not found at its original site and there are no indications as to precisely which temple it came from. However, it is noted as being discovered close to TW4, which has yielded by far the most imposing monumental remains on the East Canopus site (p. 89).   Z. K.

following double page:

27 *Calathos*
Marble
Roman period?
H. 24 cm | diam. 26.5 cm

20 **Head of Sarapis**
Marble
2nd cent. BC
H. 59 cm | w. 34 cm | d. 34 cm

PERSONAL PIETY

Religious cults were highly institutionalised in the shrines where divine effigies were Location. In order to maintain the precarious balance between the earth and the cosmos it was necessary to satisfy the gods through systematic rituals passed down through the ages. This daily divine worship was the prerogative of the pharaoh, who delegated the powers and duties associated with it to the local priests. The Egyptian people, excluded from the temples, were not involved at all in this system, except for being themselves a part of cosmic law and order. There was a tacit consensus by the whole of society, which meant that the temple was recognised by all for what it was, that is, a part necessary to keep the world running smoothly. In actual fact, ordinary people did play a part in temple life, but it was indirect and incomplete, and this would not have satisfied many persons' aspirations to a life of religion, or a personal relationship with the deity.

THE CLOTHED STATUES OF CANOPUS AND HERAKLEION Although it is true that the running of the temple excluded the presence of any person not authorised to carry out the ritual acts, the people were allowed to enter as far as the courtyards and forecourts. Individuals were able to have their statue placed in these sacred areas and thus participate indirectly in the life of the holy building, a practice that had been increasing rapidly from the time of the New Kingdom. The representations of clothed figures discovered in Herakleion and Canopus are certainly descendants of this practice. In spite of their incomplete state these sculptures of individuals (cat. nos. 115; 21, 111, p. 238; 109, 110, p. 239) fit the criteria of traditional statuary: the left leg is extended forward and the figures are standing against a dorsal pillar. What is new about them is their three-part costume, composed of a chemise, a skirt and a fringed shawl. The clothing is most probably not of Egyptian origin, but it was characteristic of Egypt in the latter part of the Late Dynastic period and the Ptolemaic period. The introduction of this form of dress meant that a posture that had not previously been seen had to be invented at the same time. While the right arm rested alongside the body as usual, the left arm held the edge of the shawl level with the groin, a position not seen in any other statues.

These remarkable pieces were produced in Egyptian workshops during the Ptolemaic period by sculptors who remained faithful to the Egyptian norms, whilst adopting some detail here and there borrowed from contemporary Greek culture, and occasionally reinterpreting it. On the one hand, these images fitted in perfectly with earlier purely Egyptian traditions, and on the other, introduced a different way of representing individuals, influenced by Greek art. The heads of the statues from Canopus and Herakleion have disappeared but it is highly likely that they were very realistic portraits, similar to the magnificent green Berlin head.

Although the value of the found pieces as works of art is great, it was not the primary purpose; their true significance was in their role as ceremonial and cultic objects, particularly important for the *post mortem* afterlife of their owner. Indeed, one's own presentation of himself by means of a statue, or even better a statue with an autobiographical inscription, was one of the surest and most valued ways of leaving one's mark on earth after death and keeping one's name alive.

These great dignitaries must certainly have paid dearly for the luxury of owning their own effigies and putting them in the temples. These persons were probably administrators and builders, as they would have had the financial means necessary to undertake large-scale works. Even though it is expressed in a standardised way, such acts of evergetism also represent a form of personal piety.

Some private effigies of this kind were found on the site at Herakleion. The most interesting is undoubtedly the fragment of a masculine votive statue in black granite (cat. no.111). The head and the whole of the lower part of the body have disappeared. The right hand is broken at the wrist and there is a triangular piece missing from the bent elbow of the left arm. The dimensions of the fragment show that the figure was life-size. The whole surface of the sculpture is very corroded.

A BRIEF PICTURE OF PROCESSIONAL CEREMONIES IN PRIVATE PIETY The shrines sheltered the image of a god, hidden almost the whole year long in his *naos*, or inner sanctuary. No-one except for his prophet was allowed to enter this area, and everyone else had to be content with experiencing the sacred character of these places by approaching the entrances or the outer courtyards

115 **Torso of a clothed man**
Black granite
2nd cent. BC
H. 152 cm

The size of the figure shows that it was life-size. The whole surface of the sculpture is worn, particularly from the thighs upwards. It is represented in the traditional manner: the left leg forward, the right arm resting down the side, the left arm bent at the elbow, the hand holding the folds of the draped cloth on the stomach. There is a long rectangular pillar in the back. The cloak is held by the finely-carved fingers of the clenched left hand. It is noted that there is a deep vertical cylindrical hole at the base of the neck, which still contains mortar. This shows that the head was attached separately. The round surface at the base of the neck is very rough around the fixing hole. This technique of assembling elements of a sculpture was common with marble but is surprising in the case of granite. This probably did not occur when the work was created but is more likely to have taken place during a repair or possibly use for another purpose. Z. K.

21 **Torso of a clothed man**
Pink granite
2nd cent. BC
H. 120 cm

This is a life-size statue of a man in traditional Egyptian style. In spite of the wear to the surface some parts of the clothing can be distinguished. A narrow cloak hugs the side and the left leg. There is a long pillar on the back of the sculpture.   Z. K.

111 **Torso of a clothed man**
Black granite
Ptolemaic period
H. 42 cm

This is one of the many examples of 'clothed statues'. The pillar passes behind the back through a rectangular cut at the rear. The composition is typical of all the monuments in this category. The interesting feature of this sculpture is the fact that it bears three hieroglyphic inscriptions on the chest and both upper arms. The symbols of the inscription, typically Ptolemaic in style, are clumsy and some are almost ill-formed: *'The noble (?) benefactor, who gave generously to the lord gods of Gereb N (?), son of …'* The name of the figure has been damaged and is illegible. That of his father, which is completely intact, seems to be absolutely unique, so that the meaning is uncertain. In any case, this short message left on the man's chest lets us know that he was a benefactor who had made donations to the major deities of the temple of Herakleion (H1, p. 289).   Z. K. | J. Y.

109 **Torso of a clothed man**

Black granite
Ptolemaic period
H. 45.5 cm

The lower torso has been preserved in one piece from the left elbow to the lower thigh. The surface is worn and pitted and the breaks at both the thighs and torso are well worn by the water. The shawl is grasped by the proper left hand tightly against the body, creating a dramatic affect across the thighs and abdomen that continues in modelling across the backside of the statue. The clothing is of interest since it is the most elaborate from the examples recovered at Herakleion. The trapezoidal fringed edges of the shawl hang above the left arm's elbow and like the ones on the skirt are flanged at the tips. This high placement of the shawl's fringes on the arm is a local variation of the costume. Part of the rectangular pillar is visible on the back of the fragment.   E. L.

110 **Torso of a clothed man**

Black granite
Ptolemaic period
H. 77 cm

The intact lower torso from mid-abdomen to mid-thigh has sustained substantial damage to the proper left arm and hand. The figure is wearing the tripartite costume but in contrast to the previous examples it is less finely executed and the fringes are only delineated without further decorative aspects.   E. L.

and looking at the relief images of the god. However, on special occasions the desire to 'see the god', so often expressed in prayers, was satisfied. In fact, if the daily worship of the holy of holies took place in darkness concealing him from view, the god would come out into the open for important solemn liturgies, which often took place only once a year. These took place at great celebrations in which not only the court officials and the members of the priesthood took part, but also the entire population of the surrounding area and sometimes people from further afield. Reliefs in the temples, the inscriptions that accompany them, feast calendars in the Ptolemaic temples and finally the accounts of Herodotus give quite a precise description of these festivities. The ceremonies that took place on the route between Canopus and Herakleion in the month of Khoiak are a perfect illustration of this (p. 195).

Many people went on a pilgrimage to the temples; those who could write left their name and sometimes a message of adoration or thanksgiving on the walls of the building. Acts of worship could also be carried out in private. Many people wore amulets representing their favourite gods, often in animal form, or even sacred objects with great symbolic and protective powers. These amulets were usually made from inexpensive material, such as faience, and therefore anyone could afford them; for the more wealthy people they were also made in metal. Many people must also have had images of gods in their homes or given them as offerings.

The finds at Herakleion included many statuettes and amulets made from gold, bronze, lead and earthenware. This collection of small objects in itself tells an equally important story about Egyptian religion and the hopes of each individual. It seems that the entire pantheon of gods and sacred beasts will be unveiled to us when the water in the bay at Aboukir finally clears. This private worship was a daily activity since it was practised outside the strict temple circuit. However, it was no less codified and corresponded to the universally accepted norms, which were the required channels of communication between man and god. The individual called on the god on his own behalf, in contrast to the priest, who acted in the name of the pharaoh in order to maintain the cosmic and terrestrial equilibrium.

Royal emblems, such as the falcon Horus wearing the double crown or *uraeus*-snake, in amulet form, conferred the superhuman strength of the pharaoh (cat. no. *202*). Stone hieroglyphics guaranteed life or youthfulness. The most powerful and the most common talismans were the scarab (cat. no. 130), the *djed* pillar, the Isis knot and the *oudjat* – that is, the outlined eye of the celestial god with the strange mark decorating the falcon's cheek, which signifies clairvoyance, physical prowess and universal fertility (cat. no. 170, p. 243). These wonder-working talismans armed both the living and the dead and were true receptacles of protective beneficial charms (cat. nos. 327; 131, 323, p. 243; 205, 326, p. 368; *340–343, 375*).

A vast number of 'popular' images of the Egyptian gods and sacred animals, such as Bastet the cat, (cat. nos. 173, 174, p. 243; 195, p. 246; 172, p. 367), the lion Sachmet (cat. no. 176, p. 246), the vulture goddess Nechbet (cat. no. 198, p. 246), Apis the bull (cat. no. *203*), Thoth the baboon (cat. nos. *324, 325*, p. 246) or ibis (cat. no. 175, p. 250) and the jackal-headed Anubis (cat. nos. 171, p. 250; *200, 201*) have been discovered at Canopus and Herakleion (compare such figures of

130 Scarab
Stone
6th – 2nd cent. BC
H. 1.6 cm | w. 4.8 cm | d. 3.4 cm

Isis *lactans* (p. 105) of Harpokrates (p. 125) or of Osiris (p. 197). They are made of a mixed material, clay or bronze, and the use of moulds allowed them to be mass-produced. Workshops produced large numbers of small bronzes showing traditional depictions of Egyptian gods (p. 366).

Making *ex-voto* offerings in order to obtain a cure or a guarantee of fertility (cat. nos. 113, 331, p. 250; *132, 339*), or to thank the god for his blessings was normal practice. The healing cults, moreover, particularly flourished in the shrine of Sarapis in Canopus. Near Canopus, on the present-day site of Ras el-Soda, a pit (*favissa*) was filled with a collection of various Egyptian amulets, Hermaic pillars, figurines of Isis Aphrodite and so-called 'grotesques'; amongst the latter, deformed ugly statuettes evoke well-established examples of disfiguring disease. Could it have been the case that depositing images of the sick and infirm in sacred pits was considered an excellent way of protecting oneself against the moral decay and physical ills of which these objects bore the marks? Canopus, therefore, had a very special place in the religious landscape of the Alexandrian region. The identity of the Egyptian cults and the expression of private worship seem to confirm this in a very marked fashion. The practice of inducing dreams in places of incubation by the temples was very widely developed during the Ptolemaic period, perhaps as a result of the Greek influence. It opened up a vast area to oniromancy, the interpretation of dreams to divine the future, to which

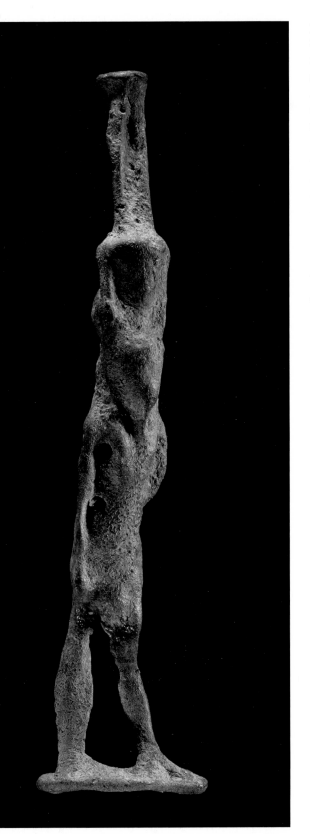

priests, scribes and laymen devoted themselves fully from then on, in oratories reserved for incubation and in sanatoriums. People often came to spend the night in consultation with the god to beg for a cure, or for a child in the case of sterility, although the questions they asked could relate to other subjects such as the construction of a temple, for example. The headrests discovered in the Canopus region, both full-size (cat. nos. 148–151, p. 353) or in miniature (cat. no. 360, p. 250), are perhaps the ultimate proof of this.

All things considered, the faithful had many ways of showing their fidelity to the religious world in which they lived, even if they did not participate in worship in the temples. The majority of those who lived outside the temples had other desires than the priests and were not preoccupied by the same things as those who lived in the shrines, being less interested in knowledge of the world and the gods described in the great theological texts. Nevertheless, the many offertory stations, touching in their modesty, illustrate the importance of the presence of the gods in everyday life and the trust that the faithful had in their beneficial intervention (cat. nos. 128, 129, 351, p. 250; *114, 328, 332, 333, 348–350, 353, 356–359*).   D. F.

327   Statuette of a deity
Lead
6th – 2nd cent. BC
H. 9.4 cm | w. 2.2 cm

Standing with the left foot advanced in the characteristic pose for gods and men, this hollow-cast figure sports an elaborate, but very worn, headdress. It seems to be the lotus flower surmounted by high plumes worn by Nefertem, son of Ptah and Sachmet, the embodiment of the primeval lotus out of which the sun first rises. A figure this size is unlikely to have been suspended as an amulet around its owner's neck, as the ring at the back suggests; perhaps just the reference to suspension itself was enough to protect its owner or dedicator.   T. H.

170

170 **Bead in the form of the eye of Horus or *oudjat***

Gold
Late Pharaonic–Ptolemaic
H. 0.68 cm

The bead is made from two identically shaped pieces of metal in the form of an Eye of Horus, or *oudjat*, and a strip of metal, which forms the sides. There is an opening in each of the narrow sides of this strip of metal. The metal on the front is decorated with filigree wire and a flat golden sphere for the pupil.
Beads or pendants in the form of the Eye of Horus, or *oudjat*, were popular in ancient Egypt from the time of the pharaohs until Roman times. They are often found on necklaces, where they hang alongside other amulets. The majority of the Eyes of Horus are moulded or beaten and are not decorated with filigree work or granulation like the piece from Herakleion. The word *oudja* means affluence and well-being; the name *oudjat* means the intact, healthy eye. *Oudjat* is also the symbol of the moon, which waxes time and again – the perfect eye is equated with the full-moon and is the reason why it is depicted on hand-held mirrors whose rounded shape symbolises a full face. These mirrors often have a handle shaped like a papyrus stalk, which is also referred to as a *ouadj* – something that is 'green, fresh and renewed'.
Y. S.

131

131 **Amulet**

Steatite
6th – 2nd cent. BC
H. 1.35 cm | w. 1 cm | d. 0.6 cm

Incised on one side of this rectangular plaque is a kneeling figure, his arms raised in rejoicing, surmounted by a sun-disc. The plaque is pierced vertically for suspension. Steatite is a soft stone which can be easily carved, but becomes much harder once fired and glazed, a technique which is closely related to the production of faience.   T. H.

323 **Statuette of Horus-Falcon**

Lead
6th – 2nd cent. BC
H. 2.5 cm | w. 1.4 cm | d. 0.7 cm

The amulet with flat base and hanging ring represents Horus in the form of a falcon wearing the double crown of Upper and Lower Egypt.   D. F.

following double page:

323

following double page:

173 **Statuette of Bastet**

Bronze
6th – 2nd cent. BC
H. 19 cm | w. 4.3 cm | d. 7.1 cm

There are holes corroded into the base of the neck of this piece; the lower part of the animal is missing.   D. F.

174 **Statuette of Bastet**

Bronze
6th – 2nd cent. BC
H. 7.1 cm | w. 3.9 cm | d. 1.6 cm

The deity is represented with the body of a human and the head of a cat. The body of the goddess is cut off at the pelvis. A circular hole cut out of the right hand shows that the goddess was holding an object. The great number of known examples shows that this was a *sistrum*.   D. F.

173

176 **Statuette of Sachmet**

Bronze
6th – 2nd cent. BC
H. 16.7 cm | w. 3.7 cm | d. 1.7 cm

The statuette represents Sachmet: a deity with the body of a woman and the head of a lioness.   D. F.

195 **Base of figurine**

Bronze
6th – 2nd cent. BC

The small base of statue contains the fragmentary feet of the missing deity. In contrast to cat. nos. 172, 173 or 174 (pp. 244, 245, 367), which were made in hollow cast, this is in solid cast. The position of these feet demonstrates that the missing god was seated, because the majority of standing gods were represented with the left leg advanced forward. Under the base, there is a projected part which possibly served to fix the statue on another wider base. The base is rectangular and covered on sides by hieroglyphic relief. Most of the inscriptions are effaced, and only the frontal side of the base could be read as following: '*Bastet who gives life (to) Isis the daughter...* ' These few words represent the beginning of the text which started with the name of the goddess and followed with the name of the votarist who offered the statue. This formula was common in bronze statues of the Late Pharaonic period onward.   A. A-R. R.

198 **Image of Nechbet**

Bronze
6th – 2nd cent. BC
H. 17 cm | w. 10 cm | d. 3 cm

Like the Falcon, the vulture, Egypt's largest bird, lives high in the limestone cliffs and soars over the desert and alluvial land in search of food. Although Nechbet, the goddess of Upper Egypt was sometimes presented as a falcon, or a woman with a falcon's head, the main representation of Nechbet was the vulture, which was always represented as a vulture with widespread wings. The vulture's head and wings had served as an inspiration for the headdress of Egyptian queens from the fourth dynasty, and sometimes the bird was shown spreading her wings on the sides of the queen's head, with the vulture head descending on the front and surrounded by two cobras. This bronze head represents the goddess Nechbet wearing the *atef* crown which is composed of the white crown of Upper Egypt surrounded by two feathers. The lower projecting part served to attach the head to the missing body of the statue.   A. A-R. R.

325 **Statuette of Thoth the Baboon**

Lead
6th – 2nd cent. BC
H. 2.8 cm | w. 1.5 cm

The amulet of a baboon crowned with a lunar disc represents Thoth. A fastener can be seen under the base. The baboon, together with the ibis, is the sacred animal of the god Thoth.   D. F.

198

195

325

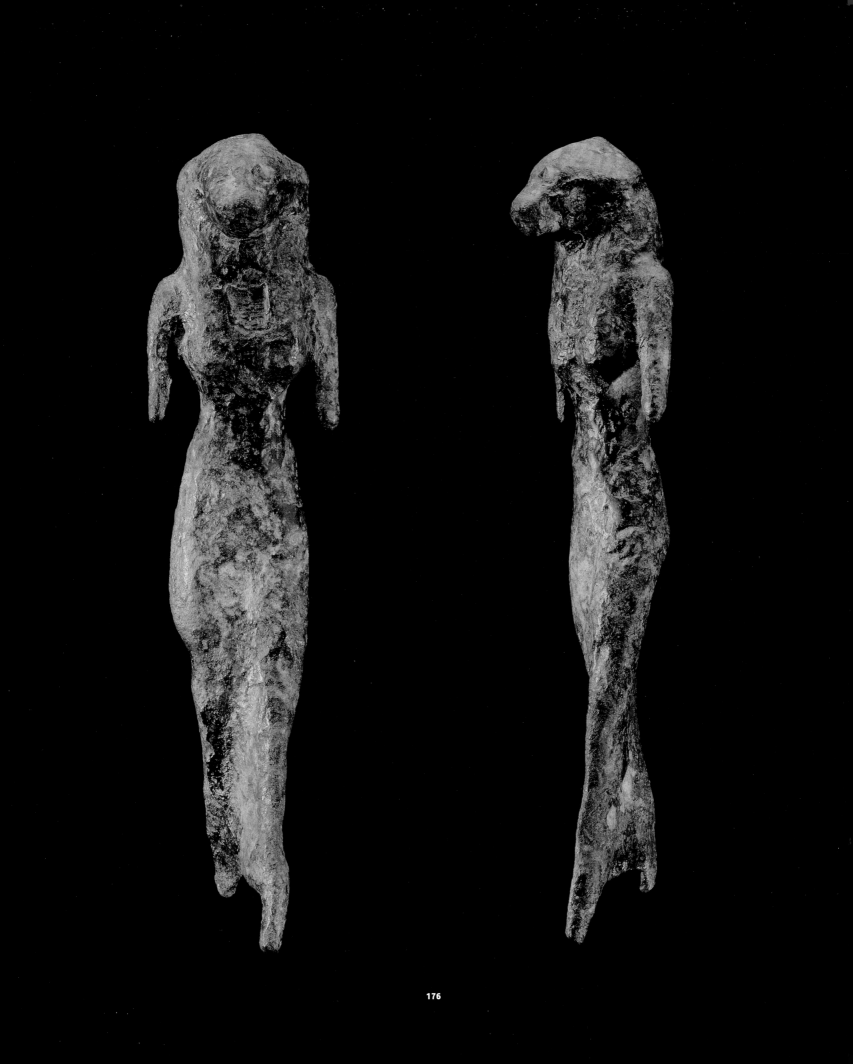

175

171

113

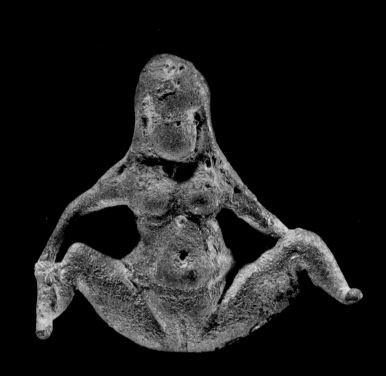

331

previous double page:

175 Statuette of an ibis
Bronze
6th – 2nd cent. BC
H. 10 cm | w. 8.8 cm | d. 3.3 cm

In the past there were three types of ibis in Egypt: the glossy ibis, with brown plumage, the cattle egret and the sacred ibis, which had a white body and black head and tail. It is probably the latter that is represented here.   D. F.

171 Statuette of Anubis
Bronze
6th – 2nd cent. BC
H. 18 cm | w. 22.7 cm | d. 3.7 cm

The piece is beautifully made. The hind legs rest on a tenon probably designed to fit exactly into a plinth. Square areas stand out slightly from the body of the animal. They are probably signs of repairs.   D. F.

113 Statue of a pregnant woman
Limestone
Ptolemaic period
H. 14 cm | w. 5 cm

The completely naked female figure is standing. The thighs are parted a little and slightly crouching in a posture characteristic of Bes and Beset. The face, whose features are curtly schematised, is reminiscent of certain statues attributable to the Ptolemaic period. Striking are the right ear, the breasts, which are prominent but not drooping, and the stomach, rounded like that of a pregnant woman. A small figure built like a child or a dwarf sits astride the woman's shoulders leaning against the nape of her neck. Her right arm is clasped round an elongated object that seems to protrude from beneath her belly and clearly appears to be an erect phallus with the glans clearly defined.
This limestone statue can perhaps be classified as one of the objects known as *erotica*, of which many different types have been found on the sites of several temples. Many examples show a small figure (sometimes with the plaited hair of a child) coupling with a partner of adult appearance. The young partner is usually endowed with an oversized phallus.   J. Y.

331 Statuette of a woman
Lead
Ptolemaic period
H. 3.2 cm | w. 3.6 cm | d. 1 cm

Figurine with parted legs, either in childbirth or in an erotic posture. The breasts as well as the genitals are visible. The woman seems to be wearing a belt around her waist.   D. F.

360 Miniature headrest
Lead
6th – 2nd cent. BC
H. 1.8 cm | w. 2.6 cm

351 Small vessel containing an offering
Lead
6th – 2nd cent. BC
H. 2.8 cm | diam. 7 cm

128 Votive anchor
Limestone
6th – 2nd cent. BC
H. 12.6 cm | w. 2.1 – 2.8 cm | d. 3.7 cm

129 Votive anchor
Limestone
6th – 2nd cent. BC
H. 9 cm | w. 2.4 – 6.6 cm | d. 3.7 cm

The model of the miniature anchor from a sea-going ship is a reproduction of the full-size anchors discovered on the site and represented on Egyptian monuments. Votive anchors illustrate the thanks given to the god for allowing the safe undertaking of a voyage, whether safely completed or about to take place.   D. F.

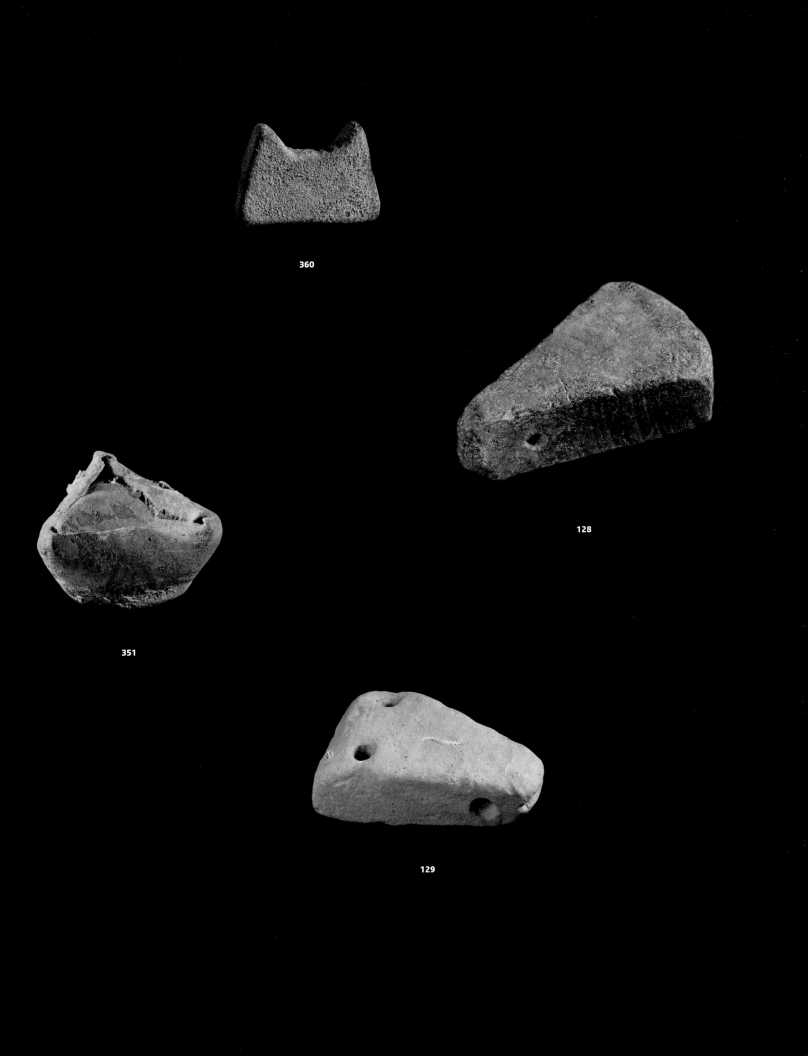

360

128

351

129

GOLD FOR THE GODS
STONE WITH GOLD FRAGMENTS

A simple stone chest, without any inscription, but with spectacular contents: filled with gold, the ore of the gods. Perhaps it was in gratitude to a deity for a deed well done. In such a case, any inscription would have been superfluous – both the donor and the god would have known what it was for.

120   **Stone**
6th – 2nd cent. BC
H. 15 cm | w. 30 cm | d. 30 cm

121   **Gold fragments**

TEMPLES AND WORKSHOPS

THE HISTORY OF PILGRIMAGE Parallel to the retreat of pagan cults, monastic and pilgrimage life flourished in late antiquity and the early Byzantine period. The origins of the former lie in the late third century when, to start with, individual Christians sought solitude in order to devote their lives to God and their belief. Soon, monastic communities – the so-called *Koinobia* – developed. The earliest known founder was Pachomios who lived in Egypt in the late third, and first half of the fourth, century. The rules for communal life are attributed to him. At approximately the same time, around the middle of the fourth century, Basilius the Great, Bishop of Caesarea and one of the fathers of the Cappadocian Church, set down similar rules. Among other things, these regulations foresaw monks and nuns providing for themselves. For this reason, monasteries often possessed installations such as wine and oil presses as well as kilns for ceramic-making. According to Pachomios, monks and nuns were also occupied with spinning, tailoring, shoemaking, and mat weaving. In the so-called Kellia, a monastery complex in the western Nile delta (p. 200), there were workshops where the monks produced and sold straw mats and baskets. It seems that a goldsmith studio was also situated at the sanctuary of Cyrus and John at Menouthis in Egypt (p. 278).

Some monasteries were, at the same time, places of pilgrimage. St Catherine's monastery on Sinai, supposedly located on the site of the burning bush, is one of these and is still active today. As is the case with St Catherine's, many places of pilgrimage were located at sites mentioned in the Old Testament and where members of the holy family, famous ascetics, monks, nuns and monastery founders lived, were active or died. Because of its background in the history of religion, most of these pilgrimage sanctuaries were located in the Holy Land. The church on Mount Nebo, the Church of the Holy Sepulchre in Jerusalem and the Church of the Nativity in Bethlehem are among the most famous examples.

Particularly from the fourth to seventh century, pilgrimages to such holy sites were especially in vogue. One of the first Christian pilgrims was Helena, the mother of Constantine the Great, who set out on a journey to the Holy Land in 325 AD. Many Christians followed her example and, already in the fourth century, it seems that the church authorities in Jerusalem had to cope with problems of security and crowd control.

Famous pilgrimage sanctuaries outside of the Holy Land included the shrine of Saint Menas at the south-west of Lake Mareotis in Egypt (p. 200) and that of the Saints Cyrus and John in Menouthis. As with the pilgrimage centres in the Holy Land, it appears that these two shrines also attracted visitors from all over the world. That this applied to Menouthis was confirmed by Sophronios, who was originally a pilgrim and later became Patriarch of

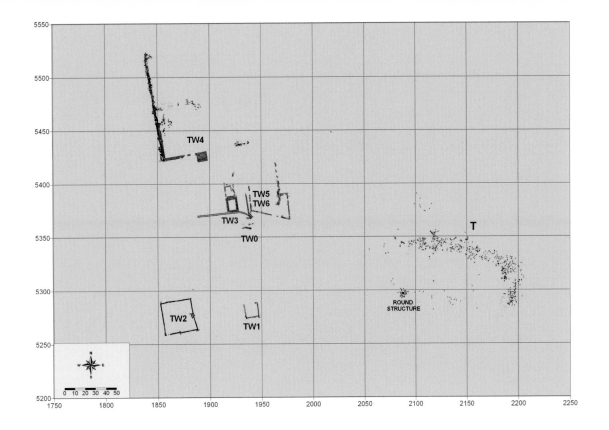

Chart of discoveries made
in East Canopus

Jerusalem: 'I am talking of Romans and Galatians and Kilikiens, and also of peoples from Asia, inhabitants of islands and Phoenicians, Byzantines and Bithynians and Ethiopians, Thracians, Meder and Arabs, inhabitants of Palestine and Syrians and Elamites, really of all nations which exist beneath the heavens.'

THE ARCHITECTURE AND CULT OF A BYZANTINE PILGRIMAGE SHRINE

At this point, three reasons justify speaking about the architecture and cult of a Christian sanctuary. Firstly, the excavated sector T in East Canopus could have been part of a pilgrimage shrine or of a monastery complex such as the one of the Methanoia. The latter had been built close to the pagan temple of Serapis, after its destruction by the Christians in 391. Secondly, the places mentioned must have been located in the immediate vicinity of T. Thirdly, the documentation on these sites, which must be counted among the most important and fascinating in Egypt, provides information on the architecture of the pilgrimage centres and the character of pilgrimage in general.

In the early fifth century, Patriarch Cyril of Alexandria disapproved of the fact that Christians were still visiting the pagan pilgrimage shrines in the region of Canopus. He, therefore deemed it necessary, after being requested to do so by an angel in a dream, to initiate a competing Christian pilgrimage sanctuary there. Due to a lack of suitable relics, it seems that Cyril invented – or rediscovered – two martyrs Cyrus and John. The new Christian cultic site was installed in an older church dedicated to the evangelists and located in Menouthis two Roman miles from Canopus. This soon developed into a large-scale institution and a famous shrine of pilgrimage.

The Sophronios mentioned above, who visited the shrine in the early seventh century, was among the numerous believers. He was suffering from an eye ailment, and sought and found a cure. Out of gratefulness, he later wrote seventy chapters with stories of miracles and anecdotes about pilgrims and their healings. It seems that Sophronios witnessed some of these in person; he learned of others by hearsay and from the votive tablets on the walls of the shrine. In any case, the stories provide us with a lively view of the cult in Menouthis.

In addition, Sophronios gives us information on the location and composition of the complex: sea voyagers, travelling to or from Alexandria, could see it from afar. It seems likely that it was located on a hill, namely, between the sea in the east and a sandy area in the west. It was surrounded by an enclosing wall, one of its gates opened towards the sea. The grave of the saints, a baptistery and a treasury were located within the church or in the immediate vicinity. A fountain, bathhouses, latrines and guesthouses and inns were located outside of the church. It seems likely that a goldsmith atelier was also part of the facilities of the pilgrimage shrine.

Many pilgrims visited Menouthis to seek healing from their acute or chronic disorders such as eye illnesses or constipation. A blind pilgrim from Rome supposedly waited for eight years to be healed. Overflowing with the ill and suffering, the place appeared more like a hospital than a place of pilgrimage.

Healing sleep, the so-called incubation, was still a component of most cures (p. 59). For this purpose, the pilgrims camped in the church – the closer to the saint's grave the better. A rich pilgrim named Juliana is supposed to have paid for a space to sleep near the holy tomb. While they were sleeping, some pilgrims had visions: the saint appeared before them and either healed them personally or gave them advice on the medicine required for their cure. Usually, the recommended medicine consisted of oil and wax from the lamps and candles which stood or hung close to the shrine. This kind of use of oil and wax was common in the Byzantine period and there are many records of this. It is also possible that the oil was filled into small bottles, similar to the well-known Menas ampoules.

It appears that treatment and accommodation at those places of pilgrimage were free of charge. However, as a token of their gratitude, several pilgrims left inscriptions or graffiti on the walls of the shrines and possibly also donated a coin (cat. nos. 83, 84, 87, 89, 90, 92; 85, 86, 88, 93, 434–436, p. 260; *437, 452*). Others remained in the sanctuaries after being cured in order to help with the organisation or nursing. A female pilgrim was cured of constipation caused by a stone in her intestines. She dedicated this stone to the shrine and it was hung above the grave of the saint. Other pilgrims showed their thanks through gifts of money, silk clothing or other textiles, liturgical vessels or pieces of golden jewellery – Sophronios described these as glittering, gold pebbles. Jewelled votive pictures were as common in ancient times as they are today: for example, they were found during the excavations carried out at a temple on the Greek island of Kythnos and are supposed to have hung from the ceiling above the grave of Jesus in the Church of the Holy Sepulchre in Jerusalem. These precious votive gifts also included bracelets, necklaces, rings, belts and votive crowns. The palette of the finds from Canopus and Herakleion look similar and range from earrings (cat. nos. 41, 154, 155, p. 266; 39, 40, 156–158, p. 267; 37, 45, 46, 54, 159, p. 268; *42–44, 160*), pendants (cat. nos. 164, *162, 163*), chains (cat. no. 47, p. 268), rings (cat. nos. 60, 166, 168, p. 270; 165, 167, p. 271; *57, 69*), crosses (cat. nos. 63, 70–72, p. 272) to jewellery fragments (cat. nos. 52, 64, 169, p. 272; *61, 62*).   Y. S.

Menas ampoule, 6th cent. AD

92   Solidus
Gold
Heraclius (637–638 AD)
Diam. 2.1 cm | wt. 4.38 g

Obverse: In the middle, Heraclius with a long beard, to the right Heraclius Constantinus beardless, left Heraclonas. All three wear crown and cloak and have an orb with cross in the hand (cf. cat. no. 93).
Reverse: Cross potent above three degrees [?]. In the field VICTORIA AVGVS(TORVM) (Victory of the emperor)/CONOB (refers to the location of mint: Constantinople); monogram (Z and ?).   C. M.

83   Solidus
Gold
Anthemius (467–472 AD)
Diam. 2 cm | wt. 3.25 g

Obverse: Armed bust facing, D(OMINVS) N(OSTER) ANTHEMIVS PERPET(VVS) AVG(VSTVS) – Our Lord Anthemius, perpetual emperor.
Reverse: Two emperors standing facing holding a spear and between them an orb mounted on a large cross; monogram MD/CONOB (cf. cat. no. 92).   C. M.

89   Semissis
Gold
Heraclius (613–641 AD)
Diam. 1.86 cm | wt. 2.2 g

Obverse: diademed bust, [D(OMINVS)] N(OSTER) [H]EPACLIVS T P(ER)P(ETVVS) AVG(VSTVS); cf. cat. no. 91, p. 71; monogram Z.
Reverse: Cross potent, VICTORIA AVGVS(TORVM) – Victory of the emperor; monogram Δ.   C. M.

90   Tremissis
Gold
Heraclius (613–641 AD)
Diam. 1.85 cm | wt. 1.45 g

Obverse: diademed bust, [D(OMINVS)] N(OSTER) [H]EPACLIVS T P(ER)P(ETVVS) AVG(VSTVS); cf. cat. no. 91, p. 71; monogram Z.
Reverse: Cross potent, VICTORIA AVGVS(TORVM) – Victory of the emperor; monogram X.   C. H.

87   Tremissis
Gold
Heraclius (610–613 AD)
Diam. 1.63 cm | wt. 1.38 g

Obverse: diademed bust, [D(OMINVS)] N(OSTER) [H]EPACLIVS T P(ER)P(ETVVS) AVG(VSTVS); cf. cat. no. 91, p. 71.
Reverse: Cross potent on an orb, VICTORIA AVGVS(TORVM) – Victory of the emperor; monogram Δ.   C. M.

84   Tremissis
Gold
Anastasius (491–518 AD)
Diam. 1.4 cm | wt. 1.37 g

Obverse: Diademed bust, [D(OMINVS)] N(OSTER) ANASTASIVS P(ER)P(ETVVS) AVG(VSTVS) – Our Lord Anastasius, perpetual emperor.
Reverse: Victory advancing, VICTORIA AVGVSTORVM – Victory of the emperor.   C. M.

92

83

89

90

87

84

85   **Semissis**
Gold
Mauricius (582–583 AD)
Diam. 1.7 cm | wt. 1.41 g

Obverse: Diademed bust, the inscription is no longer legible.
Reverse: Cross potent, VICTORIA [AVGVSTORVM?] – Victory
of the emperor.   C. M.

86   **Semissis**
Gold
Heraclius (610–641 AD)
Diam. 1.83 cm | wt. 2.15 g

Obverse: Diademed bust, the inscription is no longer legible.
Reverse: Cross potent on an orb, VICTORIA AVGVS(TORVM) – Victory of the
emperor.   C. M.

88   **Semissis**
Gold
Heraclius (610–613 AD)
Diam. 1.93 cm | wt. 2.13 g

Obverse: Diademed bust, [D(OMINVS)] N(OSTER) HEPACLIVS T P(ER)P(ETVVS)
AVG(VSTVS); cf. cat. no. 91, p. 71.
Reverse: potent cross on an orb, VICTORIA AVGVS(TORVM) – Victory of the
emperor; monogram.   C. M.

93   **Solidus**
Gold
Heraclius (639–641 AD)
Diam. 2 cm | wt. 4.3 g

Obverse: In centre, Heraclius with long beard, on right Heraclius Constantinus
beardless, on left Heracleonas. All three wear crown and cloak and hold an orb
with cross in left hand. Reverse: Cross potent on base and three steps, beneath
CONOB; cf. cat. no. 92, p. 71. In field left crossed *h* (monogram of Heraclius).
VICTORIA AVGV(STORVM) – Victory of the emperor; monogram Z.
This is the last gold issue of the reign. It shows Heraclius with Heraclius
Constantinus, his son by his first wife, and Heracleonas, born in 626 to his second
wife Martina. Heracleonas was proclaimed *caesar* in 632 and *augustus* in 638. From
632 he was shown on the coins but smaller and with no crown. On the issues
dating after 638 he is represented, like on this coin, taller and wearing a crown.
The second marriage of Heraclius was deemed incestuous because Martina was
the emperor's niece and caused much trouble at the end of the reign and after
Heraclius's death.

434   **Tremissis**
Gold
Pulcheria (414–453 AD)
Diam. 1.3 cm | wt. 1.3 g

Obverse: Bust right of the empress with diadem and cloak. AEL(IA) PVLCHERIA
AVG(VSTA) –Aelia Pulcheria empress.
Reverse: Cross in wreath, beneath CONOB; cf. cat. no. 92, p. 258.   C. M.

436   **Solidus**
Gold
Heraclius (616–625 AD)
Diam. 2 cm | wt. 4.35 g

Obverse: To left, bust of Heraclius facing with crown and cloak. To right, similar
but smaller bust of Heraclius Constantinus. DD(OMINI) NN(OSTRI) [H]EPACLIVS
ET [H]ERA(CLIVS) CONS(TANTINVS) [T] P(ER)P(ETVI) AVG(VSTI) – Our Lords
Heraclius and Heraclius Constantinus, perpetual emperors; compare cf. cat. no. 91,
p. 71. The duplication of the beginning letters indicates the plural of the word.
Reverse: Cross potent on base and three steps, beneath CONOB; cf. cat. no. 92,
p. 258. VICTORIA AVGV(STORVM) – Victory of the emperor; monogram I Θ.   C. M.

following double page:

435   **Tremissis**
Gold
Justinus II (565–578 AD)
Diam. 1.5 cm | wt. 1.3 g

Obverse: Bust right of the emperor with diadem, armour and general's cloak.
D(OMINVS) N(OSTER) IVSTINVS P(ER)P(ETVVS) AV(GVSTVS) – Our Lord Iustinus,
perpetual Kaiser.
Reverse: Victory holding wreath and orb with cross advancing right, beneath;
cf. cat. no. 92, p. 258. At right a star. VICTORIA AAVGVSTORV(M) – Victory of the
emperor; monogram I.   C. M.

85

86

88

93

434

436

435

155 **Lion-head earring**

Gold
Possibly 3rd cent. BC
Diam. 2.76 cm | d. 1.1 cm

On the earring with a tapering band made of a sheet gold tube entwined with wire, a sleeve, topped with a lion's head of sheet gold, is attached to the wide end of the band. The sleeve has an arch-shaped base and is decorated with two s-formed overlays, decorated with volutes. The volutes both end with a granule. Additional granules fill in the space between the s-formed overlays. The head and mane of the lion are formed from a modelled, engraved sheet of gold. The animal's snout is open and obviously intended to hold the top of the ring.   Y. S.

154 **Lion-head earring**

Gold
Possibly late 4th or 3rd cent. BC
Diam. 1.9 cm | d. 0.89 cm

The earring consists of a tapering ring of four twisted gold sheet tubes. A sleeve and a lion-head ornament made of sheet gold are attached to the wider end of the ring.   Y. S.

41 **Earring with two pendants**

Gold and pearls
6th–early 8th cent. AD
L. 1.87 cm | w. 1.46 cm | d. 0.31 cm

The lower end of the golden earring made of a band with pin clasp broadens double-conically. A wire, on which a golden bead and a pearl are strung, is soldered on here. A second pendant, in addition to this one, was attached in the same fashion. This second pendant is lost, but evidence of its existence can be seen from the traces of soldering on the double-conical broadening.

A detached pendant was found, together with the earring, at the same site. This pendant consists of a wire with two beads separated by a granule wreath. This cannot be the lost pendant of the earring as the wire used for the preserved earring pendant and that of the pendant found separately have differing diameters and are bent at the lower end in a different manner. Y. S.

156   **Animal-head earring**
Gold
Possibly 3rd cent. BC
Diam. 1.9 cm | d. 0.38 cm

The earring is made of a tapering ring of four entwined sheet gold tubes. A sleeve and an animal-head ornament made of gold sheet are attached to the wider end of the ring. The eyes and mouth of the animal are indicated by simple chiselling, ears of sheet gold and horns of grooved gold sheet tubes are attached to the head.
Y. S.

39   **Earring with decorative disc**
Gold
6th–early 8th cent. AD
Diam. 1.89 cm | w. 1.82 cm | d. 0.85 cm

The ornamental disc is decorated with an engraved Greek cross in a wreath of triangular chased decorations.   Y. S.

40   **Pendant of an earring**
Gold and pearls
6th–early 8th cent. AD
L. 8.7 cm | w. 0.95 cm | d. 0.7 cm

The pendant of a golden earring consists of a foxtail chain ending on both sides in cylindrical, grooved ornaments with an eyelet of wire and granules welded to them, and of a piece of wire which begins with a similar eyelet on which two pearls, separated by a filigree sphere, are attached.   Y. S.

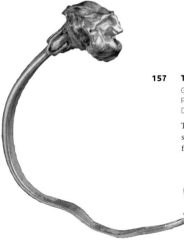

157   **Twined earring**
Gold
Ptolemaic (?)
Diam. 0.52 cm | d. 0.18 cm

The tubes are surrounded by a sleeve on the outside. The sleeve is decorated with a five-leaved flower of sheet gold, filigree wire and a small golden ball.   Y. S.

158   **Golden earring with a granule pyramid**
Gold
Diam. 1.71 cm | d. 0.55 cm

A three-sided pyramid, formed from eighteen granules of the same size and one larger stone, is soldered to the ring.   Y. S.

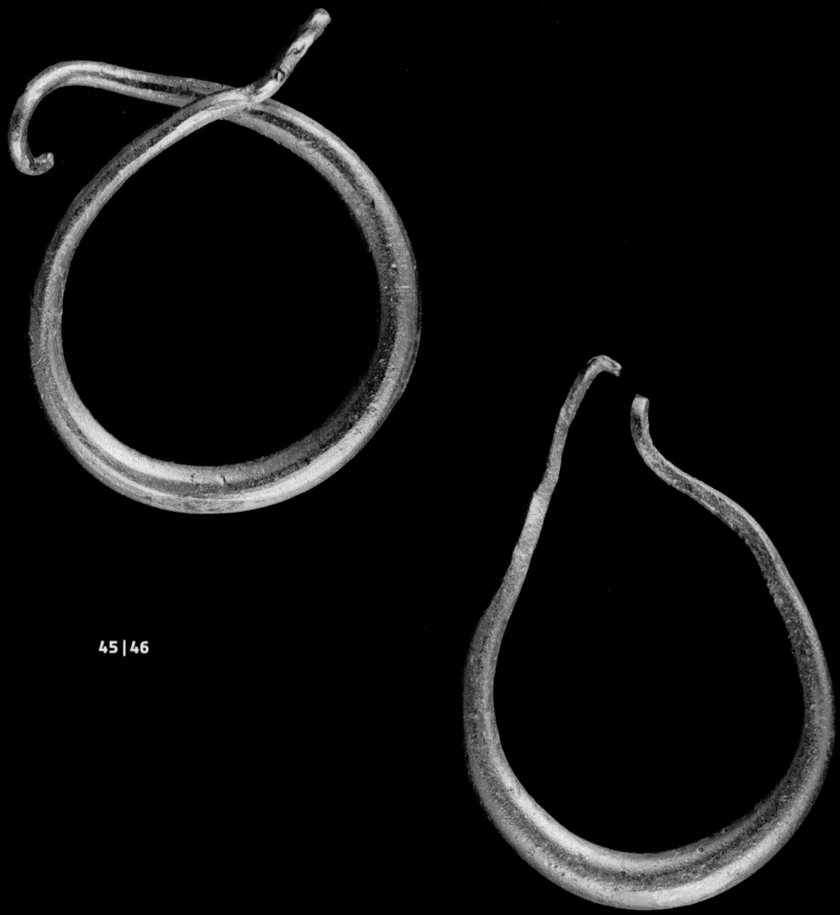

45 | 46

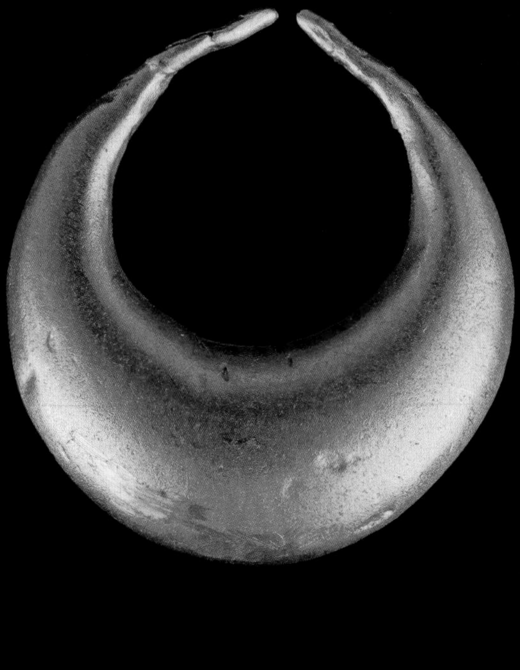

45 | 46 Pair of earrings
Gold
Late Roman or Byzantine
Diam. 1.3 cm | d. 0.18 cm

159 Sickle-shaped earring
Gold and filling material
Ptolemaic period (?)
Diam. 2.65 cm | d. 0.83 cm

37 Earring with setting and two glass beads
Gold and glass
5th–early 8th cent. AD (?)
H. 2.8 cm | w. 1.06 cm | d. 0.07 cm

The earring is made of bent wire the diameter of which narrows
towards the end. Two dark glass pearls are attached to the wire
as well as a strip of sheet gold and a rhombic box setting with a
profiled mirror. An eyelet is soldered to the lower corner of the
setting and the joint is covered by a granule. Remains of a white
substance, possibly plaster or beeswax, can be discerned within
the settings. Such substances were used for fixing stone and
glass fillings.   Y. S.

47 Necklace with drop-shaped glass beads
Gold and glass
6th–early 8th cent. AD
L. 3.3 cm | w. 0.8 cm | d. 0.8 cm

Two similar chain links of wire from the necklace are preserved.
The two ends of the wire are bent to form eyelets and a violet,
drop-shaped glass bead is attached to each chain link.   Y. S.

**54 Golden pendant with a drop-shaped sapphire
and pearl**
Gold, sapphire and pearl
6th–late 8th cent. AD
L. 1.88 cm | w. 0.61 cm | d. 0.54 cm

159

168 **Ring with a quadratic bezel**
Gold
Diam. 1.32 cm | d. 0.63 cm

60 **Finger ring with two twisted wires**
Gold
Diam. 1.56 cm | d. 0.4 cm

166 **Golden ring with oval widening**
Gold
Ptolemaic (?)
Diam. 1.8 cm | d. 0.71 cm

167 Finger ring with oval glass or stone cabochon
Gold, glass or stone
Ptolemaic
Ring: diam. 2.68 cm | d. 1.89 cm
Cabochon: h. 1.45 cm | w. 0.96 cm | d. 0.35 cm

This ring consists of an oval hoop and a high superstructure
with an oval bezel setting on a fluted base. An oval glass
or stone cabochon of a dark red, almost black colour was
found together with the ring. Similar rings were popular
in the Hellenistic period.   Y. S.

165 Finger ring with engraved Nike
Gold
Possibly second half of the 4th or 3rd cent. BC
Diam. 2.97 cm | d. 2.8 cm

This ring consists of a hoop with a rectangular square section,
broad shoulders, and a circular engraved and punched bezel.
The engraving shows Nike, the personification of victory, standing next to a censer and making an offering. The ring could
have been used as a seal ring.   BC. Y. S.

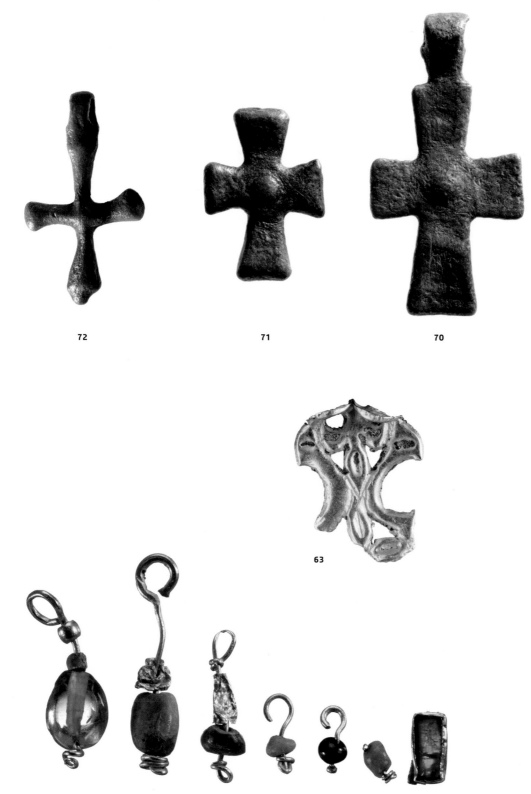

72

71

70

63

52

72   Cross pendant
Lead
6th–early 8th cent. AD
H. 2.42 cm | w. 1.4 cm | d. 0.22 cm

71   Cross pendant
Lead
5th–early 8th cent. AD
H. 1.97 cm | w. 1.41 cm | d. 0.21 cm

70   Cross pendant
Lead
5th–early 8th cent. AD
H. 3.42 cm | w.1.78 cm | d. 0.15 cm

63   Cross fragment
Gold
Late 6th–7th cent. AD
H. 1.1 cm. w. 0.89 cm | d. 0.03 cm

52   Six pendants and a setting
Gold, one amethyst, one green stone
(possibly emerald), pearls
Roman–Byzantine
Measurements (from left to right):
L. 1.81 cm | w. 0.68 cm | d. 0.47 cm
L. 2.28 cm | w. 0.50 cm | d. 0.40 cm
L. 1.56 cm | w. 0.49 cm | d. 0.41 cm
L. 0.83 cm | w. 0.33 cm | d. 0.28 cm
L. 0.67 cm | w. 0.30 cm | d. 0.30 cm
L. 0.50 cm | w. 0.30 cm | d. 0.25 cm
L. 0.71 cm | w. 0.38 cm | d. 0.24 cm

The pendants each consist of a
wire on which various decorative
links are attached. These are
drop-formed amethysts, beads
and gold links of different
shapes. The rectangular setting
is made of sheet gold and contains a green stone, possibly an
emerald.   Y. S.

**169   Forty-two golden
elements of
different shapes**
Gold
Ptolemaic period (?)
Various measurements and weights

**64   Sixty-three golden
elements of
different shapes**
Gold
Ptolemaic period (?)
Various measurements and weights

169

64

A BEAUTY FROM THE DEPTHS
THE DARK QUEEN

One of the finest finds from the bay of Aboukir is a remarkable Graeco-Egyptian product of the Ptolemaic era – a queen in dark stone wearing the usual robe that identifies the sovereigns of Isis incarnate. The hair, whose plaited tresses are handled with entirely naturalistic detail, is crowned with a diadem decorated with the *uraeus*-snake.

The effigy is larger than life-size, and represents a female figure standing with her arms at her sides and the left foot slightly forward. This position respects the canons of the pharaonic style, but the way the surface and the physiognomy are modelled bears witness to a different artistic influence. The queen holds an *ankh* (the symbol of life) in her left hand, and on her chest her dress carries the 'Isis knot'. She is dressed in a fine shirt with a low-cut circular neckline. The fabric moulds the breasts closely, forming delicate vertical folds. On top, the goddess is wrapped in an ample piece of fabric knotted in the centre of the chest. The material passes below the breasts, creating more strongly arched folds. A shawl of this kind rises to the right shoulder. Two thick folds descend vertically on the axis of the figure, rounded off in high relief. At the top, the knot forms a loop, and a carefully modelled flap end falls from it forming a zigzag fold. The modelling of the clothing and the woman's anatomy is extremely soft and indicates the hand of a master.

On the side of the left thigh is a flat relief of an *ankh* symbol that the queen holds in her left hand, the phalanxes of which are carefully modelled. At the back of the sculpture is a smooth rectangular dorsal pillar.

Despite its smooth appearance, the face manifests certain characteristic features in shape, chin and mouth. The wrinkles of the neck show that she is no longer a young woman. The *uraeus*-snake and wide flat headband are royal attributes of Hellenistic rulers. All these features together suggest that the statue in Herakleion is an image of Cleopatra III, who died in 101 BC (or possibly her mother) assimilated to Isis, a notion that is supported by the presence of the *ankh* symbol.   Z. K.

112 **Statue of a queen**
Black granite
Ptolemaic period
H. 220 cm

JEWELS, GOLD AND FAITH Although a period of several hundred years lies between Ptolemaic Herakleion and Byzantine East Canopus, both locations have more in common than appears likely at first glance: the pieces of goldsmith's work found at both sites provide proof that they were both important religious centres. In addition, they are confirmation of already known facts, namely that Byzantine culture was, at least partially, founded on older traditions. This can be recognised in individual pieces of goldsmith's work and the overall character of the finds presented here.

Only two pieces of jewellery from Herakleion have an unquestionably symbolic content: These are two golden beads in the form of a Horus eye or *oudjat* (cat. no. 170, p. 242) and a leaden Byzantine crucifix (cat. no. 345).

Horus was the ancient Egyptian god of heaven and light. During a battle with Seth, one of his two eyes was wounded and, later, magically healed. The *oudjat* symbolises this eye. Seeing that, according to what has been passed down, Horus cared for the souls of the dead, the Horus eye can also be regarded as a symbol for life after death. As such, it is often depicted on the sarcophaguses, masks and jewellery of mummies. The Horus eye, therefore, has a significance similar to that of the Byzantine cross.

Not only the meaning, but also the form, of several Byzantine symbols can be traced back to older prototypes: one example is the wedding ring from East Canopus (cat. no. 59). Its iconography is based on a Roman wedding ceremony, the *dextrarum iunctio*, the joining of both right hands. In these depictions, Juno, Pronuba or Concordia are usually shown between the bride and groom. In late antiquity, the rite was Christianised and its iconography adapted: Christ now takes over the role of the Roman goddesses.

At both locations, Herakleion and East Canopus, an exceptionally large number of pieces of goldsmith's work were found, in Herakleion, the majority in and around the temple and in the 'great canal'. As in many other places, jewelled votive gifts were probably also donated in these two. The same could apply for the 'great canal' where other possible votive gifts, including miniature anchors and barks, were found (pp. 198, 251).

Several leaden crosses were excavated in East Canopus – one of these is exhibited (cat. no. 72, p. 272). These crosses have no function as jewellery and can only be explained as being votive gifts. A small lead tablet with a raised cross must have fulfilled a similar purpose: this tablet has two corroded holes, possibly used to nail it to a venerated object. In addition, the pendant in the form of a *tabula ansata* was probably a votive gift (cat. no. 53). Small sheets of gold, in the same shape and with inscriptions, were traditionally dedicated to various gods during Roman times. On the other hand, other pieces of goldsmith's work show signs of having been worn (cat. no. 56) and may also have been votive gifts. This indicates that both places were sanctuaries where jewelled votive gifts, possibly made locally, were common.

345 Cross pendant
Lead
5th–8th cent. AD
H. 3.02 cm | w. 2.17 cm | d. 0.17 cm

59 Wedding ring
Gold
7th–early 8th cent. AD
Diam. 1.96 cm | d. 0.42 cm

An engraved inscription, framed at the top and bottom by a frieze of circular design, runs around the ring: HPHNHN THN EMHN ΔIΔOME VMIN AMH[N], I give you my peace, Amen (a passage from John 14:27). The ornament on the ring is decorated with a wreath of triangular design and, within this, from the bottom upwards, an engraved inscription OMONOIA, harmony, a base line and a wedding scene. It shows the bridegroom on the left, the bride on the right with Christ between them. The bridegroom has short hair, is wearing a short tunic and a cloak, which appears to be held together on his right side by a fibula. The bride has long hair and is wearing a long dress. Christ is dressed in a long, belted garment; His long hair is framed by the aura of the cross. There are lenticular notches above the heads of the bride and groom, probably representing the sun and moon, which often appear on wedding rings.   M.T. | Y. S.

53 Pendant in the shape of a *tabula ansata*
Gold
Late Roman or Byzantine
H. 0.66 cm | w. 1.34 cm | d. 0.04 cm

The engraved inscription NAI/NAI can be seen on the obverse, the second NAI is in mirror image.   Y. S.

56 Finger ring with circular ornament
Gold
6th–early 8th cent. AD
Diam. 1.29 cm | d. 0.54 cm

Because of its size, this might have been a child's ring.   Y. S.

59

53

56

76   Seal
Lead
6th–7th cent. AD
Diam. 2,8 cm | d. 0.4 cm

Obverse: Two saints and angels on both sides of an image Christ (?) above a cross.
Reverse: Cruciform monogram, Γαβριηλ – Gabriel.   C. M.

ON DATING THE GOLDSMITH'S WORK FROM EAST CANOPUS The gold-smith's work from the T sector of East Canopus was found dispersed over the entire area. The same applies to the coins and seals, which date from the Roman to the Umayyad period, the majority from between the sixth and early eighth century AD. All pieces of goldsmith's work found there must have been created at the beginning of the eighth century, at the latest. A more precise dating can only be made through comparisons with dateable pieces of goldsmith's work from all regions of the Byzantine Empire and further afield.

FASHION IN EARLY BYZANTINE GOLDSMITH'S ART It is *communis opinio* that Byzantine jewellery from the sixth and seventh centuries AD forms a unity formally and technically and as far as motifs are concerned. This has the consequence that, for example, a chain from the sixth century, produced in an atelier in Constantinople cannot be distinguished from a chain produced at the same time in another workshop in the Byzantine Empire. Some forms of jew-ellery were actually widespread throughout the empire and beyond. Among these forms are the crescent shaped, perforated earring (cat. no. 38, p. 285), the pendant and the preserved fragments of a necklace. The wide geographical distribution appears attributable to a single, influential atelier, possibly the workshop of the palace in Constantinople. But why should there also not have been regional and local schools in the art of the goldsmiths in the sixth and seventh centuries as there were in other art forms?

In order to determine such local workshops, it is necessary that the greatest possible number of pieces of goldsmith's work be found at one location as in Canopus. If there is an accumulation of forms,

79 **Seal**
Lead
7th cent. AD
Diam. 2.5 cm | d. 0.5 cm

Obverse: Monogram.
Reverse: Cruciform monogram.   C. M.

75 **Seal**
Lead
6th cent. AD
Diam. 1.8 cm | d. 0.5 cm

Obverse: CON[S]TAN[TI]N(I) – perhaps (seal) of Constantinus.
Reverse: Cruciform monogram, Κωνσταντινου
– (seal) of Konstantinus.   C. M.

80 **Seal**
Lead
7th cent. AD
Diam. 2.5 cm | d. 0.5 cm

Obverse: Illegible.
Reverse: Cruciform monogram, Ευτυχιανου
– (seal) of Eutychianos.   C. M.

74 **Seal**
Lead
Early 6th cent. AD
Diam. 2.2 cm | d. 0.4 cm

Obverse: Square monogram made up
of A Ω E N T.
Reverse: Square monogram poorly
preserved, made up of A N.   C. M.

77 **Seal**
Lead
6th–7th cent. AD
Diam. 2.1 cm | d. 0.2 cm

Obverse: Monogram.
Reverse: Monogram, Σεργι(ου)
– (seal) of Sergios.   C. M.

78 **Seal**
Lead
6th–7th cent. AD
Diam. 2.1 cm | d. 0.4 cm

Obverse: Haloed bust of saint.
Reverse: Cruciform monogram.   C. M.

38

48

49-51

58 **Ring with ornament in the form of a small oil lamp**
Gold
Late 6th–early 8th cent. AD
L. 3.81 cm | w. 1.74 cm | d. 1.08 cm

The ring is made of a perforated band with an ornament in the form of a small oil lamp. The band is decorated with a wave-shaped tendril, bound at regular intervals. Two leaves grow out of each of these bindings: a small simple leaf alternates with a three-part, ivy-like leaf. The oil lamp has a double spout and an onion-shaped lid attached to the body with a hinge. It also has a drop-form mirror, made of a strip of lead and pearl-wire, as well as a handle in the form of a simple eyelet. Y. S.

38 **Crescent-shaped earring**
Gold
6th–early 8th cent. AD
L. 2.65 cm | w. 2.18 cm | d. 0.17 cm

The perforated work shows a cantharos emerging from the tendrils; some engravings add structure to the cantharos and the leaves of the vines. Y. S.

48 **Necklace with circular links**
Gold
6th–early 8th cent. AD
L. 2.27 cm | w. 1.34 cm | d. 0.14 cm

The larger chain link is decorated with a four-part leaf in the centre, framed by two intertwined triangles and surrounded by a raised, cordlike setting. The second link or the pendant also appears to have been circular but its diameter is smaller. It is possible that this link was decorated with a leaf consisting of several parts and surrounded with a similar cordlike setting. Y. S.

49–51 **Necklace with cylindrical and semi-globular links**
Gold
Late 6th–early 8th cent. AD
Fragment 1 (49): l. 0.60 cm | w. 0.95 cm | d. 0.20 cm
Fragment 2 (50): l. 3 cm | w. 1 cm | d. 0.13 cm
Fragment 3 (51): l. 5 cm | w. 0.57 cm | d. 0.25 cm

The links of the chain are joined together with simple wire eyelets. A perforated Greek cross, surrounded by a raised meander, decorates the large circular link of fragment 1. Y. S.

motifs and techniques which do not occur in the pieces from other provinces it can be assumed with a high level of certainty that we are dealing with regional characteristics. The fragment of a necklace with hemispheric links (cat. nos. 49–51), the fragment of a necklace with circular links (cat. no. 48), and the cross pendant belong in this category. Parallels to certain details in these pieces of gold-smith's work can be found in Egyptian jewellery. It therefore seems probable that they were produced in that country, possibly at the site of discovery, where a goldsmith's workshop almost certainly existed. Exclusively non-Egyptian gold-smith's works were used as models for the unique ring crowned with a figure in the shape of a small oil lamp (cat. no. 58) but that does not rule out the possibility that it was produced in Egypt. If this ring does, in fact, have a connection with the cult of a Christian pilgrimage sanctuary, such as that of the saints Cyrus and John, it could have been produced locally. Y. S.

III. TRADE AND EVERYDAY LIFE

THONIS-HERAKLEION

PORT AND COMMERCE

Statements and digs by the IEASM have confirmed references by classic authors to the site of Thonis-Herakleion. To the east of Canopus and the Mediterranean waterside, it was situated in a zone, now underwater, close to the mouth of the western branch of the Nile, known by the names 'Canopic mouth' and 'Herakleopolite mouth'. Owing to its geographical position, it was the main port to engage in commerce with the Greek seas, under the pharaohs, and the centre from which foreign ships were surveyed. Under the Saiten and the Persians, and then under the three last indigenous dynasties, Thonis was the border-police and customs post, and the emporium through which products imported by the Greeks would pass, bound for their trading posts in Naukratis.

During the course of the reign of Psammetichos I (664–610 BC) Greek soldiers had been stationed near a city bearing the Egyptian name Nokratj, which in Greek is transcribed as Naukratis, on the Canopic branch of the Nile, some one hundred kilometres from the river's mouth. Naukratis belonged to the district of Sais and was only about twenty kilometres away from the hub of the twenty-sixth dynasty and its temple to Neith, the patroness of the Saitic dynasty. The Greek settlement rapidly transformed itself into an active site of commerce and manufacturing. Several Greek cities obtained

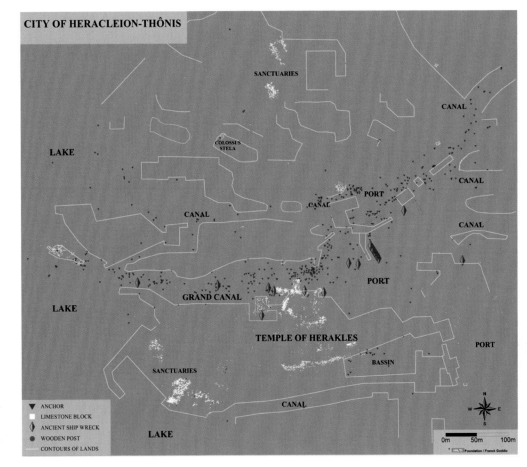

Discovery sites in Herakleion

Miniature anchor as offering (cat. no. 129, p. 251)

concessions there, the organisation of which was regulated under Amasis (*c.* 570–526 BC). The carriages of merchandise imported by the Greeks, heading for their trading posts and workshops, entered Egyptian territory via the Canopic mouth and travelled up the branch of the same name. Archaeological evidence shows relatively clearly that Naukratis was founded well before the reign of Amasis. Archaeological remains impart information to us about sanctuaries, not about warehouses, even though we might well hypothesise that every city had not only its own sanctuary but also its own commercial quarter. Furthermore, Naukratis was not exactly an ordinary Greek township with its own citizens, comparable to the colonies of Sicily and Italy. Its existence depended on the permanence of the Egyptian king's favour (and his interest) for its monopoly on the Egyptian market to remain unquestioned. Naukratis, which most likely suffered financial troubles at the time of the revolts against the Persians in western Lower Egypt, reprised its prosperous activities – duly controlled by the pharaonic administration – under the last indigenous dynasties, as the Stele of Naukratis illustrates (p. 318).

Topographical surveys carried out in the Bay of Aboukir culminated in the discovery of the site of Thonis-Herakleion. At around 6,500 metres from the eastern bank of the peninsula, covering an area of 1,000 × 1,200 metres, the site took shape as a town, with buildings; to the south was the temple district of a significant shrine in pharaonic style; to the north and east, the basins of a vast port.

There was also a central promontory, from which the temple, with annexes, rose up, surrounded by the city, and with a lake on the inner west side. On the other side of the temple, quays and a vast inner port opened into the Nile via a narrow passage (p. 93). The whole ensemble was protected by a cordon, in the form of a sand dune, on the west bank of the river. In maritime terms, its position was ideal: at once sheltered from the dominant north-west winds and from storms from the north-east. Material discovered through excavations shows how this port, made up of several large basins, and fitted out with a significant infrastructure, must have experienced intense activity, making for the city's prosperity. More than seven hundred diversely-shaped antique anchors and sixteen wrecks dating from the sixth to the second centuries BC, discovered recumbent on the seabed, bear eloquent testimony to this fact (cat. no. 321).

Jean Yoyotte points out that the most astonishing and crucial find is a stele that is almost the

321 **Anchor fragment**
Bronze
6th–2nd cent. BC
L. 21 cm

The fragment in bronze, fairly conical in shape, was designed in all likelihood to reinforce the wooden tip of the anchor. Circular holes are visible in the upper part of the object; a square one in the lower part; they were probably destined to receive fixing nails. The bronze plaque was curved into a cone, flattened and bent to the level of the tip, thus reinforcing the part that would grip to the seabed.   D. F.

duplicate of another that was found in 1890 in Naukratis; it is described in detail below (p. 316).

The statues in the temple district date, for the most part, from the Ptolemaic period. However, soundings have freed an abundance of ritual implements, bronze figurines, and ceramic and limestone vases from the ground. The bronzes include a classical *sistrum*, the pedestal of a Harpokrates statue and an image of Chons with the head of a falcon (p. 124); the dates of the large majority of these artefacts are spread from over the course of the sixth through the first centuries BC. An incense-burner in the form of a little Greek female sphinx can be dated to the sixth century (cat. no. 136, p. 351).

Just as at Naukratis, digs at Thonis-Herakleion, through which merchants from Naukratis and Greek travellers and mercenaries used to pass, have succeeded in bringing concrete information to light about economic and cultural relations between Egypt and Hellas. In fact, according to a tradition relayed by Herodotus, Psammetichos, the first king of the twenty-sixth dynasty, would have called on Greek mercenaries to drive out the Assyrians and re-establish the unity of Egypt for him, posting them, subsequently, in strategic places, especially in the eastern part of the Delta, a region open to invasions. The presence of Greek mercenaries at this time in Egypt is not the stuff of legend only; some of them, most often originating from Asia Minor, inscribed their names on the legs of the colossal statues in Abu Simbel on the way back from an expedition to Nubia led by the Egyptian general under Psammeti-

chos II (595–589 BC). These Greeks from Asia were numerous enough to 'colonise' several quarters of Memphis, whose dwellers were called 'Helleno-Memphites' and 'Carian-Memphites'. The merchants must have followed soon after the soldiers. Greek mercenaries and tradesmen were definitely occupants of the city of Naukratis, but they were likewise present in Thonis-Herakleion. This fact is borne out by the discovery on the site of fragments of arms of hoplite soldiers such as helmets (cat. nos. 311, 313, p. 295), spearheads (cat. nos. 314–317, p. 295), arrowheads (cat. nos. 318, 319, p. 295), catapult projectiles (cat. no. 361, p. 295) and axes (cat. nos. *308, 309*), as well as Athens-style tetradrachms (cat. nos. 441, 442, p. 295).

It turns out that the Athenian coins featuring an owl, actually a tawny owl, were the object of numerous imitations in the course of the fourth century BC, instigated by Persian satraps, Anatolian or Phoenician cities, and even the sovereigns of Egypt. The first person, according to Herodotus, to have struck money in the country of the pharaohs was Aryandes, satrap of Egypt under the Persian ruler Kambyses and Darius I. However, not one of these coins has been preserved. They must have been issued between 500 and 492 BC, since the production of imitations of Attic tetradrachms began towards the end of the fifth century. When, in 407 and 405, Athens was no longer able to strike coins because the Laurian mines had stopped producing as a result of the war against Sparta, the import of owls, so beloved in Egypt, came to a halt. It was then that the pharaohs of the twenty-eighth, twenty-ninth and thirtieth dynasties had imitations of Athenian tetradrachms struck. A coin weight featuring an owl, with a hawk's head (of Amon) on the reverse, was amongst the finds made in Herakleion (cat. no. 372, p. 296). It is notable that a patch of these coins was discovered at Athribis in the Delta. A treasury of money, found in Fayum, confirms how thousands of this type were struck, and an Athenian law of 375–374 BC reveals how these imitations were already in circulation in Athens. This coinage was probably minted in order to pay the many Greek mercenaries serving in the Egyptian armies. With Achoris (393–380 BC) having concluded an alliance with Athens in the fourth year of his reign, it seems that the city provided him with standards and templates. So the coins obtained from money produced by Achoris displayed

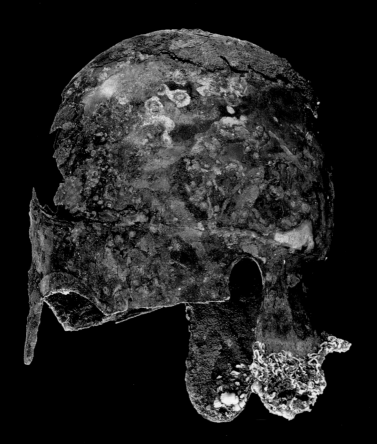

311

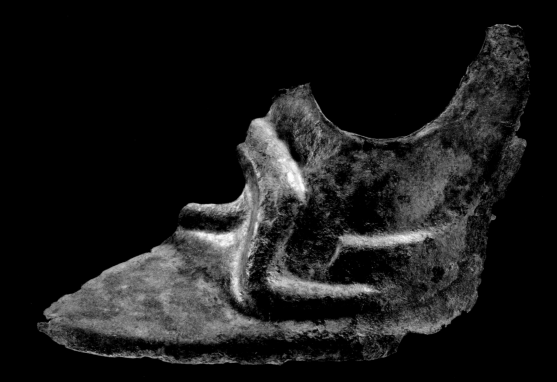

313

314

316

315

317

319

318

361

previous double page:

311 Helmet

Bronze
5th–4th cent. BC
H. 34 cm | w. 23.5 cm

This bronze helmet is of the 'Chalcidian' type. It is so-named as
it appears first on the so-called 'Chalcidian' pottery of the late Archaic
period. It now seems that the pottery of this name was made in Italy,
and it is possible that an analogous type of helmet first evolved in
greater Greece and south Italy, as many examples have been found
there. Later on this type of helmet becomes very common in Athenian
representational evidence, and must have been popular at Athens. The
'Chalcidian' helmet resembles the well-known Corinthian helmet in
many respects. A curving ridge separates the upper from the lower
skull of the helmet, and decorative eyebrows are worked on the skull
above either side of the nasal. The part of the helmet covering the
cheeks found in the Corinthian helmet are, however, absend. This helmet originally had hinged cheek-pieces, which have now become separated from the helmed. N. S.

313 Helmet cheek-piece

Bronze
4th cent. BC
H. 14 cm | w. 7.5 cm

The bronze cheek-piece of a helmet of the 'Phrygian' type had hinged
cheek-pieces, with two curves cut out of the front edge, one in the
upper part leaving the eye uncovered, and
a second curve further down in front of the mouth to ease breathing.
N. S.

314 Javelin tip/spear tip

Bronze
5th–4th cent. BC
L. 13.3 cm

316 Spear tip

Bronze
5th–4th cent. BC
L. 35 cm | w. 2.5 cm | diam. 2.5 cm

315 Lance tip

Bronze
5th–4th cent. BC
L. 27 cm | w. 2.5 cm. diam. 2.4 cm

317 Javelin tip

Bronze
6th–2nd cent. BC
L. 18 cm | w. 3 cm

This type of leaf-shaped spearhead is typical for the Greek hoplite spear
and they are found produced in both bronze and iron. The leaf-shaped
blade is sharpened on both sides, has a central rib and occupies about
half of the total length of the spearhead. The rest of the spearhead consists of a cylindrical tube, into which the wooden shaft, typically made
of strong but light ash-wood, was fixed.   N. S.

319 Arrowhead

Bronze
6th–2nd cent. BC
L. 3 cm | diam. 1.8 cm

318 Arrowhead

Bronze
6th–2nd cent. BC
L. 3.3 cm | w. 1.3 cm | d. 0.9 cm

This arrowhead is of a type popularly called 'Cretan' at the time. Cretan archers were famous and served throughout the Mediterranean as
mercenaries. The blade of the arrow ends in two barbs, in between
which is a boss, to help prevent the shaft of the arrow from splitting on
impacd. Below the blade is a tang for fitting the head into the shafd. In
this case, as in many other examples, the tang would originally have
been much longer, and has been broken off. The point of the arrowhead is also missing, and appears to have been re-sharpened later (?).
N. S.

361 Catapult projectiles

Lead
6th–2nd cent. BC
L. 3–4 cm | d. 2–3 cm

441 Coin

Silver
4th cent. BC (?)
Diam. 2.1 cm | wt. 15.42 g

Tetradrachm of Athens
Obverse: Head of Athena facing right in crested Attic helmet
Reverse: Owl standing to the right; behind, an olive branch.
ΑΘΕ – (Coin) of Ath(ens).   A. M.

442 Coin

Silver
4th cent. BC (?)
Diam. 2.4 cm | wt. 15.16 g

Tetradrachm of Athens
Obverse: Head of Athena facing right in crested Attic helmet
Reverse: Owl standing to the right; behind, an olive branch. ΑΘΕ
– (Coin) of Ath(ens).   A. M.

great finesse, to the point of being no longer distinguishable from Athenian coins. A hoard buried in Tell el-Maskhuta contained many of this type of tetradrachms, which might be of Egyptian origin. Cruder Egyptian copies would have been fashioned during the era of Nektanabo I (380–362 BC) and then Nektanabo II (360–343 BC). Under Nektanabo II the striking of Athenian coinage continued, alongside gold Egyptian staters and small hybrid silver coins. In 343, Artaxerxes III Ochos, who re-conquered Egypt, had tetradrachms of the Attic type struck once again, but with an inscription on the reverse in demotic Egyptian meaning "Artaxerxes pharaoh". Under Darius II, the satraps Sabazes (334–333 BC) and Mazakes (333–332 BC) issued imitations of owls with their name in Aramaic letters on the reverse. Towards the middle of the fourth century, small coins in silver appeared in Egypt, with Attic and Egyptian characters.

If the coinage was at the nerve centre of the war, it no less constituted a means of exchange too. Recovered ceramics reveal the intense activity of such exchange between Egypt and the lands of the eastern Mediterranean. The imports that have been collected confirm how the extent of contacts grew towards the middle of the first millennium (sixth to fourth century BC). The documentation available mirrors these great commercial currents (cat. nos. 381, 384, 405, 409; 383, 385, 393, 398, p. 300; 413, p. 301; 388, p. 303; 397, p. 339). According to the literature on ceramics, these were as follows: a Corinthian current, perceptible above all at the beginning of the period when Corinth ruled the seas; an Ionian current, a Cycladic current, then an Attic current that can be seen emerging primarily from the Persian period onwards. A Phoenician current can also be added to this list, whose strong point, apart from Phoenicia, seems to have been the island of Cyprus. This latter current can be observed, most notably, in the exports of numerous torpedo-style amphoras (cat. no. 382, p. 302).

372 Coin weight

Lead
4th cent. BC
H. 2.6 cm | w. 2.6 cm | d. 0.6 cm | wt. 41.6 g

This coin weight is particularly important for our appreciation of the monetary activity in the Classical period. On one side there has been stamped into the metal a design of ram's head. This, the symbol of the god Amon, perhaps signifies the context in which the weight was used. It may, for example, have served the priests of the temple, or others on business to do with the god. The other side of the weight has had hammered into it the reverse of an Athenian tetradrachm, of the type in production at Athens between around 350 and 290 BC. The weight amounts to 41.6 grams and thus equates closely to the theoretical weight of ten Athenian drachmas (approximately 43 grams). The choice of a ten-drachma weight is interesting, since the most common Athenian denomination in use at this period was a four-drachma coin. Ten drachmas, though not the most convenient weight for checking Athenian coin, may have been adopted for this weight because it provides a useful bridging point between the Persian weight standard and the Athenian: ten Attic drachmas were equivalent to eight Persian sigloi. This may suggest, as might the date of the coin stamped into the weight, that it was produced during the period of the Persian occupation of Egypt (343–332 BC).   A. M.

In parallel with large figurative vases, diverse and varied products such as wine, oil or pitch were also imported in large quantities. Whether originating on the Levantine coast or in eastern Greece, wine, oil and olive amphoras counted amongst the most distributed products of the archaic Mediterranean, imported not only in order to satisfy the needs of Greek colonisers but also those of the local population. If oil, which played an essential role in the Greek diet, was principally imported to meet the Greeks' daily needs, wine was also regularly imported for Egyptian leaders, who could appreciate its taste. Great amateurs of wine like the Persian kings, the pharaohs of the last indigenous dynasties, were familiar with the best *grands crus* of the Mediterranean basin.

These observations cut to the core of the problem: for whose benefit were imports made? The massive presence of foreign products on a site does not constitute sufficient proof that regular commerce was made with diverse social groups, and does not necessarily indicate a foreign presence. With research as it stands currently, we can not accept the hypothesis that Greek commerce, for example, was limited almost exclusively to those cities founded by the Greeks. This also explains the existence of several sites based around ports, probably in order to control the arrival of merchandise coming from the most outlying regions of the Mediterranean basin. Generally speaking, documentation reveals the existence and vitality of cultural and commercial exchanges at this time, and in so doing invites questions about borrowing and influences, and the cultural integration of customs and tastes, up to the Ptolemaic period. This is especially the case with reference to certain objects known as 'Persian' and those of the 'Achaemenid' type, whose technical and artistic influence is felt up until the Ptolemaic period (cat. nos. 344; 154–156; pp. 266–67; *229–232, 243–251, 352, p.303*).

D. F.

344 **Plaque showing a griffin**
Lead
Late period (?)
L. 4.9 cm | w. 3.8 cm

409

381   Amphora

Ceramic
6th cent. BC
H. 42.5 cm | diam. 10.5 cm

This amphora hearkens back to Klazomenain ceramic, which was produced primarily in the sixth century BC in north Ionian Asia Minor.   C. G.

409   Ionian goblet

Ceramic
End of 7th–mid-6th cent. BC
H. 6.3 cm | diam. 15.7 cm

The high quality drinking vessel belongs to a long tradition in the eastern Greek world. Amphoras and goblets are often characteristic of the Ionian and Cycladic commercial currents.   C. G.

384   Amphora

Ceramic
End of 5th–mid-4th cent. BC
H. 32 cm | diam. 22.5 cm

The Lekythos is decorated with a geometric palmette (palm-leaf) decoration.   C. G.

405   Fat-bellied lekythos

Ceramic
End of 5th–mid-6th cent. BC
H. 9.6 cm | diam. 5.1 cm

The lekythos is decorated with a geometric palmette (palm-leaf) decoration.   C. G.

384

405

393   Bolsal
Ceramic
End of 5th cent. BC
H.. 4.5 cm | diam. 9.7 cm

On the floor of the interior is a stamped decoration: four palms radiating out from a circle. The vessel has a brilliant black coating of thin slip to smooth the surface and prepare it for painting. The decoration stamped on it is a significant element in dating id.   C. G.

398   Kotyle (vessel)
Ceramic
End of 5th – beginning of 4th cent. BC
H. 10 cm | diam. 14.4 cm

The ceramic from Asia Minor has a painted geometric decoration.   C. G.

385   Amphora
Ceramic
End of 5th – mid-4th cent. BC
H. 28.5 cm | diam. 11 cm

The amphora contained hazelnut shells.   C. G.

383   Amphora
Ceramic
5th cent. BC
H. 65 cm | diam. 40 cm

The amphora, although without the classic strie (combed lines) under its edge, belongs to productions originating in Mende, a city well known for having widely exported one of the most famous wines in antiquity at the end of the fifth century BC.   C. G.

413 **Bowl**
Ceramic
Mid-4th cent. BC
H. 4.5 cm | diam. 13.4 cm

The interior decoration is of linked palms surrounded by a circular guilloche
pattern. There is a graffito including a Greek letter rho (name or start of name?)
around the belly of the imported bowl. C. G.

382   **Torpedo amphora**

Ceramic
Persian period
H. 56 cm | diam. 30 cm

The black painted decoration on the upper part of the belly
represents a star, a pentagram.   C. G.

388 **Fragment of an askos**
Ceramic
End of 5th–mid-4th cent. BC
Diam. 3.5 cm | diam. medallion 7.7 cm

The medallion with a man's bearded face
and hair in wavy curls, probably represented
Boreas, incarnation of the north wind for
the Greeks.   C. G.

352 **Dish**
Lead
Late period (?)
H. 5 cm | diam. 15 cm

This flat dish displays a Persian-style decoration.   C. G.

COLOSSAL, FAT AND FECUND
HAPI, THE INUNDATION OF THE NILE

The iconography of this uninscribed colossus is that regularly found with fecundity figures. The statue shows a fat male who has large, pendant breasts with prominent nipples. He holds before him an offering table with a central lip for a water channel at the front. The offering table rests on his forearms and on the palms of his hands, the damaged fingers of which protrude beyond the table itself; his nipples rest on the surface of the offering table. He has a tripartite wig of the type worn by both male and female deities as well as by elite women.

The figure was found in seven pieces. It had already been broken in antiquity and shows traces of repair work from that time. His straight false beard, for example, is quite untypical of deities, who almost always have a much longer beard with an outcurved end. The original beard had been damaged and was remodelled to form an intact shape; in the process, the edges were chamfered geometrically, creating a profile that is unnatural for anything made of hair. Above the wig rises a clump of papyrus, representing the heraldic plant of Lower Egypt, which was also particularly associated with Hapi, the inundation of the Nile. This element too had broken in antiquity. The top piece of the plant was found in the excavations and is now reassembled with the rest of the statue.

The offering table is reassembled from several parts. It is sculpted on top in relief with the shapes of four loaves along the top left edge, but the rest of the surface is smoothed into a slightly concave shape, probably where larger elements, such as per-haps the libation tables often carried by fecundity figures, had been irretrievably damaged. The thickness of the offering table obscures the normally bulbous stomach of a fecundity figure. The bulge of the abdomen is visible below. Pendant strips that form part of the minimal garment are carved in relief on the right thigh and where the legs meet. The left leg, part of the calf of which is a separate fragment, is advanced in a strongly striding pose comparable with that of the colossus of the king (cat. no.106, p. 165). The principal function of fecundity figures is to bring offerings, and the striding pose can express movement, but it can also render a general male figure without such an implication.

Like almost all Egyptian statues of any size, the colossus has a back pillar which one would expect to be inscribed. The absence of inscriptions on all three colossal statues (cat. nos. 106, 107, p. 165) raises the question of whether they were ever completely finished. In this connection, it is striking that the original surface of the fecundity figure is much rougher than the re-smoothed areas.

This statue is almost identical in scale to the colossal statues of a king and queen near which it was found, but it is uncertain whether they form a true set. This statue is thus the largest known Egyptian statue of a being who is identified as a deity.

Many such statues were set up facing outward in front of temples or in their outer areas, and so addressed those who saw or entered. Because Egyptian temples were not accessible to a broad public, many of those entering would have been priests. By

contrast, colossal figures of deities are known in the relief decoration of pylons, in scenes where they are offered to by the king. Some lifesize figures of deities form part of group statues with kings, notably in New Kingdom temples (cf. representation on the *naos*, p. 48). The most important figures of deities, however, were the small precious cult statues kept in sanctuaries. This pattern is very different from that of the Classical world, where some of the most renowned cult statues were colossal in scale.

Fecundity figures are not deities in a straightforward sense. They personify fertile aspects of the natural and cultivated world, among which by far the most prominent was Hapi, the inundation of the Nile, who was often divided into Upper and Lower Egyptian forms, with the Lower Egyptian one bearing a heraldic papyrus clump, as on the present statue. Hapi was almost the only being depicted as a fecundity figure who received any kind of cult. Typically, fecundity figures were grouped in pairs, but in this case no trace of a companion has been found. Since the statue was set up at Herakleion, at one of the mouths of the Nile, its identification with Hapi is particularly plausible.

The principal function of fecundity figures was to bring offerings to the temple for the king to present them to the gods. They therefore belong more with the king as representative of this world than with the gods, whose domain was more cosmic. In the first millennium BC in particular, there was a close identification between the king and

fecundity figures, who were often depicted in very long sequences on temple walls and whose actions were attributed to the king. A couple of images of King Amenhotep III (1391–1353 BC) even have the form of fecundity figures.

The water and the products that fecundity figures were shown bringing were presented to the gods, who in turn provided for the well-being of Egypt as a whole; the figures could therefore be suitably directed out from the temple as well as in toward it, and would convey a message of royal as well as divine provision for the country. The Herakleion statue, which is one of very few that are likely to have faced outward, displayed ideas like these on a colossal scale.   J. B.

103 **Colossal statue of a god of fertility, probably Hapi**
Pink granite
4th cent. BC–early Ptolemaic period
H. 540 cm | wt. 6 t.

A CUSTOMS POST IN THE MEDITERRANEAN

PLACES OF CUSTOMS TAXATION Because of it geographical position, Herakleion was the principal port under the pharaohs to engage in commerce with the Greek seas and the centre from which foreign ships were surveyed. It was here that the 'officer at the door to foreign peoples from Ouadj-our' would act, to use the title borne under the twenty-sixth dynasty by those officials in charge of policing the borders at the entrance to the river, where boats coming from Hellas would arrive.

As the Stele of Naukratis informs us, a cut would be taken from the quantity of taxes regularly collected for the state's benefit from, on the one hand, the goods and products of the Greeks in Naukratis and, on the other hand, imports reaching them from the sea via the Canopic branch of the Nile. The tithes would be used for the benefit of the Sais temple of Neith, serving as an additional offering, in other words as a resource in kind to benefit the local priesthood. Two places of taxation were envisaged then: Naukratis and Herakleion.

A customs register of the Egyptian satraps from the Persian era enables us to envisage the procedures involved in customs taxation: 'Firstly, ships pay their customs dues at the mouth of the Canopic branch, that is to say, it seems, that the port of entry and taxation was, quite simply, Thonis, both in the Saitic period and in the fourth century – a port that the Achaemenid administration quite simply just preserved in the same state... Next, once the ships paid their customs dues, they were free to continue up the Nile, as far as Naukratis and Memphis, where the size of the markets (most particularly Memphis in the Persian era) allowed them to sell their products (wines, oil, iron, wood) at profit.' Once they have sold their merchandise, 'the traders fill the holds of the ships with local products, especially natron, which they can effectively load up in one

320 **Plaques**
Bronze
Ptolemaic period.
H. 15 cm | w. 14 cm | d. 1 cm (A)
H. 21.5 cm | w. 15.5 cm | d. 1 cm (B)

Of the two plaques recovered between sectors H1 and H7, the first is completely corroded, the second bears a horizontal inscription in large hieroglyphics bordered by two 'threads'. Two square conduits certainly destined for solid tenons are cut through the upper thread; both are hollowed at a point 2.5 centimetres from the top of the plaque and 3 centimetres from the edge. This symmetry, and the fact that the threads appear to end a little before the edge, suggest that the plaque is complete.

The beginning of the text has been destroyed. What follows, *'in the mouth of the Haou-Nebouy'* can be clearly made out. Beyond that, possibly traces of 'the hoe'.

The term *Haou-nebouy* means literally 'those who are behind the nebout', this last word referring to a place, in all probability a group of islands. Since the Ancient Empire, from amongst the people that the pharaoh intended to subjugate, Haou-nebout has designated those on the northern confines of Egypt. This archaic ethnonym would survive, with a figurative meaning, in the classical language used on official and religious occasions. Thus, in the triumphalist rhetoric that sings of the power of the conquering kings of the New Empire, nebout is applied to the peoples of Syria-Palestine. Under the Saitic kings, it designates the Phoenicians, Carians and Greeks recruited as soldiers. In trilingual sacerdotal decrees in honour of the Ptolemies, according to the demotic version, the Greek text is *'in the writing of the Iouwein [Ionians]'*, whereas in the version in hieroglyphic writing it appears as *'in the writing of the Haou-Nebouy'*. It is worth remembering, in this respect, that Greek was the daily language of the Macedonian rulers as well as all those minorities established in the Egypt of the Lagides. Literally, we should translate *Haou-nebouy* as *'Those who are behind (or around) the Two Lords'*. On our bronze plaque, the word nbwy, *'the Two Lords'* appears supported by two falcons bearing the royal decoration (we encounter a similar form in the Satrap Stele, dating from the governance of Ptolemy I). The pair of divine birds of prey represents, quite simply, Horus and Seth, the two gods whose attributes are united in the persona of the king. The etymological word-play simply encompasses a designation of the Lagide pharaoh, who was effectively *'surrounded by Greeks'*. It should be understood that the fragment from Herakleion talks about *'the estuary of the Greeks'*, which gave the position of Thonis-Herakleion specified in the decree of Nektanabo I discovered on the site.

The tenons indicate quite evidently that the plaques must have been adapted for, and probably embedded in a support that, given the weight of each, would have had to be solid, either a stone wall, or a very thick wooden support (just like the monumental double-doors of propylaea and the access doors to temples). The narrow band left empty above the line of text and the likewise empty field underneath suggest that the long text was intended to fill a dado or base strip, where dedications to, and emphatic definitions of, the temple and its divinities were situated. It is therefore probable that the two objects are the survivors of a series of bronze plaques, the only ones to have escaped salvage and melting down when the monument was destroyed.   J. Y.

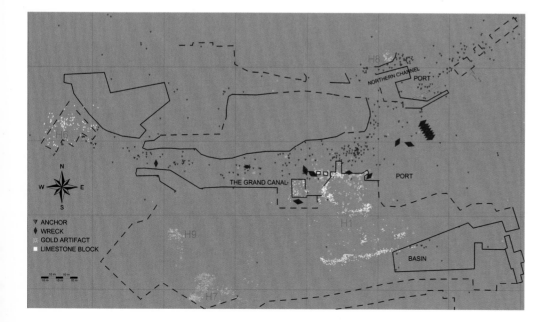

ANCHOR
WRECK
GOLD ARTIFACT
LIMESTONE BLOCK

Discovery sites in the harbour basin of Herakleion

port or another, as they travel down the Nile. Then they travel through Thonis once again, where they pay tax on the natron.'

TYPES OF TAXES The Nektanabo decree makes reference to several types of tax, including imports heading for Naukratis passing through Thonis, which was inevitably, then, a place for customs taxations; transactions within Naukratis; and 'all the things that arise in Per-meryt', an expression that can be understood to mean a tax on productions (crafts) produced by the people of Naukratis.

The royal decree laid down that ten per cent of all royal taxes globally registered at the royal treasury should be transferred to Neith. So this was not a tax of ten per cent, but rather ten per cent of royal taxes. Other Ptolemaic and Roman inscriptions allocate the same rights from the same products to Isis of Philae, making it clear that such an act was not new. A comparison of these documents reveals a constant level of ten per cent, and the transfer of a part of the regal dues to temples situated in the neighbouring areas of the customs ports. This transfer was justified by the mastery of the beneficiary gods over the trade route, Neith being the mistress of the sea.

For Greek ships, the main tax consisted of a quantity of gold and silver, which varied according to the type of boat. For larger Greek ships, part of the cargo of oil had to be added. A complementary tax, called 'men's money', consisted of a tax in money and in kind for the big boats; this was a sort of 'toll', almost akin to a port tax, levied on crew members. On leaving Egypt, the Greeks, without exception, would pay a monetary tax proportional to the value of the natron that they were carrying from Egypt and nothing else. There was no significant difference in the payment of tax according to the ships' tonnage. This would imply that the ships did not only transport natron on the return journey, otherwise the differences between tonnage amounts would have been systematic. Only natron seems then to have been subject to a specific tax, other merchandise was not taxed. Whatever their loads, all boats, on the other hand, had to pay the 'men's money'.

AN EXTRAORDINARY PAIR OF TWINS
THE STELES OF THE PHARAOH NEKTANABO I

The 210-centimetre-high stele known as the Stele of Naukratis has survived in a perfect state of preservation. This stone was discovered by chance in 1899 on a site of Hussein Kamel, uncle of Khedive, otherwise known as *Kom Halfaya*, in the remains of a 'public building on the south of the tell'. In explanation of its perfect state of preservation we can only imagine that the stone had remained hidden when paving or masonry was reused.

Hewn in a beautiful hard stone and engraved with elegance, the stele features fourteen columns of hieroglyphic text, skilfully composed, using a particular graphic system that had been fashionable in the Saitic period, and magnificently inscribed. The text, in Egyptian, according to tradition, consecrates a decision taken by the founder of the thirtieth dynasty, Nektanabo I in the first year of his reign (November 380), shortly after his accession, in favour of the temple of Neith (Neith being the protectress of Sais and of the preceding dynasties). Henceforth, a cut would be taken from the volume of taxes regularly collected for the state's benefit from, on the one hand, the goods and products of the Greeks in Naukratis and, on the other, imports reaching them from the sea via the Canopic branch. These tithes would serve as an additional offering to the temple of Neith, in other words as a resource in kind benefiting the local clergy, whom the new king hoped to rally to him. In the top part of the stele, above the fourteen columns of text, there is an engraving of a scene, which shows the king making an offering to Neith: on one side a plated meal and,

on the other, a great gold necklace. The Greeks were very familiar with the Egyptian image of the goddess, which they had long since assimilated to their Athena, and the message contained in the imagery of this scene must have been as clear to them as foreigners, as it would have been for illiterate Egyptians.

Two realms were targeted for taxation, then: on the one hand Naukratis itself, the very place in which the stele had been erected, on the other 'in a township called Înt', which meant 'everything that came from the Sea of the Greeks'. This mysterious place name, was none other than the Thonis of Greek texts. IEASM's task was to culminate, in 1999, with the discovery of the site of Thonis-Herakleion, and with an amazingly fruitful initial exploration. The most surprising and critical of the finds was a stele that was the double or, to be more precise, almost the double, of the stele from the first year of Nektanabo found in Naukratis: the same materials, same dimensions, same quality of execution, and same picture. Identical to the last detail, it, too, featured fourteen columns of vertical text. At the very most, there were just five variations in the written forms of five words. The stone was as perfectly preserved as its sister stone from Naukratis.

Though nothing unexpected in itself, the find was enough to make any classicist and historian of Egypt very happy, since the fiscal measures it outlined concerned the customs set-up of both Thonis/Herakleion and the Greek settlements in Naukratis. It was no less than an extremely rare event in the

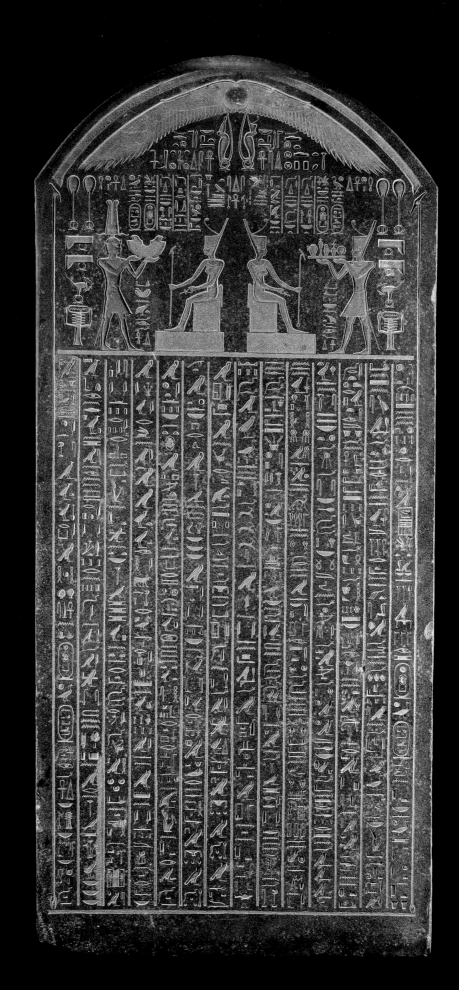

history of the field. Here were two versions of the same document, concerning two distant townships, preserved intact, by chance, in the very places they had been displayed in antiquity, and almost certainly not very far from the point where each was initially erected. One might even call it a miracle, bearing in mind the destruction inflicted by nature and by man on the monuments of the two sites and the disconcerting disorder of shattered, dispersed and dismembered stones encountered in most parts of Lower Egypt and the region of Alexandria.

There is one difference, however, between the two versions. The end of the text reads 'His Majesty has said: Let this be established on the present stele ...'. The Naukratic example (line 13) goes on to specify: 'on the present stele that stands in Nokratis, on the bank of the Ânou canal (Canopian branch of the Nile).' The Herakleion example specifies, however: 'on the present stele at the mouth of the Sea of the Greeks, in the city whose name is The Hôné of Sais.' Here we have the full form of the original name for Herakleion, which is distinguished from that of other *Thôné* townships of the lower Delta by mention of the district capital in whose domain Naukratis fell, and which was also the privileged beneficiary of taxes levied on Canopic commerce.

These two twin steles are both splendid examples of the art of engraving on hard stone in which the artists of the fourth century excelled. The way in which the workshops of Sais succeeded in producing two practically identical works by hand is quite astonishing. A particular detail reveals to us an aspect of fine 'editorial' technique employed by the designer-scribes of the temple of Neith: the base of column thirteen of the Herakleion example was underscored by a thread of fine lines and the begin-

**118   Stele of Thonis-
       Herakleion**
Black granite
380 BC
H. 195 cm | w. 88 cm |
d. 34 cm

Stele of Naukratis
Black granite
380 BC
H. 195 cm | w. 88 cm |
d. 34 cm

ning of column fourteen minutely dotted, in order to indicate each place where the name Thonis should be substituted for that of Naukratis, which had featured on the first model.

Both steles with their texts illustrate the refined art of communication mastered by those in the service of the divine pharaohs: a communication between the state and its subjects, between Egypt and its foreign partners and between the world of men and the world of the gods. By means of sacred writing, politics and economics were ideally integrated into a conception of the cosmos that we might call religious.

Furthermore, these two steles are the only preserved indigenous sources concerning the economy of the Greek emporium. The content of the texts was meant as a signpost, erected with the motivation of making known, in a durable way, the former and recent advantages enjoyed by the Neith temple in Sais and maintaining the memory of Nektanabo in Naukratis and Thonis/Herakleion.

If reading and translating the inscription present no more than a few points of difficulty now, interpreting its form and its content still raises a considerable number of questions. These documents effectively suppose the existence of a royal decree, which must have been formulated in demotic Egyptian, but which would only have summed up the essential facts. The function of such a stele with its inscription was to make the royal decision sacred. Its declaration ties in with the political logic of the *Königsnovelle* and effects an edifying theological demonstration. The double image that occupies the upper quarter of the stele, within an arched cosmic frame, like the long text below, communicates the same fundamental information. The two scenes show the king making an offering to Mistress Neith, Mother of God and protectress of Sais, on the one hand a plate of food, on the other hand a precious gold necklace. The meal would be a symbol for everyday food, and the service of divine offering. As for the jewellery, one might wonder whether it does not symbolise, here, the treasury of Neith's rich store of metals. In any case, the message contained in the summit of the stele must have imposed itself on every passer-by, whether Egyptian or Greek.

The same could not have been said for the text, accessible only to hierogrammats. Compared to other inscriptions from the thirtieth dynasty, the stele of Naukratis immediately caused surprise, or indeed difficulties, because of the frequent use it makes of transcribing words using only one-letter signs. G. Maspéro, the first editor, assumed that these 'alphabetical', as it were, written forms were due to the drafter's familiarity with the Greeks but this theory can not be sustained. In fact, whether or not the principle was initially suggested by the model of an alphabetical writing (Phoenician or Greek), this purely phonetic genre of written forms can be seen sporadically in lapidary texts from the fourth century and even from as early as the seventh century. This could well be an attempt to increase once more the recourse to the past, as was usual in the Saitic period, in the thirtieth dynasty. The approach of our hierogrammat goes against the search for a system to facilitate the automatic recognition of words and as far as possible against classical orthographic norms. The so-called 'alphabetism' is just one of the procedures maintained here to emphasise the text's rare and singular lessons, including: different signs to denote the same sound, the introduction of proto-Ptolemaic words, the invention of unedited multi-letter signs using puns, and discrepancies, consisting of the use, in a single text, of between two and five ways of writing the same word. According to received wisdom, the aim of this florid style was to retain the attention of the literate on the text on display. From this, we can deduce that scribes, experts in sacred writing, were present in, and passed through, Naukratis and Herakleion during the fourth century.

The text arranged in columns covers three quarters of the slab. It is made up of two parts of pretty much equal length. Firstly, following the full protocol of Nektanabo, 'beloved of Neith, mistress of Sais', an elegy by the king in poetic form (col. 1–7), then a narration, based on the enunciation of two declarations, placed in the king's mouth (col. 7–14), which concludes with a standardised wish for the prosperity of the sovereign (col. 14). So far, this narrative has held our attention almost solely because of the crucial information it includes about Naukratis. However, even the theme of the initial encomium is not enough to conceal from us that very specific content is meant to be conveyed, perceptible in the choice and ordering of motifs. This preamble seems to express the ideological principles and balance of power that governed the relationship between the powerful priesthood of the Saitic domain and the general who had become pharaoh several months previously. Nektanabo, in the image of Re, is assumed here to have been elected by Neith, mother of the sun, who won the good opinion of the Egyptians for him and eliminated his competitors. An intrepid warrior, he will defend Egypt and assure the tranquillity of those who follow him in full confidence, being, like Re, the source of his subjects' well being. In accordance with common convention, he will assiduously maintain the buildings, equipment and services in the temples but, in a rare acknowledgement of prevailing circumstances, he has consulted the local priests and 'is doing things conforming to their wishes'. Finally, the poem, evoking the sun, the land and the water, sings about how the whole of Nature lavishes her resources on the 'only god, rich in (exotic?) *marvels*' and concludes with two lines of verse about deliveries received from foreign countries and about Nektanabo's favourable conduct regarding these deliveries (by means of his payments to the deity?).

The prose narration begins with a dry account of the new king's entry into Sais, using sacramental terms: his ritual ascent to the palace at the sanctuary, installation and crowning before Neith, and libations in front of a statue of Osiris, the other master of the Saitic shrine. Two speeches, both introduced by 'Then his Majesty says' follow on, in the interlude. The second, in two sentences (col. 13–14), simply ordains the erection of the stele. The first, in one long uninterrupted phrase, sets out the steps for consecration to perpetuity (col. 8–13). The king's words are translated into an artificial language, which is both classical and neo-Egyptian. Nektanabo is allocating a tenth of the income from taxes destined for the king to the goddess of Neith: this from taxes levied on Greek imports passing through Thonis/Herakleion and on production and transactions in Naukratis.

It is highly likely that, at the time, taxes levied on the commerce of the people of Naukratis would have been in Greek money rather than in kind. Ultimately, the theological justification for this decision was that the goddess was 'mistress of the Great Green (Sea)' and therefore the dispensary of provisions and goods coming from outside. The function of Neith-Methyer to order the world, figurehead of all great bodies of water, effectively qualified her as the sovereign of the seas from which Greek imports came.   J.Y.

Stele of Nektanebo I,
Line 13 (right) und 14 (below)

MONETARY HABITS

BEFORE THE CONQUEST BY ALEXANDER THE GREAT in 332 BC and the Establishment of the Ptolemaic Kingdom. The orthodox view of monetary behaviour in Egypt over this period is essentially as follows. Whereas many states and peoples around the eastern Mediterranean began the production of silver coinage in the late sixth to fifth centuries BC, coinage was not produced during this period in Egypt. During the fifth century BC, foreign silver coinages travelled there, entering an economy in which they were valued not by virtue of the monetary form they took – coins – but for their weight as silver bullion. Thus fifth-century hoards of coins found in Egypt are characterised by numbers of pieces that have been cut up and used as makeweight silver, rather than as coin. This pattern began to change in the fourth century BC when there is a certain amount of evidence to suggest that imitations of Athenian tetradrachms began to be produced in Egypt. Amongst these are certain issues signed by Persian governors of the province, as well as some signed in demotic Egyptian by the great king of Persia himself. It is possible, therefore, that it was at Persian instigation that this production began. However, not all Athenian imitations produced in the province were signed by Persians, and it might equally be suggested that the Persian overlords of Egypt were in fact responding with their issues to a phenomenon that was arising spontaneously within the province. Certainly, the phenomenon of imitation of Athenian coinage is best explained as an attempt by local coin issuers of the fourth century BC to plug the gap left by the fall-off in supply of genuine Athenian coinage at this period. This presupposes that Athenian coins were a widely used and generally accepted medium of exchange in the areas where imitations were produced and circulated. Thus by the late fifth or early fourth century BC parts of Egypt at least had started to use coins as coins, not just as bullion.

There is a relatively high representation of Alexander's coinage (one silver, seven bronze) which may have entered Herakleion with the conquest, or in the years immediately afterwards. The four silver coins of Athens are all tetradrachms, either of Athens itself or fourth century imitations. The four bronze coins of Kos are all of the same type and may belong to the late fourth century or the early Hellenistic period. These, together with single finds of bronzes of Chios, Elaea, Rhodes, Salamis and Sidon, are all indicative of, if anything, a port well connected with the Greek and Phoenician world of the eastern Mediterranean.

Quite astonishing, however, is the number of bronze coins that have been found with the types of a lion walking right or left with a ram's head above on the obverse, and a horse walking left with an ankh above on the reverse. Thirty have thus far been identified, accounting for almost seventy per cent of the coins dating to the period before the arrival of Alexander the Great. Both this large number and the predominance of these pieces are remarkable and require some comment. Four such coins were excavated at the site of Naukratis in the Nile Delta and their origin has been debated over the years. Either they have been attributed to King Euagoras of Salamis or to an unknown city on Cyprus or to the city of Kition. Defending this last attribution, O. Callot has recently noted that no such bronzes have ever been found at Salamis. One is known from Kourion on the island, while twenty-five have been found in three separate excavations in the region of Kition. He concludes: 'All this leads us to doubt the attribution to Salamis, especially if one accepts that the small bronze units were scarcely circulating outside of the issuing sites, where they were reserved for minor local transactions. Consequently, it seems to me to be more sensible to attribute these issues to the kingdom of Kition.' In the light of the Herakleion finds, coupled with the coins from Naukratis, it must be questioned whether the Cypriote attribution of these coins is correct.

As Callot notes, bronze coinage did not normally travel far in the ancient world, since its value was confined to the area in which it was produced and familiar. Thus the find of a substantial number of bronzes of the same type at one particular site would usually indicate that those bronzes were produced at or near that site. In the case of the lion/horse bronzes, however we encounter a problem. How are we to interpret the find of a large number of these coins at Herakleion?

Two possibilities suggest themselves. The coinage might be reattributed to Egypt, rather than to Cyprus. Given the appearance of the ram's head on the obverse it might be attractive to attribute the coins to Herakleion itself with its major temple of Amon. This would be a bold step, since virtually no other bronze coinage is known from Egypt in the fourth century. Nonetheless, it should not be forgotten that the thirty coins so far known from Herakleion are likely to increase as work continues on the identification of coins in the Maritime Museum. The case for reattribution may come to seem overwhelming on sheer numbers alone. Alternatively, if the coins have been correctly attributed to Kition, the presence of large numbers of them at Herakleion, and perhaps too at Naukratis might be indicative of some form of 'special relationship' between one Cypriot city and the Nile delta, such that its bronze coinage became familiar in Egypt and could circulate in territory outside that of the city of issue (p. 130). This too is a bold suggestion that finds no clear support in the literary record, but a bold suggestion will undoubtedly be necessary to explain this phenomenon.

Ptolemaic and Roman Coins Archaeologists, when invited to study the coin finds from the excavation of an ancient city are often presented with a mass of poorly preserved, base-metal, low value coinage. The stuff of day-to-day transactions, to be sure, this is important material for the interpretation of the ancient economy, but it is only one half of the story. So often the precious metal finds, the silver and gold coins that formed the main-stay of another part of the economy are absent from excavated finds. In part this may be because their ancient owners took far better care of their high value coins than the lower. It is also the result of centuries of opportunistic burrowing by poorer modern inhabitants in search of the imagined wealth of their richer predecessors.

From the coins presented in the pages that follow, it will be clear immediately how the picture offered by the Canopic sites differs from the norm. Hidden for centuries under the sea, and undisturbed by the prying hands of intruders, the cities of Canopus and Herakleion have retained the full range of the ancient coinage used and lost there. The result is a golden opportunity in more ways than one. We find, on the one hand, the spectacular evidence for the wealth of these cities and their inhabitants, in the gold coinages that circulated from the early fourth century BC to the eighth AD (p. 71). These were high-value, and once prized possessions. The gold aureii from the period of the Roman Empire represented about a month's wages to the soldiers who once owned them (cat. no. 494, p. 331). The silver from the fourth century BC, imitations of the coins of Athens (p. 295), the tetradrachms of the great Macedonian general Alexander are less in value, perhaps a week's pay, but demonstrate how Canopus and Herakleion were linked to a broader economy, where silver was the popular medium for monetary exchange. Merchants from around the Mediterranean could call at the harbours of Alexandria and Herakleion and conduct their business in silver coins, and undoubtedly did.

Herakleion and Canopus are uncharacteristically rich in the finds of precious metal coins they have yielded, but the base metal coinages should not be forgotten. Here we are in the realm of everyday exchange. The Ptolemaic kings who succeeded Alexander as rulers of Egypt, closed their borders to foreign coinage and stimulated the use of bronze currency. This trend would continue for over 500 years, through to the Roman province of Egypt. The vast majority of finds from the two sites bear witness to the busy economic activity of this period, and offer a glittering prospect of a reconstruction of the vibrant economic life of the two cities that their appearance belies.

As a whole the coinage from Canopus and Herakleion bears witness, more clearly than any other form of evidence, to the political vicissitudes of the two cities. From their origins in the Pharaonic period as important trading centres, through the conquest of Egypt by Alexander the Great, through the rule of the Macedonian dynasty of the Ptolemies, ending with the fall of the last of their line, the famous Queen Cleopatra, the history is laid out in the coinage. Then came the empires of Rome and Byzantium, continuing the remarkable blend of local productivity and foreign rule that has been the fate of Egypt at so many times in her history.

Precisely, the coin finds from across a city-site such as Herakleion hold out the prospect of tackling broader questions. Herakleion's status as a port inhabited before and after the conquest of Egypt by Alexander the Great in 332 BC offers a – thus far – unique opportunity to examine the change in monetary habit effected by the conquest and the subsequent establishment of the Ptolemaic kingdom and, thereafter, the Roman province of Egypt.

With Alexander in 332 BC the arrival of coinage in the province becomes relatively clear. The establishment of the Ptolemaic dynasty in Egypt initially saw a continuation of Alexander's minting practice, even down to the posthumous use of his coin types. But shortly after his assumption of the royal title in 305 BC Ptolemy I appears to have moved to establish Egypt as a closed monetary zone (cat. nos. 429–433; 443, 446–449, p. 328). All foreigners coming to Egypt were required to exchange their coinage for the official coin of the Ptolemaic realm. This royal coinage was produced, initially at least, in gold, silver and bronze. The evidence for this closed system comes essentially from a single documentary source. A famous papyrus letter of 258 BC from a local official to his superior describes the difficulty he was experiencing in administering the system.

The question that must be asked, however, is how far the bureaucratic theory and intent of the central administration actually obtained in monetary practice within Ptolemaic Egypt. The evidence of coin finds within Egypt offers the only possible test. Against the background of a limited number of published sites and hoards in and from Egypt, Herakleion will offer key evidence for the success of the royal attempt to monopolise coinage. Such a site, situated on the coast and with a pre- and post-Ptolemaic existence, offers a potentially powerful test for the behaviour of coin-users in an area where coinage should have been a familiar phenomenon before the appearance of the Ptolemaic bureaucracy.

The Ptolemaic dynasty's production of coinage was far from uniform, however. Following the creation of a distinctive Ptolemaic coinage in the latter years of Ptolemy I's reign, the silver coinage minted on an idiosyncratic 'Ptolemaic' standard remained in production down to the end of the dynasty. For the most

429 Coin

Gold
Ptolemaic period; Ptolemy I Soter (306–283 BC)
Diam. 1 cm

Gold six-drachma coin of Ptolemy I Soter,
mint of Alexandria.
Obverse: Head of Ptolemy I Soter facing to
the right with diadem and aegis.
Reverse: Eagle left on thunderbolt, wings
open. ΠΤΟΛΕΜΑΙΟΥ ΒΑΣΙΛΕΩΣ.   A. M.

430 Coin

Gold
Ptolemaic period, Ptolemy I Soter (306–283 BC)
Diam. 1 cm

See cat. no. 429.

431 Coin

Gold
Ptolemaic period, Ptolemy I Soter (306–283 BC)
Diam. 0.9 cm

See cat. no. 429.

432 Coin

Gold
Ptolemaic period, Ptolemy I Soter (306–283 BC)
Diam. 1 cm

See cat. no. 429.

433 Coin

Gold
Ptolemaic period, Ptolemy I Soter (306–283 BC)
Diam. 1.1 cm

See cat. no. 429.

429

430

431

432

433

443

446

443 Coin

Silver
Ptolemaic period,
Ptolemy I Soter
(306–283 BC)
Diam. 1.8 cm | wt. 3.83 g

Bronze coin of Ptolemy I
Soter, mint of Alexandria.
Obverse: Head of Alexander facing right with
diadem and ram's horn.
Reverse: Eagle facing left
on thunderbolt, wings
open; to the left, aphlaston. ΠΤΟΛΕΜΑΙΟΥ.
A. M.

446 Coin

Bronze
Ptolemaic period,
Ptolemy I Soter
(306–283 BC)
Diam. 1.7 cm

See cat. no. 443.
Obverse: Head of Alexander facing right with
diadem and ram's horn.
Reverse: Eagle left on
thunderbolt, wings open.
ΑΛΕΞΑΝΔΡΟΥ. (Coin) of
King Ptolemy.   A. M.

447 Coin

Bronze
Ptolemaic period,
Ptolemy I Soter
(306–283 BC)
Diam. 2.73 cm

Silver tetradrachm of
Ptolemy I Soter, mint
of Alexandria.
Obverse Head of Ptolemy
I Soter facing to the right
with diadem and aegis.
Reverse Eagle left on
thunderbolt, wings
closed. ΠΤΟΛΕΜΑΙΟΥ
ΒΑΣΙΛΕΩΣ. (Coin) of
King Ptolemy.   A. M.

448 Coin

Bronze
Ptolemaic period,
Ptolemy I Soter
(306–283 BC)
Diam. 2.75 cm

Obverse: Head of Zeus
facing right, laureate.
Reverse: Eagle standing
left on thunderbolt,
wings open.
ΠΤΟΛΕΜΑΙΟΥ
ΒΑΣΙΛΕΩΣ. (Coin) of
King Ptolemy.   A. M.

449 Coin

Bronze
Ptolemaic period,
Ptolemy I Soter
(306–283 BC)
Diam. 2.75 cm

See cat. no. 448.

447

448

449

part the designs of this coinage remained unchanged, with a head of Ptolemy I on the obverse and the Ptolemaic badge of an eagle on thunderbolt on the reverse. Gold coinage was issued down, probably to the reign of Ptolemy VIII, but almost always has the air of the ceremonial or commemoration in the choice of designs adopted by the issuers. Until the 260s BC, Ptolemaic bronze coinage followed the model of other Greek states, being issued in apparently low denominations to serve as fractions of the higher value precious metal coinage. Under Ptolemy Philadelphos, however, a reform of the bronze led to the introduction of a new bronze system with, most probably, denominations up to the value of one third of a silver tetradrachm. These distinctive large coins, weighing around ninety-six grams, were accompanied by a range of lower denominations. This system remained in place probably until late in the reign of Ptolemy Philopator. From this point the weight of the Ptolemaic bronze coinage began to decline. By the middle of the second century, it seems, only a fraction of the quantity of bronze coinage was being produced that had been in the third century BC. Under the last Ptolemaic ruler, Cleopatra VII, there was something of a revival in the production of bronze, but on a wholly new system. Her coinage, relatively common in collections today, was much reduced in weight and marked with denominational indicators to clarify its worth.

Nevertheless, the finds from the Hellenistic period thus far examined conform to expectations. Of the 222 pieces identified, 219 (ninety-nine per cent) are coins of the Ptolemaic rulers. With the exception of four silver tetradrachms, one gold stater and five gold quarter staters all of these coins are of bronze. The precious metal coins all belong to the reign of Ptolemy I. The bronze is far more difficult to summarise, for two reasons. First, the coins are often in an appalling state of preservation and while it has been possible to attribute them to the Ptolemaic kingdom, it is impossible to read the control marks or form an opinion of their style that would allow closer identification. Second, our understanding of Ptolemaic bronze coinage, though recently improved, is still far from perfect, and uncertainties of attribution exist even for the best-preserved coins. Nonetheless, a few general observations are possible.

While there is a large amount of coinage that can with confidence be contributed to the rules of the third century BC, there is less that can with certainty be attributed to the second century and less still to the first. In part this observation will be a function, perhaps, of the differing amounts of bronze coinage produced over these different periods. A notable absence is the bronze coinage of Cleopatra VII. Numbers of coins of this ruler have now been discovered at Canopus; none have yet been identified from Herakleion. These are still early days for the interpretation of this material, but the current pattern seems to be of a fall off in loss of Ptolemaic bronze coin at Herakleion, perhaps beginning in the early second century BC.

Under Rome, the status of Egypt as a closed currency system is clear from the coinage produced there and again from finds. The Roman administration continued the production of the Ptolemaic silver tetradrachm, which had become heavily debased under Cleopatra VII, and debased it further. These 'Alexandrian tetradrachms' were issued in huge numbers through the second and third centuries AD coming finally to a halt in the reign of Diocletian (284–305 AD). Bronze coins were produced alongside this notionally silver coinage, but petered out as a regular part of the Egyptian monetary system in the reign of Commodus (180–192 AD). These Egyptian coinages were the media by which a closed currency system was maintained in Egypt, uniquely within the Roman Empire, for the best part of three centuries. The Roman silver denarius, which was a standard element of the monetary system throughout the rest of the empire over much the same period, never circulated within Egypt. Following the reforms of Diocletian, Egypt, like the rest of the Roman Empire, was flooded in the fourth century with the standardised Roman bronze coinage.

At Herakleion, the relative absence of Roman material is in stark contrast to other sites excavated in Egypt, and surprising too in the context of the vast emission of coinage by the Roman administration in the province. The (elsewhere) near omnipresent billon tetradrachms of Roman Alexandria are almost entirely absent (only two have so far been observed). The coins of the Roman period are mainly bronze and all but two are from the Antonine period or earlier. Wholly absent thus far is the otherwise ubiquitous fourth-century imperial bronze coinage. On the basis of the numismatic evidence as it currently appears it is difficult to believe that there was significant occupation of, or commercial activity at, the site in the Roman period.

It should be stressed once more, however, that the above discussion, while based on a representative sample of the coins currently excavated from the site, may not necessarily be representative of the site as a whole. Leaving aside the problem of the wrecks still to be excavated from the waterways of the city, the occurrence of which may not necessarily have mirrored the occupation patterns of the city, it is quite possible that the areas of the city currently explored are not wholly representative of the city as a whole. Only time and further excavation will help to resolve this uncertainty. There is much to look forward to. A. M.

494 **Aureus**

Gold
Antoninus Pius (155/156 AD)
Diam. 2 cm

Obverse: Head of Antoninus
laureate facing right. ANTONINVS AVG(VSTVS) PIVS P(ATER) P(ATRIAE)
IMP(ERATOR) II – Emperor Antoninus Pius, Father of the Fatherland, twice
distinguished as conquering commander.
Reverse: Victory advancing left holding wreath and palm. TR(IBVNICIA)
POT(ESTATE) XX CO(N)S(VL) IIII – with tribunal strength for the twentieth
time (155/156 AD), four times consul.   A. M.

98 **Coin**

Bronze
Faustina II (163–170 AD)
Diam. 2.2 cm

Bronze coin in the name of Faustina II, wife of Marcus Aurelius
Antonius   A. M.

EVERYDAY LIFE IN THE CANOPIC AREA

CERAMICS

The explorations and excavations carried out by the IEASM on the sites of Herakleion and Canopus to the east of the Aboukir peninsula and in the port of Alexandria have begun to bring to light some remarkable pottery material, both entire and as sherds. So often the first datable remains of occupation, ceramics, by dint of their manufacture and function, also bear silent witness to daily life. They represent a link in a chain constituted by other archaeological materials, be they small, such as part of an earring, or more imposing, such as a statue or an architectural element.

The ceramics of the region provide a material that has in part, already been investigated for a long time, and in part, has only very recently been the object of research. The ceramics unearthed belong to two categories: Egyptian and imported. Beyond this criterion based on origin, the material may be everyday or else fine ware, as well as amphorae. At this stage in the investigation of this immense site, the first chronological indications, supplied by the study of the ceramics, testify to the occupation of the Herakleion site from the twenty-sixth dynasty to Ptolemaic times. This material is significant because its analysis is of essential importance for the Delta, and, therefore, for Egypt generally. Analogous evidence at East Canopus, at least as available to us presently, starts later, in the fourth century

BC, and demonstrates occupation to the Byzantine period, with significant settlement in the Ptolemaic era on certain excavated zones. In the port of Alexandria, ceramics now encompass a chronological spread from the Ptolemaic period to the Byzantine.

If the underwater archaeological excavations often present specific and disturbed contexts of immersion, it remains nonetheless true that the material recovered to date has revealed coherent ceramological ensembles. Significantly it has permitted an internal chronology to be pinpointed for three sites, further interpretations of their significance to be brought to light, and an approach to the study of the contacts Herakleion and East Canopus had forged with the Mediterranean world prior and subsequent to the foundation of Alexandria to be formulated.

As regards the area of the site prospected to date, it is in the northeast zone of Herakleion that twenty-sixth dynasty (664–525 BC) ceramics are attested. Settlement can be attested through the preponderance of amphorae from Samos, from Milet, renowned for its oil, from Lesbos, from Chios or from Klazomenai (cat. no. 381, p. 299), celebrated for its spiced wine and oil but also for fine ceramics such as the Ionian bowl (cat. no. 409, p. 298) or the fragment of a cup from Chios and of an one-handled

399 Juglet
Ceramic
End of 5th–mid-4th cent. BC
H. 7.6 cm

Caught in a concretion of sand, this piece shows the influence of Greek ceramics. The type and its variants, were common at the time in the area of Herakleion and Canopus. C. G.

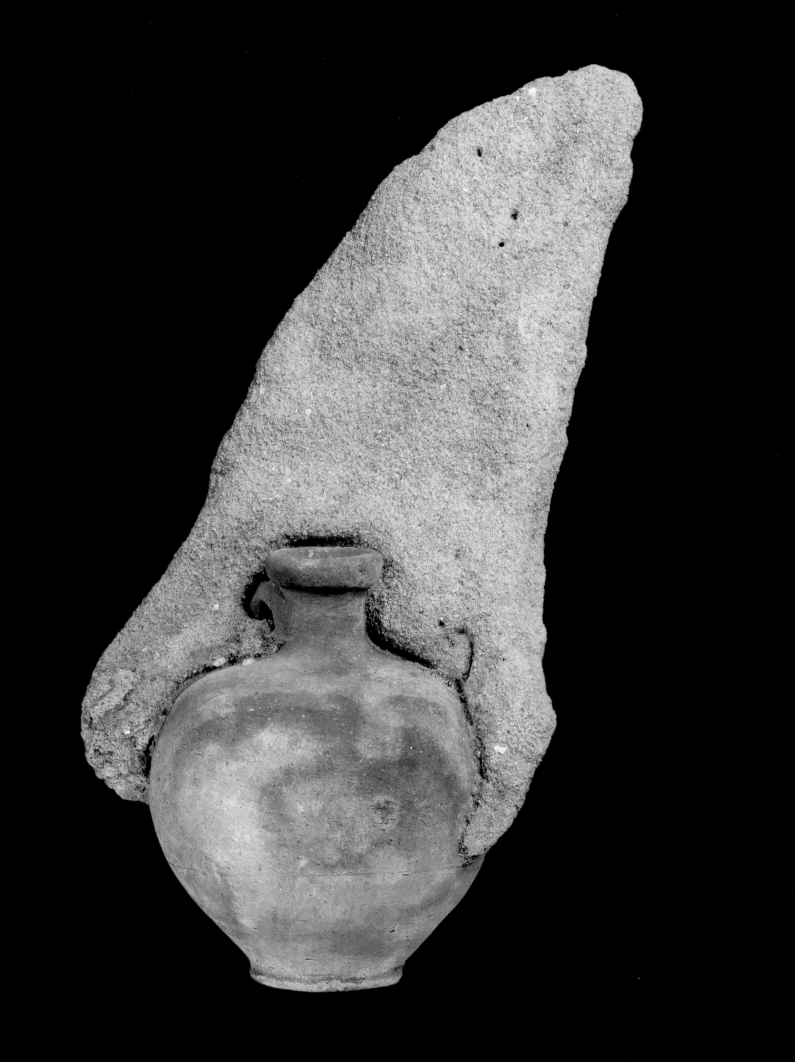

wine jar from northern Ionia in the so-called 'wild goat style', a term for the decoration of ceramic vessels with animal friezes in which the wild goat dominates. Such quantitative superiority is a reflection of the role of the eastern Greeks in the creation, or the development, of Herakleion. Less numerous but no less assured, Corinthian ceramics, in the form of numerous sherds from the beginning of the sixth century BC, manifest contact, direct or not, with the Peloponnesian city, which produced small oil or perfume vases that were widely exported. The end of the Saite era saw more specific relations established with other areas on the borders such as the Levant and Cyprus.

Domestic Egyptian products, manufactured in Nile silt paste from the river's alluvium, are represented by products made for cooking purposes, for example, a cylindrical earthenware jar for storage (cat. no. 403) or a hemispherical one for cooking. The question remains as to whether these local ceramics represent the punctual traces of Egyptian settlement or instead point to relations with the surrounding area.

In contrast the local domestic ware is more frequent (pan, bowl, mortar) in the western zone of the northern canal, with dates ranging between the end of the sixth century BC and the beginning of the fourth century BC. Here can be found not only manifestations of the maintenance of maritime trade with the Levant but equally links with Greece. This is also the case for certain vases for liquids, such as the small marl ware jugs (cat. no. 399, p. 332) in imitation of red-figure fat-bellied *lekythoi*.

But, it is above all the area between the northern and central basins where the vestiges of a port, the foundations of a monument, and the main canal have been discovered, more precisely to the north of the temple district (p. 289), that demonstrates not only the richness and variety of the ceramics brought to this harbour site of cultic importance from the end of the first period of Persian domination around 400 BC and, more especially, during the indigenous dynasties, but also the vitality of the domestic workshops. Hence, primarily in the harbour zones, amphorae originating from the Levant, from Cyprus, from the north of the Aegean Sea, from Thassos, from Mendes (cat. no. 383, p. 300) in Khalkidhikí, have been found. On the other hand, fine ceramics, representing the majority, are more closely associated with sacred sites. There are numerous Attic drinking vessels with black varnish (cat. no. 393, p. 300), bowls, as well as the so-called plain fine ware imported for its quality or aesthetic value. These characteristics are noted in particular on the medallion applied on a vessel with a spout (cat. no. 388, p. 303), a form and motif that also existed in Cyprus. Red-figure ceramics, except for some *krater* fragments from the Classic period (cat. no. 424, p. 44), generally survive in the guise of fat-bellied *lekythoi*. They present a varied gamut of decoration: ornamental bands, palmettes (cat. no. 405, p. 298), a lattice of white dots, or figurative illustration, such as a girl carrying a cosmetic box, or a panther (cat. no. 404, p. 199). But the presence of these Greek imports should not obscure the relations with the eastern zone of the Mediterranean that indeed remain paramount. Herakleion obtained painted table amphorae (cat. no. 384, p. 298) from various centres of production. Such vessels are seldom identified in Egypt, yet are regularly found in Herakleion in contexts from the end of the fifth to the mid-fourth century BC. There is also cup (cat. no. 398, p. 300) from the same decorative repertory.

This distinctive painted decoration is generally associated with eastern Greece, sometimes with Cyprus. If this island does not appear to have been a major import centre for Herakleion, it seems at least to have served as an intermediary zone, providing a stopping-place in the trade with the eastern half of the Mediterranean. This was apparently the origin of an amphoriskos (cat. no. 385, p. 300), which, at the time of its discovery, still contained hazelnut shells – a telling snapshot of daily life that is similarly conveyed by the mortar (cat. no. 406) or basin sometimes called the 'Persian bowl'. Particularly widespread in the fifth and fourth centuries BC, it is equally met with in many sites on the eastern Mediterranean as well as in Egypt.

The presence of Cypriot pottery at Herakleion and at other Delta sites corresponds to the regular exchanges this island maintained with Egypt in spite of the political circumstances. Rarer were contacts with the western Mediterranean, as illustrated by the presence of a vessel from the fourth century BC (cat. no. 408), a product peculiar to the Greek towns of Sicily. The iconography of this vessel corresponds to the status of Dionysos in the Herakleion pantheon (p. 200).

The vitality of certain Egyptian workshops is evident in the frequency of marl ware in clay. Examples number not only juglets of Greek inspiration (cat. no. 400), but also goblets or mugs (cat. nos. 389, 390, p. 343) and bowls (cat. nos. 410, 411, 418, p. 336) that appear recurrently in the same contexts. Many consider these drinking vessels to be particularly thin walled and finely made imitations of metal vases of Persian Achaemenid tradition. A number of imperfectly fired examples betray the proximity of pottery workshops whose presence close to a religious, economic, or administrative centre is hardly surprising, since they manufactured products for everyday needs. The wealth of this imported and local material which was popularly used as votive offerings must be related to the religious complex of the temple area of Amon of the Gereb.

In comparison, the external zones bordering the main canal have yielded far less homogeneous finds. This fact has provided evidence of frequentation in the eastern zone, which due to its proximity to the eastern basins is not surprising, but also in the western zone; in both there are ceramics finds

406 Mortar
Ceramic
Beginning of 5th – beginning
of 4th cent. BC
H. 9.8 cm | diam. 32 cm

400 Juglet
Ceramic
4th cent. BC
H. 10 cm

The ceramic is Egyptian.   C. G.

402 Juglet
Ceramic
4th cent. BC
H. 11.4 cm | diam. 8.8 cm

This is possibly an import from
the Levant.   C. G.

410 **Bowl**
Ceramic
End of 5th–mid-4th cent. BC
H. 9.3 cm | diam. 14.3 cm

411 **Bowl**
Ceramic
Persian period
H.. 5.5 cm | diam. 11.2 cm

This is an imported bowl of Achaemenid type.
C. G.

412 **Bowl**
Ceramic
4th cent. BC
H. 4.8 cm | diam. 13.8 cm

The ceramic is Egyptian.
C. G.

418 **Bowl**
Ceramic
3rd cent. BC
H.. 5.5 cm | diam. 12.6 cm

This is an imported piece from the area of the Aegean.
C. G.

425 **Oil lamp**
Ceramic
End of 6th–5th cent. BC
H.. 2.2 cm | diam. 5.2 cm

426 **Oil lamp**
Ceramic
Mid-4th–beginning of 3rd cent. BC
H. 4.3 cm | diam. 3.4 cm

Like all the lamps found on the site
with their spout intact, this example
bears traces of use. It is finely made
and is of Alexandrian manufacture
based on Athenian examples.   C. G.

from the fifth century BC to the beginning of the Ptolemaic period. Eastern imports have been found here, amphorae from the Levant (cat. no. 382, p. 302), a lamp (cat. no. 425, p. 337), a pot with a high handle (cat. no. 407), and a drinking vessel (cat. no. 397) but also more usual local ware: basins, a 'bread plate' (cat. no. 419), a bowl (cat. no. 412, p. 336), probable evidence of nearby zones of domestic character, notably to the west. Ptolemaic ceramics have also been found here, such as a lamp from Alexandria (cat. no. 426).

From the reigns of the Ptolemies onwards, the ceramic facies at Herakleion alters and can now be compared with material discovered along the entire length of the canal between Herakleion and Canopus. Noteworthy is the preponderant presence of Egyptian ceramics, and, therefore the lower number of imports, except in the case of amphorae from the main centres of Hellenistic production. These 'packaging materials' are of particular interest because of their stamps, which became widespread from the end of the fourth century BC on, when a large number of export cities flourished in the Aegean world. Thanks to the fragments of amphorae issuing from several workshops in southwest Asia Minor, specimens from Knidos with an overhanging lip and imprinted with monograms – examples of early stampings (cat. no. 386, p. 340) – or from Rhodes, it can be observed that Herakleion was maintaining its role as centre of trade. By the second century BC, it can be clearly seen at Canopus how great a role the

coastal region was playing in the Rhodes market; this picture is strengthened by the excavations in Alexandria, where some amphorae from Kos or Knidos have been unearthed, but most of them from Rhodes.

Since the end of the fourth/beginning of the third century BC, the repertoire of Egyptian ceramics for daily use as well as luxury products was inspired primarily by classic Greek pottery, which had hardly been the case before Alexander the Great. The influence and adoption of these imported models surface in changes affecting both the forms and manufacturing processes that had been usual up to that time. Hemispherical bowls with or without stamped palmette decoration (cat. nos. 415, 416, p. 341; 414, 417, p. 343), plates (cat. no. 420, p. 343), fish dishes and cooking ceramics (cat. no. 394) come from Delta workshops that probably lay close to the city, as was the case at Naukratis. In imitation of black glaze, some examples were made without the introduction of oxygen while cooling so as to stain the vase black. Ceramic goblets, of which also examples in bronze were discovered, were found not only in one of these blackened variants (cat. no. 391, p. 344), but also in a form fired in the normal way with oxygen being introduced and with a partial slip (cat. no. 81, p. 344). This kind

397   Kantharos (vessel)
Ceramic
4th cent. BC
H. 8.9 cm | diam. 8.3 cm

Two divided handles begin at the shoulder and end in a (Herakles) knot, a symbol of good fortune. This drinking vessel was only produced over a short period and thus represents an interesting chronological point of reference.   C. G.

407   Olpe
Ceramic
4th cent. BC
H. 15.5 cm

419   Bread plate
Ceramic
Ptolemaic period
H. 17 cm | diam. 2.5 cm

The ceramic is Egyptian.   C. G.

397

407

386 Amphora neck
Ceramic
2nd half of 4th cent. BC
H. 22 cm | diam. 17 cm

On the handle there is a round
monogram stamp. C. G.

394 Chytra
Ceramic
3rd cent. BC
H. 8.5 cm | diam. 7.2 cm

The vessel, with one or two handles, was used for boiling or simmering foodstuffs.
C. G.

416 Bowl
Ceramic
End of 3rd–2nd cent. BC
H. 5.5 cm | diam. 11.2 cm

The ceramic is Egyptian.   C. G.

415 Bowl
Ceramic
Ptolemaic period
H. 4.3 cm | diam. 13 cm

The ceramic is Egyptian.   C. G.

of drinking vessel, which would become a specific dating marker at the beginning of the Roman era, appears in Herakleion from Ptolemaic contexts. Similarly from the start of production in Ptolemaic times, one also notes the use of a red slip that associates these ceramics with *sigillata* products manufactured in the East which, by 125 BC, represent the lion's share of imported ceramics at Alexandria. In the same connection, Alexandrine workshops used a partial slip layer, a technique that appeared at the beginning of the second century BC in several centres of the eastern Mediterranean. Beside such ceramics marked by foreign influences, there were primarily kitchen utensils (cat. no. 392) that have gradually evolved from the pre-Ptolemaic period to our own day.

At Canopus, but not in Herakleion, *sigillata*, a fine ceramic primarily used for tableware, was found in two forms, dating to the time from the end of the second century BC to the beginning of the Roman emperors. The comparison between ceramic material from Canopus and that from Herakleion in the Ptolemaic phase provides evidence that Herakleion was occupied until the second half of the second century BC and then transferred part of its activity to Canopus and Alexandria. Investigations

on Canopus have not yet brought up Roman ceramics of the empire. If the so-called *gawadis* (cat. no. 82) belong to a machine which took water from a well through a lifting-wheel system on which these pots were hung and poured it into the channels through which the land was irrigated, this would show how little such ceramic forms, which are still used, have changed up to the present day.

The most recent ceramic discoveries are amphorae from the late antique period, such as the wine amphora from the region of Gaza (cat. no. 387, p. 346), as well as Byzantine examples manufactured in the eastern Mediterranean between the fourth and seventh centuries BC.

If we turn to the east harbour of Alexandria, a ceramic appears clearly bearing the imprint of the early empire. Testimony from the end of the Ptolemaic period is to date less frequent, but it is attested more particularly in the area around the island of Antirhodos, while excavations of the Timonium have exposed a majority of items dating from the first and second centuries.

Contact with the eastern basin of the Mediterranean is represented by fine ceramics imported from Cyprus, Knidos (cat. nos. 481, 485, p. 384), Asia Minor, and

420 Plate
Ceramic
Ptolemaic period
H. 4 cm | diam. 21.6 cm

390 Mug
Ceramic
End of 5th–mid.-4th cent. BC
H. 13.5 cm
The ceramic is Egyptian.　C.G.

389 Mug
Ceramic
End of 5th–1st half of 4th cent. BC
H. 13 cm | diam. 7.5 cm

The ceramic is Egyptian.　C. G.

414 Bowl
Ceramic
Ptolemaic period
H. 6 cm | diam. 11.2 cm

417 Bowl
Ceramic
2nd cent. BC
H. 6 cm | diam. 13 cm

The ceramic is Egyptian.　C. G.

391 **Mug**
Ceramic
Ptolemaic period
H. 8.7 cm | diam. 5.1 cm

The type of mug or goblet is a relatively infrequent Hellenistic form attested by the occasional specimen from the southern
part of Egypt in Ptolemaic contexts.   C. G.

81 **Mug**
Ceramic
2nd cent. BC
H. 9.3 cm | diam. 5.7 cm

The form is probably inspired by metal models similar to
those found at Herakleion.   C. G.

423 **Unguentarium**
Ceramic
5th–4th cent. BC
H. 9.5 cm | diam. 2.5 cm

This salve bottle is Egyptian ceramic.   C. G.

392 **Bowl**
Ceramic
5th–4th cent. BC
H. 9 cm | diam. 35 cm

Of Pharaonic tradition, this bowl modelled out of a clay made from Nile silt was probably used in making bread.   C. G.

82   Gawadis (Ladle)
Roman-Byzantine
H. 27 cm | diam. 14.2 cm

amphorae from Rhodes, for example. Such an import profile is not specific to pottery in Alexandria, being found on other sites to the east of Alexandria and, in addition, in the northern Sinai peninsula.

Yet, even if these bonds were sustained, an opening to the western arena of the Roman world could be felt, which was not unconnected with the annexation of Egypt to the Roman Empire in 30 BC and to the Roman peace reigning over the entire Mediterranean basin. Evidence of this is provided by the wine amphorae from Crete (cat. no. 486, p. 385), the *sigillatae* and amphorae from Gaul, amphorae from Beatica, in which the famous fish sauce was presented, and those from Tripolitania, exported, especially between the second and the beginning of the third centuries AD for the oil trade. Everyday pottery associated with this commerce, such as oil lamps, have also survived (cat. nos. 492, 493, p. 347). It should be remarked that at the beginning of the early empire, fine ceramic products were mainly imported, a situation that was to change essentially about the middle of the second century.

At this time, new forms of local cookware products emerged that were inspired by Hellenistic models but reveal particular developments, as demonstrated by the cooking pots, for example (cat. nos. 482, 483, p. 348).

The repertory of fine ceramics was also renewed at the beginning of the empire, as can be observed on a goblet (cat. no. 487, p. 349) or an oil lamp (cat. no. 491, p. 347), but the most significant witnesses for a revival of local products are, on the one hand, the imitations of Cypriot *sigillata* (cat. no. 488, p. 349), such as bowls, some decorated with *guilloches*, which appeared by the first half of the second century BC, and on the other, containers for liquids with a striated bowl marked by characteristic elongation (cat. no. 490, p. 349). A mortar is among the few discoveries from the late antique (cat. no. 484, p. 348).

Continuing excavations will surely yield much additional information about the daily life of this site; ceramic research could contribute by showing possible developments in the trade relations of the Egyptian delta with the whole of the Mediterranean basin and connecting these with the commercial and political developments of the region.   C. G.

387

491 **Oil lamp**
Ceramic
Roman period
H. 3 cm | diam. 7.5 cm

Despite its common
form, the imagery on
this lamp is intriguing.
It can be identified as
a drinking vessel of
Herakles flanked by a
pair of cudgels.   C. G.

493 **Oil lamp**
Ceramic
End of 2nd cent. AD
H. 4 cm | diam. 5.7 cm

492 **Oil lamp**
Ceramic
2nd cent. AD
H. 4.6 cm | diam. 5.7 cm

The lamp is decorated
with the profile bust of
a male figure wearing
a toga.   C. G.

387 **Gaza amphora**
Ceramic
4th–mid-5th cent. AD
H. 46.5 cm

482 Chytra (pot)
Ceramic
Second half of 1st cent. BC
H. 28 cm | diam. 17.5 cm

The cooking pot is of fine craftsmanship and perfectly preserved, and, in its characteristics, particularly the rim, is typical of Egyptian production from the end of the Ptolemaic period that can also be found in Upper Egypt.   C. G.

483 Cooking pot
Ceramic
1st–3rd cent. AD
H. 12.2 cm | diam. 14 cm

484 Mortar
Ceramic
Roman period
H. 9.5 cm | diam. 37.8 cm

This mortar bears the name of its maker, KACCI \ ANOY, (work) of Kassianos, whose exports from Syria reoccur in Cyprus and Alexandria.   C. G.

487 Mug
Ceramic
1st cent. AD
H. 6.8 cm | diam. 6.4 cm

488 Bowl
Ceramic
2nd cent. AD
H. 5.9 cm | diam. 10.8 cm

This bowl is a local imitation of sigillata produced in Cyprus at the beginning of the first century.   C. G.

490 Jug
Ceramic
2nd cent. AD
H. 35 cm

This jug with grooves characteristic of certain Alexandrine products from the early empire was probably produced by two people; the rather fine work of the grooves contrasts strikingly with the heavy neck that is roughly connected with the body. This is most probably explained by the fact that 'two hands' were involved in its production.   C. G.

THE BEGUILING SCENT OF ARABIA
AN INCENSE BURNER

In contrast to the multitude of Egyptian-style sphinxes in the exhibition, this piece depicts a common form of the Greek-style sphinx: feminine, winged, crowned and sitting upon its splayed haunches. The piece is broken at the front legs and at the hind legs where the statue would have been the most vulnerable. The proper right side has suffered serious corrosion from underwater exposure including the erosion of all of the finer details. The left side and front of the piece show that the sickle-shaped wings were divided into schematic feathered sections which were likely painted to add more intricate detail. There is the bare suggestion of the chest cavity's ribs and on the lower abdomen attention was paid to modelling eight teats. The shoulders project beyond the chest, while the neck and head are set back from it, creating the disjunctive anatomy common on Attic sphinxes. The facial features consist of wide almond-shaped eyes and a broad full-lipped smile. The sphinx wears a collar of rounded shapes from which long, lozenge-shaped pendants hang. The hairstyle consists of a single row of tightly curled ringlets, which fall backwards over the shoulders in a similar style to the archaic *kourai*. The crenellated crown and the wings of the piece support the incense dish.

Greek sphinxes are commonly feminine, as opposed to the male Egyptian sphinxes. However their meaning was similar: in Greece the sphinx was a guardian, commonly used in the Archaic period as a decoration on grave steles and as free standing commemoration of battles. The details of the incense burner, compared to the dimensions of archaic sphinx statues from Attica, date the piece to the sixth century BC.   E. L.

136   **Incense burner**
Limestone
6th cent. BC
H. 24.2 cm | w. 9 cm |
d. 12 cm | diam. bowl 13.5 cm

EGYPTIAN STONE AND METAL ITEMS

In ancient Egypt stone supplied a natural material with a wide range of uses and colours to suit any taste. The geographical positioning of the land allowed various natural veins of stone to be explored and mined as early as the pre-dynastic period. Due to the landscape of Egypt, limestone is the most ubiquitous rock found and was the stone most used for building construction and some statuary. Harder stones which were more costly, such as granite and diorite, were often laboriously quarried in Assuan at the southern border of the country or in the Sinai peninsula. Many of the mining sites of the pre-dynastic period and Old Kingdom remained in use during the New Kingdom and possibly into the Graeco-Roman period.

While gold and hard stone such as granite were more often used to fashion the images of the ruler and the gods, less costly stones were available to the common people. Semi-precious stones such as carnelian and garnet were commonly drilled to make beads, along with the common beads of faience. Besides their use for jewellery, these stones were worked into statues for temple use, into amulets for the petitioners, as well as into jars, bowls and vessels for private and royal use. Depictions in tombs at Sakkara and Thebes depict the use of spiral drills or bow-drills to hollow out the stones which would later become bowls, jars and vases. The representation of the use of these drills can be found in tombs ranging in time from between the sixth to the twenty-sixth dynasties (around 2100–525 BC) The painting illustrated here from a tomb of the fifteenth century BC shows carpenters using this device.

Polishing of the exterior of the vessel would have been done with sand and chunks of stone. The production of long-held Egyptian traditions and crafts, such as the making of stoneware would have changed little since the Old Kingdom while artistic taste for the market changed rapidly during the Hellenistic and Roman periods.

A few of the stone vessels in this exhibition, in particular those with square lug handles (cat. no. *139*; cat. nos. 138, 140, 142, p. 354), portray an artistic taste prevalent during the Ptolemaic and Roman periods. The remainder of the vessels shown here are not of Egyptian late period styles but rather of standard shapes which had been made there for ages (cat. nos. 122, 126, p. 196; 134, p. 354; *123*). Stoneware found in Herakleion bears witness to a variety of forms such as were in daily use during the Late Pharaonic and Graeco-Roman period. Finer stones, such as alabaster would have been used for ointment and perfume bottles (cat. nos. 147, p. 354) associated with the bedroom or toiletries.

Carpenters at work with a spiral drill or bow-drill, fifteenth century BC

150 **Headrest**
Limestone
6th – 2nd cent. BC
H. 18 cm | w. 26.5 cm

149 **Headrest**
Limestone
6th – 2nd cent. BC
H. 17 cm | w. 26.5 cm

148 **Headrest**
Limestone
6th – 2nd cent. BC
H. 19.5 cm | w. 27 cm

The form is known for headrests of smaller size from the Old Kingdom on.   D. F.

133 **Gravestone**
Marble
Ptolemaic period
H. 20 cm | w. 45 cm | d. 20 cm

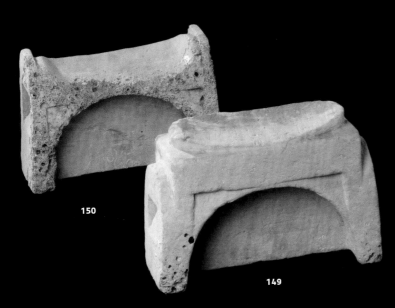

150

148

149

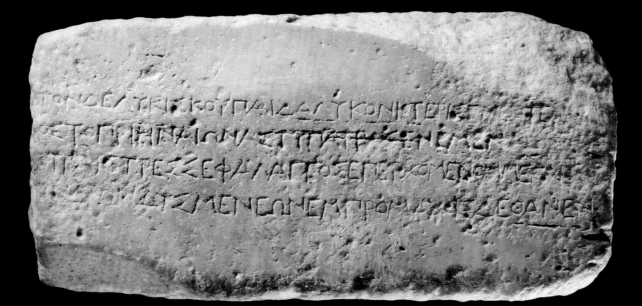

133

138 **Mortar**
Black granite
6th–2nd cent. BC
H. 14 cm | diam. 37.5 cm

134 **Pot**
Alabaster
6th–2nd cent. BC
H. 6.7 cm | diam. 7.5 cm

147 **Ointment vessel**
Alabaster
6th–2nd cent. BC
L. 15 cm | diam. 2 cm

140 **Mortar**
Black granite
6th–2nd cent. BC
H. 30 cm | diam. 32 cm

142 **Pestle**
Black granite
6th–2nd cent. BC
L. 27 cm | diam. 9.1 cm

134

147

143

135 Pot
Alabaster
6th–2nd cent. BC
H. 9.8 cm | diam. 13.5 cm

143 Millstone
Red granite
6th–2nd cent. BC
Diam. 120 cm | d. 28 cm

145 Grindstone
Volcanic stone
6th–2nd cent. BC
H. 10 cm w. 65 cm | d. 42 cm

322 **Bronze utensil**

Bronze
5th–2nd cent. BC
H. 6.7 cm | l. 35.8 cm | d. 2.8 cm

The object has an oval-shapped flattened section, a long handle and animal protome. Its flattened end is a little worn but the main details of the pattern, repeated on both of its surfaces, can be made out. The shape is suggestive of a recumbent figure or cat. Another animal, resembling a lion with horns, adorns the end of the handle, its shoulders rising out of a ribbed section at the end of the handle. The figure is very detailed. The teeth and mane, for example, have been clearly marked, the tongue lolls out of its mouth as if panting, one of the horns is now missing. A shallow hole has been bored into its back, near the handle, possibly as a means of attaching a protome. There is a second, deeper hole between the legs of the animal. A small triangular piece of metal, drawn out to a point, projects downwards from the chest of the lion.

The function of the object is uncertain. It bears a resemblance to censer arms, seen depicted on the walls of temples. However the object highlighted here does not have the characteristic hand shape usually found at the end of the censer arm, nor a storage area for incense pellets. The marks underneath the protome suggest that it may once have been attached to something else.   Z. C. | D. F.

299 **Ring**

Bronze
6th–2nd cent. BC
L. 9.5 cm | diam. 4.3 cm | d. 1.2 cm

The bronze ring with short hook has the form of a duck's head, whose details are well modelled. Each eye is stamped as one circle with a point inside each circle. During the late Pharaonic, Ptolemaic and Roman periods, the head and neck of ducks were the most common form in decorations, particularly ladles' handles (p. 196). The offerings tables from the Old Kingdom downward show that ducks and geese were among the different offerings. Various scenes show also that these birds were sacrificed by twisting their necks. So it is probable that making the handles in the form of bird's necks and heads symbolises that ceremonial tradition in ancient Egypt.   A. A–R. R.

294 **Weights**

Bronze
6th–2nd cent. BC
L. 03–1.2 cm | w. 0.3–1.2 cm | wt. 0.45–7.13g

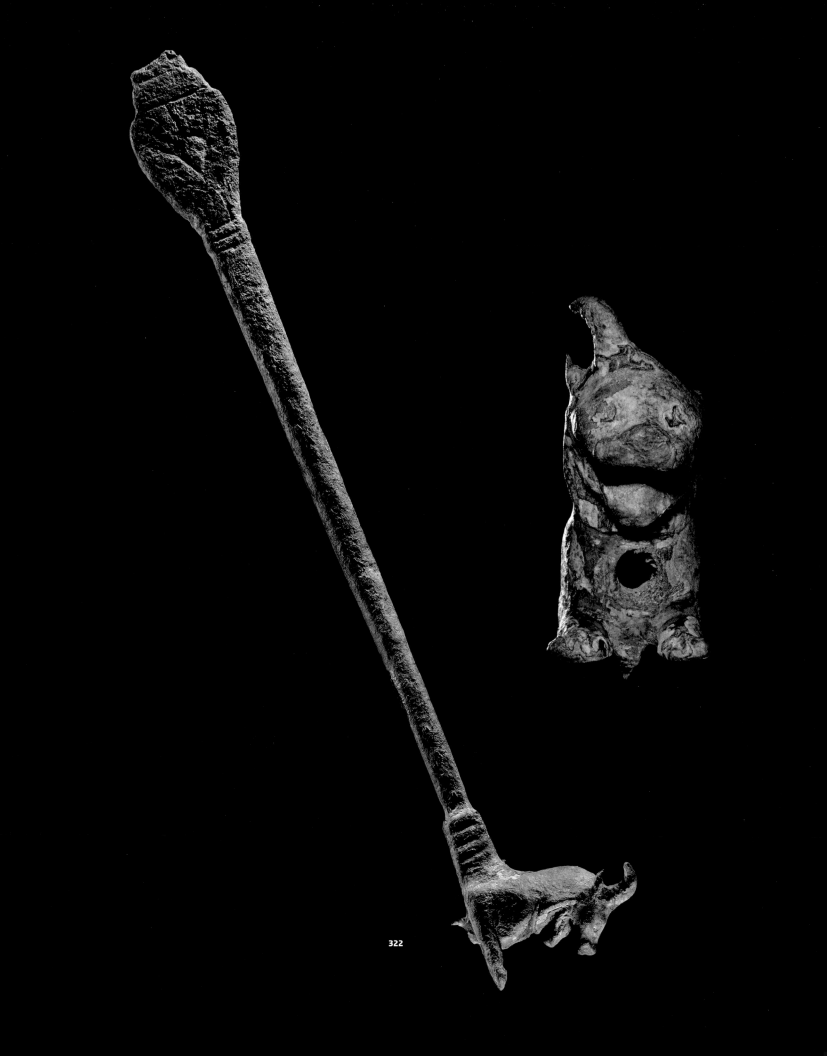

362 Ingot

Lead
6th–2nd cent. BC
H. 11 cm | w. 47 cm | d. 16.5 cm

Ingot marked with three stamps reproduced in pairs: the letters VA and depictions of a flute-player and an acrobat (?).   D. F.

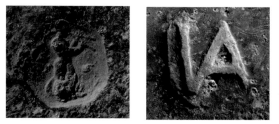

355 Feeding-bottle

Lead
6th–2nd cent. BC
H. 2.5 cm | diam. 5 cm

73 Miniature mirror

Lead
Roman period
H. 2.5 cm | diam. 4.4 cm | d. 0.3 cm

The mirror depicts the Three Graces.   D. F.

Other objects such as a mill stone (cat. no. 143, p. 357), a grindstone (cat. no. 145, p. 357), mortars and pestles or plates made of granite and volcanic hard stone would have been used for food preparation in open areas such as the kitchen or courtyard.

The collection of metal artefacts within this exhibition accurately mirrors the amount of these metals in use in ancient Egypt: During the Pharaonic period, the main metals used would have been gold, silver, copper (and bronze; cat. nos. 294, 299, 322, p. 358) and more rarely lead (cat. nos. 355, 362, p. 360) or iron. The introduction of both iron goods and lead came about in the later New Kingdom during a period of interactions between the court of Amenophis III and the Hittites of present-day Turkey (1391–1353 BC). Metals were often used to cover temple doors and cult statues or amulets for the elite of the society, much as semi-precious stones would have functioned for the commoner's pendants. Although scarce, examples of beads with silver or gold foil are known from both Egyptian and Nubian cemeteries during this period.

The majority of metal objects displayed here are examples of votive statuettes either used by petitioners of deities at local temples or worn during daily life for protection and blessings. Such bronze statuettes would have been made by the hollow cast method (p. 366). Such a process not only allowed for satisfactory methods of ancient 'mass-production' but also allowed for fine details rendered in the wax model to be retained. As with the stone artefacts mentioned above, little innovation would have been used in the construction of such objects, only changing the current jewellery or clothing styles. Of particular note is a Roman mirror from the city of Canopus (cat. no. 73, p. 360). The use of lead alone dates the mirror to the very late Ptolemaic period at earliest. The scene on the back is of the Three Graces, beautiful maidens, personifying Youth, Beauty and Purity. These three goddesses, popular throughout the ancient Hellenistic and Roman world, were often depicted in sculpture, painting and jewellery.   E. M.

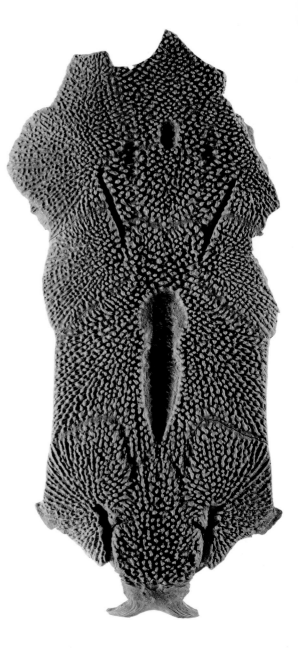

455   **Bone from the skull of a Nile catfish**

6th – 2nd cent. BC

The Nile catfish was a frequent food and entered into cycles of barter in the eastern Mediterranean.   D. F.

Four fish-hooks (cat. nos. 304–307) were found at a warehouse site in Alexandria. Some corrosion is evident, but the hooks are remarkably well preserved. All are fashioned in bronze and display a typical J-form used by present-day fishermen. Bronze or copper alloy wire provided ancient hook makers with a low corrosive material with significant tensile strength and malleability to produce a hook with curved definition and a sharp barb to increase catching potential and on which to attach bait.

Although similar in profile, each hook displays variations in size and thickness. The shanks are straight or slightly curved with a sharp barb visible on the inner side. The shaft-tips end in a flattened spade to facilitate line attachment, rather than the more common eyed-ring found in many modern fish-hooks. Variations in shaft dimensions are evident, from the extended length of cat. no. 304 to the relatively short cat. no. 305. Hooks with longer shafts would have been used in rod fishing or handlining in which many hooks could be attached one after another, and the long shaft would have prevented aggressive fish from biting the line to escape. The smaller hooks could similarly have been used in rod fishing and handlining and possibly on longlines. These examples display what, in present-day fishing parlance, would be termed an 'ideal' form, demonstrating that Alexandrian fishermen had access to high quality fishing gear.

In an archaeological context, the fish-hooks offer a valuable glimpse of contemporary fishing practices. The length, thickness and curvature of the shaft, and the weight and placement of the barbs are clear indications that the profile of the hooks were made for a specific fish or body of water. A. A-R. R.

305 **Fish-hook**
Bronze
6th–2nd cent. BC
L. 2.4 cm | d. 0.2 cm

306 **Fish-hook**
Bronze
6th–2nd cent. BC
L. 5.9 cm | d. 0.3 cm

307 **Fish-hook**
Bronze
6th–2nd cent. BC
L. 2.9 cm | d. 0.2 cm

304 **Fish-hook**
Bronze
6th–2nd cent. BC
L. 12 cm | d. 0.35 cm

LET IT BE RECOGNISABLE TO ALL
ATHENA'S DECORATIVE HELMET CREST

193   Statuette of Athena
Bronze
Ptolemaic period
H. 9.2 cm | w. 2.8 cm | d. 1.4 cm

Athena is recognisable by her hairstyle, helmet and the drape of her dress.

312   Helmet crest
Bronze
4th cent. BC
H. 81 cm | w. 34 cm | d. 5 cm

Athena, c. 370 BC
(ill. p. 365, left)

At the top of the Corinthian-style helmet crest is an arched band, linking it to the helmet and supporting an arched rectangular holster, in which horse hairs were implanted, in imitation of a horse's mane. From the back of the holster a long horse's tail falls softly, the tufts of hair in tangled waves. The workmanship is of exceptional technical and artistic quality. It must have belonged to a statue of incredible dimensions, raising the question as to who the personality was whose importance would have justified such a monument. Without being able to fully rule out a deserving general or a sovereign displaying his military worth, such an honour usually fell to a divinity. Much more than Aries, god of war, it was the goddess of the army, Athena, who enjoyed great popularity. She was usually represented with a Corinthian-style helmet on her head (or in her hand). More particularly, we see her in a helmet with a crest of this type, furnished with a long wavy horse's tail, on Apulian vases from the fourth century BC and on terracotta figurines in from the third century BC Athens.

Of course, it is not possible to date the effigy from which this crest came on the sole basis of this kind of information, but its style and the high quality of its execution might well suggest that it came from an enormous bronze effigy of Athena, perhaps either an original from the fourth century BC or an excellent replica.

212 **Miniature sarcophagus with**
a figurine of a shrew
Bronze
6th – 2nd cent. BC
H. 3.5 cm | w. 7 cm | d. 1.7 cm

Mummified shrews were common and they were carefully
looked after in boxes made of bronze or wood. D. F.

216 **Seat**
Bronze
6th – 2nd cent. BC
H. 9.3 cm | w. 15 cm | d. 3.9 cm

The armrests and the back of this seat for a statuette are
decorated with various carved designs. The seat rests on a
base, which would have been inserted into another piece.
The base appears to be inscribed with hieroglyphics,
though these are no longer legible. D. F.

172 **Statuette of Bastet**
Bronze
6th – 2nd cent. BC
H. 16 cm | w. 10 cm

This is the lower part of a cast statuette of a cat sitting down
whose head and front paws are missing. Cat statuettes like
this, the image of Bastet of Bubastis, were very popular during
the late Dynastic period and the Ptolemaic era. A. A-R. R.

EXCURSUS:
EGYPTIAN METALWORK

Among the easiest Egyptian objects to recognise are
deities in human and animal form, which were produced in their thousands as bronze figures in the
Late period and Ptolemaic period and, nowadays,
turn up in more or less every museum collection.
Widely varying in size, style, material and quality,
the works offer a glimpse of the artistic and religious practices of the Egyptians.

Bronze is a general term for alloys of copper
and tin, to which lead and zinc can be added. There
are great reserves of copper ore in the Sinai Peninsula and the Egyptian eastern desert, and the earliest examples of copper workings in Egypt go back to
the pre-dynastic period. If copper is mixed with
about ten per cent tin, a metal is created that has
a lower melting point, is hard, flows more easily
and produces sharper edges. Although bronze was
known in the Old Empire, it found more widespread
use only in the New Empire. In the Third Intermediate Period, the Egyptians learnt how to use different
alloys for different purposes. Bronze mixtures containing up to thirty per cent lead were not suitable
for weapons or tools but were easy to cast in moulds.

212

216

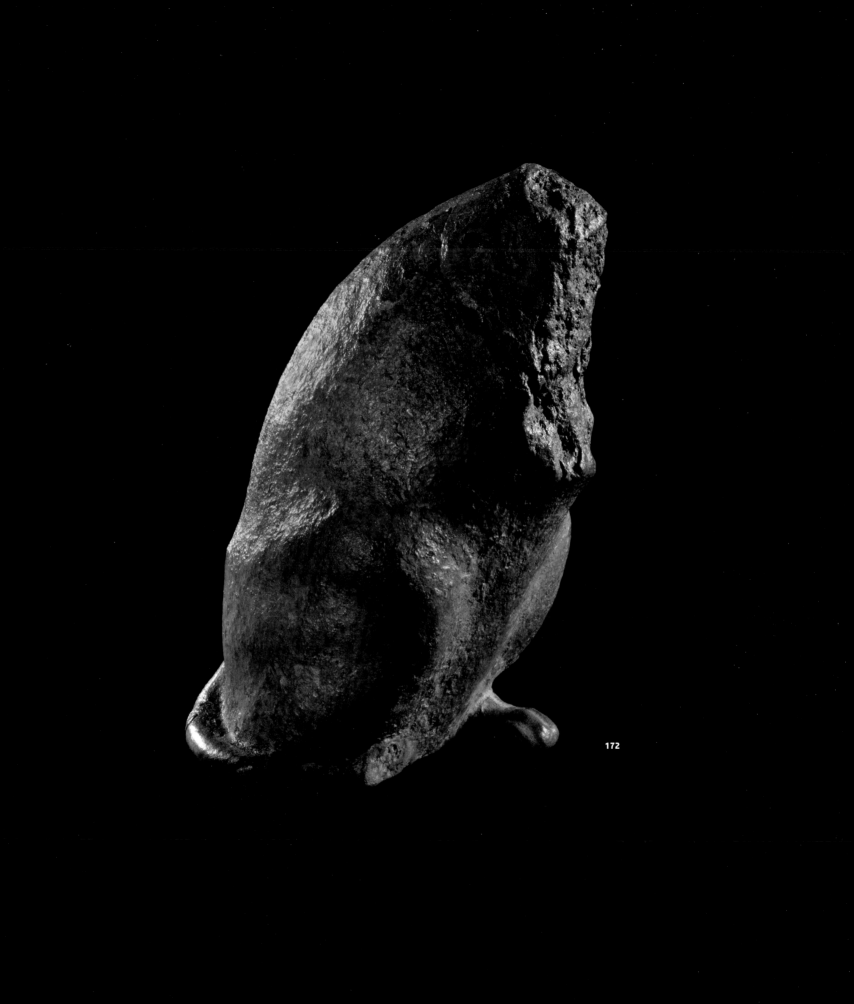

172

Pure lead objects such as those also exhibited here (cat. no. 213, p. 125; 330, p. 124) come from the late phase of the Ptolemaic/Roman period. Different colour metals could be produced by means of other alloy ratios, and thoroughly polished bronze with a high tin content looks almost like much more expensive gold. The products of Egyptian metalworkers were valued not only in Egypt – a considerable number of Egyptian bronzes were for example found buried in the Temple of Hera on Samos as well.

The most widespread method of manufacturing metal statues was the lost wax process. In this, a wax model was covered in a casing of clay, and then heated so that the wax melted and ran out. Subsequently, liquid metal was poured into the empty cavity to produce a metal replica of the wax original. Once this was removed from the mould, the metal could be further processed. Details could be brought out and surfaces polished, gilded and provided with inlays, although processing refinements of this kind are largely missing from the objects now recovered from the sea. Objects involving complex manufacturing processes such as the *atef* crown of Osiris were cast in several parts and then put together (cat. nos. 205–208, 326). To get at the object, the clay mould had to be broken, so that each cast is in principle a one-off. But in the case of more

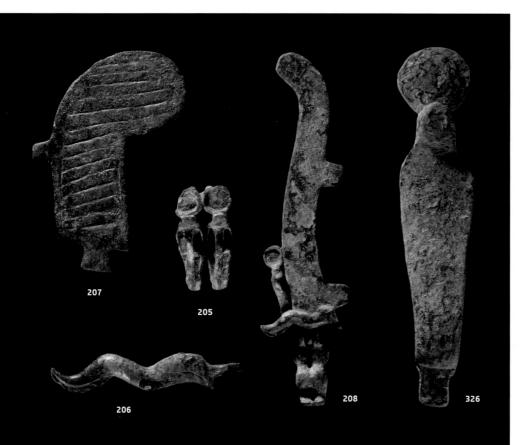

207 **Part of a crown**
Bronze
6th–2nd cent. BC
H. 12.3 cm | d. 0.7 cm

Bronze ostrich feather from an *atef* crown. T. H.

206 **Part of a crown**
Bronze
H. 10.7 cm | w. 1.3 cm
6th–2nd cent. BC

The ram's horn from the *atef* crown has a tenon with which it was fixed to the central part of the crown, while the ostrich feather was inserted into a groove. D. F.

205 **Part of a crown**
Bronze
6th–2nd cent. BC
H. 6.1 cm | w. 3.1 cm | d. 1.8 cm

Double *uraeus*-snake with solar discs. At the back of the latter are two hanging rings, which form part of a hinge usually attached under the ram's horn of the *atef* crown. Note that the cobra tails stretch vertically along the body to the top of the head, where they finally coil up and link together, thus forming the two hanging rings. D. F.

208 **Part of a crown**
Bronze
6th–2nd cent. BC
H. 18.9 cm | w. 4.2 cm | d. 0.6 cm

This formed part of a crown, probably the *atef* crown worn by Osiris and other deities, made separately and attached by the tenons at top and bottom. T. H.

326 *Uraeus*-snake
Lead
6th–2nd cent. BC
H. 19 cm | w. 4.2 cm

The fire-spitting *uraeus* serpent, associated with a number of powerful goddesses, was placed on royal crowns to protect the wearer. In an architectural context, shrines and royal baldachins could also be protected by rows of guardian *uraei*. The tenon on the bottom of this specimen, and its large size, suggest that it was mounted in such a setting. T. H.

ordinary types of object such as the statues depicted here, it is more probable that the wax originals were themselves at least partly cast in moulds so as to enable the production of large numbers of similar works.

In its simplest form, the lost wax process produces a solid cast, but this is a waste of metal and also produces extremely heavy objects. A more economical use of the technique is hollow casting. The wax model is built round a solid core normally made of sand or clay, which is fixed by pegs projecting into the clay casing. After casting, the core could be left in place, or removed if the remaining cavity could be used as a container (cat. nos. 212, 172).

Inscriptions that record the contents of a treasury or the royal gifts for a temple show what enormous quantities of gold, silver and bronze were in circulation in Egypt, even though only a tiny fraction of these precious metal items of antiquity have survived unchanged to the present time, since in times of emergency objects were melted down for their metal content. For this reason, statues of divinities and parts of temple fittings have survived better than images of individuals and domestic objects. If shrines were reconstructed or cleared of old objects, the sacred character of the sacrifices and fittings required them to be got rid of in a respectful fashion within the temple precinct – as it were, buried with due ritual rather than melted down and used them for something else. Troves of this kind were for example found in Karnak and Saqqara.

Whereas some of the statuettes were part of clothing or worn as amulets, there were counterparts among the bronzes listed here, mainly among the votive offerings – gifts to shrines to secure the goodwill of a particular deity or made in fulfilment of a vow. Inscriptions on the base of votive offerings (cat. nos. 216, p. 366; *185*) normally contain a formulaic text: 'May God X grant life to Person A, the son/daughter of B and C.' In many cases, the object also served as a reliquary and contains the mummified remains of an animal that was linked with the deity depicted, cats sacred to Bastet, falcons sacred to Horus and/or ibises sacred to Thoth. Votive images were made of many diverse materials such as clay, wood, earthenware and glass, but metal was particularly suitable. Gold and silver were con-

sidered to be the skin and bones of the gods, and a series of particularly splendid figures were manufactured in this way. The number of votive gifts found illustrates the popularity of the cults of particular gods. Most commonly Osiris, god of the dead, must have been depicted. But also Osiris's wife Isis and her Horus were popular subjects and were normally represented in the shape of Isis as Harpocrates (p. 117), as the Greeks transcribed the Egyptian term *Hor-pa-hered*, i.e. Horus as a child. The earthly incarnation of Horus was Pharaoh himself, and from the Ptolemaic time on, the royal iconography often stressed the relationship between the kind and queen and Horus and Isis.

The sheer number of votive bronzes of this kind often create an impression of paralytic uniformity, and they are therefore difficult to date. Some pieces can be labelled with the name of a king or donor whose career can be definitely attributed to a particular period. A chronological attribution on the basis of style is however difficult. Pictures of gods are standardised and less subject to variations than personal portraits. A clear stylistic development is the introduction of Hellenistic motifs from the Ptolemaic period. Compare the Greek-inspired pictures of Harpocrates (cat. nos. 329, 330, p. 124) with their counterparts in the Egyptian style. Apart from that, from the Egyptian Late Period until well into the Roman period small uninscribed bronzes of deities such as those exhibited here were made in large quantity. However, the precise dating is dependent on the context in which they were discovered.   T. H.

THE 'ROYAL QUARTERS' OF ALEXANDRIA

Underwater excavations off Alexandria have facilitated a detailed cartography of the eastern port and its approaches. This research has been instrumental in determining its basic shape and, in places, in acquiring a picture of the installations and buildings that at one time rose near the palace: the royal port, the Timonium, the island of Antirhodos and the ancient breakwaters. This has transformed our topographical knowledge of the harbour infrastructure that served the city. Lying on the seafront, this complex comprised a succession of government buildings and cultural facilities. The Ptolemies, in choosing to have close by them scholars of the Greek world, expressed both their desire to yoke knowledge to power and their concern to keep abreast of Greek culture.

This said, a rapid overview of the plans drawn up by the IEASM and the photographs taken by its divers does not permit the debris of the various palaces and temples to be identified precisely. What could be seen were stretches of waste ground littered with more or less dense concentrations of collapsed constructions and half-abandoned demolition sites strewn with sculptures and inscribed blocks predating Alexander. Limestone blocks seemed few and far between, while chunks of harder stones were more plentiful. In fact the appearance of the submerged 'royal quarters' of Alexandria that had been saved from the invasions of the modern city very closely resembled sites of large stone temples, themselves preserved from medieval or more recent occupation, in Lower Egypt. Nevertheless, these vast underwater clumps of remains, the columns and capitals, the blocks of granite, basalt, calcite, limestone, and the sculptures, amphorae, and anchors, have now been surveyed and have been identified as belonging to dams, moles, harbour basins, as well as to the pavements and colonnades of palatial monuments.

The many dives required by the IEASM program have confirmed the locality of the sunken palaces and ports, though initially these dream-like landscapes seemed little more than mysterious-looking debris. What had the sculptures and inscriptions encountered represented in their time? How, when, and by what natural or manmade processes had the crowning glory of the pharaonic world been reduced to such a dilapidated state? The results obtained from successive campaigns have radically overhauled our knowledge of the topography of the ports and palaces of Alexandria. Study of the harbour basins was extended in an effort to determine the depth and type of sedimentation and locate wrecks, as well as to draw up an adequate plan of the quays. The survey and inspection of the many architectural elements found in the palace zone were accompanied by excavations designed to determine the chronology of the buildings and of the abandonment and destruction of the various sites.

Technically speaking, the ports were rationally arranged. The entrance to the basins was well protected from swell and waves and the island of Antirhodos possessed its own small port serving as an ideal haven. The Poseidium would have been located on the peninsula. This new topographic map, corresponding on the whole to indications in the ancient authors, was based directly on concrete realities as measured in the field. These observations have made it possible to account for the choice of the site of the ancient port and its architecture in engineering terms.

The rock crests that lie flush and those which emerged in ancient times are characterised by the presence or absence of a sap line. Cleared ground from vast construction zones has been identified, preserved by immersion from being covered or subsiding like the parts of the ancient city that remained above the surface in medieval, modern, or contemporary times. It is as yet far from possible to date the installations and the transformations of each sector, to designate or name the constructions which might have existed, or to determine or date the circumstances which brought them to their present ruined and disorderly state.

Important observations may nonetheless be advanced: on the western slope of Cape Lochias, the ancient coast with its peninsula and the island, the ground is strewn with limestone pavements that have preserved continuity and coherence, except in a few places where they have suffered marginal crumbling or localised break-up. The esplanades themselves bear only ruins, huge architectural fragments with a peppering of sculptural remnants forming a massive and more or less dispersed heap of stone.

The now immersed ancient shore, including its two peninsular prolongations, is thus covered in an almost continuous series of layers of blocks lying every which way, with whole or fragmented column barrels of various types and modules, capitals and bases of scattered columns, chunks of entablature, and ashlar. These architectural elements were cut from rocks such as limestone, marble, red granite and other diverse granitoids, and quartzite. In places, there are monoliths from pre-Alexandrine pharaonic temples that were obviously reemployed as rough work in walls. At one point, brash from a

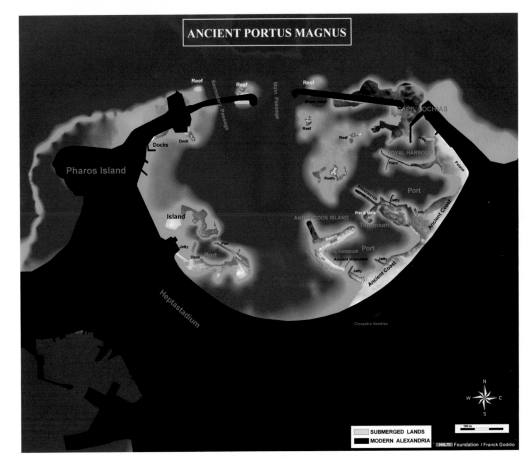

Chart showing the sunken areas, buildings and monuments around the harbour of Alexandria, based on research and excavation work carried out by IEASM.

stonecutting shop can be discerned. Between the concentrations of stone blocks, a few structures can be localised in situ from the sturdy limestone walls remaining in place or, more less frequently, from remnants of fired-brick walls. All in all the ancient coast possesses much the same appearance as the contiguous band of shore remaining on land as it was described by members of the Egyptian Expedition and by nineteenth-century visitors.

Even in antiquity, monuments built under the Ptolemies and Roman emperors suffered terrible depredations, the direct or indirect consequences of tectonic and human phenomena by which they were periodically upended or devastated (pp. 58–70). As a result, elements originally from the same monument were found at different sites sometimes extremely distant from one another. In the Ptolemaic and Roman periods blocks removed from older monuments were incorporated in new structures. Columns were reused either in situ, or after removal, first in churches and then in mosques. In the Arab period large stone objects were removed en masse of to be used in defensive structures, as attested by the materials reemployed in the great Tulunid enclosures and by Abd el-Latif's famous text relating to the removal of columns from the Sarapeum for coastal defences at the time of Saladin in the twelfth century.

On the south-west branch of the island of Antirhodos, by the side of the still intact pavement and some fallen debris, three sculptures in an excellent state of conservation have been exhumed from beneath some architectural brash: two sphinxes (cat. nos. 461 and 462, pp. 57, 147) and the statue of a priest (cat. no. 464, p. 215). Crushed beneath the blocks, ceramics have emerged which are datable from the first century BC to the second century AD.

466

469

457

previous double page:

466   **Fragment of an obelisk**

Black granite
Sethos I (1293–1279 BC)
H. 56 cm | w. 200 cm | d. 78 cm

It is possible to deduce the original structure of the decoration of the whole obelisk from this fragment, part of the barrel interior. On each face, a broad, axial column of hieroglyphics contained a titulary of the king. Below, this column bisected a picture showing the king (kneeling rather than in the form of a sphinx) in the presence of a standing divinity. Beneath the king, in a frame, his two cartouches are affronted by a qualifier proclaiming that he is 'beloved' of the divinity.
Side A
Axial column: 'Sti-Merenptah'
Right, the king: 'Lord of the Two Menmare lands, lord of the Seti-Merenptah crowns, beloved of Amon-Re, Lord of the Thrones of the Two Lands'
Left, the god: 'Amon-Re, Lord of the Thrones of the Two Lands'
Side B
Axial column: 'Beloved of the Lords of the Great Castle'
Left, the king: only the qualifier, 'beloved of [Ptah in] Heliopolis,' remains.
Right, god Ptah in his chapel: 'Ptah, Lord of Ma'at'
Side C
Axial column: 'Beloved of [Re-Hor] akhti, endowed with life'
Right, the king: only the qualifier, 'beloved of Atum-khepri, the great god,' remains.
Left, the god Atum with human face, wearing the solar disc on his head: 'Words spoken by Atum-khepri: I give you life.'
Neither the iconography nor the designation of Atum is particularly frequent. Whereas the god is generally represented wearing the pschent, he sports a wig surmounted by the solar disc that distinguishes certain images of Re-Horakhti. The name affirming the identity of the evening sun with the sun that reappears in the morning is very seldom attested.
The three pictures thus presented three of the first four gods of the Ramessian state, the Theban Amon, the Heliopolitan sun in its form of Atum-khepri and Ptah of Memphis (a fourth, which would have been either Seth or another form of the sun was reproduced on the side missing).
In any case, vertical mentions of Re-Horakhti and the divinities of the Great House, i. e. the main temple at Heliopolis, make it possible to number this block among the remnants of Seti I's monumental works in the city.   J. Y.

469   **Inscribed block**

Pink granite
Apries 589–570 BC
H. 105 cm | w. 140 cm | d. 55 cm

A horizontal line of hieroglyphs can be discerned on vertical face A: 'Son of Atum, [his] beloved'. Mention of Atum brings back to us to Heliopolis, as does the allusion to the gods of Ker-aha (cat. no. 470).
In point of fact, the place of that name located on the site of what is now Old Cairo, and which was known to the Greeks by the name of Babylon of Egypt, was administratively dependent on Heliopolis and theologically closely associated with the temple of Re.   J. Y.

457   **Inscribed statue base**

Black granite
Merenptah 1213–1203 BC
H. 70 cm | w. 95 cm | d. 50 cm

Cut into a parallelepiped, this block represents about a quarter of the base of a statue of a walking male figure. On the inner face (D), to either side of the axis, two cartouches of king Merenptah placed on the ideogram meaning gold and surmounted by the sign for the sky.
Right, the first name: 'the Lord of the Two Lands, Ba-en-Re, beloved of the gods'.
Left, the birth name: 'the Lord of the Crowns, Merenptah who is in peace according to Ma'at.'
From either side of this central panel sprung two horizontally written titularies that continued over the lateral faces. Only the beginning remains, containing the first name introduced by 'Long live the King of Upper and Lower Egypt, Lord of the Two Lands'.
Note the coexistence of two alternatives for this first name: in C 'Ba-n-Re [beloved of] amon'; and in B 'Ba-n-Re [beloved of gods]'.
On section A, a scene in a rectangle with the sky above contained two cartouches arranged over three columns and preceded by the usual titles juxtaposed with the titulary of a god; here the king is '[beloved of…] Ptah, king of the gods'.
As the usual qualifier for Amon-Re of Thebes is only very seldom given to Ptah of Memphis, this must be a peculiar form or idol of the latter.
Moreover, this text is equally unusual in that, instead of being turned as is normal on bases of royal statues so it may be read by the viewer, it faces towards the back of the statue. It is not inconceivable that the statue represented not Merenptah, but a non-mummiform guise of Ptah. Mention of Ptah suggests a source in Memphis, where Merenptah was particularly active, but a quite different origin, including Heliopolis, cannot be excluded.   J. Y.

Three fragments of an obelisk (cat. no. 466, p. 373), a plinth and a statue dating from the Ramessesian epoch (1291–1204 BC; cat. no. 457, p. 373) and several elements from a building erected by the Saite king Apries (589–570 BC) were reused late on in monuments from dynasties before the arrival of Alexander (cat. nos. 467–469; 470, p. 376; 471, p. 377). Thanks to these discoveries, it can be confirmed that the majority of works of pharaonic antiquity found in Graeco-Roman Alexandria were taken from the temples of Heliopolis, just as many pieces collected from all over the continental parts of the city have hinted for around a century.

These Egyptian monuments in Greek and Roman Alexandria offer a glimpse into the cultural relationships between the old pharaonic and the young Hellenistic worlds. The number and quality of Egyptian vestiges recovered from Alexandria have increased significantly thanks to the extensive sub-aquatic topographical survey undertaken by the IEASM in the east sector of the eastern harbour and, still more, through the intensive salvage work taking place on the closest of the vast concentrations of large stones from antiquity languishing underwater at the foot of the Qait Bey. As regards *pharaonica*, it seems reasonable to suppose that the special temples, typical works of art, distinctive ritual practices and traditional religious conceptions of the Egyptians were far from marginal in Greek Alexandria and this from the time of the first Ptolemies. With respect to such *pharaonica*, two principal questions arise: does the context of their deposit and their material state reveal anything of the monumental topography and history of Alexandria? And more especially what is the meaning of the omnipresence of the colonised peoples' 'barbarian' artefacts in the metropolis of their Greek conquerors? In other words, what do they reveal about the relations between the two cultural traditions? What then did the builders of the Greek city mean by bringing parts of Egyptian temples and statuary from the interior? 'What was', to echo the terms used by Letronne 'the outcome of the incessant battle waged in a civilisation whose origins reach back to the cradle of the world?' And perhaps first one should ascertain whether this really was a 'battle' at all, and not a less fraught symbiosis between the culture of the Hellenes and the immemorial inheri-

471   **Inscribed block**

Pink granite
Apries 589–570 BC
H. 130 cm | w. 120 cm | d. 60 cm

This piece appears to be an architrave or a lintel from a door, the horizontal inscription in A corresponding to the vertical side visible frontally of the stone in place, the vertical inscription in C, apparently of similar workmanship, adorning the underside (?). One reads on C, vertical: the end of a cartouche, followed by 'living eternally'; on A, horizontal: '… Haab-ib-[Re], that of the Two Ladies, the Lord of the Arm (Khepesh)'. The five architectural elements from a construction by Apries belonged originally to one and the same monument.

Be they the components of a room built on square pillars, or more likely from a doorframe, these large monoliths removed from a Heliopolitan building embellished under Apries were later deposited in an Alexandrine temple. At some unspecified date, they were sectioned for use as building material for some construction and presumably this latter was subsequently itself exploited as a source of stone for two new structures. In fact, of these five vestiges of Apries, two (cat. nos. 467, 471) lie on the paved esplanade in the centre of the island, approximately five metres apart on a piece of ground strewn with truncated Roman columns, two of which bear votive inscriptions dating from the beginning of the third century.

The other three (cat. nos. 468–470) lie on the southern coast of the royal port, opposite one another on a paved zone among a jumble of diverse stone blocks and barrels of Roman columns.

Still better (or worse), the two halves of the riser, snapped through by an earth tremor or by an accident during transport, ended up, one on the southern side of the port (cat. no. 468), the other on the island (cat. no. 467).

It is instructive to note that the surface and inscription of the first has been severely corroded, while on the second they appear almost fresh. One plausible assumption might run as follows: Apries' Heliopolitan blocks were re-erected, as they were or already sectioned into masonry blocks, in some Alexandrine building. On the occasion of a rebuilding drive during the Roman or Byzantine era, this building was in turn plundered as a source of stone and shared out among a number of new constructions. Thus, the blocks tend to turn up randomly in various more or less contemporary building programs, scattering our Heliopolitan stones so that they ended their days on deserted demolition sites as they appear, underwater, in their present abandoned state. This is then an exemplary case of the enigmatic vicissitudes suffered by these stones as they were removed, recycled, and misappropriated countless times.

J. Y.

470   **Inscribed block from Heliopolis**

Pink granite
Apries 589–570 BC
H. 167 cm | w. 77 cm | d. 50 cm

On side A, there are remains of two affronted
columns of hieroglyphs: '[the son of Re] Apries,
endowed [with life and power] … beloved [of the Gods],
Lord of Kher-aha'.   J. Y.

467   **Fragment of a door jamb**

Pink granite
Apries 589–570 BC
H. 115 cm | w. 60 cm | d. 45 cm

This segment builds into an oblong block, 2.50 metres high
and approximately square in section, cut from a pillar or
more probably from a door stile.
On side A, remnants of a column of hieroglyphics: 'the King
of Upper and Lower Egypt Haa-ib-Re, endowed with life and
power'.
It can be deduced from a comparison with block cat. no. 470
that a parallel column opposite has since vanished together
with the other half. The block connects flush with cat.
no. 468.   J. Y.

468   **Fragment of a door jamb**

Pink granite
Apries 589–570 BC
H.. 150 cm | w. 60 cm | d. 45 cm

This block fits side by side with block cat. no. 467.   J. Y.

470

467

468

tance of a still vigorous Egyptian culture. We are accustomed to imagining Hellenistic Alexandria as a city whose environment was purely Greek, where the temples looked like those in Athens or Ephesus, where the dominant population, manners and taste, all Greek, had little to do with the exotic practices and artefacts of the natives of the *chora*, even rejecting them outright. The presence of people of Egyptian stock has been ascertained among the city's population, but the generally accepted idea is that there is no evidence of an indigenous cult organised according to the Egyptian tradition in Alexandria. How then is Alexandria's *pharaonica* to be accounted for? What was its visible or tacit role in cult-related beliefs, practices, and architectural complexion of the city?

It has been noted that many of the products of traditional pharaonic sacred art collected from all over Alexandria date from dynasties before the foundation of the city brought there from temples of the *chora*. In point of fact, the original provenance of many of the monuments, obelisks, statues, low-reliefs, and architectural members can be determined from the names of places and/or of local divinities appearing on their hieroglyphic inscriptions. Further rare cases where monuments have been removed from temples in Memphis or Sais should also be noted. As has been recognised for at least a century, however, an appreciable majority of Alexandria's pre-Ptolemaic *pharaonica* whose origin can be determined had been at the outset at Heliopolis, the venerable seat of sun worship located to the north-east of modern Cairo. They include relatively movable objects such as obelisks, statues of kings, sphinxes, and monolithic elements, and parts of monumental constructions, such as architraves, door stiles or lintels and intercolumnar partitions. On them only the characteristic names of the city and of the holy places at Heliopolis can be read. The divinities illustrated or named, those whose king is known as 'the beloved', are the sun, Re, under various names and in the guise of images that theology conferred on the creator star, and Heliopolis mythology's community of primordial powers (or 'souls').

The sculptures and blocks themselves are made of granite or granitoids from Aswan, as well as some pieces of greywacke from Wadi Hammamat; the high proportion of quartzite from the Gebel Ahmar, the 'Red Mountain', near Heliopolis, is remarkable. The collection of Alexandrine relics affords a significant list of the pharaohs who had adorned the House of Re over the ages: Sesostris III (1878–1841), Thutmosis III (1479–1425), Sethos I (1293–1279) and Ramesses II (1279–1213), and the Psammetics, Apries (589–570) and Amasis (570–526), Nektanabo I (380–362) and Nektanabo II (360–343). The materials employed, the divinities invoked, the founding kings, form approximately the same selection as that revealed by the analysis of the few remaining vestiges (found in situ or as reused in Arab-Islamic Cairo) of great and famous buildings in the City of the Sun, today likewise almost entirely absorbed by the encroachments of the modern metropolis.

As the present inventory stands, the most substantial batch of pieces of demonstrably Heliopolitan origin has been recovered from the area of the Sarapeum. A considerable number have recently been brought up from among the vast and mysterious concentrations of stone in the immersed shore zones. Some have been collected, in inadequately determined contexts, from the centre of the city; a handful of others come from the eastern areas. Everywhere such *pharaon-*

ica is embedded in a of a mix of Graeco-Roman remains. Contrary to what a rapid overview of the map might have one believe, it is obvious that for centuries Heliopolis was not used as a quarry for erecting or decorating all buildings in all sectors of Alexandria. A more likely supposition is that the authorities undertook wholesale transfers of stones, followed by gradual, more localised dispersion, though the monuments in Alexandria remained grouped in a few temples dedicated to the Egyptian rite or featuring partially pharaonic ornamentation.

One thing should be observed, however: the percentage of monuments used as spolia in Heliopolis from among pharaonic antiquities of every kind whose origin can be guaranteed is overwhelming and this percentage has only been increased by recent sub-aquatic discoveries. Unless for some reason the profile of the corpus presently being drawn up alters radically, for the moment it seems as if the vast temples of the *temenos* of the sun had at one point constituted the main if not only depository whence obelisks, statues, sphinxes might be removed, a storehouse of readymade architectural members that could be reemployed in the construction and adornment of Alexandrine temples in an 'old style'. It should be remarked in passing that the word spolia in this context should not be taken pejoratively, as though scornful Greeks and overbearing Romans should be berated for their unthinking depredations of the subjected Egyptian 'barbarian'. The term spoliation is in point of fact appropriate in cases where intact walls are demolished so as to recuperate the dressed stone, or, at a push, when a victor makes off with obelisks as trophies. On the other hand, the transfer and reemployment of movable monuments from an antique holy site to another recently set up (a process the Egyptians themselves had long practised) may imply, not contempt for the beliefs attached to these works, but a genuine religious concern. Such 'cherry-picking' from among the temples of the *chora* at a time when Egyptian hierogrammates officiated in Rome might have been felt by their colleagues back home not as sacrilegious violation but, one might almost say, as something approaching missionary zeal.

The architectural elements were variously redeployed. A block detached from a wall implies the demolition of this wall, while a section of a column or a block taken from an architrave presupposes the initial monolith was sawn up. Another type of reuse from one temple to another has to be envisaged, however. This has nothing to do with utilitarian vandalism and its effect, on the contrary, is one of conservation: rather as with a kit, colonnades and granite door-cases alike can be converted into monolithic supports and beams, which are then set up and re-erected at some other site.

Investigation piece by piece or category by category is complicated by the well-rehearsed fact that very little Alexandrian *pharaonica* has been found complete or in an adequate state of preservation. Worse still, apart from the Sarapeum where the statues and fragments, although visibly manhandled and disturbed, at least remain in the enclosure or on the periphery of the *temenos*, it can be affirmed *a priori* that no stone of any size remains close to the neighbourhood of any Alexandrine monument of which it might initially or subsequently have formed a part. The appearance and context of the layers, as well as the material state of certain pieces, paints a picture of a confused series of accidental breakage, deliberate dismemberment, manipulation, or all three. On one and the same site *materia aegyptica* is everywhere associated with *materia hellenica*, generally far more abundant, in a combination of architectural elements, Greek inscriptions, and pieces of sculpture dating, *pêle-mêle*, from the later period and the Lagid epoch, the entirety abandoned in or on surfaces datable to the Arab or Ottoman era.

In the process, it has been ascertained that several Egyptian blocks encountered long ago or more recently are simply remnants of larger monoliths and that they present scoring marks for hewing, mortises, bore-holes, and other technical alterations. Some monuments were clearly sectioned at some as yet indeterminate date into ashlar or for recycling and eventually fulfilled functions quite different to those they had at the outset. A priori, one would be inclined to date these reemployments to a point following the desacralisation of what had become idolatrous temples and ascribe them to Christians or Moslems. It is well known, however, that sectioning stones with a view to deploying them elsewhere was a recurrent practice in pagan

antiquity also. Once again, the question is whether Greek or Roman pieces display traces of reuse or adaptations of a similar type, as it is crucial to discover whether solely the products of the indigenous culture fell victim to such destructive reuse, sharing with Greek creations only the misadventure of ultimate dispersal. Columns, capitals, friezes and the like, set up by Greeks and Romans (cat. nos. 472, 477, p. 382) were readily purloined by Christians. The ostensibly idolatrous images and hieroglyphics could of course only be recuperated if buried in carcass work.

The constant transport and dispersal that has occurred since the end of paganism is such that, in pharaonic strata as they are at present, it is not possible to infer the site or identity of the temples in which they were housed. Were the temple of Isis in the royal quarters and the temple of Isis on the island of Pharos, for example, Egyptian or 'Isiac'?

The layers immediately accessible to investigation and underwater excavation are only the ultimate resting-place, more or less posterior to the end of antiquity, but certainly prior to the Ottoman era and to the final state of the *pharaonica* generally. Indeed, it will be no easy task to chronologically pinpoint the final chapter prior to abandonment and immersion.

Between the time they arrived in the Hellenistic city and when they were found, any objects in the pharaonic style are likely to have experienced all or part of the following series of adventures and mishaps. In accordance with their original function and significance, they could have been consecrated after being placed in an Alexandrine temple, hewn into masonry blocks or sawn up, processes which would have utterly destroyed any number of monuments, or at least deprived them of epigraphy; the resulting blocks might be reused in several ways. They could have suffered individual or massive displacement, the parts of a single unit ending up relatively near their original location or scattered far and wide. On top of this there were general breakages or mutilation due to a natural agency, or as a result of subsequent handling or iconoclastic assault. *Pharaonica* thus shared in the trials and tribulations of monuments of the Hellenistic and Graeco-Roman styles and bear the traces of various misadventures that occurred during the construction of ancient Alexandria.

Indications that might allow the stratigraphic chronology of the events and mishaps of the zone of the *basileia* to be arrived at remain few and far between. The fact that the statues there are in a broken state implies that the present appearance of the sites should be dated to after the iconoclastic upheavals of the fourth century AD. The cases of dispersion, such as that of the monoliths of Apries divided between the coast and the island (cat. nos. 467, 471, pp. 375–377), suggest that buildings, whether they had collapsed in situ or not, were used as a source at one moment or another, as confirmed by the remains of a stonecutting works. Moreover, it is surely probable that one of the stone concentrations on the peninsula represents remains from the temple of Poseidon, though not the Lagid temple Strabo had seen around 27 BC.

Nevertheless, one cannot go so far as to describe the debris along the coast as belonging to the 'palaces' of the Ptolemies. Even if the *temenos* probably continued celebrating the cult in Roman times and if some of the *basileia* might have been placed at the service of the prefects of Egypt, that is, become basilicas, major programs of urban and monumental restoration are likely to have modi-

477

472

fied the purpose assigned to the various spaces and eliminated constructions from the Hellenistic dynasty.

On the map as we presently have it, the palace Strabo had seen on Antirhodos three years after the death of Cleopatra and which might well have sheltered the queen before she withdrew to her mausoleum, stands facing the Timonium, the palace that the deposed Mark Antony built as a refuge in his dejection. Thus the spectres of the two lovers continue to haunt this submerged domain.

Some might think it a pity that the mission was not fortunate enough to recover in Antirhodos the traces of Cleopatra or unearth in the royal port the wreck of the splendid floating palace or barge which in 41 BC had conveyed the queen to Mark Antony in Cilicia. We did though begin to dream when, in the little port of Antirhodos, a wreck was discovered containing, among other items, a splendid intaglio with a religious motif mounted on a gold ring (cat. no. 478, p. 384). Further on, other jewels hint at further mysteries (cat. nos. 479, 480, p. 384), all the more remarkable as remnants of both pharaonic style and Hellenistic and Graeco-Roman style statuary have been discovered in various sites. Plunged into the murky depths, the sheer beauty of a female head in marble that can be identified as a Roman empress is deeply moving (cat. no. 465).

Excavations have also made it possible to establish a chronology for settlements and activities from successive periods on Antirhodos. The pier at the eastern tip of the island dates to the fifth to fourth centuries BC, a surprising fact if the historian adopts an oversimplified image of coastal occupation prior to Alexander. The last indigenous dynasties maintained the police and customs controls introduced by the Saites and Persian dynasties for Greek navigators and tradesmen, while some Hellenes returned to serve the pharaohs as mercenaries. The shelter afforded by the cove might very well have been developed for them. The paving on the esplanade was laid under the first Ptolemies, since the formwork for the raft foundation has been dated (by carbon-14 analysis) to the third century.

On the west-east branch of Antirhodos, an axial strip of the paved terrain is covered with more or less dense groups of smooth granite columns together with a few blocks of various hard rocks, including some reused from pharaonic times. These layers appear to have been a quarry abandoned following its exploitation. At three points, they feature granite plinths bearing a Greek dedication, including seven dating from the principate of Caracalla (around 213 AD). In the absence of architectural elements that can be ascribed to the Ptolemaic era, the picture is of a building erected in the imperial period on the spot where 'the palace of Cleopatra' once stood and subsequently refurbished at the beginning of the third century with monuments to the honour of the emperor. The preservation of eight mostly complete inscriptions from a single period, scattered but over one and the same stretch of ground – the fortuitous upshot of the complicated vicissitudes of the site – is a miraculous event and has contributed incalculably to our knowledge of the dramatic relations between the city and Emperor Caracalla (pp. 60–64).

In the context of the international exchanges promoted by Alexandria (cat. nos. 425, 486, p. 384), means of payment took on major importance, as much for foreign trade as for transactions at home. With the arrival of the Greeks, the minting and use of currency underwent considerable development in the Nile Valley. In 326/325 BC, a workshop was set up in Alexandria, probably close to the royal quarter of the *basileia*, in which gold and silver coin was minted conforming to the Attic standard. A monetary policy was instituted from 306 by Ptolemy I and consolidated subsequently by his successors (p. 325).

The mints were supplied by the gold mines of the eastern desert and Nubia, while the system of obligatory conversion of external moneys added to the quantity of noble metal required for coining Lagid currency with extra from abroad. Melting down money in this way made it possible to mint, *inter alia*, the splendid silver tetradrachms – a metal unusual in Egypt – issued by Ptolemy I Soter whose longevity turned them into the Lagid currency par excellence. The obverse of the silver and gold coinage was struck with the profiles of the king, queen, or royal couple. The reverse featured either the eagle of Zeus that had become the symbol of the Lagid dynasty, or the horn of plenty, simple or double, in reference to the kingdom's prosperity based on its agricultural resources, first and foremost wheat.

Bronze coins were generally used in day-to-day affairs, although beginning in the second half of the third century the uptake of bronze coinage widened considerably. If the term by which they

previous double page:

477 Capital
Pink granite
c. 250–350 AD
H. 50 cm | w. 68 cm | d. 68 cm

A Corinthian capital with double rows of acanthus leaves of alternating heights. The corner volutes have secondary decorative curls at the top and at the centre. The boss in the centre of the column capital is worn but likely was a highly stylised flower. E. L. | J. M.

472 Capital
Pink granite
c. 100–250 AD
H. 85 cm | w. 130 cm | d. 130 cm

A large Corinthian capital with a double rowed collar of simplified and rounded acanthus leaves. The capital in general is very simple and schematic in execution. The two capitals recovered from Alexandria harbour are consistent with known architectural types occurring throughout Egypt in the Roman period. The use of Egyptian hard stone, such as grandiorite or red granite, is a distinctive characteristic of capital manufacture in the Ptolemaic and Roman periods. E. L. | J. M.

were designated, chalkos, evokes copper, they were in fact an alloy of copper, lead and tin. From 260 BC, eight bronze classes or denominations exist, distinguished by diameter, weight and iconography (p. 330). The obverse of these eight denominations generally sports the bearded head of Zeus-Amon, with, on the reverse, the eagle with outspread or folded wings. The legend is unremarkable: *Ptolemaiou Basileios* ('From Ptolemy, king').

J. Y. | D. F. | F. G.

465 **Head of Antonia Minor**

Marble
1st cent. AD
H. 35 cm

The hairstyle is difficult to make out: the locks are parted down the middle of the forehead, forming to the side two wavy clumps that extend down to the nape of the neck. The hair is flattened down on the top of the head. Two thick bands to the side cover half of each ear before meeting behind at the base of the skull. They cover the start of some long, thick strands (rolled or braided) that run down the nape to the base of the neck. This hair arrangement is characteristic and can be observed on currency adorned with the head of Antonia Minor, mother of Germanicus and Claudius. This fashion was widely followed in private portraiture and many examples of pictures of women with hairstyles of this kind have survived. Nevertheless, the size of the sculpture is more in keeping with an official portrait, in point of fact one of Antonia Minor herself who had been honoured in the Roman Empire from Tiberius her brother-in-law until the reign of her son Claudius.   Z. K.

478 Ring

Gold and semi-precious stone (intaglio)
1st cent. BC–1st cent. AD
Diam. ring: 2.95 cm, diam. setting 1.8 cm

Gold ring with a three-quarter hoop made of
three solid beaded wires. One granule is
attached to each end of every wire. An oval bezel
setting with a flat intaglio in dark blue and
white is soldered to the hoop. The intaglio
shows a bird standing on a ground line and
playing with a ribbon.   S. H. B. | Y. S.

479 Ring

Gold
1st cent. BC–1st cent. AD
Diam. 2.53 cm

Polygonal finger-ring with a tiered bezel on
a quadratic base. The surface of the bezel is
undecorated, but every edge of the polygon is
accentuated with engraved lines.   S. H. B. | Y. S.

480 Ring

Gold and agate
Roman period
Diam. 2.29 cm

Gold ring with a circular hoop made of
gold sheet and a recessing oval setting. The
latter contains a curved, white and red agate.
Rings like this were popular in the early
imperial time, as suggested by finds from
Pompeii and elsewhere in the Roman Empire.
S. H. B. | Y. S.

481 Bowl

Ceramic
Ist cent. BC
H. 5.1 cm | diam. 9.3 cm

486 Cretan amphora

Ceramic
Roman period
H. 46 cm | diam. 12.8 cm

485 Rhodian amphora

Ceramic
Roman period
H. 98.5 cm | diam. 29.5 cm.

478

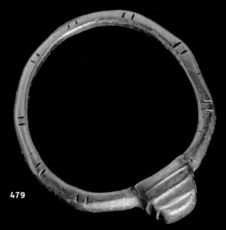

479

480

481

486

485

THE GUARDIAN GENIE FOR TOWN AND COUNTRY

AGATHODAIMON

The fragment represents a coiled serpent whose four smoothly cut superimposed rings can be clearly differentiated. This is Agathodaimon, the 'good genie'. A guardian genie responsible for happiness was worshipped in every person's home and every town's temple. Alexandria's Agathodaimon guaranteed prosperity for the metropolis and its inhabitants and had a famous temple in the Graeco-Roman era.   Z. K.

The central importance of this protective god is further emphasised by the siting of the temple: it was located in the middle of Alexandria at the junction of the two main thoroughfares through the city. The citizens of Alexandria even named the nearest arm of the Nile after their guardian – a tributary that had been called Canopic. The stretch of water

subsequently named Agathodaimon formed the eastern border of Alexandria, the inhabitants of which placed themselves in the protection this name-giving god. Before visiting the Egyptian capital, the Roman emperor Nero (54–68 BC) had himself depicted on Alexandian coins as the new Agathodaimon, thus proclaiming to the people of the metropole that they now stood under the special protection of the emperor. The importance of this god which has survived to this day documents an episode at the end of the fifth century AD. Among the heathen cult objects which were burnt by Christians on the spot where the guardian deity's temple once stood, was a cult statue. With the words of the patriarch Peter: "And here is the treacherous snake!" the cult statue of Agathodaimon was thrown onto the pyre.   Z. K.–M. C.

459   Agathodaimon
Black granite
3rd–2nd cent. BC
H. 30 cm | w. 25 cm

Isis and Sarapis from Oxyrhynchus, 2nd cent. BC

30 **Stele of Isis-Thermoutis**
Marble
2nd cent. AD
H. 32 cm | w. 23 cm | d. 6 cm

This modest marble stele, discovered on site T in Canopus, is a typical example of piety towards Isis. It consists of a flat rectangular stone, the top of which may have been arched since it bears traces of the lower half of a winged disk. At the top and on the sides the framework is baton-shaped, whilst the base is slightly broader. The bottom of the resulting panel is hollowed out, almost entirely carved with the image of a cobra. The head is in profile and wears a crown in the form of a solar disk with bovine horns.

The rearing cobra wearing the *Hathoric* crown is a well-known symbol of Isis Thermoutis, thus the Isis assimilated with the pharaonic Renenutet, the goddess of fertility. This representation was particularly popular in Roman Alexandria, as its presence on Alexandrian coins proves, for example. On a marble base in the Graeco-Roman Museum in Alexandria there is a cobra with the inscription Agathodaimon. It is, in fact, sometimes difficult to distinguish Isis Thermoutis in the form of a cobra from Agathodaimon represented in the same form; only the Isis crown allows the distinction to be made. Nevertheless, on monuments Isis Thermoutis normally appears in a pair with Agathodaimon likened to Sarapis, or with Sarapis himself.   Z. K.

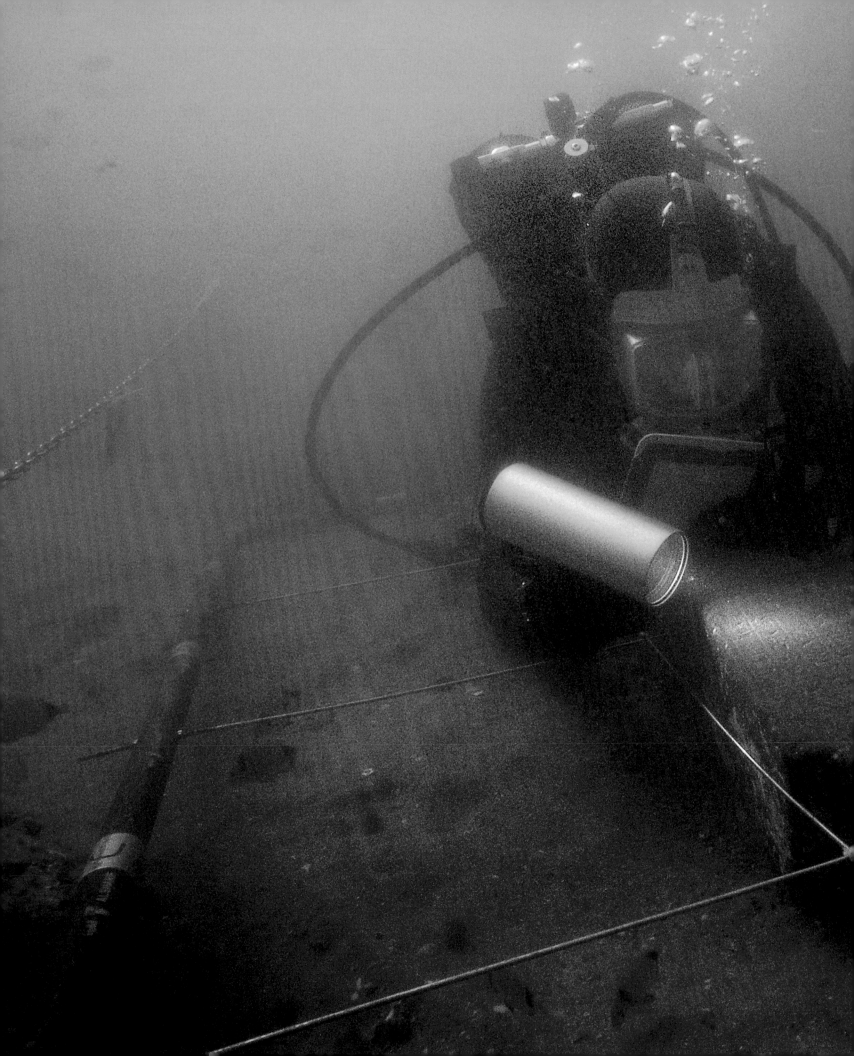

IV. FROM EXCAVATION TO EXHIBITION

RESTORATION AND CONSERVATION

241 Bowl
Bronze
Late Pharaonic period
H. 6 cm | diam. 13.3 cm

Much of the upper part of the bowl is
now obscured by shelly remains and
little can be said with certainty about
its original form. However, it is possible
to surmise that the vessel had a short
neck which flares outwards from the
bowl and probably had no pronounced
rim, thus identifiable as a calyx cup.
Z. C.

"… underwater excavation should only take place
once it is certain that the objects exhumed may be
adequately treated, for otherwise one risks watching them deteriorate and disappear." (P. Pomey)

The archaeological excavations undertaken in
Egypt by the IEASM benefit from an on board conservation-restoration laboratory that allows for
immediate treatment of the objects as they leave the
water. Initial stages of conservation can thus be carried out on ship while complementary approaches
necessitating heavier equipment are carried out on
land, in the laboratory in Alexandria.

ABOARD SHIP

As far as possible the removal of delicate objects
calls for the intervention of the conservator underwater, although it is on the surface that the objects
are dealt with in earnest. The object is initially cleaned of sediment, then identified and inventoried.
The programme of conditioning carried out
depends on the materials concerned. On board storage makes it possible to start the first stage of the
treatment, eliminating the salts impregnating the
objects. Salts are harmful to the long-term conservation of the artefacts: as objects in stone or ceramics dry, they crystallise and crack open, causing
lift or material loss. In metals such as bronze, salts
and especially chlorides cause cyclical corrosion
that may cause the object to vanish entirely. Initi-

left: Osiris (cat. no. 185) being cleaned

right: Isis (cat. no. 182, p. 105) and Osiris (cat. 185)
before cleaning

ally, the salts are eliminated by simple osmosis, immersing the objects in rinsing vats containing regularly renewed fresh water. This extraction is controlled and monitored by measuring the electrical conductivity.

The optimum salt content during the desalination process is 50 Microsiemens (50 µS / cm) for tap water. Only towards the end of this stage, before the drying process is started, is the value reduced to (30 µS / cm). The electrical conductivity of water is measured in Microsiemens per centimetre, its intensity being dependent on the ions present in the solute.

Objects found under the sea are the most often covered with agglomerates of sediment associated with marine organisms. These concretions of limestone, sometimes very thick and hard, not only render the object unrecognisable, they also retain high concentrations of salt. To allow the article to be identified and to facilitate desalinisation, mechanical "surgical" cleaning, sometimes under the binocular microscope, is carried out using pneumatic micro-engravers and scalpels. These mechanical processes are sometimes deployed in conjunction with chemical treatments, since objects with a fragile surface cannot sustain the repeated vibration and pressure applied. Stone objects bearing inscriptions or decorations, such as the large stele (p. 183), are examples of objects that call for especially delicate handling.

As a general rule, chemical treatments are seldom employed on the boat, except for the objects in lead which are severely affected by changes in environment. For them, the shift from sea to fresh water triggers rapid corrosion and the formation of a white efflorescence. To avoid this, they are preserved in a solution of sodium sulphate before being treated electrochemically in the laboratory in Alexandria.

THE LABORATORY AT ALEXANDRIA

The meticulous work of conservation-restoration continues in the laboratory in Alexandria which possesses a considerable range of equipment making it possible to forestall many of the types of deterioration affecting the archaeological material. These treatments can be mechanical, chemical, or electrochemical in nature.

METALS Restoration and conservation of metals is a complex issue. If gold, the noble metal par excellence, undergoes no alteration, bronze, silver, iron and lead corrode rapidly since the emergence into the open air upsets the balance they gradually acquire with respect to their medium. For certain metal objects desalinisation by osmosis is insufficient. If the internal structure allows, these treatments must be supplemented by a controlled and precise polarisation of the object in a chemical solution (electrochemical stabilising treatment). Once the salts contained in the metal have been eliminated, sub-deposit surface of the object can be precisely determined. This original surface is identified by observing the stratigraphy of the corrosion products through a binocular microscope. A given treatment then selectively eliminates the corrosion products by use of chemical solutions of various acids, bases, reducers, or complexing agents. Mechanical cleaning using ultrasound scalpels, fibreglass brushes, pneumatic micro-engraver, micro-lathe fitted with a diamond wheel, mounted brushes and abrasive gums complement these surface treatments that slowly expose the original surface of the object. This lengthy and painstaking process is generally carried out under a binocular microscope. The fragility of the surface sometimes requires impregnation by consolidant. In certain cases, resin reinforcements or fibreglass fabric linings can be deployed. Metal objects are then chemically sta-

bilised by a corrosion inhibitor, before being coated in an acrylic varnish and a mineral wax to protect them from air moisture, furthering their long-term conservation. Finally, they are stored at a constant temperature and humidity level so as to prevent corrosion setting in again.

CERAMICS To completely desalinate ceramics, the initial treatment is followed by immersion in a bath of distilled water, thereby reducing the salt content to a more acceptable level less damaging to the object, a process that facilitates stabilisation and long-term conservation. After desalting, the ceramic can be restored: fragments are stuck back together, gaps are filled and tinted, while underfired, and thus fragile pastes are impregnated with a consolidating material. To avoid any possible recrystallisation of the salts, it is advisable to store this type of archaeological material in a room of constant hygrometry and temperature where it can be conditioned prior to eventual public exhibition.

STONEWORK The process adopted is substantially the same for statues and architectural members in stone. First of all, the procedure consists in the removal of concretions by chemical and mechanical means. However, marble, limestone and sandstone require a longer desalinisation time than basalt or granite, which are relatively impermeable to salts. The elements disengaged are consolidated by means of infiltration with reversible acrylic resin. A cement made of crushed stone similar to that constituting the object with a binder of reversible resin is used to fill and consolidate the surface. When necessary, statue fragments may be bolted together.

ORGANIC MATERIALS Once on the surface, organic archaeological material (wood, leather, basketry, textiles, bone, etc.) requires rapid and painstaking treatment. In other materials, deterioration of an organic object is not always visible. In many cases waterlogged timber, for example, can preserve its original form, but internal degradation may be underway and the physical and chemical properties may have changed radically. As it deteriorates, wood tends to become soft and spongy; once

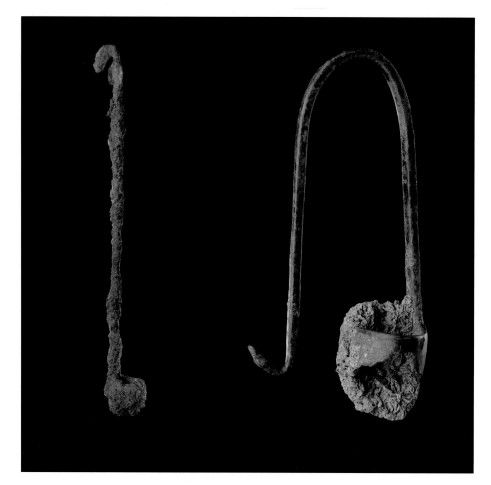

out of the water, it contracts, splits, and twists. Previously sustained by the water, the cells break down and the wood loses its original shape quickly and irreversibly. To prevent this, it is widely accepted that wood must undergo consolidation prior to drying. Thus, following cleaning and desalinisation, the water saturating these artefacts has gradually to be replaced by resin. This maintains the initial shape of the cells, preventing their collapse as they dry during what is slow and closely monitored procedure.

Conservation should not be regarded as the application of techniques and treatment processes, but as an essential stage in the excavation. Sometimes, in the case of fragile objects, the conservator is both the first and the last to see some minute technological or historical detail. As the archaeological excavation unfolds, it is his or her task to record all the information the object conveys. Sometimes based on analysis, this documentation is though not the ultimate goal, as the object must also be stabilised to ensure its survival, as well as occasionally being improved aesthetically on museological grounds. The objects displayed in this exhibition, which come from the port of Alexandria and Aboukir Bay, represent solely the last stage in a lengthy process of conservation and restoration.

A. A. B. E-K. | O. B.

257 Simpulum
Bronze
6th–2nd cent. BC
L. 46.5 cm | diam. 5.3 cm

The ladle is completely covered in the remains of sea life so that little can be made of its original features. However, the object does adequately demonstrate the extent to which conditions in the water can affect the archaeological artefacts.
Z. C.

258 Simpulum
Bronze
6th–2nd cent. BC
L. 48 cm | diam. 6 cm

The ladle has a large square-sectioned handle with a duck's head terminal and a large bowl. Complete. Poor condition. Large amount covered with remains of sea-life. Large part of bowl missing. Rim distorted. Handle bent at the centre.   Z. C.

A LARGE-SCALE PROJECT: THE CONSERVATION-RESTORATION AND PRESENTATION OF THE HEAVY STONE PIECES

The vertical presentation at the exhibition of the great royal stele and the three colossal statues has called for a series of carefully considered interventions, as well as close co-operation between various disciplines.

DISCOVERY AND CONSERVATION At the time of their discovery, the three fragmentary colossi were readily identifiable thanks to their reliefs. All the pink granite fragments were easily recovered with the exception of the queen's right arm (cat. no, 107, p. 165). The situation with the large royal stele was very different and the various fragments were not easy to locate (cat. no, 119, p. 183). The seventeen fragments, with masses ranging from 100 kg to 5 tonnes, were carved in a heterogeneous gneiss (black- and pink-coloured inclusions in a grey matrix), of highly varied appearance. The blocks were scattered over a relatively large excavation surface and were all covered with thick layers of deposit. The general state of conservation of the stele quickly appeared problematic as its fall and stint underwater had significantly deteriorated the material.

The stone was compromised by a copious network of structural fissures and surface peeling, and the inscriptions reappeared only after the particularly tough and adherent concretions were chemically eliminated. Any attempt at removing the concretion mechanically was likely to rip off fragments of the surface and to jeopardise decipherment of the text. So, after the blocks had been assembled on a barge, a silicone cast was applied to preserve evidence of the fragile inscription and aid its epigraphic study (p. 179).

The salts were eliminated by immersing the various fragments in a vat measuring some 20 m³. Salt extraction is normally controlled and monitored by measuring the electric conductivity, allowing the water to be replenished with care and ending the treatment at the correct moment – in this case after ten months.

RESTORATION Even with the conservation phase over, the restoration and mounting of the great stele and the three colossal statues required months of research and close co-operation was called for to solve the puzzle of how best to handle the artefacts and bring the project to a satisfactory conclusion. It was a collaboration that involved conservator-restorers, specialists in stonework, metal constructors, art removers, and engineering contractors specialising in metal and stone structures.

The prime objective was to return this colossal piece to its onetime vertical position, but it was necessary to fulfil several additional imperatives as well. The elements also had to be sufficiently well consolidated and stable so as to be safely transported and mounted in the context of a travelling exhibition. We had moreover to respect the ethics of conservation, respond to various aesthetic criteria, fulfil the safety requirements laid down for public display, and facilitate the artefacts' transport to and installation in the exhibition space.

The stele fragments bear a lattice of gaping cracks, the majority being located down within the material, though some run perpendicular to the surface. To reinforce the cleaving, holes were bored in the back of the stele into which resin was vacuum injected so as to consolidate the cracks. The restorers then filled the holes by inserting fibreglass plugs. Adapted to each particular case, the innovative injection system allowed the material to regain its cohesion. Meticulous soundings revealed that a third of the surface of the stele was on the brink of falling away. To counter that problem, we patiently consolidated the surface scaling and flaking by injecting it by syringe drop by drop with an acrylic resin in a volatile solvent. The cracks that had opened up at the surface were in-filled by a granite powder preparation bound with reversible synthetic resin.

ASSEMBLY AND PRESENTATION Once the restoration phase was complete, the stele and the colossi were affixed to metal structures to enable them to be

stainless-steel anchors were fixed to the rear of the segments and screwed to a large metal armature erected in the exhibition space.

Thanks to many months of research and collaboration on these four enormous objects, all the demands of conservation, transport and public display have been respected. The stele and colossi now stand as they used to before a sleep that had lasted more than two millennia and continue, as admiring museum-goers pass by, to stare out into eternity. L.T.

displayed vertically as in the past. By modelling the artefacts in 3D on a computer, the connections between the various elements were simulated, so locating their centres of gravity and determining the optimum positions for the anchors. At length, this procedure made it possible to devise a metal armature adapted to the thickness, cracks and structural shortcomings of each stone.

All the holes were pierced without percussion to avoid opening up fresh cracks. For this purpose, we had an auger-machine with a diamond bit mounted on a sliding system of axles and rollers specially made. This system of drilling in parallax makes it possible at the outset to adjust the placing of the fragments to the nearest millimetre, to move them about, bore them, and finally to replace them exactly as they were, and thus position the unit extremely accurately. For the stele, the fragments to be connected were aligned on a laser plane to ensure perfect flatness. In certain cases, in order to safeguard the integrity of the fragments, stainless-steel sleeves were introduced into the boring holes. To ensure the pieces remain in perfect position relative to one another, stainless-steel dowels are then introduced into the sleeves, a method that allows the elements to be separated if need be. It is interesting to note that the sculpture of the queen had been restored in antiquity by a similar process using steel pins in parallax drill holes closed by lead.

The idea of transporting a stele 6 m by 3.5 m and weighing some 15 tonnes in a single piece was out of the question; it was thus necessary to design a metal fastening and transport system that would allow it to be split into five independent elements. To enable the five elements to be handled and reassembled,

V. CATALOGUE OF WORKS

Compiled by Cornelia Ewigleben, Kirsten Groß-Albenhausen and
Manfred Clauss

h. = height, w. = width, l. = length, d. = depth / thickness,
wt. = weight

Catalogue numbers set in italics on pages 26–401 refer to the
Catalogue of Works below.

EAST CANOPUS

1 (p. 144)
Sphinx
Amenemhat IV, 1798–1789 BC
Quartzite
H. 53 cm | w. 142 cm | d. 70 cm
Location: Excavations warehouse,
Alexandria (SCA 1162)

2 (p. 133)
Portrait of a Pharaoh
25th dynasty (712–664 BC)
Quartzite
H. 38 cm | w. 31.5 cm | d. 34.5 cm
Location: Great Library, Alexandria
(SCA 166)

3 (p. 43)
Portrait of a Pharaoh
Saitic dynasty (664–525 BC)
Diorite
H. 35 cm | w. 30 cm | d. 29 cm
Location: Great Library, Alexandria
(SCA 167)

4 (p. 133)
Portrait of a Pharaoh
30th dynasty (380–343 BC)
Black granite
H. 37 cm | w. 17 cm | d. 14 cm
Location: Great Library, Alexandria
(SCA 168)

5 (p. 154)
Sphinx
End of late period—Ptolemaic period
Diorite
W. 115 cm | d. 50 cm
Location: Excavations warehouse,
Alexandria (SCA 1158)

6 (p. 155)
Sphinx
End of late period to early Ptolemaic
period
Black granite
H. 65 cm | w. 145 cm | d. 50 cm
Location: Roman Theatre, Alexandria
(SCA 1173)

7 (p. 158)
Sphinx
End of late period to early Ptolemaic
period
Black granite
H. 28 cm | w. 75 cm | d. 23.5 cm
Location: Roman Theatre, Alexandria
(SCA 1164)

8 (p. 155)
Sphinx
Ptolemaic period
Pink granite
H. 46 cm | w. 114 cm | d. 36 cm
Location: Excavations warehouse,
Alexandria (SCA 1159)

9 (p. 159)
Sphinx
Ptolemaic period
Pink granite
H. 44 cm, l. 120 cm, b. 36.5 cm
Location: Excavations warehouse,
Alexandria (SCA 1161)

10 (p. 151)
Head of a sphinx
Ptolemaic period
Pink granite
H. 31 cm | w. 27 cm | d. 29 cm
Location: Excavations warehouse,
Alexandria (SCA 174)

11 (p. 150)
Head of a sphinx
Ptolemaic period
Pink granite
H. 27.5 cm | w. 18.5 cm | d. 23 cm
Location: Excavations warehouse,
Alexandria (SCA 172)

12 (p. 152)
Head of a sphinx
Ptolemaic period
Pink granite
H. 26.5 cm | w. 31 cm | d. 24.5 cm
Location: Excavations warehouse,
Alexandria (SCA 176)

13 (p. 150)
Head of a sphinx
Ptolemaic period
Pink granite
H. 30 cm | w. 22 cm | d. 23 cm
Location: Excavations warehouse,
Alexandria (SCA 177)

16 (p. 148)
Head of a sphinx
Ptolemaic period
Diorite
H. 54 cm | w. 33 cm | d. 29 cm
Location: Excavations warehouse,
Alexandria (SCA 202)

20 (p. 235)
Head of Sarapis
2nd cent. BC
Marble
H. 59 cm | w. 34 cm | d. 34 cm
Location: Great Library, Alexandria
(SCA 169)

14 (p. 151)
Head of a sphinx
Ptolemaic period
Pink granite
H. 28 cm | w. 21 cm | d. 23 cm
Location: Excavations warehouse,
Alexandria (SCA 175)

17 (p. 161)
Portrait of Berenice II
3rd cent. BC
Diorite
H. 13.7 cm | w. 11.4 cm | d. 9 cm
Location: Great Library, Alexandria
(SCA 204)

18 (p. 173)
Statue of a queen
3rd cent. BC
Black granite
H. 150 cm | w. 55 cm | d. 28 cm
Location: Great Library, Alexandria
(SCA 208)

19
Head of Sarapis
2nd cent. AD
Marble
H. 27 cm | w. 18 cm | d. 13.5 cm
Location: Great Library, Alexandria
(SCA 165)

15 (p. 153)
Head of a sphinx
Ptolemaic period
Pink granite
H. 27.5 cm | w. 26 cm | d. 23 cm
Location: Excavations warehouse,
Alexandria (SCA 173)

21 (p. 238)
Torso of a clothed man
2nd cent. BC
Pink granite
H. 120 cm
Location: Maritime Museum,
Alexandria (SCA 1160)

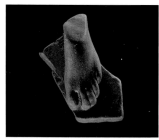

22
Fragment of base with foot
Ptolemaic period–Roman period
Diorite
H. 15 cm | w. 25.5 cm | d. 19 cm
Location: Excavations warehouse,
Alexandria (SCA 1165)

25 (p. 134)
Fragment of base with foot
Roman period
Marble
H. 2.9 cm | w. 6.7 cm | d. 3.8 cm
Location: Excavations warehouse,
Alexandria (SCA 170)

27 (p. 234)
Calathos
Roman period
Marble
H. 24 cm | diam. 26.5 cm
Location: Excavations warehouse,
Alexandria (SCA 206)

29 (p. 40)
Bust of the Nile god
Roman period (2nd cent. AD)
Greywacke
H. 67 cm | w. 56 cm | d. 30 cm
Location: Excavations warehouse,
Alexandria (SCA 842)

23
Fragment of base with foot
Ptolemaic period–Roman period
Diorite
H. 28 cm | w. 22 cm | d. 19 cm
Location: Excavations warehouse,
Alexandria (SCA 180)

26 (p. 118)
Isis
Roman period
Marble
H. 130 cm | w. 63 cm
Location: Maritime Museum,
Alexandria (Nr. 56)

28 (p. 114)
Osiris-Canobos
1st to 2nd cent. AD
Marble
Vase: H. 24 cm | diam. 21.2 cm
Head: H. 13.3 cm | w. 12.6 cm | d.
11.1 cm
Location: Great Library, Alexandria
(SCA 205)

30 (p. 391)
Stele of Isis-Thermoutis
2nd cent. AD
Marble
H. 32 cm | w. 23 cm | d. 6 cm
Location: Great Library, Alexandria
(SCA 207)

24 (p. 121)
Harpokrates
Roman period
Marble
H. 15 cm | w. 34.5 cm | d. 20.5 cm
Location: Excavations warehouse,
Alexandria (SCA 171)

31–34 (p. 48)
Naos of the Decades
380–362 BC
Black granite
Canopos
H. 178 cm | w. 88 cm | d. 80 cm
Location: Musée du Louvre, Paris
(D 37); base and rear wall: Graeco-
Roman Museum, Alexandria
(JE 25774);
newly-found sections 31 and 33, two
large, contiguous fragments of left
wall, 34, small, third fragment of left
wall, and 32, fragment from centre of
right wall: Graeco-Roman Museum,
Alexandria (SCA 161–164)

36 (p. 217)
Offering table
Ptolemaic period-Roman period
Black granite
H. 17 cm | w. 61.5 cm | d. 59 cm
Location: Maritime Museum,
Alexandria (SCA 1163)

37 (p. 269)
Earring with setting and two glass beads
5th to early 8th cent. AD (?)
Gold and glass
To the east of the temple T
H. 2.8 cm | w. 1.06 cm | d. 0.07 cm
Location: Graeco-Roman Museum,
Alexandria (SCA 109)

39 (p. 267)
Earring with decorative disc
6th to early 8th cent. AD
Gold
To the east of the temple T
L. 1.89 cm | w. 1.82 cm | d. 0.85 cm
Location: Great Library, Alexandria
(SCA 197)

40 (p. 267)
Pendant of an earring
6th to early 8th cent. AD
Gold and pearls
To the east of the temple T
L. 8.7 cm | w. 0.95 cm | d. 0.70 cm
Location: Great Library, Alexandria
(SCA 195)

42
Earring with hemispheric ornament
6th to early 8th cent. AD
Gold
To the east of the temple T
Diam. 2.2 cm | d. 0.5 cm
Location: Great Library, Alexandria
(SCA 191)

43
Pendant of an earring
6th to early 8th cent. AD
Gold and pearls
To the east of the temple T
L. 5.25 cm | w. 0.5 cm | d. 0.5 cm
Location: Great Library, Alexandria
(SCA 194)

35 (p. 231)
Console or table-leg
Ptolemaic period
Black granite
H. 70 cm | w. 21 cm
Location: Roman Theatre, Alexandria
(SCA 1166)

38 (p. 284)
Crescent-shaped earring
6th to early 8th cent. AD
Gold
To the east of the temple T
L. 2.65 cm | w. 2.18 cm | d. 0.17 cm
Location: Great Library, Alexandria
(SCA 102)

41 (p. 266)
Earring with two pendants
6th to early 8th cent. AD
Gold and pearls
To the east of the temple T
L. 1.87 cm | w. 1.46 cm | d. 0.31 cm
Location: Great Library, Alexandria
(SCA 108)

44
Earring with granule pyramid
7th or early 8th cent. AD
Gold
To the east of the temple T
Diam. 1.4 cm | d. 0.11 cm
Location: Graeco-Roman Museum,
Alexandria (SCA 105)

62

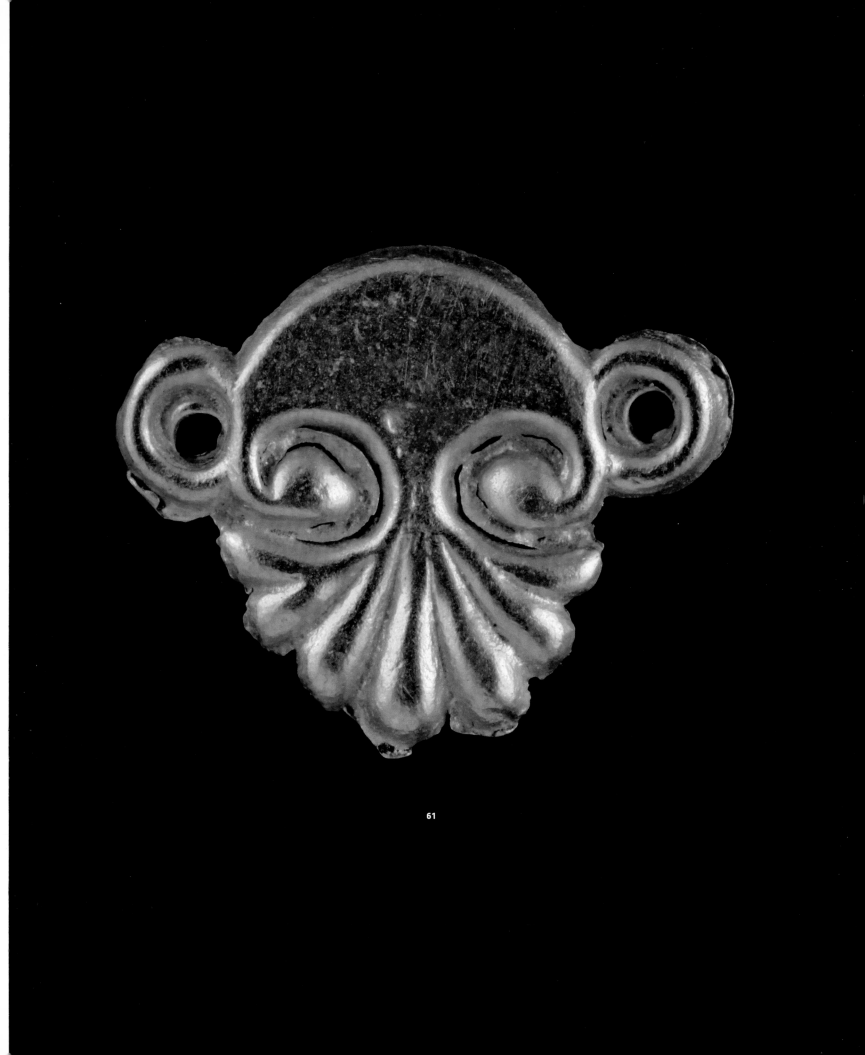

61

71 (p. 272)
Cross pendant
5th to early 8th cent. AD
Lead
To the east of the temple T
H. 1.97 cm | w. 1.41 cm | d. 0.21 cm
Location: Maritime Museum,
Alexandria (SCA 464)

74 (p. 283)
Seal
Early 6th cent. AD
Lead
Diam. 2.2 cm | d. 0.4 cm
Location: Excavations warehouse,
Alexandria (SCA 486)

77 (p. 283)
Seal
6th to 7th cent. AD
Lead
Diam. 2.1 cm | d. 0.2 cm
Location: Excavations warehouse,
Alexandria (SCA 487)

80 (p. 282)
Seal
7th cent. AD
Lead
Diam. 2.5 cm | d. 0.5 cm
Location: Excavations warehouse,
Alexandria (SCA 485)

75 (p. 282)
Seal
6th cent. AD
Lead
Diam. 1.8 cm | d. 0.5 cm
Location: Excavations warehouse,
Alexandria (SCA 484)

78 (p. 283)
Seal
6th to 7th cent. AD
Lead
Diam. 2.1 cm | d. 0.4 cm
Location: Excavations warehouse,
Alexandria (SCA 488)

81 (p. 344)
Mug
2nd cent. BC
Ceramic
H. 9.3 cm | diam. 5.7 cm
Location: Excavations warehouse,
Alexandria (SCA 1132)

72 (p. 272)
Cross pendant
6th to early 8th cent. AD
Lead
To the east of the temple T
H. 2.42 cm | w. 1.40 cm | d. 0.22 cm
Location: Maritime Museum,
Alexandria (SCA 468)

73 (p. 361)
Miniature mirror
Roman period
Lead
H. 2.5 cm | diam. 4.4 cm | d. 0.3 cm
Location: Excavations warehouse,
Alexandria (SCA 1170)

76 (p. 280)
Seal
6th to 7th cent. AD
Lead
Diam. 2.8 cm | d. 0.4 cm
Location: Excavations warehouse,
Alexandria (SCA 500)

79 (p. 282)
Seal
7th cent. AD
Lead
Diam. 2.5 cm | d. 0.5 cm
Location: Excavations warehouse,
Alexandria (SCA 483)

82 (p. 345)
Gawadis (Scoop)
Roman—Byzantine period
Ceramic
H. 27 cm | diam. 14.2 cm
Location: Excavations warehouse,
Alexandria (SCA 89)

83 (p. 259)
Solidus
Anthemius (467–472 AD)
Gold
Diam. 2 cm | wt. 3.25 g
Location: Great Library, Alexandria
(SCA 200)

86 (p. 261)
Semissis
Heraclius (610–641 AD)
Gold
Diam. 1.83 cm | wt. 2.15 g
Location: Graeco-Roman Museum,
Alexandria (SCA 94)

89 (p. 259)
Semissis
Heraclius (613–641 AD)
Gold
Diam. 1.86 cm | wt. 2.2 g
Location: National Museum,
Alexandria (SCA 99)

92 (p. 259)
Solidus
Heraclius (637–638 AD)
Gold
Diam. 2.1 cm | wt. 4.38 g
Location: Great Library, Alexandria
(SCA 201)

84 (p. 259)
Tremissis
Anastasius (491–518 AD)
Gold
Diam. 1.4 cm | wt. 1.37 g
Location: National Museum,
Alexandria (SCA 96)

87 (p. 259)
Tremissis
Heraclius (610–613 AD)
Gold
Diam. 1.63 cm | wt. 1.38 g
Location: Graeco-Roman Museum,
Alexandria (SCA 97)

90 (p. 259)
Tremissis
Heraclius (613–641 AD)
Gold
Diam. 1.85 cm | wt. 1.45 g
Location: Graeco-Roman Museum,
Alexandria (SCA 98)

93 (p. 261)
Solidus
Heraclius (639–641 AD)
Gold
Diam. 2 cm | wt. 4.3 g
Location: Graeco-Roman Museum,
Alexandria (SCA 319)

85 (p. 260)
Semissis
Mauricius (582–583 AD)
Gold
Diam. 1.7 cm | wt. 1.41 g
Location: Graeco-Roman Museum,
Alexandria (SCA 95)

88 (p. 261)
Semissis
Heraclius (610–613 AD)
Gold
Diam. 1.93 cm | wt. 2.13 g
Location: National Museum,
Alexandria (SCA 93)

91 (p. 71)
Tremissis
Heraclius (613–641 AD)
Gold
Diam. 1.69 cm | wt. 1.31 g
Location: Great Library, Alexandria
(SCA 199)

94 (p. 71)
Umayyad dinar
729–730 AD
Gold
Diam. 2 cm | wt. 4.25 g
Location: Great Library, Alexandria
(SCA 101)

95 (p. 71)
Umayyad third-dinar
718–719 AD
Gold
Diam. 1.37 cm | wt. 1.43 g
Location: Great Library, Alexandria
(SCA 100)

96
Coin
Cleopatra VII (718–719 AD)
Bronze
Diam. 2.1 cm | wt. 8.37 g
Location: Excavations warehouse,
Alexandria (SCA 1167)

97 (p. 54)
Coin
Cleopatra VII (51–30 BC)
Bronze
Diam. 2.5 cm
Location: Maritime Museum,
Alexandria (SCA 1169)

98 (p. 331)
Coin
Faustina II (163–170 AD)
Bronze
Diam. 2.2 cm
Location: Maritime Museum,
Alexandria (SCA 1168)

HERAKLEION

99 (p. 139)
Statue of Sethos II (A)
1203–1196 BC
Black granite
H. 127 cm | w. 60 cm | d. 30 cm
Location: Maritime Museum,
Alexandria (SCA 454)

100 (p. 139)
Statue of Sethos II (B)
1203–1196 BC
Black granite
H. 112 cm | w. 50 cm | d. 30 cm
Location: Maritime Museum,
Alexandria (SCA 453)

101 (p. 135)
Statue of Horus as a falcon
Late period–Ptolemaic period
Black granite
H. 68 cm | w. 23 cm | d. 54 cm
Location: Excavations warehouse,
Alexandria (SCA 278)

102 (p. 44)
Sphinx
4th cent. BC
Black granite
H. 98 cm | w. 147 cm | d. 58 cm
Location: Maritime Museum,
Alexandria (SCA 282)

105 (p. 146)
Sphinx
Ptolemaic period
Pink granite
H. body 40.5 cm | h. head 31 cm | w.
124 cm | d. 42.5 cm
Location: Maritime Museum,
Alexandria (SCA 625)

103 (p. 311)
**Colossal statue of
a god of fertility
probably Hapi**
4th cent. BC to early Ptolemaic period
Pink granite
H. 540 cm | wt. 6 t
Location: Maritime Museum,
Alexandria (SCA 281)

107 (p. 165)
Colossus of a Ptolemaic queen
Ptolemaic period
Pink granite
H. 490 cm | w. 120 cm | d. 75 cm | wt.
4 t
Location: Maritime Museum,
Alexandria (SCA 280)

108 (p. 205)
Statue of Thoth-Hermes
Ptolemaic period
Marble
H. 170 cm | w. 60 cm | d. 50 cm
Location: Roman Theatre, Alexandria
(SCA 532)

104 (p. 146)
Sphinx
Ptolemaic period
Pink granite
H. 139 cm | w. 36 cm | d. 68 cm
Location: Maritime Museum,
Alexandria (SCA 461)

106 (p. 165)
Colossus of a Ptolemaic king
Ptolemaic period
Pink granite
H. 500 cm | w. 150 cm | d. 75 cm | wt.
5.5 t
Location: Maritime Museum,
Alexandria (SCA 279)

109 (p. 239)
Torso of a clothed man
Ptolemaic period
Black granite
H. 45.5 cm
Location: Maritime Museum,
Alexandria (SCA 607)

114

358

328

353

110 (p. 239)
Torso of a clothed man
Ptolemaic period
Black granite
H. 77 cm
Location: Maritime Museum,
Alexandria (SCA 460)

111 (p. 238)
Torso of a clothed man
Ptolemaic period
Black granite
H. 42 cm
Location: Excavations warehouse,
Alexandria (SCA 455)

112 (p. 276)
Statue of a queen
Ptolemaic period
Black granite
H. 220 cm
Location: National Museum,
Alexandria (SCA 283)

113 (p. 249)
Statuette of a pregnant woman
Ptolemaic period
Limestone
H. 14 cm | w. 5 cm
Location: Excavations warehouse,
Alexandria (SCA 383)

114
Statuette with the head of an owl (?)
(left)
Ptolemaic period
Limestone
Votive depot
H. 11.5 cm | diam. 4.1 cm
Location: Excavations warehouse,
Alexandria (SCA 1050)

115 (p. 237)
Torso of a clothed man
2nd cent. BC
Black granite
H. 152 cm
Location: Maritime Museum,
Alexandria (SCA 452)

116 (p. 126)
Naos
Ptolemaic period
Pink granite
H. 110 cm | w. 53 cm | d. 63 cm
Location: Maritime Museum,
Alexandria (SCA 456)

117 (p. 127)
Naos from the Temple of Amon-gereb
Ptolemaic period
Pink granite
H. 174 cm | w. 93 cm | d. 100 cm
Location: Maritime Museum,
Alexandria (SCA 457)

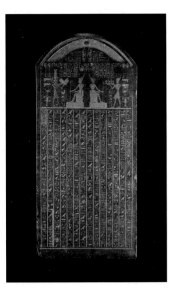

118 (p. 318)
Stele of Thonis-Herakleion
380 BC
Black granite
H. 195 cm | w. 88 cm | d. 34 cm
Location: National Museum,
Alexandria (SCA 277)

119 (p. 183)
Stele of Ptolemy VIII Euergetes II
2nd cent. BC
Pink granite
H. 610 cm | w. 310 cm | d. 40 cm |
wt. 15.7 t
Location: Maritime Museum,
Alexandria (SCA 529)

120 | 121 (p. 254)
Stone with gold fragments
6th to 2nd cent. BC
H. 15 cm | w. 30 cm | d. 30 cm
Location: Excavations warehouse,
Alexandria (SCA 381, 550)

122 (p. 196)
Oblatory dish
(bottom)
6th to 2nd cent. BC
Quartzite
H. 6.5 cm | diam. 46 cm
Location: Excavations warehouse,
Alexandria (SCA 364)

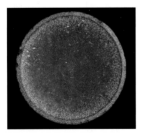

123
Oblatory dish
6th to 2nd cent. BC
Black granite
H. 4.4 cm | diam. 46 cm
Location: Excavations warehouse,
Alexandria (SCA 265)

124 (p. 196)
Oblatory dish
6th to 2nd cent. BC
Black granite
H. 6 cm | diam. 31.5 cm
Location: Excavations warehouse,
Alexandria (SCA 373)

125 (p. 196)
Oblatory dish
(top)
6th to 2nd cent. BC
Black granite
H. 6.3 cm | diam. 30 cm
Location: Excavations warehouse,
Alexandria (SCA 374)

126 (p. 196)
Oblatory dish
6th to 2nd cent. BC
Black granite
H. 5 cm | diam. 28.5 cm
Location: Excavations warehouse,
Alexandria (SCA 358)

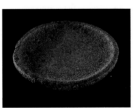

127
Oblatory dish
6th to 2nd cent. BC
Black granite
H. 6 cm | diam. 35 cm
Location: Excavations warehouse,
Alexandria (SCA 365)

128 (p. 251)
Votive anchor
6th to 2nd cent. BC
Limestone
H. 12.6 cm | w. 2.1–8 cm | d. 3.7 cm
Location: Excavations warehouse,
Alexandria (SCA 370)

129 (p. 251)
Votive anchor
6th to 2nd cent. BC
Limestone
H. 9 cm | w. 2.4–6.6 cm | d. 3.7 cm
Location: Excavations warehouse,
Alexandria (SCA 371)

130 (p. 240)
Scarab
6th to 2nd cent. BC
Stone
H. 1.6 cm | w. 4.8 cm | d. 3.4 cm
Location: Excavations warehouse,
Alexandria (SCA 523)

131 (p. 243)
Amulet
6th to 2nd cent. BC
Steatite
H. 1.35 cm | w. 1 cm | d. 0.6 cm
Location: Excavations warehouse,
Alexandria (SCA 841)

134 (p. 355)
Pot
6th to 2nd cent. BC
Alabaster
H. 6.7 cm | diam. 7.5 cm
Location: Excavations warehouse,
Alexandria (SCA 430)

137 (p. 230)
Bowl
Ptolemaic period
Stein
H. 5.3 cm | diam. 14 cm
Location: Excavations warehouse,
Alexandria (SCA 433)

140 (p. 354)
Mortar
6th to 2nd cent. BC
Black granite
H. 30 cm | diam. 32 cm
Location: Excavations warehouse,
Alexandria (SCA 367)

132
Phallus
Ptolemaic period
Limestone
L. 6.2 cm | diam. 2.9 cm
Location: Excavations warehouse,
Alexandria (SCA 528)

135 (p. 357)
Pot
6th to 2nd cent. BC
Alabaster
H. 9.8 cm | diam. 13.5 cm
Location: Excavations warehouse,
Alexandria (SCA 429)

138 (p. 354)
Mortar
6th to 2nd cent. BC
Black granite
H. 14 cm | diam. 37.5 cm
Location: Excavations warehouse,
Alexandria (SCA 268)

141
Mortar
6th to 2nd cent. BC
Black granite
H. 7.5 cm | w. 39 cm | d. 27 cm
Location: Excavations warehouse,
Alexandria (SCA 366)

133 (p. 353)
Gravestone
Ptolemaic period
Marble
H. 20 cm | w. 45 cm | d. 20 cm
Location: Excavations warehouse,
Alexandria (SCA 382)

136 (p. 351)
Incense burner
6th cent. BC
Limestone
H. 24.2 cm | w. 9 cm | d.12 cm | diam.
bowl: 13.5 cm
Location: Excavations warehouse,
Alexandria (SCA 270)

139
Mortar
6th to 2nd cent. BC
Black granite
H. 20 cm | diam. 20 cm
Location: Excavations warehouse,
Alexandria (SCA 267)

142 (p. 354)
Pestle
6th to 2nd cent. BC
Black granite
L. 27 cm | diam. 9.1 cm
Location: Excavations warehouse,
Alexandria (SCA 269)

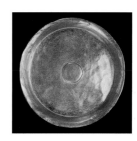

143 (p. 356)
Millstone
6th to 2nd cent. BC
Red granite
Diam. 120 cm | d. 28 cm
Location: Excavations warehouse,
Alexandria (SCA 458)

146 (p. 194)
Vat
Ptolemaic period
Pink granite
H. 63 cm | w. 205 cm | d. 90 cm
Location: Maritime Museum,
Alexandria (SCA 459)

149 (p. 353)
Headrest
6th to 2nd cent. BC
Limestone
H. 17 cm | w. 26.5 cm
Location: Excavations warehouse,
Alexandria (SCA 378)

152 (p. 226)
Phial
6th to 2nd cent. BC
Gold
H. 1.5 cm | diam. 18.9 cm | d. 0.1 cm
Location: Excavations warehouse,
Alexandria (SCA 296)

144
Grindstone
6th to 2nd cent. BC
Quartzite
H. 21 cm | w. 44 cm | d. 19 cm
Location: Excavations warehouse,
Alexandria (SCA 376)

147 (p. 355)
Kohl pot
6th to 2nd cent. BC
Alabaster
L. 15 cm | diam. 2 cm
Location: Excavations warehouse,
Alexandria (SCA 432)

150 (p. 353)
Headrest
(left)
6th to 2nd cent. BC
Limestone
H. 18 cm | w. 26.5 cm
Location: Excavations warehouse,
Alexandria (SCA 377)

153 (p. 228)
Bowl
6th to 2nd cent. BC
Silver
H. 6.4 cm | diam. 11 cm | d. 0.1 cm
Location: Excavations warehouse,
Alexandria (SCA 951)

145 (p. 357)
Grindstone
6th to 2nd cent. BC
Volcanic stone
H. 10 cm | w. 65 cm | d. 42 cm
Location: Excavations warehouse,
Alexandria (SCA 368)

148 (p. 353)
Headrest
6th to 2nd cent. BC
Limestone
H. 19.5 cm | w. 27 cm
Location: Excavations warehouse,
Alexandria (SCA 379)

151
Headrest
6th to 2nd cent. BC
Wood
H. 20 cm | w. 33 cm
Location: Excavations warehouse,
Alexandria (SCA 584)

154 (p. 266)
Lion-head earring
possibly 4th or 3rd cent. BC
Gold
Grand canal
Diam. 1.9 cm | d. 0.89 cm
Location: Graeco-Roman Museum,
Alexandria (SCA 298)

155   (p. 266)
Lion-head earring
possibly 3rd cent. BC
Gold
Grand canal
Diam. 2.76 cm | d. 1.1 cm
Location: Graeco-Roman Museum,
Alexandria (SCA 299)

158   (p. 267)
Earring with granule pyramid
Gold
Grand canal
Diam. 1.71 cm | d. 0.55 cm
Location: Graeco-Roman Museum,
Alexandria (SCA 308)

161   (p. 190)
Ptolemy III foundation plaque
(246–222 BC)
Gold
H. 11 cm | w. 5 cm | d. 0.1 cm
Location: Graeco-Roman Museum,
Alexandria (SCA 876)

164
Head-shaped gold pendant
3rd to 2nd cent. BC
Gold
H. 1.12 cm | w. 0.91 cm | d. 0.51 cm
Location: Graeco-Roman Museum,
Alexandria (SCA 1122)

156   (p. 267)
Animal-head earring
possibly 3rd cent. BC
Gold
Temple H1
Diam. 1.9 cm | d. 0.38 cm
Location: National Museum,
Alexandria (SCA 288)

159   (p. 268)
Sickle-shaped earring
Ptolemaic period (?)
Gold and filling material
Grand canal
Diam. 2.65 cm | d. 0.83 cm
Location: Graeco-Roman Museum,
Alexandria (SCA 297)

162
Pendant with a flexible bezel setting
Ptolemaic (?)
Gold
Grand canal
H. 2 cm | w. 1.12 cm | d. 0.64 cm
Location: Graeco-Roman Museum,
Alexandria (SCA 300)

165   (p. 271)
Finger ring with engraved Nike
possibly second half of the 4th or 3rd
cent. BC
Gold
Temple H1
Diam. 2.97 cm | d. 2.8 cm
Location: National Museum,
Alexandria (SCA 290)

157   (p. 267)
Twined earring
Ptolemaic (?)
Gold
Temple H1
Diam. 0.52 cm | d. 0.18 cm
Location: Graeco-Roman Museum,
Alexandria (SCA 292)

160
**Earring with filigree and granule
decoration**
Ptolemaic period (?)
Gold
Diam. 1.6 cm | d. 0.42 cm
Location: Graeco-Roman Museum,
Alexandria (SCA 1121)

163
Pendant with garnet bead
3rd or 2nd cent. BC
Gold and garnet
Temple H1
L. 1.35 cm | diam. pearl 0.58 cm
Location: Graeco-Roman Museum,
Alexandria (SCA 293)

166   (p. 270)
Golden ring with oval widening
Ptolemaic (?)
Gold
Grand canal
Diam. 1.8 cm | d. 0.71 cm
Location: Graeco-Roman Museum,
Alexandria (SCA 311)

167 (p. 271)
Finger ring with an oval glass or stone cabochon
Ptolemaic
Gold, glass or stone
Temple H1
Ring: diam. 2.68 cm | d. 1.89 cm
Cabochon: h. 1.45 cm | w. 0.96 cm | d. 0.35 cm
Location: National Museum, Alexandria (SCA 286)

168 (p. 270)
Ring with a quadratic bezel
Gold
Diam. 1.32 cm | d. 0.63 cm
Location: Graeco-Roman Museum, Alexandria (SCA 1118)

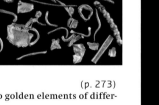

169 (p. 273)
Forty-two golden elements of different shapes
Ptolemaic period (?)
Gold
Temple H1
Various measurements and weights
Location: Graeco-Roman Museum, Alexandria (SCA 150)

170 (p. 242)
Bead in the form of the eye of Horus or Oudjat
Late Pharaonic—Ptolemaic
Gold
H. 0.68 cm
Location: Graeco-Roman Museum, Alexandria (SCA 1123)

171 (p. 248)
Statuette of Anubis
6th to 2nd cent. BC
Bronze
H. 18 cm | w. 22.7 cm | d. 3.7 cm
Location: Roman Theatre, Alexandria (SCA 975)

172 (p. 367)
Statuette of Bastet
6th to 2nd cent. BC
Bronze
H. 16 cm | w. 10 cm
Location: Excavations warehouse, Alexandria (SCA 474)

173 (p. 244)
Statuette of Bastet
6th to 2nd cent. BC
Bronze
H. 19 cm | w. 4.3 cm | d. 7.1 cm
Location: Excavations warehouse, Alexandria (SCA 930)

174 (p. 245)
Statuette of Bastet
6th to 2nd cent. BC
Bronze
H. 7.1 cm | w. 3.9 cm | d. 1.6 cm
Location: Excavations warehouse, Alexandria (SCA 968)

175 (p. 248)
Statuette of Ibis
6th to 2nd cent. BC
Bronze
H. 10 cm | w. 8.8 cm | d. 3.3 cm
Location: Roman Theatre, Alexandria (SCA 1087)

176 (p. 247)
Statuette of Sachmet
6th to 2nd cent. BC
Bronze
H. 16.7 cm | w. 3.7 cm | d. 1.7 cm
Location: Excavations warehouse, Alexandria (SCA 1041)

177 (p. 124)
Statuette of Chons with a lunar disc on his head
Late period
Bronze
H. 21.5 cm | w. 6.5 cm
Location: Excavations warehouse, Alexandria (SCA 387)

178 (p. 125)
Statuette of Harpokrates
Late period—Ptolemaic period
Bronze
H. 10.6 cm | w. 4.4 cm | d. 2 cm
Location: Excavations warehouse,
Alexandria (SCA 1022)

181 (p. 125)
Statuette of Harpokrates
Late period—Ptolemaic period
Bronze
H. 10.4 cm | w. 2.8 cm | d. 1.8 cm
Location: Excavations warehouse,
Alexandria (SCA 1008)

184 (p. 117)
Statuette of Isis *lactans*
Late period—Ptolemaic period
Bronze
H. 10 cm | w. 3.5 cm
Location: Excavations warehouse,
Alexandria (SCA 978)

187
Statuette of Osiris
Late period—Ptolemaic period
Bronze
H. 6.4 cm | w. 2 cm | d. 1 cm
Location: Excavations warehouse,
Alexandria (SCA 966)

179 (p. 125)
Statuette of Harpokrates
Late period—Ptolemaic period
Bronze
H. 9.2 cm | w. 2.7 cm | d. 1.3 cm
Location: Excavations warehouse,
Alexandria (SCA 995)

182 (p. 105)
Statuette of Isis *lactans*
Late period—Ptolemaic period
Bronze
H. 18 cm | w. 4.1 cm | d. 1.8 cm
Location: Excavations warehouse,
Alexandria (SCA 1093)

185
Statuette of Osiris
Late period—Ptolemaic period
Bronze
H. 21 cm | w. 4.3 cm | d. 2.2 cm
Location: Excavations warehouse,
Alexandria (SCA 1081)

188
Statuette of Osiris
Late period—Ptolemaic period
Bronze
H. 10.3 cm | w. 2.8 cm
Location: Excavations warehouse,
Alexandria (SCA 982)

180 (p. 125)
Statuette of Harpokrates
Late period—Ptolemaic period
Bronze
H. 8.8 cm | w. 2.7 cm | d. 1 cm
Location: Excavations warehouse,
Alexandria (SCA 1059)

183 (p. 117)
Statuette of Isis *lactans*
Late period—Ptolemaic period
Bronze
H. 11.8 cm | w. 2.8 cm
Location: Excavations warehouse,
Alexandria (SCA 972)

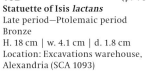

186
Statuette of Osiris
Late period—Ptolemaic period
Bronze
H. 9.1 cm | w. 2.2 cm | d. 1 cm
Location: Excavations warehouse,
Alexandria (SCA 411)

189
Statuette of Osiris
Late period—Ptolemaic period
Bronze
H. 7.9 cm | w. 2.4 cm | d. 1.2 cm
Location: Excavations warehouse,
Alexandria (SCA 1013)

190
Statuette of Osiris
Late period—Ptolemaic period
Bronze
H. 9.3 cm | w. 2.5 cm | d. 2.4 cm
Location: Excavations warehouse,
Alexandria (SCA 952)

193   (p. 364)
Statuette of Athena
Ptolemaic period
Bronze
H. 9.2 cm | w. 2.8 cm | d. 1.4 cm
Location: Excavations warehouse,
Alexandria (SCA 996)

196
Plinth of a statuette
6th to 2nd cent. BC
Bronze
H. 5 cm | w. 3 cm | d. 3 cm
Location: Roman Theatre, Alexandria
(SCA 994)

199   (p. 197)
Image of Osiris
Late period
Bronze
H. 5.5 cm | w. 1.5 cm | d. 2 cm
Location: Excavations warehouse,
Alexandria (SCA 926)

191
Statuette of Osiris
Late period—Ptolemaic period
Bronze
H. 9 cm | w. 2.7 cm | d. 0.7 cm
Location: Excavations warehouse,
Alexandria (SCA 1004)

194   (p. 220)
Base of figurine of the goddess Maat
6th to 2nd cent. BC
Bronze
H. 8.5 cm | w. 2.5 cm | d. 1.9 cm
Location: Roman Theatre, Alexandria
(SCA 1003)

197
Head of Amon (?)
6th to 2nd cent. BC
Bronze
H. 3.4 cm | w. 2.25 cm
Location: Excavations warehouse,
Alexandria (SCA 1019)

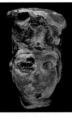

200
Anubis emblem holder
6th to 2nd cent. BC
Bronze
H. 4.7 cm | w. 4 cm | d. 0.8 cm
Location: Roman Theatre, Alexandria
(SCA 973)

192
Statuette of Osiris
Late period—Ptolemaic period
Bronze
H. 6 cm | w. 1.7 cm
Location: Excavations warehouse,
Alexandria (SCA 1031)

195   (p. 246)
Base of figurine
6th to 2nd cent. BC
Bronze
Location: Roman Theatre, Alexandria
(SCA 962)

198   (p. 246)
Image of Nechbet
6th to 2nd cent. BC
Bronze
H. 17 cm | w. 10 cm | d. 3 cm
Location: Roman Theatre, Alexandria
(SCA 895)

201
Anubis emblem
6th to 2nd cent. BC
Bronze
H. 8.6 cm | w. 4.7 cm | d. 2.7 cm
Location: Roman Theatre, Alexandria
(SCA 981)

202
Emblem of the falcon Horus
6th to 2nd cent. BC
Bronze
H. 6.9 cm | w. 4.2 cm
Location: Roman Theatre, Alexandria
(SCA 997)

203
Emblem of the sacred bull
6th to 2nd cent. BC
Bronze
H. 4.2 cm | w. 4.5 cm | d. 1.6 cm
Location: Roman Theatre, Alexandria
(SCA 1001)

204   (p. 227)
Emblem
6th to 2nd cent. BC
Bronze
H. 13.6 cm | w. 7.9 cm | diam. 2.3 cm
Location: Excavations warehouse,
Alexandria (SCA 1037)

205   (p. 368)
Part of a crown
6th to 2nd cent. BC
Bronze
H. 6.1 cm | w. 3.1 cm | d. 1.8 cm
Location: Excavations warehouse,
Alexandria (SCA 1006)

206   (p. 368)
Part of a crown
6th to 2nd cent. BC
Bronze
H. 10.7 cm | w. 1.3 cm
Location: Excavations warehouse,
Alexandria (SCA 927)

207   (p. 368)
Part of a crown
6th to 2nd cent. BC
Bronze
H. 12.3 cm | d. 0.7 cm
Location: Excavations warehouse,
Alexandria (SCA 1074)

208   (p. 368)
Part of a crown
6th to 2nd cent. BC
Bronze
H. 18.9 cm | w. 4.2 cm | d. 0.6 cm
Location: Excavations warehouse,
Alexandria (SCA 1002)

209   (p. 128)
Hem-hem crown of Chons
End of late period—early Ptolemaic
period
Bronze
H. 15 cm | w. 10 cm
Location: Excavations warehouse,
Alexandria (SCA 401)

210
Element from a crown of Amon
End of late period—Ptolemaic period
Bronze
H. 8.7 cm | w. 3.4 cm
Location: Excavations warehouse,
Alexandria (SCA 929)

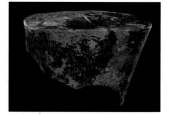

211
Crown of Amon
Ptolemaic period
Bronze
H. 15.1 cm | w. 18 cm | d. 22 cm
Location: Excavations warehouse,
Alexandria (SCA 967)

212   (p. 366)
**Miniature sarcophagus with a
figurine of a shrew**
6th to 2nd cent. BC
Bronze
H. 3.5 cm | w. 7 cm | d. 1.7 cm
Location: Excavations warehouse,
Alexandria (SCA 404)

213   (p. 125)
Amulet of Harpokrates
Late period—Ptolemaic period
Bronze
H. 3.3 cm | w. 1.3 cm | d. 0.6 cm
Location: Excavations warehouse,
Alexandria (SCA 423)

214 (p. 134)
Wig
Late period—Ptolemaic period
Bronze, silver, electrum
H. 25 cm | w. 13 cm | d. 18.5 cm
Location: Excavations warehouse,
Alexandria (SCA 976)

217 (p. 222)
Mirror
6th to 2nd cent. BC
Bronze
H. 16.3 cm | diam. 11.2 cm | d. 0.4 cm
Location: Excavations warehouse,
Alexandria (SCA 941)

220 (p. 222)
Mirror
6th to 2nd cent. BC
Bronze
H. 19.9 cm | diam. 18.2 cm | d. 1 cm
Location: Excavations warehouse,
Alexandria (SCA 934)

223 (p. 223)
Mirror
Ptolemaic period
Bronze
H. 22.6 cm | diam. 16.2 cm | d. 0.5 cm
Location: Excavations warehouse,
Alexandria (SCA 1048)

215 (p. 197)
Artificial beard
Late period—Ptolemaic period
Bronze
L. 16.6 cm | d. 4.6 cm
Location: Excavations warehouse,
Alexandria (SCA 1079)

218 (p. 222)
Mirror
6th to 2nd cent. BC
Bronze
H. 15.1 cm | diam. 11.9 cm | d. 0.4 cm
Location: Excavations warehouse,
Alexandria (SCA 1016)

221 (p. 222)
Mirror
6th to 2nd cent. BC
Bronze
H. 19.8 cm | diam. 15 cm | d. 0.6 cm
Location: Excavations warehouse,
Alexandria (SCA 985)

224 (p. 228)
Vessel
5th to 2nd cent. BC
Bronze
H. 13 cm | diam. 41.5 cm | d. 0.3 cm
Location: Excavations warehouse,
Alexandria (SCA 222)

216 (p. 366)
Seat
6th to 2nd cent. BC
Bronze
H. 9.3 cm | w. 15 cm | d. 3.9 cm
Location: Excavations warehouse,
Alexandria (SCA 905)

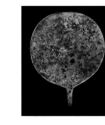

219 (p. 223)
Mirror
6th to 2nd cent. BC
Bronze
H. 14.4 cm | diam. 11.8 cm | d. 0.3 cm
Location: Excavations warehouse,
Alexandria (SCA 984)

222 (p. 223)
Mirror
6th to 2nd cent. BC
Bronze
H. 23.6 cm | diam. 17.2 cm | d. 1 cm
Location: Excavations warehouse,
Alexandria (SCA 1056)

225
Receptacle
Ptolemaic period
Bronze
H. 5.6 cm | diam. 10.2 cm | d. 0.2 cm
Location: Excavations warehouse,
Alexandria (SCA 1130)

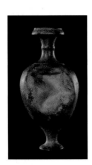

226 (p. 218)
Vessel
Ptolemaic period
Bronze
H. 10.3 cm | diam. 5.1 cm
Location: Excavations warehouse,
Alexandria (SCA 1010)

227 (p. 229)
Cauldron
Ptolemaic period
Bronze
H. 18 cm | w. incl. handles 45.4 cm |
diam. 27.9 cm
Location: Excavations warehouse,
Alexandria (SCA 407)

228
Lekythos
Late period—Ptolemaic period
Bronze
H. 20.9 cm | diam. 3.8–8.1 cm | d.
0.1 cm
Location: Excavations warehouse,
Alexandria (SCA 896)

229
Bowl
6th to 4th cent. BC
Bronze
H. 8.5 cm | diam. 9.6 cm | d. 0.1 cm
Location: Excavations warehouse,
Alexandria (SCA 904)

230
Bowl
Late period
Bronze
H. 8.2 cm | diam. 11.2 cm | d. 0.1 cm
Location: Excavations warehouse,
Alexandria (SCA 216)

231
Bowl
Late period—Ptolemaic period
Bronze
H. 7.8 cm | diam. 11.7 cm
Location: Excavations warehouse,
Alexandria (SCA 897)

232
Bowl
Late period—Ptolemaic period
Bronze
H. 9.4 cm | diam. 10.7 cm | d. 0.1 cm
Location: Excavations warehouse,
Alexandria (SCA 1023)

233
Bowl
Ptolemaic period
Bronze
H. 14.5 cm | diam. 11 cm
Location: Excavations warehouse,
Alexandria (SCA 987)

234
Bowl
Ptolemaic period
Bronze
H. 13 cm | diam. 9.7 cm
Location: Excavations warehouse,
Alexandria (SCA 992)

235
Basin
6th to 2nd cent. BC
Bronze
H. 11.9 cm | diam. 42.1 cm
Location: Excavations warehouse,
Alexandria (SCA 911)

236
Basin
6th to 2nd cent. BC
Bronze
H. 7 cm | diam. 26.7 cm
Location: Excavations warehouse,
Alexandria (SCA 1011)

237
Basin
Ptolemaic period
Bronze
H. 13.3 cm | diam. 25.8 cm
Location: Excavations warehouse,
Alexandria (SCA 899)

238
Basin
Ptolemaic period
Bronze
H. 17 cm | diam. 25.3 cm
Location: Excavations warehouse,
Alexandria (SCA 900)

239
Small dish
6th to 2nd cent. BC
Bronze
Diam. 13 cm
Location: Excavations warehouse,
Alexandria (SCA 400)

240 (p. 228)
Bowl
5th to 2nd cent. BC
Bronze
H. 6.4 cm | diam. 10.5 cm | d. 0.35 cm
Location: Excavations warehouse,
Alexandria (SCA 986)

244
Bowl
Late period
Bronze
H. 6.5 cm | diam. 12.5 cm | d. 0.1 cm
Location: Excavations warehouse,
Alexandria (SCA 586)

248
Bowl
Late period
Bronze
H. 9.8 cm | diam. 15.5 cm | d. 0.2 cm
Location: Excavations warehouse,
Alexandria (SCA 1045)

252 (p. 229)
Bowl with handle
Ptolemaic period
Bronze
H. 9.6 cm | diam. 25.2 cm
Location: Excavations warehouse,
Alexandria (SCA 406)

241 (p. 394)
Bowl
Late Pharaonic period
Bronze
H. 6 cm | diam. 13.3 cm
Location: Excavations warehouse,
Alexandria (SCA 991)

245
Bowl
Late period
Bronze
H. 7.2 cm | diam. 11.2 cm | d. 0.1 cm
Location: Excavations warehouse,
Alexandria (SCA 390)

249
Bowl
Late period
Bronze
H. 6.9 cm | diam. 13.1 cm | d. 0.2 cm
Location: Excavations warehouse,
Alexandria (SCA 964)

253 (p. 225)
Situla
Late period—Ptolemaic period
Bronze
H. 3.4 cm | diam. 3.4 cm | d. 0.4 cm
Location: Excavations warehouse,
Alexandria (SCA 1060)

242 (p. 228)
Bowl
Ptolemaic period
Bronze
H. 7 cm | diam. 12.2 cm | d. 0.2 cm
Location: Excavations warehouse,
Alexandria (SCA 566)

246
Bowl
Late period
Bronze
H. 6.5 cm | diam. 12.7 cm | d. 0.4 cm
Location: Excavations warehouse,
Alexandria (SCA 940)

250
Bowl
Late period
Bronze
H. 7.3 cm | diam. 14.6 cm | d. 0.2 cm
Location: Excavations warehouse,
Alexandria (SCA 928)

254
Situla
Ptolemaic period
Bronze
H. 7.2 cm, with handle 18.9 cm | diam.
5.7 cm | d. handle 0.2 cm
Location: Excavations warehouse,
Alexandria (SCA 1025)

243
Bowl
Late period
Bronze
H. 9.3 cm | diam. 12.1 cm | d. 0.1 cm
Location: Excavations warehouse,
Alexandria (SCA 391)

247
Bowl
(right)
Late period
Bronze
H. 9.4 cm | diam. 13.4 cm | d. 0.3 cm
Location: Excavations warehouse,
Alexandria (SCA 916)

251
Bowl
Late period—Ptolemaic period
Bronze
H. 6.5 cm | diam. 12.6 cm | d. 0.1 cm
Location: Excavations warehouse,
Alexandria (SCA 961)

255 (p. 199)
Situla
Ptolemaic period
Bronze
H. 25 cm | diam. 28.5 cm | d. 0.4 cm
Location: Excavations warehouse,
Alexandria (SCA 223)

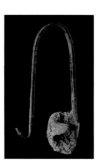

258 (p. 398)
Simpulum
6th to 2nd cent. BC
Bronze
L. 48 cm | diam. 6 cm
Location: Excavations warehouse,
Alexandria (SCA 908)

261
Simpulum
6th to 2nd cent. BC
Bronze
L. 50.4 cm | diam. 6.1 cm
Location: Excavations warehouse,
Alexandria (SCA 220)

264
Simpulum
6th to 2nd cent. BC
Bronze
L. 50.7 cm | diam. 4.2 cm
Location: Excavations warehouse,
Alexandria (SCA 397)

256
Stand
6th to 2nd cent. BC
Bronze
H. 6.8 cm | diam. 50.1 cm
Location: Excavations warehouse,
Alexandria (SCA 993)

259 (p. 201)
Simpulum
Ptolemaic period
Bronze
L. 26.5 cm | diam. 6.1 cm
Location: Excavations warehouse,
Alexandria (SCA 1064)

262
Simpulum
6th to 2nd cent. BC
Bronze
L. 55.4 cm | diam. 6.9 cm
Location: Excavations warehouse,
Alexandria (SCA 478)

265
Simpulum
6th to 2nd cent. BC
Bronze
L. 51.9 cm | diam. 6.5 cm
Location: Excavations warehouse,
Alexandria (SCA 1095)

257 (p. 398)
Simpulum
6th to 2nd cent. BC
Bronze
L. 46.5 cm | diam. 5.3 cm
Location: Excavations warehouse,
Alexandria (SCA 1071)

260 (p. 203)
Simpulum
6th to 2nd cent. BC
Bronze
L. 52.2 cm | diam. 6.7 cm
Location: Excavations warehouse,
Alexandria (SCA 395)

263
Simpulum
6th to 2nd cent. BC
Bronze
L. 50.5 cm | diam. 6.1 cm
Location: Excavations warehouse,
Alexandria (SCA 579)

266
Simpulum
6th to 2nd cent. BC
Bronze
L. 53.8 cm | diam. 4.2 cm
Location: Excavations warehouse,
Alexandria (SCA 1042)

267
Simpulum
6th to 2nd cent. BC
Bronze
L. 49.2 cm | diam. 5.8 cm
Location: Excavations warehouse,
Alexandria (SCA 909)

270   (p. 203)
Simpulum
Ptolemaic period
Bronze
L. 51.8 cm | diam. 4.2 cm
Location: Excavations warehouse,
Alexandria (SCA 1034)

273
Simpulum
Ptolemaic period
Bronze
L. 56.8 cm | diam. 4.1 cm
Location: Excavations warehouse,
Alexandria (SCA 1014)

276
Ladle
6th to 2nd cent. BC
Bronze
L. 20.3 cm | diam. 10.2 cm
Location: Excavations warehouse,
Alexandria (SCA 1057)

not illus

268
Simpulum
6th to 2nd cent. BC
Bronze
L. 51.7 cm | diam. 4.5 cm
Location: Excavations warehouse,
Alexandria (SCA 936)

271
Simpulum
Ptolemaic period
Bronze
L. 44.5 cm | diam. 7.4 cm
Location: Excavations warehouse,
Alexandria (SCA 1032)

274   (p. 218)
Spoon
6th to 2nd cent. BC
Bronze
L. 27 cm | diam. 10.2 cm
Location: Excavations warehouse,
Alexandria (SCA 1044)

277
Ladle
6th to 2nd cent. BC
Bronze
L. 27.1 cm | diam. 11.5 cm
Location: Excavations warehouse,
Alexandria (SCA 1078)

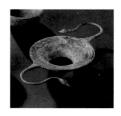

269
Simpulum
Ptolemaic period
Bronze
L. 52.3 cm | diam. 5.6 cm
Location: Excavations warehouse,
Alexandria (SCA 931)

272
Simpulum
Ptolemaic period
Bronze
L. 43.9 cm | diam. 4.4 cm
Location: Excavations warehouse,
Alexandria (SCA 1043)

275
Ladle
6th to 2nd cent. BC
Bronze
L. 25.2 cm | diam. 10.4 cm
Location: Excavations warehouse,
Alexandria (SCA 915)

278   (p. 201)
Strainer
6th to 2nd cent. BC
Bronze
H. 1.4 cm, l. 17.6 cm | diam. 8.6 cm
Location: Excavations warehouse,
Alexandria (SCA 1063)

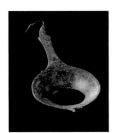

279 (p. 201)
Strainer
6th to 2nd cent. BC
Bronze
H. 2.7 cm, l. 22 cm | diam. 9.1 cm |
d. 0.1 cm
Location: Excavations warehouse,
Alexandria (SCA 1062)

280 (p. 202)
Strainer
Ptolemaic period
Bronze
H. 3.1 cm, l. 28.8 cm | diam. 14.6 cm
Location: Excavations warehouse,
Alexandria (SCA 1029)

281 | 282 (p. 219)
Candelabra
6th to 2nd cent. BC
Bronze
H. foot 18.8 cm | diam. foot
3.2–3.8 cm (281)
Diam. bowl 9.5 cm (282)
Location: Excavations warehouse,
Alexandria (SCA 1054, 1061)

283 | 284 (p. 221)
Lamp and handle
Ptolemaic period
Bronze
H. 11 cm | w. 13.2 cm | d. 7.6 cm (283)
L. 36.4 cm | d. 1.1 cm (284)
Location: Excavations warehouse,
Alexandria (SCA 1024, 1028)

285
Oil lamp
5th to 4th cent. BC
Bronze
H. 1.3 cm | diam. 12 cm
Location: Excavations warehouse,
Alexandria (SCA 980)

286
Brazier
6th to 2nd cent. BC
Bronze
H. 7.8 cm, diam: 7.4–8.6 cm
Location: Excavations warehouse,
Alexandria (SCA 1058)

287 (p. 219)
Incense burner
6th to 2nd cent. BC
Bronze
H. 9.6 cm | diam. 8.7–9.9 cm
Location: Excavations warehouse,
Alexandria (SCA 1073)

288 (p. 229)
Brazier
6th to 2nd cent. BC
Bronze
H. 23 cm | diam. 46 cm
Location: Excavations warehouse,
Alexandria (SCA 912)

289 (p. 219)
Incense burner (?)
6th to 2nd cent. BC
Bronze
H. 8.3 cm | diam. 13 cm
Location: Excavations warehouse,
Alexandria (SCA 1086)

290
Incense burner
6th to 2nd cent. BC
Bronze
H. 7.9 cm | diam. 10.4 cm
Location: Excavations warehouse,
Alexandria (SCA 392)

291
Sistrum
(lower part)
6th to 2nd cent. BC
Bronze
H. 14 cm | w. 4 cm | d. 1.2 cm
Location: Excavations warehouse,
Alexandria (SCA 581)

292
Central section of a sistrum
6th to 2nd cent. BC
Bronze
H. 8 cm | w. 4.3 cm | d. 1.3 cm
Location: Excavations warehouse,
Alexandria (SCA 977)

293
Arched sistrum
6th to 2nd cent. BC
Bronze
H. 2.7 cm, l. 12 cm | d. 4 cm
Location: Excavations warehouse,
Alexandria (SCA 906)

296   (p. 227)
Bell
6th to 2nd cent. BC
Bronze
H. 7.6 cm | diam. 4.5–5.2 cm | d.
0.4 cm
Location: Excavations warehouse,
Alexandria (SCA 385)

299   (p. 358)
Ring
6th to 2nd cent. BC
Bronze
L. 9.5 cm | diam. 4.3 cm | d. 1.2 cm
Location: Excavations warehouse,
Alexandria (SCA 393)

302
Shovel
6th to 2nd cent. BC
Bronze
L. 13 cm, l. shovel 5.2 cm | w. shovel
3.8 cm
Location: Excavations warehouse,
Alexandria (SCA 580)

294   (p. 358)
Weights
6th to 2th cent. BC
Bronze
L. 0.3–1.2 cm | w. 0.3–1.2 cm | wt.
0.45–7.13 g
Location: Excavations warehouse,
Alexandria (SCA 501)

297
Ring handle
6th to 2nd cent. BC
Bronze
Diam. 10.2 cm
Location: Excavations warehouse,
Alexandria (SCA 910)

300
Sections of a door
6th to 2nd cent. BC
Bronze
H. 12 cm | w. 12 cm
Location: Excavations warehouse,
Alexandria (SCA 564)

303   (p. 227)
Tongs
6th to 2nd cent. BC
Bronze
L. 45.9 cm | d. 0.4 cm
Location: Excavations warehouse,
Alexandria (SCA 943)

295   (p. 227)
Bell
6th to 2nd cent. BC
Bronze
H. 7.5 cm | diam. 4.3–5.2 cm | d.
0.2 cm
Location: Excavations warehouse,
Alexandria (SCA 388)

298
Handles
6th to 2nd cent. BC
Bronze
Location: Excavations warehouse,
Alexandria (SCA 1018)

301
Nails
6th to 2nd cent. BC
Bronze
L. 20–25 cm
Location: Excavations warehouse,
Alexandria (SCA 1097)

304   (p. 363)
Fish-hook
6th to 2nd cent. BC
Bronze
L. 12 cm | d. 0.35 cm
Location: Excavations warehouse,
Alexandria (SCA 495)

305   (p. 363)
Fish-hook
6th to 2nd cent. BC
Bronze
L. 2.4 cm | d. 0.2 cm
Location: Excavations warehouse,
Alexandria (SCA 492)

306   (p. 363)
Fish-hook
6th to 2nd cent. BC
Bronze
L. 5.9 cm | d. 0.3 cm
Location: Excavations warehouse,
Alexandria (SCA 493)

307   (p. 363)
Fish-hook
6th to 2nd cent. BC
Bronze
L. 2.9 cm | d. 0.2 cm
Location: Excavations warehouse,
Alexandria (SCA 503)

308
Axe blade
6th to 2nd cent. BC
Bronze
H. 2.9 cm | w. 6.8 cm
Location: Roman Theatre, Alexandria
(SCA 1066)

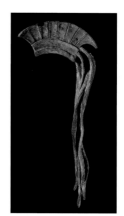

309
Axe blade
6th to 2nd cent. BC
Bronze
H. 2.9 cm | w. 9.9 cm
Location: Excavations warehouse,
Alexandria (SCA 1084)

310
Dagger
6th to 2nd cent. BC
Iron and wood
L. 15 cm
Location: Excavations warehouse,
Alexandria (SCA 1065)

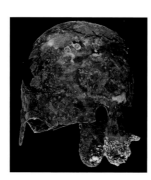

311   (p. 292)
Helmet
5th to 4th cent. BC
Bronze
H. 34 cm | w. 23.5 cm
Location: Excavations warehouse,
Alexandria (SCA 1026)

312   (p. 365)
Helmet crest
4th cent. BC
Bronze
H. 81 cm | w. 34 cm | d. 5 cm
Location: Excavations warehouse,
Alexandria (SCA 224)

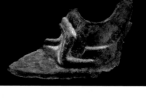

313   (p. 292)
Helmet cheek-piece
4th cent. BC
Bronze
H. 14 cm | w. 7.5 cm
Location: Excavations warehouse,
Alexandria (SCA 971)

314   (p. 293)
Javelin tip/spear tip
5th to 4th cent. BC
Bronze
L. 13.3 cm
Location: Excavations warehouse,
Alexandria (SCA 1049)

315   (p. 293)
Lance tip
5th to 4th cent. BC
Bronze
L. 27 cm | w. 2.5 cm | diam. 2.4 cm
Location: Excavations warehouse,
Alexandria (SCA 1094)

316   (p. 293)
Spear tip
5th to 4th cent. BC
Bronze
L. 35 cm | w. 2.5 cm | diam. 2.5 cm
Location: Excavations warehouse,
Alexandria (SCA 1096)

317   (p. 293)
Javelin tip
6th to 2nd cent. BC
Bronze
L. 18 cm | w. 3 cm
Location: Excavations warehouse,
Alexandria (SCA 913)

318 (p. 294)
Arrowhead
6th to 2nd cent. BC
Bronze
L. 3.3 cm | w. 1.3 cm | d. 0.9 cm
Location: Excavations warehouse,
Alexandria (SCA 499)

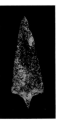

319 (p. 294)
Arrowhead
6th to 2nd cent. BC
Bronze
L. 3 cm | diam. 1.8 cm
Location: Excavations warehouse,
Alexandria (SCA 498)

320 (p. 313)
Plaques
Ptolemaic period
Bronze
H. 15 cm | w. 14 cm | d. 1 cm (A)
H. 21.5 cm | w. 15.5 cm | d. 1 cm (B)
Location: Excavations warehouse,
Alexandria (SCA 389)

321 (p. 291)
Anchor fragment
6th to 2nd cent. BC
Bronze
L. 21 cm
Location: Excavations warehouse,
Alexandria (SCA 1069)

322 (p. 359)
Bronze utensil
5th to 2nd cent. BC
Bronze
H. 6.7 cm, l. 35.8 cm | d. 2.8 cm
Location: Excavations warehouse,
Alexandria (SCA 1047)

323 (p. 243)
Statuette of Horus-Falcon
6th to 2nd cent. BC
Lead
H. 2.5 cm | w. 1.4 cm | d. 0.7 cm
Location: Excavations warehouse,
Alexandria (SCA 561)

324
Statuette of Thoth the Baboon
6th to 2nd cent. BC
Lead
H. 4.3 cm | d. 2.9 cm
Location: Excavations warehouse,
Alexandria (SCA 1098)

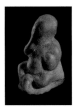

325 (p. 246)
Statuette of Thoth the Baboon
6th to 2nd cent. BC
Lead
H. 2.8 cm | w. 1.5 cm
Location: Roman Theatre, Alexandria
(SCA 1021)

326 (p. 368)
Uraeus-snake
6th to 2nd cent. BC
Lead
H. 19 cm | w. 4.2 cm
Location: Excavations warehouse,
Alexandria (SCA 990)

327 (p. 241)
Statuette of a deity
6th to 2nd cent. BC
Lead
H. 9.4 cm | w. 2.2 cm
Location: Excavations warehouse,
Alexandria (SCA 974)

328
Harpokrates
Ptolemaic period
Lead
Votive depot
H. 4.2 cm | w. 2.9 cm | d. 2 cm
Location: Excavations warehouse,
Alexandria (SCA 1052)

329 (p. 124)
Harpokrates
Ptolemaic period
Lead
H. 4 cm | w. 2.5 cm | d. 0.5 cm
Location: Excavations warehouse,
Alexandria (SCA 925)

330   (p. 124)
Statuette of Harpokrates
Ptolemaic period
Lead
H. 5 cm | w. 2.5 cm | d. 0.5 cm
Location: Excavations warehouse,
Alexandria (SCA 917)

331   (p. 249)
Statuette of a woman
Ptolemaic period
Lead
H. 3.2 cm | w. 3.6 cm | d. 1 cm
Location: Excavations warehouse,
Alexandria (SCA 1033)

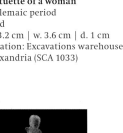

332
Statuette of an elephant
Ptolemaic period
Lead
H. 4.2 cm | w. 3.6 cm | d. 1 cm
Location: Excavations warehouse,
Alexandria (SCA 1046)

333
Figurine of an elephant
Ptolemaic period
Lead
H. 2.4 cm | w. 3 cm
Location: Excavations warehouse,
Alexandria (SCA 526)

334   (p. 198)
Votive barque
Ptolemaic period
Lead
W. 12.1 cm | d. 1.6 cm
Location: Excavations warehouse,
Alexandria (SCA 405)

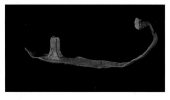

335   (p. 198)
Votive barque
Ptolemaic period
Lead
W. 21.5 cm | d. 3 cm
Location: Excavations warehouse,
Alexandria (SCA 1017)

336   (p. 198)
Votive barque
Ptolemaic period
Lead
H. 6.2 cm | w. 37.3 cm | d. 3.3 cm
Location: Excavations warehouse,
Alexandria (SCA 1039)

337   (p. 198)
Votive barque
Ptolemaic period
Lead
w. 44.5 cm | d. 3.7 cm
Location: Excavations warehouse,
Alexandria (SCA 1072)

338   (p. 187)
Uraeus amulet
Late period
Ceramic
H. 1.6 cm | w. 3.7 cm | d. 1 cm
Location: Excavations warehouse,
Alexandria (SCA 555)

339
Phallus-shaped amulet
Ptolemaic period
Lead
L. 5 cm | diam. 1.4 cm
Location: Excavations warehouse,
Alexandria (SCA 1020)

340
Amulet (?) in the shape of a coin
6th to 2nd cent. BC
Lead
H. 1.2 cm | w. 1 cm | d. 0.2 cm
Location: Excavations warehouse,
Alexandria (SCA 512)

341
Amulets (?) in the shape of coins
6th to 2nd cent. BC
Lead
H. 1.2 cm | w. 1 cm | d. 0.2 cm
Location: Excavations warehouse,
Alexandria (SCA 508)

342
Amulets (?) in the shape of coins
6th to 2nd cent. BC
Lead
H. 1.2 cm | w. 1 cm | d. 0.2 cm
Location: Excavations warehouse,
Alexandria (SCA 506)

343
Amulets in the shape of coins
6th to 2nd cent. BC
Lead
H. 1.2 cm | w. 1 cm | d. 0.2 cm
Location: Excavations warehouse,
Alexandria (SCA 507)

346   (p. 199)
Oil lamp
5th to 4th cent. BC
Lead
Location: Excavations warehouse,
Alexandria (SCA 998)

350
Box
6th to 2nd cent. BC
Lead
H. 7.3 cm | w. 6.3 cm | d. 0.3 cm
Location: Excavations warehouse,
Alexandria (SCA 914)

353
Dish
Ptolemaic period
Lead
Votive depot
H. 2 cm | diam. 7.7 cm | d. 0.3 cm
Location: Excavations warehouse,
Alexandria (SCA 1053)

344   (p. 297)
Plaque showing a griffin
Late period (?)
Lead
L. 4.9 cm | w. 3.8 cm
Location: Excavations warehouse,
Alexandria (SCA 999)

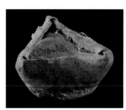

347
Basin
6th to 2nd cent. BC
Lead
H. 6.3 cm | diam. 12 cm
Location: Excavations warehouse,
Alexandria (SCA 1027)

351   (p. 251)
Vessel
6th to 2nd cent. BC
Lead
H. 2.8 cm | diam. 7 cm
Location: Excavations warehouse,
Alexandria (SCA 1077)

354
Plate
6th to 2nd cent. BC
Lead
Diam. 14.5 cm
Location: Excavations warehouse,
Alexandria (SCA 1036)

348, 349
Boxes,
6th to 2nd cent. BC
Lead
H. 3.5 cm | diam. 5 cm
Location: Excavations warehouse,
Alexandria (SCA 938, 939)

345   (p. 278)
Cross pendant
5th to 8th cent. AD
Lead
H. 3.02 cm | w. 2.17 cm | d. 0.17 cm
Location: Maritime Museum, Alexandria (SCA 427)

352   (p. 303)
Dish
Late period (?)
Lead
H. 5 cm | diam. 15 cm
Location: Excavations warehouse,
Alexandria (SCA 907)

355   (p. 360)
Feeding-bottle
6th to 2nd cent. BC
Lead
H. 2.5 cm | diam. 5 cm
Location: Excavations warehouse,
Alexandria (SCA 901)

356
Miniature amphora
6th to 2nd cent. BC
Lead
Heraklion
H. 4.2 cm | diam. 1.9 cm
Location: Excavations warehouse,
Alexandria (SCA 1009)

357
Miniature vessel
6th to 2nd cent. BC
Lead
H. 2.5 cm | diam. 3.3 cm
Location: Excavations warehouse,
Alexandria (SCA 923)

358
Miniature vase
Ptolemaic period
Lead
Votive depot
H. 3 cm | w. 4.9 cm | d. 0.15 cm
Location: Excavations warehouse,
Alexandria (SCA 1051)

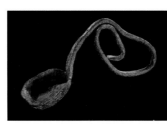

359
Miniature ladle
6th to 2nd cent. BC
Lead
L. 20 cm
Location: Excavations warehouse,
Alexandria (SCA 957)

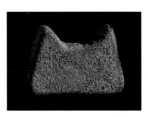

360   (p. 251)
Miniature headrest
6th to 2nd cent. BC
Lead
H. 1.8 cm | w. 2.6 cm
Location: Maritime Museum,
Alexandria (SCA 1005)

361   (p. 294)
Catapult projectiles
6th to 2nd cent. BC
Lead
L. 3–4 cm | d. 2–3 cm
Location: Excavations warehouse,
Alexandria (SCA 1104)

362   (p. 360)
Ingot
6th to 2nd cent. BC
Lead
H. 11 cm | w. 47 cm | d. 16.5 cm
Location: Excavations warehouse,
Alexandria (SCA 893)

363
Weight
6th to 2nd cent. BC
Lead
H. 5 cm | w. 5 cm | d. 0.8 cm
Location: Excavations warehouse,
Alexandria (SCA 919)

364
Weight
6th to 2nd cent. BC
Lead
H. 5 cm | w. 4 cm | d. 0.7 cm
Location: Excavations warehouse,
Alexandria (SCA 945)

365
Weight
6th to 2nd cent. BC
Lead
H. 8.8 cm | w. 8.7 cm | d. 2.2 cm
Location: Excavations warehouse,
Alexandria (SCA 958)

366
Weight
6th to 2nd cent. BC
Lead
H. 8.8 cm | w. 8.7 cm | d. 2.2 cm
Location: Excavations warehouse,
Alexandria (SCA 959)

367
Weight
6th to 2nd cent. BC
Lead
H. 3.6 cm | w. 3.6 cm | d. 1.8 cm
Location: Excavations warehouse,
Alexandria (SCA 1007)

368
Weight
6th to 2nd cent. BC
Lead
H. 5 cm | w. 4.9 cm | d. 1.7 cm
Location: Excavations warehouse,
Alexandria (SCA 1075)

369
Weight
6th to 2nd cent. BC
Lead
H. 4.7 cm | w. 4.6 cm | wt. 375 g
Location: Excavations warehouse,
Alexandria (SCA 1085)

370
Loom weight
6th to 2nd cent. BC
Lead
L. 11 cm | diam. 4 cm
Location: Excavations warehouse,
Alexandria (SCA 921)

371
Loom weight
6th to 2nd cent. BC
Lead
L. 12 cm | diam. 5.5 cm
Location: Excavations warehouse,
Alexandria (SCA 950)

372   (p. 296)
Coin weight
4th cent. BC
Lead
H. 2.6 cm | w. 2.6 cm | d. 0.6 cm | wt.
41.6 g
Location: Excavations warehouse,
Alexandria (SCA 1101)

373
Ceramic shard showing ancient repairs
6th to 2nd cent. BC
Lead and ceramic
H. 10 cm | w. 2.8 cm
Location: Excavations warehouse,
Alexandria (SCA 948)

374   (p. 187)
God-child
Late period
Faience
L. 7.9 cm | w. 2.2 cm | d. 1.8 cm
Location: Excavations warehouse,
Alexandria (SCA 562)

375
Statuette of Isis
Ptolemaic period
Faience
H. 7 cm | w. 2.1 cm
Location: Excavations warehouse,
Alexandria (SCA 522)

376   (p. 187)
Uraeus amulet
Late period
Faience
H. 4.2 cm | w. 2.2 cm | d. 1.1 cm
Location: Excavations warehouse,
Alexandria (SCA 552)

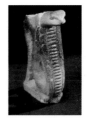

377
Uraeus amulet
Late period
Ceramic
H. 3.7 cm | w. 1.6 cm | d. 1 cm
Location: Excavations warehouse,
Alexandria (SCA 557)

378   (p. 187)
Oudjat-eye amulet
Late period
Ceramic
H. 5 cm | w. 4 cm | d. 0.9 cm
Location: Excavations warehouse,
Alexandria (SCA 558)

379   (p. 187)
Papyrus-shaped amulet
Late period
Ceramic
H. 13 cm | d. 3.6 cm
Location: Excavations warehouse,
Alexandria (SCA 565)

380   (p. 187)
Plaque
Late period
Faience
H. 8.4 cm | w. 3.6 cm | d. 1 cm
Location: Excavations warehouse,
Alexandria (SCA 560)

381   (p. 299)
Amphora
6th cent. BC
Ceramic
H. 42.5 cm | diam. 10.5 cm
Location: Excavations warehouse,
Alexandria (SCA 846)

382   (p. 302)
Torpedo amphora
Persian period
Ceramic
H. 56 cm | diam. 30 cm
Location: Excavations warehouse,
Alexandria (SCA 548)

383   (p. 300)
Amphora
5th cent. BC
Ceramic
H. 65 cm | diam. 40 cm
Location: Excavations warehouse,
Alexandria (SCA 357)

384   (p. 298)
Amphora
End of 5th to mid-4th cent. BC
Ceramic
H. 32 cm | diam. 22.5 cm
Location: Excavations warehouse,
Alexandria (SCA 591)

385   (p. 300)
Amphora
End of 5th to mid-4th cent. BC
Ceramic
H. 28.5 cm | diam. 11 cm
Location: Excavations warehouse,
Alexandria (SCA 1089)

386   (p. 340)
Amphora neck
2nd half of 4th cent. BC
Ceramic
H. 22 cm | diam. 17 cm
Location: Excavations warehouse,
Alexandria (SCA 609)

387   (p. 346)
Gaza amphora
4th to mid-5th cent. AD
Ceramic
H. 46.5 cm
Location: Excavations warehouse,
Alexandria (SCA 865)

388   (p. 303)
Fragment of an askos
End of 5th to mid-4th cent. BC
Ceramic
Diam. 3.5 cm | diam. medallion 7.7 cm
Location: Excavations warehouse,
Alexandria (SCA 1067)

389   (p. 342)
Mug
End of 5th to first half of 4th cent. BC
Ceramic
H. 13 cm
Location: Excavations warehouse,
Alexandria (SCA 245)

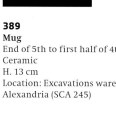

390   (p. 342)
Mug
(left)
End of 5th to mid-4th cent. BC
Ceramic
H. 13.5 cm
Location: Excavations warehouse,
Alexandria (SCA 594)

391   (p. 344)
Mug
Ptolemaic period
Ceramic
H. 8.7 cm | diam. 5.1 cm
Location: Excavations warehouse,
Alexandria (SCA 251)

392 (p. 344)
Bowl
5th to 4th cent. BC
Ceramic
H. 9 cm | open diam. 35 cm
Location: Excavations warehouse,
Alexandria (SCA 356)

395
Lid
Ptolemaic period
Ceramic
H. 6 cm | diam. 13.8 cm | d. 3.3 cm
Location: Excavations warehouse,
Alexandria (SCA 596)

398 (p. 300)
Kotyle (vessel)
End of 5th to early of 4th cent. BC
Ceramic
H. 10 cm | diam. 14.4 cm
Location: Excavations warehouse,
Alexandria (SCA 260)

401
Jug
4th cent. BC
Ceramic
H. 24.5 cm | diam. 9.8 cm
Location: Excavations warehouse,
Alexandria (SCA 244)

393 (p. 300)
Bolsal
End of 5th cent. BC
Ceramic
H. 4.5 cm | diam. 9.7 cm
Location: Excavations warehouse,
Alexandria (SCA 1080)

396 (p. 187)
Double ewer
Late period
Ceramic
H. 7.3 cm | w. 3.2 cm | d. 1.6 cm
Location: Excavations warehouse,
Alexandria (SCA 559)

399 (p. 333)
Juglet
End of 5th to mid-4th cent. BC
Ceramic
H. 7.6 cm
Location: Excavations warehouse,
Alexandria (SCA 1030)

402 (p. 335)
Juglet
4th cent. BC
Ceramic
H. 11.4 cm | diam. 8.8 cm
Location: Excavations warehouse,
Alexandria (SCA 242)

394 (p. 341)
Pot
3rd cent. BC
Ceramic
H. 8.5 cm | diam. 7.2 cm
Location: Excavations warehouse,
Alexandria (SCA 258)

397 (p. 339)
Kantharos (vessel)
4th cent. BC
Ceramic
H. 8.9 cm | diam. 8.3 cm
Location: Excavations warehouse,
Alexandria (SCA 1040)

400 (p. 335)
Juglet
4th cent. BC
Ceramic
H. 10 cm
Location: Excavations warehouse,
Alexandria (SCA 336)

403
Pot
4th cent. BC
Ceramic
H. 31.5 cm | diam. 8.5 cm
Location: Excavations warehouse,
Alexandria (SCA 848)

404 (p. 199)
Big-bellied lekythos
End of 5th to mid-4th cent. BC
Clay
H. 8.3 cm | diam. 5.4 cm
Location: National Museum,
Alexandria (SCA 247)

407 (p. 339)
Olpe
4th cent. BC
Ceramic
H. 15.5 cm
Location: Excavations warehouse,
Alexandria (SCA 339)

410 (p. 336)
Bowl
End of 5th to mid-4th cent. BC
Ceramic
H. 9.3 cm | diam. 14.3 cm
Location: Excavations warehouse,
Alexandria (SCA 228)

414 (p. 343)
Bowl
Ptolemaic period
Ceramic
H. 6 cm | diam. 11.2 cm
Location: Excavations warehouse,
Alexandria (SCA 226)

405 (p. 298)
Fat-bellied lekythos
End of 5th to mid-4th cent. BC
Ceramic
H. 9.6 cm | diam. 5.1 cm
Location: National Museum,
Alexandria (SCA 610)

408 (p. 298)
Pyxis
Early 4th cent. BC
Ceramic
H. 15.5 cm | diam. 17 cm
Location: Excavations warehouse,
Alexandria (SCA 590)

411 (p. 336)
Bowl
Persian period
Ceramic
H. 5.5 cm | diam. 11.2 cm
Location: Excavations warehouse,
Alexandria (SCA 1082)

415 (p. 341)
Bowl
Ptolemaic period
Ceramic
H. 4.3 cm | diam. 13 cm
Location: Excavations warehouse,
Alexandria (SCA 236)

412 (p. 336)
Bowl
4th cent. BC
Ceramic
H. 4.8 cm | diam. 13.8 cm
Location: Excavations warehouse,
Alexandria (SCA 345)

416 (p. 341)
Bowl
End of 3rd to 2nd cent. BC
Ceramic
H. 5.5 cm | diam. 11.2 cm
Location: Excavations warehouse,
Alexandria (SCA 227)

406 (p. 335)
Mortar
Early 5th to early 4th cent. BC
Ceramic
H. 9.8 cm | diam. 32 cm
Location: Excavations warehouse,
Alexandria (SCA 261)

409 (p. 298)
Ionian goblet
End of 7th to mid-6th cent. BC
Ceramic
H. 6.3 cm | diam. 15.7 cm
Location: Excavations warehouse,
Alexandria (SCA 597)

413 (p. 301)
Bowl
Mid-4th cent. BC
Ceramic
H. 4.5 cm | diam. 13.4 cm
Location: Excavations warehouse,
Alexandria (SCA 237)

417 (p. 343)
Bowl
(right)
2nd cent. BC
Ceramic
H. 6 cm | diam. 13 cm
Location: Excavations warehouse,
Alexandria (SCA 611)

418 (p. 336)
Bowl
3rd cent. BC
Ceramic
H. 5.5 cm | diam. 12.6 cm
Location: Excavations warehouse,
Alexandria (SCA 595)

421 (p. 336)
Miniature pot
4th cent. BC
Ceramic
H. 7.8 cm | diam. 5.6 cm | d. 0.5 cm
Location: Excavations warehouse,
Alexandria (SCA 259)

424 (p. 45)
Fragments of a red-figure vessel
4th cent. BC
Ceramic
H. 12 cm | w. 7 cm
Location: Excavations warehouse,
Alexandria (SCA 1076)

427 (p. 131)
Hemistater from Cyprus
Pumiathon (*c.* 355/354 BC)
Gold
Diam. 1.4 cm | wt. 4.10 g
Location: National Museum,
Alexandria (SCA 287)

419 (p. 338)
Bread plate
Ptolemaic period
Ceramic
H. 17 cm | diam. 2.5 cm
Location: Excavations warehouse,
Alexandria (SCA 351)

422
Unguentarium
6th to 3rd cent. BC
Ceramic
H. 16.5 cm | diam. 4 cm
Location: Excavations warehouse,
Alexandria (SCA 337)

425 (p. 337)
Oil lamp
End of 6th to 5th cent. BC
Ceramic
H. 2.2 cm | diam. 5.2 cm
Location: Excavations warehouse,
Alexandria (SCA 598)

428 (p. 54)
Stater from Cyrene
c. 310–306 BC
Gold
Diam. 1.74 cm | wt. 7.14 g
Location: Great Library, Alexandria
(SCA 284)

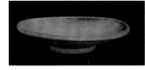

420 (p. 342)
Plate
Ptolemaic period
Ceramic
H. 4 cm | diam. 21.6 cm
Location: Excavations warehouse,
Alexandria (SCA 1131)

423 (p. 344)
Unguentarium
5th to 4th cent. BC
Ceramic
H. 9.5 cm | diam. 2.5 cm
Location: Excavations warehouse,
Alexandria (SCA 252)

426 (p. 337)
Oil lamp
Mid-4th to early 3rd cent. BC
Ceramic
H. 4.3 cm | diam. 3.4 cm
Location: Excavations warehouse,
Alexandria (SCA 342)

429 (p. 326)
Coin
Ptolemaic period, Ptolemy I Soter
(306–283 BC)
Gold
Diam. 1 cm
Location: Graeco-Roman Museum,
Alexandria (SCA 318)

430 (p. 326)
Coin
Ptolemaic period, Ptolemy I Soter
(306–283 BC)
Gold
Diam. 1 cm
Location: Graeco-Roman Museum,
Alexandria (SCA 313)

433 (p. 327)
Coin
Ptolemaic period, Ptolemy I Soter
(306–283 BC)
Gold
Diam. 1.1 cm
Location: Graeco-Roman Museum,
Alexandria (SCA 307)

436 (p. 261)
Solidus
Heraclius (616–625 AD)
Gold
Diam. 2 cm | wt. 4.35 g
Location: Graeco-Roman Museum,
Alexandria (SCA 315)

439 (p. 192)
Coin
Alexander the Great (336–323 BC)
Silver
Diam. 2.4 cm | wt. 11.85 g
Location: Excavations warehouse,
Alexandria (SCA 614)

431 (p. 326)
Coin
Ptolemaic period, Ptolemy I Soter
(306–283 BC)
Gold
Diam. 0.9 cm
Location: Graeco-Roman Museum,
Alexandria (SCA 312)

434 (p. 261)
Tremissis
Pulcheria (414–453 AD)
Gold
Diam. 1.3 cm | wt. 1.3 g
Location: Graeco-Roman Museum,
Alexandria (SCA 316)

not illus

437
Coin
Byzantine period
Gold
Diam. 2 cm
Location: Graeco-Roman Museum,
Alexandria (SCA 1119)

440 (p. 192)
Tetradrachm
Ptolemy I Soter (310–306 BC)
Silver
Diam. 2.7 cm
Location: Excavations warehouse,
Alexandria (SCA 554)

432 (p. 327)
Coin
Ptolemaic period, Ptolemy I Soter
(306–283 BC)
Gold
Diam. 1 cm
Location: Graeco-Roman Museum,
Alexandria (SCA 304)

435 (p. 262)
Tremissis
Justinus II (565–578 AD)
Gold
Diam. 1.5 cm | wt. 1.3 g
Location: Graeco-Roman Museum,
Alexandria (SCA 314)

438 (p. 71)
Abbassid dinar
785 AD
Gold
Diam. 1.90 cm
Location: Graeco-Roman Museum,
Alexandria (SCA 317)

441 (p. 295)
Coin
4th cent. BC (?)
Silver
Diam. 2.1 cm | wt. 15.42 g
Location: Excavations warehouse,
Alexandria (SCA 1000)

442   (p. 295)
Coin
4th cent. BC (?)
Silver
Diam. 2.4 cm | wt. 15.16 g
Location: Excavations warehouse,
Alexandria (SCA 1035)

445   (p. 192)
Coin
Pumiathon (361–312 BC)
Bronze
Diam. 1.8 cm
Location. Excavations warehouse,
Alexandria (SCA 438)

448   (p. 329)
Coin
Ptolemaic period, Ptolemy I Soter
(306–283 BC)
Bronze
Diam. 2.75 cm
Location: Excavations warehouse,
Alexandria (SCA 272)

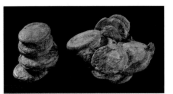

451
Coins
Ptolemaic period
Bronze
Location: Excavations warehouse,
Alexandria (SCA 937)

443   (p. 328)
Coin
Ptolemaic period, Ptolemy I Soter
(306–283 BC)
Silver
Diam. 1.8 cm | wt. 3.83 g
Location: Excavations warehouse,
Alexandria (SCA 616)

446   (p. 328)
Coin
Ptolemaic period, Ptolemy I Soter
(306–283 BC)
Bronze
Diam. 1.7 cm
Location: Excavations warehouse,
Alexandria (SCA 416)

449   (p. 329)
Coin
Ptolemaic period, Ptolemy I Soter
(306–283 BC)
Bronze
Diam. 2.75 cm
Location: Excavations warehouse,
Alexandria (SCA 275)

452
Coin
Byzantine period
Bronze
Diam. 0.8 cm
Location: Graeco-Roman Museum,
Alexandria (SCA 513)

444
Coins
Ptolemaic period
Silver and bronze
Location: Excavations warehouse,
Alexandria (SCA 1099)

447   (p. 329)
Coin
Ptolemaic period, Ptolemy I Soter
(306–283 BC)
Bronze
Diam. 2.73 cm
Location: Excavations warehouse,
Alexandria (SCA 271)

450
Coin
Ptolemy II Philadelphos (280–279 BC)
Bronze
Diam. 2.7 cm | wt. 10.53 g
Location: Excavations warehouse,
Alexandria (SCA 623)

453   (p. 187)
Naos figurine
(centre)
Late period
Holz
H. 13 cm | w. 6 cm | d. 7 cm
Location: Roman Theatre, Alexandria
(SCA 583)

495

478

ALEXANDRIA

454
Box
Ptolemaic period
Bone
H. 6.7 cm | diam. 3.5 cm
Location: Roman Theatre, Alexandria
(SCA 965)

455 (p. 362)
Bone from the skull of a Nile catfish
6th to 2nd cent. BC
Location: Excavations warehouse,
Alexandria (SCA 1015)

456
Grape pips
6th to 2nd cent. BC
Location: Excavations warehouse,
Alexandria (SCA 490)

457 (p. 373)
Inscribed statue base
1213–1203 BC
Black granite
H. 70 cm | w. 95 cm | d. 50 cm
Location: Roman Theatre, Alexandria
(SCA 542)

458 (p. 206)
Falcon-headed crocodile
7th to 6th cent. BC (?)
Black granite
H. 70 cm | w. 43 cm | d. 70 cm
Location: Maritime Museum,
Alexandria (SCA 541)

459 (p. 387)
Agathodaimon
3rd to 2nd cent. BC
Black granite
H. 30 cm | w. 25 cm
Location: Roman Theatre, Alexandria
(SCA 543)

460 (p. 209)
Ibis
Ptolemaic period
Limestone
H. 40 cm | w. 55 cm | d. 21 cm
Location: Great Library, Alexandria
(SCA 87)

461 (p. 147)
Sphinx
1st cent. BC
Diorite
H. 75 cm | w. 140 cm
Location: Maritime Museum,
Alexandria (SCA 451)

462 (p. 57)
Sphinx
1. cent. BC
Grauer Granit
H. 70 cm | w. 150 cm
Location: Roman Theatre, Alexandria
(SCA 450)

463 (p. 55)
Colossal head
Caesarion (?), 1st cent. BC
Grey granite
H. 80 cm | w. 60 cm | d. 50 cm
Location: Roman Theatre, Alexandria
(SCA 88)

464 (p. 215)
Priest with Osiris-Canobos
1st cent. BC
Black granite
H. 122 cm
Location: National Museum,
Alexandria (SCA 449)

465 (p. 383)
Head of Antonia Minor
1st cent. AD
Marble
H. 35 cm
Location: Great Library, Alexandria
(SCA 86)

453

466 (p. 372)
Fragment of an obelisk of Sethos I
1293–1279 BC
Black granite
H. 56 cm | w. 200 cm | d. 78 cm
Location: Roman Theatre, Alexandria
(SCA 544)

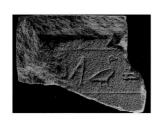

469 (p. 373)
Inscribed block
589–570 BC
Pink granite
H. 105 cm | w. 140 cm | d. 55 cm
Location: Roman Theatre, Alexandria
(SCA 546)

472 (p. 381)
Capital
c. 100–250 AD
Pink granite
H. 85 cm | w. 130 cm | d. 130 cm
Location: Roman Theatre, Alexandria
(SCA 533)

475 (p. 64)
Column with Greek inscription
Caracalla (211–217 AD)
Red granite
H. 155 cm | diam. 105 cm
Location: Roman Theatre, Alexandria
(SCA 537)

467 (p. 377)
Fragment of a door jamb
589–570 BC
Pink granite
H. 115 cm | w. 60 cm | d. 45 cm
Location: Roman Theatre, Alexandria
(SCA 539)

470 (p. 376)
Inscribed block from Heliopolis
589–570 BC
Pink granite
H. 167 cm | w. 77 cm | d. 50 cm
Location: Roman Theatre, Alexandria
(SCA 545)

473 (p. 62)
Column with Greek inscription
Caracalla (211–217 AD)
Red granite
H. 160 cm | diam. 105 cm
Location: Roman Theatre, Alexandria
(SCA 535)

476 (p. 65)
Column with Greek inscription
Caracalla (211–217 AD)
Red granite
H. 150 cm | diam. 105 cm
Location: Roman Theatre, Alexandria
(SCA 547)

468 (p. 377)
Fragment of a door jamb
589–570 BC
Pink granite
H. 150 cm | w. 60 cm | d. 45 cm
Location: Roman Theatre, Alexandria
(SCA 538)

471 (p. 375)
Inscribed block
589–570 BC
Pink granite
H. 130 cm | w. 120 cm | d. 60 cm
Location: Roman Theatre, Alexandria
(SCA 548)

474 (p. 63)
Column with Greek inscription
Caracalla (211–217 AD)
Red granite
H. 85 cm | diam. 105 cm
Location: Roman Theatre, Alexandria
(SCA 536)

477 (p. 380)
Capital
c. 250–350 AD
Pink granite
H. 50 cm | w. 68 cm | d. 68 cm
Location: Roman Theatre, Alexandria
(SCA 534)

478 (p. 384)
Ring
1st cent. BC—1st cent. AD
Gold and semi-precious stone
(Intaglio)
Diam. ring: 2.95 cm, setting: 1.8 cm
Location: Great Library, Alexandria
(SCA 84)

481 (p. 385)
Bowl
1st cent. BC
Ceramic
H. 5.1 cm | diam. 9.3 cm
Location: Excavations warehouse,
Alexandria (SCA 23)

484 (p. 348)
Mortar
Roman period
Ceramic
H. 9.5 cm | diam. 37.8 cm
Location: Excavations warehouse,
Alexandria (SCA 72)

487 (p. 349)
Mug
1st cent. AD
Ceramic
H. 6.8 cm | diam. 6.4 cm
Location: Excavations warehouse,
Alexandria (SCA 15)

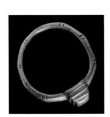

479 (p. 384)
Ring
1st cent. BC—1st cent. AD
Gold
Diam. 2.53 cm
Location: National Museum,
Alexandria (SCA 85)

482 (p. 348)
Chytra (pot)
Second half of 1st cent. BC
Ceramic
H. 28 cm | diam. 17.5 cm
Location: Great Library, Alexandria
(SCA 82)

485 (p. 385)
Rhodian amphora
Roman period
H. 98.5 cm | diam. 29.5 cm
Ceramic
Location: National Museum,
Alexandria (SCA 32)

488 (p. 349)
Bowl
2nd cent. AD
Ceramic
H. 5.9 cm | diam. 10.8 cm
Location: Excavations warehouse,
Alexandria (SCA 45)

480 (p. 384)
Ring
Roman period
Gold and agate
Diam. 2.29 cm
Location: Great Library, Alexandria
(SCA 626)

483 (p. 348)
Cooking pot
1st to 3rd cent. AD
Ceramic
H. 12.2 cm | diam. 14 cm
Location: Excavations warehouse,
Alexandria (SCA 46)

486 (p. 385)
Cretan amphora
Roman period
Ceramic
H. 46 cm | diam. 12.8 cm
Location: Great Library, Alexandria
(SCA 81)

489
Measuring pot
2nd cent. AD
Ceramic
H. 4.8 cm | diam. 3.3 cm
Location: Excavations warehouse,
Alexandria (SCA 698)

490 (p. 349)
Jug
2nd cent. AD
Ceramic
H. 35 cm
Location: Excavations warehouse,
Alexandria (SCA 1117)

491 (p. 347)
Oil lamp
Roman period
Ceramic
H. 3 cm | diam. 7.5 cm
Location: Excavations warehouse,
Alexandria (SCA 13)

492 (p. 347)
Oil lamp
2nd cent. AD
Ceramic
H. 4.6 cm | diam. 5.7 cm
Location: Excavations warehouse,
Alexandria (SCA 448)

493 (p. 347)
Oil lamp
End of 2nd cent. AD
Ceramic
H. 4 cm | diam. 5.7 cm
Location: Excavations warehouse,
Alexandria (SCA 612)

494 (p. 331)
Aureus
Antoninus Pius (155/56 AD)
Gold
Diam. 2 cm
Location: National Museum,
Alexandria (SCA 295)

495 (p. 60)
Aureus
Caracalla (206 AD)
Gold
Diam. 2 cm
Location: National Museum,
Alexandria (SCA 294)

VI. APPENDICES

LIST OF CONTRIBUTORS

A.A.E-F.Y.: Ahmed abd el Fattah Yussef
A.A-R.R.: Ashraf Abdel-Raouf Ragheb,
Department of Underwater Archaeology, Alexandria
A.B.: André Bernand, Professor emeritus
A.A.B.E-K.: Amira Abou Bakr El-Khoust
A.M.: Andrew Meadows
A.S.v.B.: A. Sophie von Bomhard
B.L.: From the studies of Barbara Lichocka, Polish
Centre of Mediterranean Archaeology, Warsaw
C.B.: From the studies of Cécile Bresc,
British Museum
C.G.: From the studies of Catherine Grataloup,
ceramic specialist
C.M.: From the studies of Cécile Morrisson,
CNRS, Collège de France
C.T.: Christophe Thiers, Egyptologist, CNRS
C.W.: From the studies of Caroline Williams
D.F.: From the studies of David Fabre,
Egyptologist
E.B.: Étienne Bernand, Honorary Professor
E.L.: From the studies of Emma Libonati,
Institute of Archaeology, University College London
E.M.: From the studies of Eric McCann, Institute of
Archaeology, University College London
F.D.: From the studies of Françoise Dunand,
Professor emeritus
F.G.: Franck Goddio, Director of Institut Européen
d'Archéologie Sous-Marine
J.B.: From the studies of John Baines, Egyptologist
J.Y.: From the studies of Jean Yoyotte,
Honorary Professor at Collège de France,
Chair of Egyptology
K.A.: From the studies of Kim Ayodeji
L.E.: Luc Eyzenschneyder
L.T.: Luc Tamborero
M.C.: Manfred Clauss, Professor for Ancient History
M.T.: From the studies of Michel Tardieu,
Professor at Collège de France
N.S.: From the studies of Nicholas Victor Secunda
O.B.: Olivier Berger
R.R.R.S.: From the studies of R.R.R. Smith
S.-A.A.: From the studies of S.-A. Ashton
S.H.B.: Salwa Hussein Bakr, Egyptologist,
Tanta University

S.W.: From the studies of Susan Walker,
Ashmolean Museum
T.H.: From the studies of Tom Hardwick,
Institute of Archaeology, University College London
Y.S.: From the studies of Yvonne Stolz,
Institute of Archaeology, University College London
Z.C.: From the studies of Zoe Cox,
Institute of Archaeology, University College London
Z.K.: From the studies of Zsolt Kiss,
Polish Centre of Mediterranean Archaeology,
Warsaw

ACKNOWLEDGEMENTS

Franck Goddio, President of the Institut d'Archéologie Sous-Marine and director of excavations would like to thank all those
who have contributed to the success of the excavations in Egypt and, consequently, to the realisation of this exhibition.

Egypt
H.E. Farouk Hosny, Minister of Culture of the Arab Republic of Egypt
H.E. Mohamed Abdel Salam el Mahgoub, Governor of Alexandria

Supreme Council for Antiquities
Prof. Zahi Hawass, Secretary General
Mohamed Abd el Maksoud: Director General for Maritime Archaeology
Mohamed Abd el Fatah: Director of Egyptian Museums
Magdi el Gandour: Director of Foreign Archaeological Missions
Hany Abou el Azm: Exhibition Committee
Sabri Abd el Aziz: Director General of Egyptian Archaeology
Ahmed Abd el Fattah: Director General of Museums in Alexandria
Ibrahim Abd El Galil Ibrahim: Responsible for exhibitions abroad
Azziza Said: Director of the Graeco-Roman Department of Archaeology, Faculty of Art Alexandria, Director of Museums
Dorreya Said
Emad Maklad
Dr. Gaballah Ali Gaballah, former Secretary General

Egyptian Museum Cairo
Dr. Wafaa Siddik: Director of the Egyptian Museum and of the Exhibition Committee, Curator for the Cairo Museum, responsible for foreign exhibitions
Albert Ghaly: responsible for foreign exhibitions
Lotfi Abdel Hamid: responsible for foreign exhibitions
Akmal Mohamed: responsible for foreign exhibitions

National Museum, Alexandria
Dr. Ibrahim Darwish, Director

Maritime Museum, Alexandria
Dr. Soad Rochdy, Director

The Graeco-Roman Museum, Alexandria
Dr. Mervat Seif El Dine

Bibliotheca Alexandrina, Alexandria
H.E. Ismail Serageldin, General Director
Dr. Badrya Sary, Director of the Museum

Restoration Department of the Supreme Council for Antiquities, Alexandria
Amira Abou Bakr, Chief Restorer
Dr. Tahany Moustafa, Director of Laboratory Chemistry
Mamdouh Mohamed, Specialised restorer
Hassa Ibrahim, Assistant restorer
Nabila Loundry, Specialist restorer

Special thanks go to the Egyptian coast guards and the Navy as well as to the archaeologists, inspectors and co-workers without whom the excavations would not have been possible.

France
H.E. Philippe Coste, French Ambassador to the Arab Republic of Egypt
H.E. Marie Christine Glas, Consul General of France in Alexandria
Denis Louche, Counsellor for Co-operation and Cultural Service
Dominique Blay, Science and Technology Mission Attaché
Louis Blin, Consul General of France in Alexandria from 2003 to 2005
Gilles Gauthier, Consul General of France in Alexandria from 2001 to 2003

Ministry for Foreign Affairs
General Direction for Cooperation, Development and Francophony

Musée du Louvre, Paris
Henri Loyrette, President
Christiane Ziegler, Director of Dept. of Egyptian
Antiquities

Germany
H.E. Mohamed Al-Orabi, Egyptian Ambassador to
Germany

Berliner Festspiele
Joachim Sartorius, Director-General

Martin-Gropius-Bau
Gereon Sievernich, Director

**Participants on the various missions in Egypt
organised by the Institut d'Archéologie Sous-
Marine:**

**Supreme Council for Antiquities, Arab Republic
of Egypt
Team:**

Alaa Eldin Mahrous
Mohamed Abd Elhamid
Dr. Ahmed Sameh Ramsis
Abd El-Hamid Abd El Maguid
Mohamed Moustafa Abd Elmaguid
Mohamed El said Mohamed
Dr. Ashraf Abd Elraouf Ragab
Osama Mousatafa Elnahas
Ahmed Shoukry Mohamed Omar
Ehab Mahmoud Fahmy
Ibrahim Ahmed Metwalli
Magdy Abdalla Gazala
Moustafa Elsouky Abas
Atef Ibrahim Ali
Timour Mahmoud Abdou
Islam Abd Elgawad Selim
Saad Ahmed Fashal
Ahmed Adel salem
Mohamed Elsaid Sultan
Basem Ahmed Fashal
Basem Ibrahhim Ibrahim
Mahmoud Mohamed Abd Elhamid
Mohamed Ali Mohamed
Mahmoud Said Maged
Belall Saad Eldin Mohamed
Wael Fathy Moursy
Adel Abd Elsalam Moubarak
Fathy Mohamed Bahig
Youssria el Gandour

**Institut Européen d'Archéologie Sous-Marine
Team:**

Amani Badr
Alexander Belov
Olivier Berger
Jean-Paul Blancan
Georges Brocot
Stéphane Brousse
Bernard Camier
Guy de Casteja
Jean Castéra
Christelle Chartier
Jonathan Cole
Tatiana Curchod
Grégory Dalex
Jérôme Delafosse
Alain Denaix
David Fabre
Michael Fitzgerald
Mohamed Mahmoud Galal
Patrick Gay
Christoph Gerigk
Catherine Grataloup
Jean-Jacques Groussard
Antoine Guillain
Susan Hendrickson
Lionel Julien
Gildas Lesouef
Zizi Louxor
Henri Bernard Maugiron
Mahmoud Mohammed Aly
Pascal Morisset
Bobby Orillanena
Frédéric Osada
Rosario Palacios de Montarco
Laurent Pellemoine
Fernando Peirera
Alain Peton
Nicholas Ponzone
Michel Revest
Pablo Rodriguez
Jean-Claude Roubaud
Philippe Rousseau
Arnaud Roy
Patrice Sandrin

Roland Savoye
Gérard Schnepp
Eric Smith
Keith Smith
Yann Streiff
Jean-Louis de Talancé
Emily Teeter
Daniel Visnikar

Franck Goddio would like to dedicate this publication to the memory of Fernando Pereira whose contribution and dedication to the missions in Egypt was immense. He is sorely missed.

**Hilti Foundation
Team:**

Andrea Mähr
Dagmar Wocher
Alfred Knauer
Harry Pfleger

EXHIBITION

Curator
Franck Goddio

Idea, Concept and General Direction
Franck Goddio
Cornelia Ewigleben
Georg Rosenbauer
Hans Saxer

Scientific Support
OCMA, Oxford Centre for Maritime Archaeology at Oxford University's Institute of Archaeology
Manfred Clauss

Project Management
Arab Republic of Egypt:
Amani Badr

Federal Republic of Germany:
Ines Kausch

Exhibition architecture and artistic direction
Philippe Délis, integral

Museography and texts:
Martine Thomas-Bourgneuf
Scenography: Tobias Grimminger
Production Berlin: scala, Günter Krüger

Press and Public Relations
salaction public relations GmbH
Dieter A. Irion, Daniela Bühe
Katrin Wollgast, Susanne von Karstedt

Martin-Gropius-Bau, Berlin
Berliner Festspiele
Director-General: Joachim Sartorius

Martin-Gropius-Bau
Gereon Sievernich

Office: Sandra Müller, Anna Shigweda
Organisation: Sabine Hollburg, Katrin Mundorf
Assistance: Filippa Carlini, Elena Montini, Ellen Riewe

Public Relations: Katrin Mundorf
Press: Ute Weingarten
Sales: Carlos Rodriguez
Technical Office: Norbert Hiersick, Bert Schülke, Torsten Seehawer

The Martin-Gropius-Bau is run by the Berliner Festspiele (a division of Kulturveranstaltungen des Bundes in Berlin GmbH) on behalf of the Commissioner for Cultural and Media Affairs for the Federal Chancellor.

Kulturveranstaltungen des Bundes in Berlin GmbH
Managing Director: Thomas Köstlin

Exhibitions Office: *Egypt's Sunken Treasures*
Rachel Riddell, Gregor Lersch, Amely Bey

Many others have contributed to the realisation of this exhibition:

Exhibition Design
Exhibition architecture, design and artistic direction: Philippe Délis, architect, integral

Scenography and Design, Tobias Grimminger
Architecture: Dominique Rouhier
Graphic Design, Catherine Petter, Laurent Henriot, Noémie Lelièvre
Assistance: Edith Clavel, Nicolas Brifault, Claire Emmanuelle Hue, Akos Gerle, Guylaine De Souza, Fabienne Dupuy

Museography and texts:
Martine Thomas-Bourgneuf
Assistance for museography: Ludovic Bablon, Vesna Jovovic, Pascale Perroud, Nathalie Puzenat, Agathe Utard
Assistance on texts: Catherine Gonnard, Barbara Grinberg, François Trassard, Anne Yanover
Translations: Zoé Andreiev, Elisabeth Donahoe, Ulrich Forderer, Astrid Forstbauer

AV Media: Les Films d'Ici
AV advisor: Harouth Bezdjian, Passage
Sound design: Diasonic, Louis Dandrel with Alain Richon

CATALOGUE

Lights: Thierry d'Oliveira,
assisted by Jacques Biderman
Models: Philippe Le Heuzey
Anchoring: Gilbert Della Noce

Production Berlin: scala, Günter Krüger
Assistance: Boris Borowski

Conservation / Restoration
Supreme Council for Antiquities, Arab Republic
of Egypt:
General Director for Restoration, Alexandria:
Amira Abu Bakr
Director of metal restoration workshops,
Alexandria: Nabila Foad
Conservators: Mona Ahmed, Shara Ramadan,
Mohamed Mahmad, Mohamed Elwardeny,
Nasrin Mohmad, Mohamed Ragab

International restoration team:
Olivier Berger, Claire Piffaut, Violaine Pillard,
David Cuendet, Luc Tamborero, Alberto del
Gil-Ricart, Rüdiger Tertel

Press and Public Relations
salaction public relations GmbH
Dieter A. Irioin, Daniela Bühe
Katrin Wollgast, Susanne von Karstedt

Transport
Hasenkamp Internationale Transporte GmbH,
Berlin
Fred Pawlitzki, Frances Brady

Guided Tours
FührungsNetz des Museumspädagogischen
Dienstes Berlin

Audio-guide
tonwelt professional media GmbH, Berlin

Communication Design
LIQUID Agentur für Gestaltung GbR, Augsburg

Website
oha werbeagentur für visuelle gestaltung,
Buchs/Switzerland

Editors
Franck Goddio
Manfred Clauss

With the assistance of:
Jonathan Cole
David Fabre
Sophie Lalbat

Photography
Christoph Gerigk

Assistance
Sonja Dräger
Gülten Hamidanoglu

© Prestel, Munich · Berlin · London · New York 2006
© for Photographs: Franck Goddio / Hilti Foundation.
All Photos are from Christoph Gerigk with the exception of
pp. 12/13, 85: Jérôme Delafosse; pp. 69, 175, 224, 391: akg-images;
pp. 35 top, 59, 60: akg-images/Erich Lessing; p. 129: akg-images/
Werner Forman; pp. 145, 166: Hervé Champollion/akg.images;
p. 365 left: akg-images/Nimatallah; p. 49: RMN/Musée du Louvre/
Hervé Lewandowski/Vertrieb bpk Berlin; p. 99: Sopraintendenza
per i Beni Archeologici del Lazio, Rome; p. 258: Sammlung Kauf-
mann, Liebighaus, Frankfurt am Main; p. 319: Antike Welt, 3/2006

Front cover: A diver illuminating the colossal statue of God Hapi
(see cat. no. 103)
Back cover: The golden ring has a chalzedony inlay showing a
bird with a crest (see cat. no. 48)
Front endpapers: Three divers illuminating the colossal statue of
God Hapi (see cat. no. 103)
Back endpapers: A console of the Byzantine period (see cat. no. 35)
Pages 6/7: The mission ships in the bay of Aboukir
Pages 8/9: A diver face to face with Sarapis (see cat. no. 19)
Pages 10/11: Sarapis is lifted to the surface (see cat. no. 19)
Pages 12/13: A diver on the seabed
Pages 14/15: The bust of Father Nile on the seabed (see cat. no. 29)
Page 16: A diver approaches the portraited head of a pharaoh
from the XXX dynasty (see cat. no. 4)
Page 18: A diver lights up the area around the Naos of the
Decades (cf. cat. no. 103)
Pages 32/33: A Pharaonic head of the XXV dynasty (see cat. no. 2)
Pages 102/103: A magic scene of the Osiris priest holding a
canopic jar (see cat. nos. 31-34) between two sphinx on the sunken
Island of Antirhodos.
Pages 286/287: A bronze bowl of the late Pharaonic period (see cat.
no. 586)
Pages 392/393: A diver is positioning the exact location of the
Naos of the Decades (see cat. nos. 31-34) on the archaeological site
of Canopus with the help of a grid system.
Pages 402/403: A diver displays a small statue of Bastet (see cat.
no. 173)
Pages 456/457: The huge statue of the god Hapy lying undisturbed
in the sea (see cat. no. 103)

Prestel Verlag
Königinstrasse 9, 80539 Munich
Tel. +49 (89) 38 17 09-0
Fax +49 (89) 38 17 09-35
www.prestel.de

Prestel Publishing Ltd.
4, Bloomsbury Place, London WC1A 2QA
Tel. +44 (020) 73 23-50 04
Fax +44 (020) 76 36-80 04

Prestel Publishing
900 Broadway, Suite 603, New York, NY 10003
Tel. +1 (212) 9 95-27 20; Fax +1 (212) 9 95-27 33
www.prestel.com

Library of Congress Control Number: 2006903484
British Library Cataloguing-in-Publication Data: a catalogue
record for this book is available from the British Library
Deutsche Bibliothek holds a record of this publication in the
Deutsche Nationalbibliografie

Project management: Victoria Salley
Translated from the French and/or German into English by:
Paul Aston, Kirstie Coughtrie, Ruth Hemus, Jenny Marsh,
Robert McInnes, David Radzinowicz, Bronwen Saunders,
Stephen Telfer
Editorial direction: Gabriele Ebbecke
Copy-editing: Cynthia Hall, Danko Szabo, Christopher Wynne
Editorial assistance: Beate Besserer, Mirela Proske

Design: LIQUID Agentur für Gestaltung GbR,
Augsburg
Layout: Cilly Klotz, Andrea Mogwitz, Munich
Typesetting: Vornehm Setzerei, Munich
Production: Cilly Klotz, Matthias Hauer
Origination: Repro Ludwig, Zell am See
Printing: Appl, Wemding
Binding: Conzella, Pfarrkirchen

Printed in Germany on acid-free paper

ISBN 978-3-7913-3545-2 / 3-7913-3545-6 (trade edition)
ISBN 978-3-7913-6078-2 / 3-7913-6078-7 (catalogue)